MODERN STUDIES IN PHILOSOPHY

PLATO

Modern Studies in Philosophy is a series of anthologies presenting contemporary interpretations and evaluations of the works of major philosophers. The editors have selected articles designed to show the systematic structure of the thought of these philosophers, and to reveal the relevance of their views to the problems of current interest. These volumes are intended to be contributions to contemporary debates as well as to the history of philosophy; they not only trace the origins of many problems important to modern philosophy, but also introduce major philosophers as interlocutors in current discussions.

Modern Studies in Philosophy is prepared under the general editorship of Amelie Oksenberg Rorty, Livingston College, Rutgers University.

Gregory Vlastos is Stuart Professor of Philosophy at Princeton University. He had previously taught philosophy at Queen's University, in Kingston, Ontario, and at Cornell University.

MODERN STUDIES IN PHILOSOPHY

Amelie Oksenberg Rorty, General Editor

PLATO

A Collection of Critical Essays

I: METAPHYSICS AND EPISTEMOLOGY

EDITED BY GREGORY VLASTOS

ANCHOR BOOKS

DOUBLEDAY AND COMPANY, INC.

GARDEN CITY, NEW YORK

1971

CONTENTS

INTRODUCTION

The last three decades have witnessed a renaissance of interest in Plato among philosophers throughout the world. This interest is still growing. Plato is being studied and argued over with greater vigor than ever before. The philosophical and even the classical journals of English-speaking countries have reflected this development. More articles and discussions of Plato have appeared in them than of any other of the great thinkers of the past. And the number of books and commentaries on Plato is also impressive, as one can see by glancing at the bibliographies at the back of each of the two volumes in this anthology.

Much of this new zeal for platonic studies has been generated by the importation of techniques of logical and semantic analysis that have proved productive in contemporary philosophy. By means of these techniques we may now better understand some of the problems Plato attempted to solve and we are, therefore, better equipped to assess the merit of his solutions. The result has been a more vivid sense of the relevance of his thought to the concerns of present-day ontologists, epistemologists, and moralists. He has become for us less of an antique monument and more of a living presence than he seemed to be in the twenties and the thirties.

With this has come a higher appreciation of his stature, in spite of the fact that the more rigorous canons of criticism by which we now judge his claims have shown errors in his thought which had not been seen, or seen clearly, by earlier scholars. Only a puerile critic would make immunity to logical error the measure of a philosopher's greatness. Can one read through a chapter in any acknowledged philosophical masterpiece—Spinoza's *Ethics*, Hume's *Treatise*, the First or the Second of Kant's *Critiques*—without spotting some error, often enough a big one? I agree with Richard Robinson that "greatness in science consists mainly in leaving the subject much more advanced than when you entered it."[1] Plato has no difficulty passing this test. He was a pioneer moving through *terra incognita*. Even a formal logic had yet to be created; Aristotle was Plato's pupil.

Extravagant claims have been made for the gains in insight

---

[1] *Plato's Earlier Dialectic*, 2nd Ed. (Oxford, 1953), p. vi of the Preface.

which have resulted from the use of more sophisticated methods of conceptual analysis in platonic exegesis. One of the distinguished advocates of this new approach once startled a seminar by declaring that these methods now enable us to understand Plato better than he was ever understood by anyone in history—better than by any of his own contemporaries, even better than by himself! One need not share the euphoria that produced this boast to insist that there is an element of truth in it after all. Take two statements, S and S', expressed by Greek sentences so similar in vocabulary and superficial syntax that they could be read in either of two different ways, the resulting difference to the sense being so great that S would, and S' would not, be consistent with major platonic theses. Alerted by our analytic tools to the ambiguity and the resulting consequences, we can tell that in a given context, where it is clear that Plato has no interest in asserting anything but S, this is the only thing he must be understood to mean. One who lacked the means to block out as clearly the difference in sense between S and S' would not be as aware of the enormous risks taken in using sentences of that form; he might, therefore, use them in cases where the context does not of itself suffice to rule out the S' reading, thereby courting grave misunderstanding by others and even by himself. If we come across such sentences in Plato, it would be plainly true to say that we can understand them better than he did and even to add that we can, therefore, understand *him* better, since we can see both what he meant to say and the logical liabilities of his incautious sentences. "Self-predication" is a fair example. Had Plato known the Russellian paradox,[2] he would have seen instantly the absurd consequences of "The *F* is *F*" for most values of *F*,[3] for example. The increment in self-understanding would have altered the texture, indeed the very substance, of his metaphysics.

Once we have made full allowance for what modern semantics and logic can do to make Plato more intelligible and alive for us

[2] Bertrand Russell, *Principles of Mathematics* (London, 1903), Chapter X, "The Contradiction." For a succinct recent discussion see the article on the Logical Paradoxes by J. van Heijenoort in the *Encyclopedia of Philosophy* (New York, 1967).

[3] Cf. G. Vlastos, "The Third Man Argument in the *Parmenides*," *Philosophical Review* 63 (1954), 319–49 at 337–38; "Self-predication in Plato's Later Dialogues," *Philosophical Review* 78 (1969), 74–78.

today, we should be quick to concede that borrowings from this quarter must be used with economy and discretion, and that continuing reliance on older linguistic and historical disciplines is as essential now as it has ever been in the past if the object of our inquiries is *Plato* himself, instead of some mock-up more pleasing to current taste. The man we have to deal with, the flesh-and-blood person whose thought we seek to comprehend, is the one who, as a young man, was the companion and admirer of Socrates, but was influenced at the same time by that bizarre metaphysician, Cratylus, and was exposed to many other philosophical currents swirling in and out of Athens. He must have fought against Sparta during the war years, even though admiring Spartan discipline and hating Athenian liberty. Although his hatred of democracy abated in his later years, he continued to oppose it on principle and tolerate it only as a lesser evil to lawless despotism. A great artist, he nevertheless feared art and clamped a moralistic strait jacket on it in his utopias. He undertook to refute not only the Sophists, like Protagoras, whom he scorned, but the greatest of his predecessors, like Parmenides, whom he revered. He was fascinated, but not mesmerized, by number theory and geometry. He did not think that empirical science deserved serious study, but he studied and wrote it just the same. He projected a physical theory which owed not less to the materialistic atomists than to Pythagorean numerological mystics. He shared Pythagoras' faith in a divine, transmigrating, soul, but his own mysticism was obstinately intellectual—for him the beatifying, immortalizing experience came through a discipline in which mind and heart were partners.

What is the bearing of these facts on the interpretation of his metaphysics and theory of knowledge, not to speak of their even more urgent import for his ethics, his moral psychology, his political theory, his theory of art? And what other facts can we extract from our textual and historical data which will make our ideas on these diverse phases of his thought more exact? Here the philosopher must look for help to the classical scholar: to the philologist, who is best fitted to recover Plato's text and to capture its sense, reading it with scrupulous care for detail, but knowing so well its entirety that he can bring to bear on the interpretation of a single sentence parallels and contrasts culled from a thousand pages of platonic text; to the historian of Greek philosophy, who has the broadest as well as the most carefully sifted knowledge of those earlier thinkers from whom Plato learned so much, and has also knowledge of the work of Aristotle, whose metaphysics, philosophy of science, cosmology, psychology, ethics and politics were formed in nearly two decades spent in the Academy and whose criticisms of Plato are instructive even when they are demonstrably tendentious in their form; and, finally, to the historian of Greek culture, who is in the best position to ascertain what it was in the science, morality, politics, art and religion of his people which presented Plato with the problems he tried to solve.

The essays in this anthology should give the reader a good idea of the variety of approaches represented in current contributions to the interpretation of Plato. Volume One is heavily weighted on the "analytical" side. All but one of its essays were written by men whose academic training was strongly philosophical (though several of them are also accomplished classicists). Volume Two is weighted on the other side, though not as heavily. There are several essays in it by distinguished hellenists, writing as pure historians, making no effort to line up platonic doctrines with their counterparts, if any, in present-day philosophizing; some of them would object on principle to this kind of effort as more likely to distort than clarify what we find in Plato. Glad though I am to illustrate this diversity of point of view, I did not make the selections with this in mind. My one concern was to bring together significant contributions to the interpretation of those aspects of Plato's thought which could be covered in this volume. Since my space was all too limited, compactness of presentation became a primary desideratum. Some fundamental work could not be represented here because it was not available in this format. For the material I looked to the classical, no less than the philosophical, books and journals, and I solicited essays from classicists as well as philosophers. It is my strong conviction that each of these two disciplines has its own indispensable place in the elucidation of Plato's thought, and I am proud that outstanding work from both appears in this anthology.

It is regrettable that limited space has crowded out other work of great intrinsic merit. For some of this the reader might turn to R. E. Allen's *Studies in Plato's Metaphysics* (Routledge and Kegan Paul, London, 1965). One should bear in mind that if the work in this present anthology and Allen's were taken together, it would still form only a small sample of the wealth of material available in books and articles. Much of this is listed in the bibliography, though this does not pretend to be complete.

For the privilege of including the selected material in this volume I wish to express my warmest thanks to those whose cooperation has made the venture possible: to Professors Moravcsik, Owen, Penner, and Wiggins for their essays written specially for this volume; to Mr. J. D. Mabbott for revising an early essay of his for its inclusion here; to Professors Ackrill, Allen, Bambrough, Cherniss, Cross, Dodds, Guthrie, Leys, Markus, Morrow, Robinson, Sparshott, Strang, Verdenius, Wedberg, Woozley for authorizing me to reprint their papers.

My warmest thanks are due to Amelie Rorty, under whose general editorship the Modern Studies in Philosophy have been prepared, and to Kay Scheuer and Paul H. Drymalski, without whose help and advice I could not have carried out the commitment. And I must not forget Gregory Zeigler, who gave up most of his Christmas holiday to prepare the *index locorum;* he has earned the thanks of those who will be using it, as well as mine.

GREGORY VLASTOS

Princeton, New Jersey

1

PLATO

R. ROBINSON AND J. D. DENNISTON

Plato ($\Pi\lambda\acute{a}\tau\omega\nu$)(1)(c. 429–347 B.C.), son of Ariston and Perictione, both Athenians of distinguished lineage. His writings show the enormous influence that Socrates had upon him both by his life and by his death. He relates in his *Seventh Letter* that the spectacle of contemporary politics, during the ascendancy of his own associates as well as under the democracy, gradually weakened his original intention to become a statesman and drove him to the paradox that there was no hope for cities until philosophers became rulers or rulers philosophers. After the execution of Socrates in 399 he retired for a time to Megara with other Socratics. In the next twelve years he perhaps travelled to many places, including Egypt. At any rate he visited Italy and Sicily in 387, where he met Dionysius I and initiated lifelong friendships with Dion of Syracuse and the Pythagorean Archytas of Tarentum. On his return he was perhaps captured and ransomed at Aegina. It was probably only a few months later that he began formal and continuous teaching at a place near the grove of Academus about a mile outside the wall of Athens. This was his chief occupation almost without interruption for the remaining forty years of his life; but he made two more visits to Syracuse. Dionysius I died in 367; and Dion thereupon summoned Plato to try to realize the philosopher-king in the person of Dionysius II, and also to strengthen Dion's declining influence at court. Plato felt bound to try; but the new ruler's suspicion of Dion was soon reinforced by jealousy of his friendship with Plato. He banished Dion and sought to retain Plato. Some years later Plato was obliged to visit Syracuse for the third and last time, because Dionysius had promised to 'do as you wish about Dion' if he came, and to do nothing of the sort if he did not. Dionysius not merely broke his promise, but practically confiscated

Article on *Plato* in *The Oxford Classical Dictionary* (Clarendon Press, Oxford, 1949). Reprinted by permission of the publishers. Paragraphs 1 to 15 are by Richard Robinson; paragraph 16 by J. D. Denniston.

Dion's money and kept Plato a prisoner until the influence of Archytas procured his release. In 357 Dion re-entered Syracuse by force and expelled Dionysius. A few years later Dion was assassinated by persons who seem to have had something to do with Plato. The *Seventh Letter* was written to Dion's party after his death, ostensibly to urge moderation and constitutional procedure, but more to explain and justify Plato's own part in the whole miserable affair.

2. His publications, which are all preserved, consist of some twenty-five dialogues and the *Apology*. There are also thirteen letters whose genuineness is much debated; but even those who reject them appear to think the *Seventh* reliable in its history. The precise order of these works is unknown; but stylometric and other inferences permit a rough division into three periods, of which the early certainly includes *Apology, Laches, Charmides, Euthyphro, Crito, Hippias Minor*, the middle certainly includes *Phaedo, Symposium, Republic*, and the late certainly includes *Sophist, Statesman, Philebus, Timaeus, Laws*.

3. The early dialogues aim primarily at portraying a character. Plato's Socrates is ugly in body but magnetic in mind; convivial and erotic, yet Spartan in habits and of enormous physical endurance. The most striking thing about him is his conversation, to which he devotes his whole life. At first appearing absurdly simple and homely, it soon becomes intensely impressive. Its main tone is great moral earnestness, often paradoxically strict; but this is seasoned with paradoxes of another sort (as that pleasure is the only good in *Protagoras*) and with an apparently mischievous treatment of his interlocutor. The main doctrine to which he tends is that virtue is knowledge. He usually does not specify what it is knowledge of, but on the whole seems to mean: of the individual's happiness or good. Hence, since real knowledge is supremely effective in practice, no one willingly does wrong; and so-called incontinence is ignorance. Hence, also, virtue should be teachable; and Socrates wonders why great statesmen have not taught it to their sons. Hence, lastly, Socrates holds it his duty to shatter the false conceit of knowledge wherever it occurs. He asks questions to which there is only one answer; and when these admissions are put together they entail the contradictory of the answerer's original assertion. He explains in Plato's *Apology* that this bewildering elenchus is an essential preliminary to the acquisition of real

knowledge and virtue; but neither there nor elsewhere does he justify his sly and mischievous manner of conducting it. The search for knowledge appears to him mostly as a question in the form: 'What is *X*?' When offered examples he says he wants 'not many *X*'s but the one *X*', '*X* itself', the 'form' or 'idea' or 'essence'. He regards this question as prior to all others, and even as answerable apart from any examples of *X*. Yet he cannot himself produce any answer, and all those proffered by others are dissolved by his elenchus. The typical form of an early Platonic work is therefore a dialogue which raises the question 'What is so and so?', refutes all suggested answers, and ends in ignorance.

4. The typical work of the middle period is a narration of an earlier conversation, and Plato makes magnificent use of the opportunity to describe the external scene. The elenchus now yields to a blaze of positive doctrine; and the combination of artistic and philosophic excellence thus achieved makes the *Republic* a very great book. Instead of pursuing some particular 'form', Socrates is now represented as concerned about the nature of a 'form' as such, about the whole collection of 'forms' as such, and about the consequences of the hypothesis that there are such entities. 'We are accustomed to posit some one form concerning each set of things to which we apply the same name', *R.* 596A. This form is the very thing itself meant by the name. Being invisible, it is grasped by thought and not by sense. It is absolutely and perfectly what it is, independent of all else, changeless, divine. The 'forms' constitute a second class of existences, more real than the changing animals and things around us. The 'form' of the Good has a unique status among them, being 'even beyond essence'; it has some of the characteristics the Christian ascribes to God, but Plato distinguishes it from God and regards all the 'forms' as quite independent of Him. He leaves the relations between 'forms' and things somewhat vague; but the 'forms' are certainly causes of things, both in that each 'form' causes the things named after it and, apparently, in that the 'form' of the Good helps to cause all things. The relation of a 'form' to its namesake is represented as that of the original to the copy, but also as that of what is shared in to what shares; and Plato apparently thought the two accounts compatible. Modern interpretations of these 'forms' as 'concepts' or 'hypotheses' are wholly mistaken; and even the terms 'substances', 'universals', and 'ideals' can be applied only with careful distinctions and reservations. The 'forms'

were 'separate' in that they were independent and self-sufficing and not parts or elements of things; but they were 'unseparated' in that Plato meant his spatial language about them to be taken metaphorically, and in that he really believed that things 'shared' in them and could not have been what they are if there had been no 'forms'.

5. As the 'forms' are absolutely distinct from things, so our apprehension of them, which is knowledge, is absolutely distinct from opinion, which is a faculty set over things. There can be no true knowledge of the changing. Opinion is changeable, fallible, irrational, and the result of persuasion; knowledge is enduring, infallible, rational, exact, clear. Knowledge comes from teaching rather than persuasion, but from recollection rather than teaching; it is our recollection of the 'forms' we saw with the mind's eye before the body imprisoned and confused us. The things we see now remind us of the 'forms' they imitate (*Phd.*); and the love of a beautiful person can lead us to the love of wisdom and of the 'form' of beauty itself (*Symp.*). In other places Plato seems to allow no part at all to sense in the creation of knowledge. Knowledge is by nature practical and commanding; for knowledge (ἐπιστήμη) and craftsmanship (τέχνη) are identical.

6. The hypothesis that there are 'forms' has among its consequences that soul is immortal; and this is elaborately argued in the *Phaedo*. Within the human soul Plato finds three parts, the natural appetites, the spirit or resolution by which we can if we will resist the appetites, and the reason that determines when we should resist (*R.* bk. 4). Virtue is the proper functioning of these three. The man is wise if his reason decides rightly, brave if his spirit carries out the decision firmly, temperate and just if the better part rules the worse and each confines itself to its own business. Vice is necessarily unhappy because it is disorder and anarchy among these parts. Analogously, the ideal city will separate from the mass a small class of soldiers, living together without private property or family, and rendered by their education completely devoted to the protection of the city. They will perpetuate themselves mostly by procreation, but occasionally by enlisting a common citizen of superior metal. Within this 'spirit' of the city a higher education in mathematics and dialectic, and a series of examinations, will gradually elevate a few philosophic souls to an understanding of the 'form' of the good; and this will give them the duty though not the desire to rule.

Plato's main political principle is that government is a science and requires expert knowledge. To this he adds a constitutional love of neatness and order. Both lead him to the strongest condemnations of democracy.

7. With the *Parmenides* and the *Theaetetus* Plato's late period approaches. In the latter he explicitly abandons narrated dialogue as cumbrous (143); in the former Socrates is for the first time a subordinate character. The *Parmenides* consists first of an apparently extremely damaging critique of the 'forms', and secondly of a sustained piece of abstract and self-contradictory dialectic. Undoubtedly Burnet and Taylor are mistaken in believing that the first part is really directed against the existence not of the 'forms' but of the sensibles. Undoubtedly also the 'forms' here attacked are those of Plato's own middle dialogues. But beyond this all is uncertain; and interpretations of the second part range from finding it a parody of some fallacious kind of reasoning to finding it an exposition of superrational truth.

8. The *Theaetetus*, applying the Socratic question to the concept of knowledge (ἐπιστήμη), examines three likely answers with great thoroughness and insight. The first, that knowing is perceiving, is developed into an elaborate relativist theory of perception and knowledge, based on Protagorean and Heraclitean notions, before being abandoned because (1) it cannot deal with the undeniable difference between the layman and the expert, and (2) being or οὐσία is grasped by 'the soul herself by herself' and not through the senses. The second, that knowledge is true opinion, is quickly dismissed, but gives occasion for a digression on false opinion, in which Plato compares the mind to a waxen tablet and to an aviary. The third, that knowledge is true opinion with λόγος, allows him to examine the meanings of λόγος, and to consider the theory that knowledge is the analysis of compounds into their unknowable elements.

9. The *Sophist*, where the leader is an unnamed Eleatic, is Plato's most intense study in metaphysics. Sophistry entails falsehood, which entails 'not-being', which seems self-contradictory. 'Being' is no better; it raises difficulties alike for pluralists, monists, materialists, and immaterialists; it is neither rest nor motion, yet everything must either rest or move. The solution is the doctrine of 'communication'. Some things communicate with each other, so that we can sometimes truly say '*A* is *B*'. Some things do not com-

municate with each other. Some things communicate with everything else; e.g. otherness, for each thing is other than each other thing. Not-being therefore exists and has being as otherness; while being itself 'is not' myriads of things. Using this discovery, Plato finds an explanation for falsehood and error.

10. Inquiring about the *Statesman*, Plato reiterates that government like medicine is a job for experts, and infers that the perfect ruler should be completely irresponsible to the people and unfettered by any inviolable constitution. Law is a second-best, useful only when science is lacking. The best constitution is simply the rule of the expert; but, failing that, we have, in order of diminishing goodness, law-abiding monarchy and aristocracy and democracy, and then lawless democracy and oligarchy and tyranny. In this dialogue, and in *Phaedrus, Sophist, Philebus*, much space goes to the method of division (διαίρεσις) and collection (συναγωγή). Διαίρεσις is occasionally analysis into elements (*Phdr.* 270–1), but oftener distinction, and especially the 'carving' of a 'form' into component 'forms', which seems to be an ancestor of Aristotle's 'genus and species'. By repeated carving until we reach an 'atomic form', Plato expects to reach a definition for any 'form', and also, apparently, to 'demonstrate' its truth. By συναγωγή he understands 'seeing the one in the many', which probably includes both our 'universal in the particulars' and our 'genus in the species' (*Phlb.* 16–18).

11. The *Philebus*, weighing the claims of pleasure and knowledge to be the good, and undertaking a close analysis of the former, rejects both, but sets knowledge nearer to that unity of 'beauty and symmetry and truth' which makes a thing good. It is hard to say whether Plato considered this a termination of the *Republic*'s quest for the 'form' of the good.

12. The *Timaeus*, devoted to natural science, describes how the creator made the world a single spherical living thing, having both soul and body, modelled upon 'the living creature that truly is', peopled with gods visible and invisible and with men. Tradition declares that this creator is only a mythical device for exhibiting the *rationality* inhering in the world, which has always existed and always will. Plato goes on to exhibit the complementary element, *necessity*. Besides the world and its model there is a third thing, the receptacle in which the copy becomes. The four elements can be analysed into the regular solids. The dialogue then deals at length

with man, his various perceptions, the irrational part of his soul, his body, his diseases, and his health. This study, being directed towards things and not 'forms', cannot achieve infallible or even perfectly consistent results (29C); but it will be as good as possible if we take care always to pursue both kinds of cause, reason and necessity (48A).

13. The *Laws*, Plato's longest and perhaps last dialogue, takes up again the question of the best constitution for a city. Though re-affirming the *Republic*'s doctrine that the ideal is perfect unity achieved through communism (739), Plato now writes in a different temper and plans a different city. Extremes are bad, whether of despotism or of freedom; so let us have a mixed constitution. The citizens shall be 5,040 persons, each supporting his family by the cultivation of two inalienable parcels of land. Trading and teaching shall be practised exclusively by resident foreigners. There shall be an 'Assembly' and 'Council'. A long panel of officers culminates in the thirty-seven 'lawguards', for whom Plato gradually accumu-lates a multifarious set of duties; their authority, constitutional from the beginning, is further limited in the last book by the institu-tion of 'Examiners' and of a 'Nocturnal Council' to revise the laws. Contrary to the *Republic* and the *Statesman*, this work values law very highly, institutes 'preambles' to the laws by which the legis-lator adds persuasion to command, and is chiefly remarkable for its immense wealth of detailed enactments, regulating every part of public and private life. Furthermore, dialectic and philosophy, which the *Republic* emphasized as the coping-stones of the constitu-tion, here yield almost entirely to religion. The reality of the divine can be proved both from the soul and from the stars, which are gods. Plato infers that everyone should be taught astronomy, and that atheists should be converted or killed.

14. Aristotle in his *Metaphysics* attributes to Plato doctrines not stated in the dialogues, especially that (1) there is a class of entities intermediate between 'forms' and things, immutable like 'forms' but plural like things, and these are what mathematics studies; (2) the 'forms' are numbers, composed of 'inassociable' units; (3) these number-forms are not ultimate, but result from the action of 'the One' upon 'the indefinite Dyad of the Great and Small'; thus pro-duced, they in turn act upon this Dyad to produce the world of changing things. This report of Aristotle's cannot be wholly mis-taken or fictitious; and something of these doctrines was probably

delivered in Plato's famous lecture on the Good, for the Good and the One were apparently identical. Plato's view on the inefficiency of writing (*Phdr.* and *Letter* 7) is sufficient explanation of their not being found in the dialogues.

15. Burnet's edition of the *Phaedo* (1911) urged that Plato must have meant this dialogue to be essentially a true account of what was said on Socrates' last day. It would follow that Socrates had studied physics in his youth, that he believed in immortality and the 'forms', and that Plato was not the inventor of the 'forms'. Burnet and Taylor have since developed this theory into the general principle that Plato aimed at historical accuracy, ascribed to famous persons only the sort of view they had really held, and expressed himself only through such characters as the 'Eleatic stranger'. The extreme consequence, that the *Timaeus* is a minute reconstruction of the state of science several decades earlier, is brilliantly drawn in Taylor's commentary; and it constitutes an adequate disproof of Burnet's hypothesis by reduction to impossibility.

16. Plato's style possesses infinite variety. He can write easy, graceful, charming narrative, lit up with flashes of humour (openings of *Protagoras* and *Republic*, *Symp.* 217A–21C) or infused with the noblest pathos (end of *Phaedo*). In another vein he is capable of the gorgeous pageantry of the *Phaedrus* myth (245C ff.), the passionate religious fervour of the address to the young atheist (*Lg.* 904E–6C), and the solemnity of the last paragraph of the *Republic*. Once or twice he recalls the statuesque grandeur of the pre-Socratics (*Phdr.* 245C–E, *R.* 617D–E), perhaps the only literary influence definitely traceable in him.

His language has a lavish fullness, sometimes amounting to redundancy. In structure he ranges from the simplest λέξις εἰρομένη (*R.* 328B–C) to very long periods, often straggling and anacoluthic (*R.* 488A–E), but sometimes even more powerful than those of Demosthenes, though quite different from them (*Criti.* 120B–C and the tremendous period at *Lg.* 865D–E). He fully appreciated the potentialities of a very short clause, closing a period or immediately following it (*Lg.* 727C, βλάπτει γάρ: *Phdr.* 238C, ἔρως ἐκλήθη). His language, as the ancient critics noted, is often deeply tinged with poetry. It is packed with metaphors (sometimes dead metaphors revived), especially from music. He will go back to a metaphor, as a dog goes back to a bone, when one thinks he has done with it.

Much of the *Sophist* is cast in the form of an extensive metaphor, the elusive Sophist, so hard to define, being represented as a hunted animal eluding chase. In his later years Plato's style shows traces of mannerism—a trick of interlacing the order of words, and some affectations of assonance (*Lg.* 657D ἡμῖν ἡμᾶς, cf. 659C; *figura etymologiae, Lg.* 868C), including the pun, which fascinated Plato, though he laughed at it in others. But all in all, from the earliest works to the latest, no other author reveals as Plato does the power, the beauty, and the flexibility of Greek prose.

Dion. Hal. *Comp.* 18, *Pomp.* passim. [Longin.] *Subl.* 12–13, 32. For an admirable discussion of P.'s style and ancient criticisms of it see E. Norden, *Antike Kunstprosa* (1898) i. 104–13.

The following works, arranged in a probable chronological order, may be confidently accepted as genuine: *Hippias Minor; Laches; Charmides; Ion; Protagoras; Euthyphro, Apology, Crito* (comm. J. Burnet, 1924); *Gorgias* (comm. W. H. Thompson, 1894); *Meno* (comm. E. S. Thompson, 1901); *Lysis; Menexenus* (*c.* 386); *Euthydemus; Cratylus; Symposium* (*c.* 384); *Phaedo* (comm. J. Burnet, 1911); *Republic* (comm. J. Adam, 1902, etc.; tr. A. D. Lindsay, 1908, etc.); *Parmenides* (*c.* 370, tr. A. E. Taylor, 1934); *Theaetetus* (*c.* 368, comm. L. Campbell, 2nd ed. 1883); *Phaedrus* (comm. W. H. Thompson, 1868); *Sophist* (360 or later) and *Statesman* (comm. L. Campbell, 1867); *Philebus* (comm. R. G. Bury, 1897); *Timaeus* (A. E. Taylor comm. 1928, tr. 1929); *Critias; Laws* (comm. E. B. England, 1921; tr. A. E. Taylor, 1934).

The following are doubtfully genuine: *Hippias Major* (comm. D. Tarrant, 1928); *Clitopho; Epinomis* (tr. with notes J. Harward, 1928); *Letters* 2–13 (comms. F. Novotny, 1930, and G. Morrow, *Illinois Univ. Studies in Lang. and Lit.* xviii, 1935; tr. L. A. Post, 1925).

The following may be confidently rejected as spurious: *Letter* 1; *Alcibiades* 1 and 2; *Hipparchus; Amatores; Theages; Minos; De Justo; De Virtute; Demodocus; Sisyphus; Eryxias; Axiochus; Definitions.*

2

THE PHILOSOPHICAL ECONOMY
OF THE THEORY OF IDEAS

H. F. CHERNISS

The objection with which in the *Metaphysics*[1] Aristotle introduces his criticism of the theory of Ideas expresses a difficulty which has tended to alienate the sympathy of most students who approach the study of Plato. The hypothesis, Aristotle says, is a superfluous duplication of the phenomenal world; it is as if one should think it impossible to count a number of objects until that number had first been multiplied. This objection, even tacitly entertained, distorts the motivation of the hypothesis; that it misrepresents Plato's express attitude towards scientific problems, the well-known statement of Eudemus quoted by Simplicius on the authority of Sosigenes amply proves.[2] The complications of the planetary movements had to be explained, Plato asserted, by working out an hypothesis of a definite number of fixed and regular motions which would 'save the phenomena'. This same attitude is expressed in the *Phaedo* where Socrates explains the method of 'hypothesis' which he used to account for the apparently disordered world of phenomena;[3] the result of this method, he says, was the Theory of Ideas.[4]

The phenomena for which Plato had to account were of three kinds, ethical, epistemological, and ontological. In each of these spheres there had been developed by the end of the fifth century doctrines so extremely paradoxical that there seemed to be no possibility of reconciling them with one another or any one of them with the observable facts of human experience.[5] The dialogues of

Originally published in *American Journal of Philology* 57(1936), 445–56. Reprinted by permission of the Johns Hopkins University Press. [English translations of a few Greek phrases in the notes have been added by the editor.]

[1] *Metaph.*, 990A34 ff. It is repeated almost exactly at 1078B34–6.
[2] Simplicius, in *De Caelo*, p. 488, 18–24 (Heiberg).
[3] *Phd.*, 99D4–100A8.   [4] *Phd.*, 100B1–102A1.
[5] Note the criticism and warning in *Phd.*, 101C: ἅμα δ' οὐκ ἂν φύροιο ὥσπερ οἱ ἀντιλογικοὶ περί τε τῆς ἀρχῆς διαλεγόμενος καὶ τῶν ἐξ ἐκείνης ὡρμημένων, εἴπερ βούλοιό τι τῶν ὄντων εὑρεῖν; ἐκείνοις μὲν γὰρ ἴσως

Plato, I believe, will furnish evidence to show that he considered it necessary to find a single hypothesis which would at once solve the problems of these several spheres and also create a rationally unified cosmos by establishing the connection among the separate phases of experience.

The interests of Socrates,[6] the subject-matter of the early dialogues, the 'practical' tone of Plato's writings throughout make it highly probable that he took his start from the ethical problems of his day. It is unnecessary to labour the point that he considered it fundamentally important to establish an absolute ethical standard; that the bearing on this point of the 'inconclusive', 'exploratory' dialogues could not have been obscure to his contemporaries is obvious to anyone who looks at such evidence of the time as is furnished by the Δισσοὶ Λόγοι (which discusses the relativity of good and evil, fair and foul, just and unjust, true and false, and the possibility of teaching wisdom and virtue) or by the papyrus fragment of Antiphon the Sophist[7] (where conventional justice is called adventitious and generally contradictory to natural justice which is defined as that which is truly advantageous to each individual). The necessity for an absolute standard of ethics which would not depend upon the contradictory phenomena of conventional conduct but would be a measure of human activities instead of being measured by them was forcibly demonstrated by the plight into which Democritus had fallen. He had bitterly opposed the relativism of Protagoras;[8] yet two of his own ethical fragments show how vulnerable he must have been to counterattack. 'They know and seek fair things,' he said, 'who are naturally disposed to them.'[9] And, attempting to reconcile conventional law and natural good,

---

οὐδὲ εἷς περὶ τούτου λόγος οὐδὲ φροντίς. ἱκανοὶ γὰρ ὑπὸ σοφίας ὁμοῦ πάντα κυκῶντες ὅμως δύνασθαι αὐτοὶ αὐτοῖς ἀρέσκειν. They do not keep the 'universes of discourse' clearly defined but think it is legitimate, for example, to drag an epistemological difficulty into an ethical problem before they have completely canvassed the ethical phenomena and have set up an hypothesis to explain them. An example of this 'childish' confusion is outlined in the *Phlb.*, (15D–16A; 17A).

[6] Cf. e.g. Aristotle, *Metaph.*, 987B1 ff.

[7] *Oxyrh. Pap.*, XI, 1364; Diels, *Fragmente der Vorsokratiker*, 4th ed., vol. II, pp. xxxii ff.

[8] Plutarch, *Adv. Colot.*, 1108F–1109A.

[9] Democritus, *fragment* 56 (Diels): τὰ καλὰ γνωρίζουσι καὶ ζηλοῦσιν οἱ εὐφυέες πρὸς αὐτά.

he remarked, 'The law seeks to benefit the life of men but can do so only when they themselves desire to fare well. For to those who obey it it indicates their proper goodness.'[10] This bald assertion of a difference between fair and foul things, virtuous and vicious actions offers no standard whereby to determine the difference, no reason for the similarity of all fair things quâ fair and for their difference from all that are foul. So long as these are only characteristics of material individuals no standard can be found, for to measure individuals against one another is to succumb to relativism. To compare and contrast one must have a definite standard of reference which must itself be underivative lest it become just another example of the characteristic in question and so lead to an infinite regress. The 'dialogues of search', by demonstrating the hopelessness of all other expedients, show that the definitions requisite to normative ethics are possible only on the assumption that there exist, apart from phenomena, substantive objects of these definitions which alone are the source of the values attaching to phenomenal existence.[11] The possibility of ethical distinctions, then, implies objective differences which can be accounted for only by the hypothesis of substantive ideas.

While this hypothesis makes an ethical system possible in the abstract, the problems raised by conscious human activity involve the construction of a complete ethical theory in the questions of epistemology. That a consistent and practical ethical theory depends upon an adequate epistemology, Plato demonstrates in the *Meno*. The subject of that dialogue is *virtue*, but it is with one of the popular practical questions about virtue that Meno opens the discussion. Socrates protests that such questions as the teachability of virtue must wait upon a satisfactory definition of virtue;[12] but

[10] Democritus, *fragment* 248 (Diels): ὁ νόμος βούλεται μὲν εὐεργετεῖν βίον ἀνθρώπων. δύναται δὲ ὅταν αὐτοὶ βούλωνται πάσχειν εὖ. τοῖσι γὰρ πειθομένοισι τὴν ἰδίην ἀρετὴν ἐνδείκνυται.

[11] *Euthd.*, 15C 11–E2; *Laches* 199E (cf. 200E–201A); *Lysis*, 222E (N.B. 218C–220B5: necessity of finding a πρῶτον φίλον which is the final cause of πάντα φίλα); *Chrm.*, (176A); *Hippias Minor* (376B: if *anyone* errs voluntarily, it must be the good man [who, of course, as good would not err at all]). Cf. *Prt.*, (361C: the difficulties into which the argument has led show that it is necessary first to discover what ἀρετή ("virtue") is and *then* discuss its teachability).

[12] *Men.*, 71A3–7. It is in the light of this that I find the key to the riddles of the *Protagoras* in Socrates' remarks at the end of that dialogue (*Prt.*, 361C2–D2).

Meno's failure to produce a definition makes him fall back upon the 'eristic argument' that one cannot search for either the known or the unknown.[13] To the implication here that ethical problems are not susceptible of investigation Socrates answers that one can escape this difficulty only by supposing that learning or discovering is really recollection of that which has already been *directly* known.[14] Here Socrates is not concerned with the details of the process; his contention is simply that, since determination of the characteristics of virtue presupposes a definition of its essential nature and to give such a definition presupposes knowledge of the essence, we must assume that essential virtue exists and has been directly known unless we are to surrender all possibility of considering ethical problems. Socrates is forced by Meno's insistence to discuss his question anyway, but his repeated objection that such questions demand a prior determination of the nature of virtue itself is a warning and an explanation of the paradoxical outcome of the consequent discussion.[15]

If men act virtuously without being able to teach virtue (that is, without being able to give a consistent account of the causes of their actions), it is because they have 'right opinions' and so are virtuous by a kind of 'divine grace'.[16] But such right opinions, though having results speciously identical with those of knowledge are unstable, for they are haphazard, being unconnected by a chain of causality with the final cause. The recognition of this causal relationship, however, is knowledge and this is just recollection.[17] Consequently until one bases his reasoning upon the knowledge of essential virtue, there can be no adequate solution of the problems of ethics.[18] So it is that by argument and example the *Meno* demonstrates how, having to distinguish knowledge and right opinion in order to save the phenomena of moral activity, the ethical philosopher is forced to face the problems of epistemology.

But Plato was not satisfied with having proved that considerations of ethics require the assumption of substantive ideas and an epistemology consistent with such an hypothesis. The pragmatic relativism of Protagoras' ethics was, after all, a necessary result of

---

[13] *Men.*, 80E–81A.

[14] *Men.*, 81D4–5. Note the word used for acquiring the knowledge in the first place: ἑωρακυῖα ("having seen") (81C6).

[15] *Men.*, 86C6–87B5.   [16] *Men.*, 99A–D.

[17] *Men.*, 97E–98B.   [18] *Men.*, 100B.

his subjective realism; and Plato had before him the example of Democritus who, though insisting upon the reality of definite moral standards, could not finally refute Protagoras since he had no adequate reason for giving mind the sovereignty over sensations. There is a winsome sadness in his confession of defeat expressed in the reply he makes the sensations give to the strictures of mind: 'unhappy Intelligence, with evidence we give you you attempt our overthrow; your victory is your defeat'.[19] The saving of the phenomena of intellection and sensation is the primary duty of epistemology; if, however, it should appear that these phenomena can be saved in their own right only by setting up the same hypothesis as was found to be essential for ethics, the coincidence of results would by the principle of scientific economy enunciated in Plato's phrasing of the astronomical problem lend added validity to the hypothesis in each sphere.

The epistemological necessity for the existence of the Ideas is proved by the same indirect method as was used in establishing the ethical necessity. Since the phenomena to be explained have first to be determined, it is essential to proceed by analysis of the psychological activities, to decide the nature of these activities and their objects. In brief, the argument turns upon the determination of intellection as an activity different from sensation and opinion. In the *Timaeus*,[20] in an avowedly brief and casual proof of the separate existence of Ideas, it is stated that if intellection is other than right opinion it follows that there exist separate substantive Ideas as the objects of intellection. The indications of the essential difference of intellection and right opinion are there said to be three. Knowledge is produced by instruction, is always accompanied by the ability to render a true account or proof, and cannot be shaken by persuasive means, whereas right opinion is the result of persuasion, is incapable of accounting for itself, and is susceptible of alteration by external influence. The difference here mentioned is vividly exemplified in the myth of Er[21] by the horrible choice of the soul concerning whom it is said: 'he was one of those who had come from heaven, having in his former life lived in a well-ordered city and shared in virtue out of habit without philosophy'.[22] The *Theaetetus*, in its attempt to define knowledge, treats as the last

---

[19] Democritus, *fragment* 125.   [20] *Ti.*, 51D–E.   [21] *R.*, 619B ff.

[2] In the parallel passage of the *Phd.* (82A–B) 'philosophy' is glossed by 'intelligence': ἄνευ φιλοσοφίας τε καὶ νοῦ.

possibility considered the suggestion that 'true opinion' may be a constitutive element of knowledge, may in conjunction with a λόγος or 'account' *be* knowledge itself.[23] As this proposal is tested, it is shown that, of the various possible meanings which λόγος might here have, the most satisfactory is 'knowledge of the proper difference of the object known'.[24] But if this 'knowledge of the difference' is not to be, in turn, mere 'right opinion' about the difference, an empty tautology, the definition is vitiated by a 'circulus in definiendo'.[25] In short, if 'true opinion' and knowledge are not identical, the former can not be an essential element of the latter, either. The common assumption of a relationship between 'right opinion' and knowledge is due to the external similarity of their results,[26] but the rightness of any particular opinion is simply accidental as Plato succinctly shows.[27] Right opinion is still essentially opinion; and this, the *Theaetetus* has already proved, cannot be knowledge, for it involves the possibility of error or wrong opinion which can be explained only as a mistaken reference to something known, although it is difficult to see how—if the term of reference be known—a mistaken identification is possible.[28] Opinion, then, is different from knowledge and secondary to it, for no satisfactory account of error can be given until the process of intellection has been explained.[29] Similarly the earlier part of the *Theaetetus* proved that knowledge can not be sensation or derived from sensation,[30] because sensation itself implies a central faculty to which all individual perceptions are referred and which passes judgement on them all.[31] As in the *Republic*[32] the proof that knowledge and opinion are different faculties is conclusive evidence for the fact that the objects with which they are concerned must be different, so here from the observation that the mind functioning directly without any intermediate organ contemplates the notions that are applicable to all things[33] proceeds the conclusion that knowledge is not to be found in the perceptions but in the reflection upon them, since only in this process is it possible to grasp reality and meaning.[34] The attempt of the *Theaetetus* to define knowledge fails, and this failure demonstrates that the λόγος, the essential characteristic of knowl-

[23] *Tht.*, 201C8 ff.   [24] *Tht.*, 208D.   [25] *Tht.*, 209D4–210A9.
[26] *Tht.*, 209E4–6.   [27] *Tht.*, 201A–C.   [28] *Tht.*, 187B4–200D4.
[29] *Tht.*, 200B–D.   [30] Cf. *Tht.*, 186E9–187A6.
[31] *Tht.*, 184B5–186E10.   [32] *R.*, 477E–478B2.   [33] *Tht.*, 185E1–2.
[34] *Tht.*, 186D2 ff.

edge, cannot be explained by any theory which takes phenomena to be the objects of intellection. That this is the purpose of the dialogue is revealed by the *Timaeus* passage above which shows that the λόγος is the δεσμός (binding) of the *Meno*,[35] the mark which distinguishes knowledge from right opinion in that dialogue and which was there identified with ἀνάμνησις (recollection). The *Theaetetus*, then, is an attempt to prove that the theory of Ideas is a necessary hypothesis for the solution of the problems of epistemology; the constructive doctrine of the *Sophist* demonstrates that it is a sufficient hypothesis for that purpose.[36] The process of abstraction and generalisation which Aristotle thought sufficient to account for knowledge[37] was recognised by Plato,[38] but he considered it to be inadequate. In the *Parmenides*,[39] after advancing all his objections to the hypothesis, Parmenides is made to assert that it is still necessary to assume the existence of Ideas if thought and reasoning are to be saved; and in the *Phaedo*[40] Socrates outlines the theory of abstraction almost in the very words which Aristotle was to use, connects it with the theories of the mechanistic physics, and rejects it in favour of the theory of separate Ideas. The possibility of abstraction itself, if it is to have any meaning, Plato believes, requires the independent reality of the object apprehended by the intellect. That is the basis of his curt refutation of mentalism in the *Parmenides*.[41] So the process of abstraction and analysis outlined in the *Philebus*, which is there said to be possible because of the participation of the phenomena in real Ideas,[42] and which in a simple example of its use in the *Republic*[43] is called 'our customary method', is in the *Phaedrus*[44] designated as ἀνάμνησις and said to require the substantial existence of the Ideas and previous direct knowledge of them by the intellect. The successful 'recollection' of the Ideas by means of the dialectical process is in the *Republic*[45] said to con-

[35] *Men.*, 98A.

[36] Cf. *Sph.*, 258D–264B and note the triumphant tone of 264B5–7.

[37] *De Anima* 432A3–14; *APo.*, 100A3–B17; cf. *Metaph.*, A, 1.

[38] *Chrm.*, 159A1–3; *Phlb.*, 38B12–13.

[39] *Prm.*, 135B5–C3.   [40] *Phd.*, 96B.   [41] *Prm.*, 132B–C.

[42] *Phlb.*, 16C10 ff. N.B. 16D2: εὑρήσειν γὰρ ἐνοῦσαν (for we shall find [the Idea] contained there).

[43] *R.*, 596A.

[44] *Phdr.*, 249B5–C4. Cf. the extended demonstration of *Phd.*, 74A9–77A5 which is based upon epistemological considerations.

[45] *R.*, 479E–480A.

stitute intellection as distinguished from opinion, and the man who is capable of such activity is there described in terms parallel to the 'mythical' description of the 'wingéd intellect' of the *Phaedrus*.[46]

The nature of the mental processes, then, can be explained only by the hypothesis of Ideas. Since no mere addition to right opinion from the sphere with which it itself deals can produce knowledge or make intelligible the fact of error and since no combination of sensations can account for apperception, knowledge cannot be synthetic or derivative. Knowledge as a special faculty dealing *directly* with its own objects must be assumed in order not only to explain the fact of cognition but also to make possible opinion and sensation as they are given by experience. The special faculty of knowledge, however, is characterised by direct contact of subject and object; since phenomena cannot enter into such a relationship with the subject, mediating organs being required in their case, it is necessary that the objects of knowledge be real entities existing apart from the phenomenal world and that the mind have been affected by them before the mental processes dealing with phenomena occur. Only so can one avoid the self-contradictory sensationalism of Protagoras, the psychological nihilism of Gorgias, and the dilemma of Democritus.

The effort to save the phenomena of mental activity leads to the same hypothesis as did the attempt to explain human conduct, and the ethical hypothesis is supported by the independent requirements of epistemology. There is, however, another sphere naturally prior to knowledge and sensation and by which finally all epistemological theories must be judged. The Ideas are necessary to account for the data of mental processes; but the physical world and its characteristics are not dependent upon these mental processes, and it is no more sufficient to assume an ontology which will fit the requirements of epistemology than it is to construct an epistemology in order to account for the phenomena of ethics. It is with this in mind that Timaeus, when in a physical discourse he uses a résumé of the epistemological proof of the existence of Ideas, apologises for his procedure with the excuse that the magnitude of his main subject requires him to give the briefest possible demonstration.[47] The very language of this passage shows that Plato considered it as

---

[46] *Phdr.*, 249C.
[47] *Ti.*, 51C5 ff.

a requirement of sound method to develop his ontological hypothesis according to the data of the physical world itself. This requirement is explained in the *Theaetetus* where a detailed theory of psychological relativism is expounded[48] by way of considering the thesis that knowledge is sensation. Such a doctrine, in spite of the objections that can be brought against its epistemological and ethical consequences, may still present a correct account of the nature of existence as nothing but a flux of motions. What seem to be individual objects and characteristics would then be merely the transitory resultants of the component motions. In that case, knowledge would really be vivid sensations which are the functions of clashing and passing movements.[49] To argue that no practical ethics or adequate epistemology can be developed from such an account is pointless, for there could be no *naturally* valid criterion by which to evaluate the different moments of evidence.[50] Such a theory as that of Ideas would be a merely pragmatic hypothesis, and distinctions of good and bad, true and false would be at best only conventional and artificial. It is, then, necessary that the study of ontology be undertaken independently of the requirements of ethics and epistemology to discover what hypothesis will explain the data of physical phenomena as such.[51] The data with which the investigation has to work are the constantly shifting phenomena of the physical world, and Plato accepts this unceasing flux as a characteristic of all phenomenal existence.[52] This flux, however, is the datum which has to be explained, and his contention is simply that change itself is intelligible and possible only if there exist entities which are not themselves involved in the change. The argument in the *Theaetetus*[53] attempts to show that the constant flux of phenomena involves alteration as well as local motion but that alteration requires the permanent subsistence of immutable abstract qualities. The relativism that asserts the constant change of everything, however, makes attributes and perceptions the simultaneous resultants of the meeting of agent and patient, while agent and patient themselves are merely complexes of change without independent existence,[54] with the result that not only are all things constantly changing their characteristics but the characteristics themselves are constantly altering, and 'whiteness' can no more be

---

[48] *Tht.*, 156A–160E. [49] *Tht.*, 179C. [50] *Tht.*, 158B–E.
[51] *Tht.*, 179D. [52] Cf. *Ti.*, 27D5–28A4. [53] *Tht.*, 181C–183B.
[54] *Tht.*, 182B.

really 'whiteness' than any other colour.[55] Similarly, if the qualities themselves are always altering, the sensations which are defined by these constantly altering qualities are undifferentiated.[56] Such an account of the world involves the denial not only of fixed states and determinable processes but also of the laws of contradiction and the excluded middle.[57] The data of phenomenal change, then, logically require the hypothesis of immutable and immaterial ideas. The argument occurs again at the end of the *Cratylus* (where, however, it is connected with one form of the epistemological proof);[58] and Aristotle accuses the Protagoreans, in the same terms as does Plato, of denying the laws of logic.[59] In a passage obviously influenced by the *Theaetetus*,[60] he explains the difficulties of the relativists as due to their failure to recognise immaterial existences and to note the distinction between quantitative and qualitative change. Like Plato, Aristotle felt that a logical account of physical nature required some hypothesis of qualitative existence as underived from quantitative distinctions.

The digression on mensuration in the *Politicus*[61] has the same intention. There Plato distinguishes between quantitative and qualitative 'measurement', the former being only relative measurement and the latter measurement against a norm,[62] and castigates those who think all the world susceptible of quantitative measurement; their error lies in the supposition that all difference can be reduced to quantitative distinctions.[63] For this reason in the *Timaeus*, where the quantitative determinations of the minima of phenomenal air, fire, water, and earth are elaborated in great detail,[64] Plato still insists that there must be substantive Ideas of air, fire, water, and earth, apart from phenomena, immutable, the objects of intellection only,[65] and that phenomenal objects are what they are because they are imitations of these real Ideas.[66] Indica-

---

[55] *Tht.*, 182D1–5.   [56] *Tht.*, 182D8–E5.   [57] *Tht.*, 183A4–B5.

[58] *Cra,.* 439D3–440C1.

[59] *Metaph.*, 1008A31–34; cf. 1009A6–12.

[60] *Metaph.*, 1010A1–37.   [61] *Pol.*, 283D–287A.

[62] *Pol.*, 283D7–284B2.

[63] *Pol.*, 284E11–285C2; cf. Rodier, *Études de philosophie grecque*, p. 48, note 1.

[64] *Ti.*, 53C4–55C5; 55D7–57C6.

[65] *Ti.*, 51A7–52A4.

[66] *Ti.*, 50C, 51A7–B1 (cf. Shorey in *Class. Phil.* XXIII [1928], p. 358).

tions of the ontological necessity of the hypothesis are not lacking in this dialogue either. The most certain and evident characteristic of phenomena is their instability; they are all involved in the process of generation[67] and so imply a cause external to themselves.[68] Apart from the 'mythical' form of the explanation to which this leads, the argument is the same as the indirect proof of the *Theaetetus*. The instability of phenomena can be explained only by assuming a world of Ideas as the source of phenomenal characteristics. To dispense with such a superphenomenal world is not only to identify right opinion and knowledge but, in fact, to say that phenomena are stable.[69] This brief remark of Timaeus sums up the results of the demonstration in the *Theaetetus* which shows that the relativistic ontology transgresses the law of the excluded middle and so can no more say that all is in motion than that all is at rest. To do away with stable qualities is tantamount to denying the possibility of change.[70] Yet it is the possibility of phenomenal alteration that was to be saved, for phenomena have no stability at all;[71] they are fleeting phrases without persistent substantiality,[72] but such they can be only if apart from them there are substances of which somehow the phenomena partake.[73]

The physical phenomena, then, considered in themselves and not as objects of sensation or cognition still can be saved only by the hypothesis of separate, substantive Ideas. That the necessary and sufficient hypothesis for this sphere turns out to be the very one needed for ethics and epistemology makes it possible to consider the three spheres of existence, cognition, and value as phases of a single unified cosmos.

---

[67] *Ti.*, 28B8–C2.

[68] *Ti.*, 28C2–3.

[69] *Ti.*, 51D6–7.

[70] Aristotle reproduces the argument in his own language in *Metaphysics*, 1010A35–7.

[71] Cf. *Ti.*, 49D4 ff. (βεβαιότητα [stability]-D7) and 51D5–7.

[72] *Ti.*, 49C7–50A4.

[73] *Ti.*, 50B–C. That the mere configuration of space is not enough to produce phenomenal fire, etc., 51B4–6 shows (N.B. καθ' ὅσον ἂν μιμήματα τούτων δέχηται [so far as it receives imitations of these]). All this, I think, makes Shorey's interpretation of 56B3–5 certain (*Class. Phil.*, XXIII [1928], pp. 357–8). To interpret στερεὸν γεγονός here as 'having received a third dimension' would be tautological, for the pyramid is *eo ipso* three-dimensional. Cf. also A. Rivaud in his introduction to his edition of the *Timaeus* (p. 26) in the Budé series.

The apparently disparate phenomena of these three orders, like the seemingly anomalous paths of the planets, had to be accounted for by a single, simple hypothesis which would not only make intelligible the appearances taken separately but at the same time establish the interconnection of them all. The problem which Plato set others in astronomy he set himself in philosophy; the resulting theory of Ideas indicates by its economy that it proceeded from the same skill of formulation which charted for all time the course of astronomical hypothesis.

3

THE THEORY OF IDEAS

A. WEDBERG

Plato's philosophical interpretation of the mathematics he knew is intimately related to his general theory of Ideas. In order to get a clear grasp of Plato's philosophical views on mathematics we must, therefore, first look at the main theses of this theory.

The problem which forms the starting-point for that theory is the problem which—ever since it was first formulated by Plato—has been the basic issue between nominalists and logical realists. Plato was the first to see this problem, and his theory of Ideas is the first attempt to solve it. Although the problem is now more than 2000 years old, it has lost none of its original interest and, alas, it has hardly been brought closer to a "definitive" solution. We can perhaps now distinguish, better than Plato could, the simple logical kernel of the problem from associated metaphysical questions, and we can accordingly separate that part of Plato's theory of Ideas which directly answers the logical problem from those parts in which he gave the reins to his speculative imagination. We shall here take a brief survey of Plato's solution of the logical problem, leaving most of the speculative superstructure out of consideration.

The problem can be formulated either in a "semantical" or in an "ontological" fashion. Both formulations were actually present to Plato's mind.

(a) Let us consider a significant subject-predicate sentence such as: "Socrates is human". Concerning the subject term, "Socrates", we know that there is something which it signifies, or designates, or is a name of, viz., the Athenian philosopher Socrates. Now, it seems reasonable to raise the question: Does also the predicate term, the adjective "human", designate something? Is there an entity of which that term is the name? The same question may be put in

Chapter III of *Plato's Philosophy of Mathematics* by Anders Wedberg (Almqvist and Wiksell, Stockholm, 1955). Reproduced by permission of author and publishers.

connection with any meaningful subject-predicate sentence of the same type. If "X is (a) Y" is a significant sentence with the expression X for its subject and the expression Y for its predicate, then does Y designate an entity of some kind?—In the modern sense of the term, this is a "semantical" question, since it is concerned with the relation between linguistic expressions and the things (entities) to which they refer.

(b) It is a fact that Socrates, Gorgias, Protagoras, etc., are all human. Does this fact mean that there is an entity, say Humanity, to which they are all related in the same manner? In general, if A, B, C, etc., are all Y, is there then some entity, say Y-ness, to which they are all related in an identical fashion?—Since here no mention is made of linguistic expressions and of their reference to things (entities), this formulation of the problem may be called "ontological" in contradistinction to the previous "semantical" formulation. However, it is easily seen that the two questions are actually equivalent. An affirmative answer to the former question implies an affirmative answer to the second, and conversely.

The two equivalent questions are here formulated in connection with what is perhaps the simplest kind of sentences, subject-predicate sentences. But the same questions can of course be raised also in connection with more complicated types of sentences, e.g., relational sentences such as: "Socrates is similar to Plato". We may ask: Does the word "similar", or perhaps the whole expression "is similar to", designate some entity? Into the fact that Socrates is similar to Plato, does there enter a third constituent, say Similarity, besides the two philosophers Socrates and Plato?

Both the semantical and the ontological formulation of the problem can be traced in Plato's dialogues, and he raised the problem with respect not only to subject-predicate sentences but also to relational sentences. Often the two formulations of the problem are inextricably combined. In the *Republic*, book X, the issue is stated thus:

> We are in the habit of postulating one unique Idea for each plurality of objects to which we apply a common name.[1]

Special cases of the problem are discussed in most of the Platonic dialogues. In the *Parmenides* the semantical problem is raised concerning the term "other":

[1] *Republic* 596A.

Must you always mean the same thing when you utter the same name, whether once or repeatedly?

The same thing, of course.

The word 'distinct' is the name of something, is it not?

Certainly.

Then when you utter it, whether once or many times, you apply it to nothing else, and you name nothing else, than that of which it is the name.

Assuredly.

Now when we say that the others are distinct from the one, and the one is distinct from the others, though we use the word 'distinct' twice, we do not for all that apply it to anything else, but we always apply it to that nature of which it is the name.[2]

In the *Hippias Major* the ontological version of the problem is debated with respect to certain ethical qualifications. The proposition that the just are just by justice is the starting-point for the following discussion:

Then this—I mean justice—is a certain thing?

Certainly.

Then, too, by wisdom the wise are wise and by the Good all good things are good?

Of course.

And these are real things, since otherwise they would not do what they do.

To be sure, they are real things.

Then are not all beautiful things beautiful by the Beautiful?

Yes, by the Beautiful.

Which is a real thing?

Yes, for what alternative is there?[3]

As is well known, Plato—the first logical realist in the history of philosophy—answers the problem in the affirmative. Besides the particulars given in sense experience there is another type of entities designated by such words as may occur as predicates in subject-predicate sentences. There is Beauty (designated by the predicate in "*X* is beautiful", or "*X* possesses beauty"), Justice (designated

[2] *Parmenides* 147D–E.
[3] *Hippias Major* 287 C–D.

by the predicate in "*X* is just"), Whiteness (designated by the predicate in "*X* is white"), and so on. There is also such a thing as Similarity (referred to by the term "similar" in the sentence "*X* is similar to *Y*"). For this type of entities Plato uses the terms "*Idea*", or "*Form*", or "*Essence*".[4]

Let the letter "*Y*" represent adjectival or abstract substantival expressions, such as "just" or "justice", "beautiful" or "beauty",

[4] Frequently occurring Platonic terms which are commonly rendered by these and similar English words are *idea, eidos, ousia, genos, fysis*. It has sometimes been argued that the word "Idea" is an appropriate translation of such Platonic terms only in contexts where the metaphysical or transcendental aspect of their connotation is especially stressed by Plato. For Plato himself, however, there was no sharp distinction, or even no distinction at all, between the more logical and the more metaphysical connotation of the terminology of the theory of Ideas. Cf., e.g., *Phaedrus* 249B–C, where the classification of sensible particulars, the grasping of their *eidos*, is said to be a recollection of those things which our soul saw when it was with God. Hence, I think, we are justified in translating the terminology of the theory of Ideas in the same manner whether the context is more logical or more metaphysical in tenor. The term "Idea" is here used merely as a convenient English substitute for a cluster of Greek words, and in any given context it is allowed to carry just as much or as little metaphysical significance as those words do. (The initial letter of "Idea" is capitalized only to call attention to this usage of the term and to obviate confusion with its current psychological usage).—It is especially common to draw a line between those occurrences of *eidos* and *genos* where they signify Idea and those occurrences where they signify class or kind. It is true that there are occurrences where we find it natural to translate these terms with our words "class" or "kind", and other occurrences where this strikes us as unnatural. But, on the whole, Plato himself made no distinction between these types of occurrences. (We have no a priori reason to believe that Plato's own conceptual distinctions were parallel to the distinctions inherent in modern English.) Of course, Plato uses such a term as *eidos* also in a sense which has nothing in common with the theory of Ideas, e.g., in the sense of concrete sensible shapes. But such usages of the term are—as far as I am aware—nowhere confounded by Plato with that usage thereof which belongs to the theory of Ideas, to his logical realism.—A phrase such as "the Idea of Beauty" likewise translates a number of different expressions used by Plato. These expressions do not all contain any of the Greek words for which "Idea" is our English substitute. The literal translation of some common types of Platonic designations for Ideas are "Beauty", "Beauty itself", "the Beautiful" or "the Beautiful itself".

and so on. Then, for appropriate substitutions for "*Y*", the theory of Ideas assumes:

(1 a) *The expression Y is the name of something, an Idea (or Form, or Essence).* •

The passage from the *Parmenides* which we just quoted shows that, for appropriate substitutions for "*Y*", the theory further assumes:

(1 b) *In each context where the expression Y occurs, it is the name of the same thing, the same Idea.*

Any satisfactory semantical theory of language, whether it is based on a philosophy of nominalism or one of logical realism, must of course take into account the fact that words are often ambiguous. Although, I think, Plato might have been prepared to agree to the qualifications of thesis (1 b) which this fact necessitates, he never himself stated them.

In connection with the term "Idea" (and its synonyms) and the names of particular Ideas Plato introduces a certain further semi-technical vocabulary. He often says that it is "by participation in", or "by the presence of", the Idea of Justice that a thing is just, that it is "by participation in", or "by the presence of", the Idea of Beauty that a thing is beautiful, and so on.[5] Using this terminology we may state the basic postulate of the theory of Ideas also in the following ontological fashion. Let the letter "*Y*" represent adjectival expressions, such as "just", "beautiful", and so on, and let "*Y*-ness" represent the corresponding abstract noun. Then, for appropriate substitutions for "*Y*", the theory of Ideas assumes:

(2 a) *It is by participation in the Idea of Y-ness that a thing is Y.*

---

[5] Of course, there is nothing like a fixed technical terminology in Plato's writings. Some of the many Greek terms which are commonly translated by "participation", or "presence", or some similar English word, are no doubt used by Plato in a consciously metaphorical manner. Cf. *Phaedo* 100D. Often Plato says simply that, e.g., good things are good "by (the Idea of) the Good", or "by a common Idea". The more elaborate terminology referred to in the text occurs prominently in the *Phaedo* and in later dialogues.

Leaving out the specification of the Idea, we may also state that, for appropriate substitutions for "Y", the theory postulates:

(2 b) *There is something, an Idea, such that it is by participation therein that a thing is Y.*

We have already quoted a passage from the *Republic* where Plato speaks of "the habit of postulating *one unique* Idea for each plurality of objects to which we apply a common name". He exemplifies the general maxim by saying that there is exactly one Idea of Bed and exactly one Idea of Table. I believe that we are justified in paraphrasing this passage as follows. For appropriate substitutions for "Y" (the passage allows any common name), the theory of Ideas assumes:

(3 a) *There is exactly one Idea such that it is by participation therein that a thing is Y.*

What this statement adds to what has already been said through (2 b) is:

(3 b) *There are never two distinct Ideas such that a thing is Y by participation in the one as well as by participation in the other.*

What does it mean to say that a thing is Y "*by* participation in" the Idea of Y-ness? From (2 a) we can no doubt infer:

(2 c) *A thing is Y if and only if it participates in the Idea of Y-ness.*

If the full meaning of (2 a) were rendered by (2 c), we could also reproduce the full meaning of (2 b) and (3 b) by the following statements:

(2) *There is an Idea such that a thing is Y if and only if it participates therein.*

(3) *There are no two distinct Ideas such that a thing is Y if and only if it participates in the one, as well as if and only if it participates in the other.*

If we are at all entitled to transcribe (2 a) in the manner of (2 c), we should, I think, at any rate have to add that the mutual implication between being Y and participating in the Idea of Y-ness is not a factual coincidence but a necessity. If the mutual implication stated in (3) comprised the merely factual and the necessary as specialised cases, (3) would be to the effect that there are no two distinct Ideas with exactly the same participants. Thus, (3) would amount to a "principle of extensionality" for Ideas: an Idea would be uniquely determined by its participants, by its "extension". If, however, the mutual implication of (3) is necessary, (3) does not exclude the possibility of two distinct Ideas which, by a factual coincidence, have exactly the same participants. The passage from the *Republic* from which we have extracted (3) is rather indefinite on this point. It could perhaps be interpreted as implying a principle of exten-sionality. But we are, I think, on safer ground if we read it as a condensed way of saying that, corresponding to each plurality of objects to which we apply a common name, there is a unique Idea which justifies the application of that name, or that, for each name "Y", there is a unique Idea such that being Y and participating in that Idea are necessarily the same. In those cases where Plato postulates the existence of the abstract entity, he even seems to employ the sentences, "X is Y" and "X participates in Y-ness", as synonymous expressions for the same proposition.

In several places of his *Metaphysics* Aristotle gives what seems to be an excellent account of the doctrine of Ideas and its origin:

> But when Socrates was occupying himself with the excellences of character, and in connection with them became the first to raise the problem of universal definition (. . .; for two things may be fairly ascribed to Socrates—inductive arguments and universal definition, both of which are concerned with the starting-point of science):—but Socrates did not make the universals or the definitions exist apart; *they* [the Platonists], however, gave them a separate existence, and this was the kind of thing they called Ideas. Therefore it followed for them, al-most by the same argument, that there must be Ideas of all things that are spoken of universally, . . . For to each thing there answers an entity which has the same name and exists apart from the substances, and so also in the case of all other

groups there is a one over many, whether these be of this world or eternal.[6]

Abstract terms designate abstract entities of some sort, and to be such and such is to be related in some way to such an abstract entity—that seems to be the basic intuition underlying the whole theory of Ideas. As Aristotle maintains, the theory seems to have grown out of the Socratic endeavour to give definitions of abstract terms. In the sequence of the early Platonic dialogues one can notice how the postulate of the existence of abstract entities, designated by the terms to be defined, gradually assumes a more and more prominent place and finally obtains an interest of its own, independent of the original interest in definitions.

Between extreme nominalism, which denies the existence of any abstract entities, and an extreme realism, which accepts more or less wholesale all significant expressions as designating entities (abstract if not concrete), there is an entire spectrum of possible positions with regard to the problem of the existence of abstract entities. Plato did never clearly define where along this spectrum he took his stand. In the critical discussion of the theory of Ideas that is contained in the *Parmenides*, one of the main objections that are put in the mouth of Parmenides is just this indefiniteness of the theory.[7] The Ideas most often referred to in Plato's writings seem to fall mainly into five (not rigidly separate) classes:

(i) Ethical and esthetical Ideas, such as the Idea of the Good, the Idea of the Just, the Idea of the Beautiful;

(ii) Ideas for certain very general notions, such as the Ideas of Sameness and Difference, Being and Not-being, Likeness and Unlikeness, One and Many;

(iii) Mathematical Ideas, such as the Idea of the Circle, the Idea of the Diameter, the Idea of Two, Three, etc.;

(iv) Ideas for natural kinds, such as the Idea of Man, the Idea of Ox, the Idea of Stone;

[6] *Metaphysics* 1078B17–1079A4. Cf. 987A29–B14. 1086A30–B13.
[7] *Parmenides* 130B–E.

(v) Ideas for kinds of artifacts, such as the Idea of the Table and that of the Couch.[8]

In the *Parmenides* Socrates professes certainty only as to the existence of Ideas of classes (i) and (ii). Concerning (iv) he confesses that he has not been able to make up his mind. Simultaneously, however, he confides that he often gets disturbed and begins to think that every general concept is an Idea.[9] From the *Republic*, book X, we have already quoted a passage, where Socrates apparently maintains a logical realism of an extreme type.

Plato's theory of Ideas is dominated by the conception of an Idea as being—to use Aristotle's expressive phrase—"one over many".[10] This conception, no doubt, covers several distinct assumptions. For the moment it is of interest to observe the implied belief that to every Idea there correspond "many" objects participating in the Idea. Hence, according to Plato, there are no Ideas in which no objects participate or which have empty classes for their extensions. The conscious recognition of empty concepts and empty classes is

---

[8] (i) The Idea of Beauty is perhaps that Idea to which Plato refers more extensively than to any other Idea. It occurs, together with various ethical Ideas, in *Euthydemus, Hippias Major, Cratylus, Protagoras, Meno, Phaedrus, Phaedo, Republic, Parmenides, Philebus, Theaetetus,* and the *Seventh Letter*.

(ii) Such general Ideas play an important role in *Parmenides, Theaetetus, Sophist* and *Timaeus*.

(iii) Mathematical Ideas occur especially in *Phaedo, Republic, Parmenides, Theaetetus, Statesman, Philebus,* and the *Seventh Letter*.

(iv) Ideas of natural kinds occur in *Parmenides, Theaetetus, Statesman, Timaeus, Philebus,* and the *Seventh Letter*.

(v) Ideas of kinds of artifacts occur in *Cratylus, Phaedo, Republic,* the *Seventh Letter* and the *Laws*.

In addition to the five types of Ideas enumerated in the text there occur several other types. In the *Phaedo*, 103C–106A, Hot and Cold, Life and Death are treated as Ideas, and in the *Seventh Letter*, 342D, such sensible qualities as colours are said to constitute Ideas. In the *Philebus*, 17A–18D, the musical notes and the types of speech-sounds for which the letters of the alphabet stand are given as instances of Ideas. In the *Theaetetus*, 202E–205E, the term *Idea* is applied to the syllable, but perhaps it may be argued that this is an altogether different usage of the word. Cf. note 15, below.

[9] *Parmenides* 130C–D. An extreme realist position is maintained also in the *Seventh Letter* 342D.

[10] *Metaphysics* 1079A2–4. Cf. the similar mode of expression in *Republic* 596A.

the result of a logical sophistication at which the Greek philosophers of Plato's time had obviously not yet arrived. This is one limitation of his logical realism.[11]

Another such limitation is apparent from the discussion in the *Statesman* of the relation between the notions of *genos* or *eidos* (or *idea*) and part (*meros*). Socrates explains that a *genos* of things belonging to a given totality of things is necessarily a part of that totality, but that a part of a totality does not have to be a *genos*. If, in dividing the set of all numbers, one were to cut off ten thousand from the rest and then give a separate name to the rest—one would, he asserts, get an instance of parts of the totality of numbers none of which is a *genos*.[12] Like Aristotle Plato seems to assume that there exists a certain privileged natural division of reality into genera, and he recognised none but such natural genera as genuine genera, as Ideas.

We have already analysed part of the significance of Plato's view that each Idea is "one over many". Another part of its significance is that each Idea is "above" each of the many objects participating in the Idea, or that the Idea is never one among those objects. The proposition:

(4) *An Idea is never one among the objects participating therein,*

is one of the most characteristic postulates of Plato's theory of Ideas. It is clearly expressed, e.g., in the following passage from the *Republic*, book V:

> Well, then, [Socrates asks] take the opposite case: the man whose thought recognizes a beauty in itself, and is able to distinguish that self-beautiful and the things that participate in it, and neither supposes the participants to be it nor it the participants—is his life, in your opinion, a waking or a dream state?

[11] Cf. *Metaphysics* 1040A25–27, where Aristotle argues that there cannot exist any Idea which can be predicated of only a single thing, since an Idea is something which is shared by several things. Cf. also *Posterior Analytics* 92B4–8, where he says that (i) to know what, e.g., the essence of humanity is implied knowing that man exists, and (ii) it is possible to understand the meaning of the phrase "goat-stag" but impossible to know the essence of goat-stag.

[12] *Statesman* 262B–263B. Cf. also *ibidem* 287C and *Phaedrus* 265E.

He is very much awake, he [Glaucon] replied.[13]

In discussing the relation between Ideas and particular things Plato frequently makes use of an assumption which may suitably be called the Platonic Principle of Similarity:

(5) *Whenever two things participate in the same Idea, they resemble each other in respect of that Idea; and whenever two things resemble each other, there is an Idea in which they both participate, and this common participation accounts for their resemblance.*

This principle is explicitly stated in the *Parmenides*.[14]

What are the Ideas and what is that relation of participation about which the previously recorded assumptions are made? It is impossible to give a single unambiguous answer to this question. Divergent conceptions of the Ideas and of the relation of participation seem to have competed with each other in Plato's mind. In modern logic we are accustomed to making a distinction between attributes (qualities, properties, relations) on one hand and classes on the other hand. Obviously, Plato's notion of an Idea is closely related to these modern concepts. As a matter of historical fact, Plato's notion of an Idea is the ancestor of which these modern concepts are the refined descendants. A fundamental distinction between attributes and classes, in the modern sense, is that the latter but not the former are subject to a principle of extensionality: whereas non-identical attributes may inhere in exactly the same things, two classes with exactly the same elements are necessarily identical. Usually we assume also a further difference between attributes and classes: the class is a collection, a bringing together (*Zusammenfassung*, says Cantor), of a number of objects, whereas an attribute is a principle according to which such a collection can be established or according to which the objects to be collected are chosen. Although proposition (3), which we have recognised as an essential part of the theory of Ideas, comes close to being a principle of extensionality for Ideas, we have not accepted the interpretation

[13] *Republic* 476C–D. Cf. also, e.g., *Euthydemus* 300E–301A (on beauty). *Parmenides* 130C (on the Idea of Man). Proposition (4) is an essential premise for the paradoxes concerning the Ideas stated in the beginning of the *Parmenides*. Further, (4) plays a role in *Republic* 597C and *Timaeus* 31A–B. Cf. note 18, below.

[14] *Parmenides* 132 D–E.

that it actually is one. Plato's usual manner of speaking suggests that he thought of the Ideas as being principles by means of which particulars are brought together into collections, rather than as being themselves collections.[15] In this respect his Ideas are more akin to our attributes than to our classes. As we shall see in a later context, he sometimes thinks of the Ideas as being, in some sense,

[15] Cf. *Phaedrus* 249B–C, 265D–C.—In *Theaetetus* 202E–205E there is a discussion of the question how a combination of given elements is related to the elements entering into the combination. The question is understood in the widest possible sense (204A), and the relation between a syllable and its letters is considered merely as a concrete example of the abstract notion of a combination of elements. Is the syllable (i) all the letters of which it consists, or (ii) a single Idea (*eidos, idea*) different from all the letters? In particular, is the first syllable of "Socrates" (i) all the letters, S and O, or (ii) a single Idea? If (i), then if it is true that S and O both have some characteristic, it appears that the syllable must likewise have that characteristic, a consequence which contradicts certain previously assumed propositions. (It has been assumed that only combinations of elements are knowable, whereas ultimate elements are unknowable.) If (ii), the syllable must be without parts, since anything which has parts is identical with all the parts; in particular, the letters cannot be parts of the syllable. An attempt is now made to eschew this conclusion by a distinction between "the whole" (*to holon*) and "all" (in the plural: *ta panta*). The whole, it is suggested, is something which has parts without being identical with all the parts. The whole is then identified with "all" in the singular (*to pan*), and the proposed distinction is rejected on the ground that there is no difference in meaning between "all" in the singular and "all" in the plural, and also on the additional ground that both the whole and the all are that from which nothing is missing. The upshot of the discussion is that if (i) the combination of certain elements is all the elements, then the combination will have any characteristic which all the elements have, whereas if (ii) the combination is a single Idea, then the combination is absolutely devoid of parts and, in particular, its elements are not parts of it.

If we are justified in interpreting this discussion as applying also to that synthesis of particulars through which we arrive at the apprehension of the Platonic Ideas, properly so called, the result of the discussion implies that an Idea is either (i) all the particulars belonging to the scope of that Idea, or (ii) a single entity devoid of parts. If we were able to ask Plato which alternative he favours, what would his answer be? The very use of the words *eidos* and *idea* to characterize alternative (ii) seems to indicate that, at least at the moment when he wrote this passage of the *Theaetetus*, Plato would have chosen alternative (ii). Thus, the passage is one—among many others— which indicates an intensional conception of the Ideas: the Idea is something else than the set of "all the things" that partake of it.

"monads" or entities not compounded out of parts.[16] This mode of thinking would seem more in agreement with our intuition of attributes than with our intuition of classes. But on the other hand he also speaks of the Idea-species as being a "part" of the Idea-genus.[17] This mode of speaking would seem more appropriate to

[16] Cf. *Philebus* 15A-B, *Phaedo* 78B-E.

[17] Cf. *Statesman* 263B. In the *Categories* there are signs that Aristotle was, however vaguely, groping his way toward a more elaborate doctrine concerning the problem of intension versus extension. In order to understand what Aristotle says, we have to review briefly some of his definitions. By a "primary substance" Aristotle means simply a concrete individual thing such as a man, a tree, or a horse. The primary substances are classified in a system of natural kinds, genera and species. Not any class, in the abstract logical sense to which we are nowadays accustomed, represents such a genus or species, and only those kinds which are genera of species are, in Aristotle's terminology, "secondary substances". As an example of a term which designates a secondary substance, Aristotle mentions "man"; his stock example of a general term which does not designate any secondary substance is "white". In the *Categories*, 3B10–23, Aristotle endeavours to explain the difference in semantic function between these two types of terms. In reading the passage one should observe that Aristotle uses "substance(s)" as an elliptical mode of referring "substance-term(s)":

"All substance appears to signify what is individual (*tode ti*). In the case of the primary substances, it is indisputably true that they signify what is individual, since their designatum is particular and one in number. In the case of the secondary substances—when we speak, e.g., of 'man' or 'animal'—our form of speech gives the impression that they, too, signify what is individual. But that is not the case: rather they signify a certain quality (*poion ti*), for the subject is not one as a primary substance is; the words 'man' and 'animal' are predicated of many subjects. Yet they do not merely signify a quality, like 'white'; 'white' signifies quality and nothing more. But species and genus determine the quality with reference to substance; they signify substance qualified in a certain manner. The determinate quality covers a larger field in the case of the genus than in that of the species: he who says 'animal' indicates a larger class than he who says 'man'."

It appears that Aristotle here assumes a twofold semantic difference between such terms as "man", "animal", on the one hand, and such terms as "white", on the other hand. (i) Whereas "white" merely indicates a certain quality, "man" signifies substance-with-a-quality, or a sort of substance. This aspect of Aristotle's thought could, I think, be expressed more clearly as follows. The statement, "X is white" (or "White is present in X"), says merely that X has a certain quality; the statement, "X is (a) man", likewise says that X has a certain quality but, in addition, that X is a primary substance. (ii)

our classes than to our attributes. We might perhaps say that the Platonic Ideas are something in between what we call attributes and what we call classes but, on the whole, closer to the former than to the latter. The Idea of Y-ness is almost the same as what we should call the attribute Y-ness, and to participate in that Idea is almost the same as having that attribute.

*

This sketchy account of the theory of Ideas has to omit many important aspects of that theory. The account would, however, be too misleading, if we did not mention the fundamental antinomy in the theory—an antinomy the absurd consequences of which Plato himself was conscious of, although he did not clearly recognize their source. In contradiction to proposition (4), which is contained in the principle of "one over many", Plato assumes that, e.g. the Idea of Beauty is itself an ideal object which is beautiful (and supremely beautiful), the Idea of Justice is itself something which is just (and supremely just), and so on. Thus, Plato believed that:

(6) *The Idea of Y-ness is (a) Y.*[18]

Aristotle seems to maintain that such terms as "man" and "animal" have an intrinsic reference to certain pluralities, or classes, of primary substances, a reference which is absent in the case of such a term as "white", which merely designates a quality. Perhaps it would be justified to say that Aristotle here vaguely envisages a distinction between an intensional and an extensional meaning, and that he assumes such expressions as "white" to have only the former kind of meaning, but such expressions as "man" and "animal" to have both kinds of meaning.

[18] Cf. *Euthydemus* 301A–B (perhaps merely a joke?), *Hippias Major* 288D–289C (Beauty itself must be beautiful in any comparison). *Protagoras* 330C (justice is just), *Symposium* 210E–211B (Beauty itself is beautiful from every point of view, at all times, in any comparison, equally throughout, for every beholder), *Phaedo* 74A–D (Equality is absolutely equal), *Parmenides* 129A–130A (Similarity, the absolute Similars, cannot be dissimilar; Plurality or the (absolute) many, cannot be one), 132A (Greatness is great), 133D–134E (Knowledge itself, the Idea of Knowledge, is knowledge of Truth itself, the Idea of Truth).—In *Republic* 597C proposition (6) is implicitly employed in proving that for each kind of things there is only one Idea, e.g., that there is only one Idea of Bed. The proof is intended as a reductio ad absurdum of the opposite assumption. If there were, e.g., two Ideas of Bed, two such "absolute beds", there would again appear one

If this proposition is combined with the previously recorded proposition (2 c), we immediately obtain the corollary:

(6') *Every Idea participates in itself.*

To be beautiful is to participate in the Idea of Beauty, to be just is to participate in the Idea of Justice, and so on. Hence if the Idea of Beauty is beautiful, the Idea of Justice is just, and so on, every Idea participates in itself. But proposition (6') directly contradicts proposition (4). This contradiction, which I choose to call the fundamental antinomy of the Platonic theory of Ideas, is the greatest logical weakness of that theory.

Plato apparently did not see the contradiction; he never saw that (6) and (2c) together entail (6') which latter proposition he never formulated. But from the contradiction he drew consequences the absurdity of which he saw. Assuming that the word "great" is a permitted substitution for "Y" in (2 a), we find that there exists an Idea of Greatness, I', participation in which makes a thing great. If C' is the set of all great things, it follows from (4) that I' is not itself an element of C'. By (6), however, I' is itself great. Thus, we get a new class of great things, C'', which in addition to all the elements of C' contains I' as an element. By (2 a), again, there exists an Idea of Greatness, I'', in which all the elements of C'' participate. By (4), I'' is not an element of C'' and, hence, distinct form I'. By (6), I'' itself is great. And so on in infinitum. Thus we obtain an infinite sequence of distinct Ideas of

---

which they would have as their common *eidos*, and this third would then be the absolute bed, the Idea of Bed, not the other two. The logic of this curious argument seems to be as follows. Suppose per impossibile that there were two Ideas of Bed, say B' and B''. By (6) each one of these is a bed, an "absolute bed". Hence, by the basic postulates of the theory of Ideas, they participate in an Idea of Bed, say B. From this point on the argument is probably a petitio principii: B which accounts for the fact that B' and B'' are both (absolute) beds, is the Idea of Bed. (If this is the premise to which Plato implicitly appeals at this stage of the argument, he is obviously presupposing the uniqueness that he is out to prove.) By (4), since B' and B'' participate in B, they are distinct from B. Consequently, neither of them is the Idea of Bed, and the assumption that there are two Ideas of Bed has been refuted.—A reasoning similar to this is hinted at in *Timaeus* 31A–B.

Greatness: *I'*, *I''*, *I'''*, . . . In the *Parmenides* Plato lets Parmenides point out this absurdity to Socrates:

> I [Parmenides] fancy your reason for postulating in each case a single Idea is something like this: When there is a number of things which seem to you to be great, you think, as you look at them all, that there is a single identical Idea for all of them, and hence you think that the Great is one.
>
> That is true, he [Socrates] said.
>
> But if with your mind's eye you regard the Great itself and these many great things in the same way, will not another Great appear beyond, by virtue of which all these must appear great?
>
> So it seems.
>
> That is, another Idea of Greatness will appear, in addition to the Greatness itself and the things which partake of it; and again above all these another, by reason of which they are all great, and each of your Ideas will no longer be one but will be infinitely multiplied.[19]

The same objection was later stressed by Aristotle in his criticism of the Platonic theory of Ideas. In contradistinction to Plato, Aristotle shows that he knew exactly how the infinite regress arises, viz. from thinking of the general Idea as a particular partaking of that Idea. In *De Sophisticis Elenchis* he discusses the argument of "the third man", which is a form of the argument stated in the *Parmenides*, and rejects it as a sophism:

> Again, there is the proof that there is a 'third man' distinct from Man and from individual men. But that is a fallacy, for 'Man', and indeed every general predicate, denotes not an individual substance, but a particular quality, or the being related to something in a particular manner, or something of that sort.

The same solution of the puzzle is emphatically restated:

> It is evident then that one must not grant that what is a common predicate applying to a class universally is an individual

---

[19] *Parmenides* 132A–B. (Jowett's translation).

substance, but must say that it denotes either a quality, or a relation or a quantity, or something of that kind.[20]

Aristotle's constant charge that in postulating the Ideas Plato mistakenly made particular substances out of universals, seems in fact to be directed mainly against Plato's proposition (6), which—as we have seen—introduces an antinomy in the theory of Ideas. By rejecting proposition (6) Aristotle definitely advanced the logical analysis of universal concepts.

Postulate (6) entails a new relationship between the Idea and the particulars comprehended under it. By virtue of (6), the Idea of Y-ness is itself a Y. If now a particular X is a Y, the Idea of Y-ness and X will resemble each other in both being Y. Thus, we obtain the consequence:

(7) *If an object participates in the Idea of Y-ness, then that object resembles the Idea (by virtue of their both being Y).*

This is frequently assumed by Plato, and it is, I think, a plausible guess that his adoption of (6) was one of the causes for his adoption of (7). More particularly, Plato often speaks of the Idea as being an archetype of which the participants are a sort of copies or imitations.[21] The Idea of Y-ness acquires for him the status of a kind of

[20] *De sophisticis elenchis* 178B36–179A10.—Cherniss (*Aristotle's criticism of Plato and the Academy*, vol. I [Baltimore 1944], pp. 289–300; *The riddle of the early Academy*, p. 70) maintains that Plato himself realized the mistake which underlies the paradoxes of the *Parmenides*. The essence of Cherniss' argumentation is: since Plato states the paradoxes and yet does not abandon the theory of Ideas, he cannot have considered the paradoxes as valid objections to the theory; hence, he must have had an answer to the objections, and he must, in fact, have known the right answer. In the elaboration of this dubious line of thought Cherniss makes important use of the assumption that the *Parmenides* paradoxes are alluded to also in *Republic* 597C and *Timaeus* 31A–B. This assumption is, I think, a mistake. Cf. note 18 above. Against Cherniss' psychological postulate it can be objected that Plato often musters arguments and counter-arguments on the same question without finding a definitive solution to the quandary, that much of his thinking is, essentially and not merely in its literary expression, the mental dialogue of a sceptic with a faith.

[21] The conception of the Idea as an archetype, of which its participants are imitations, occurs in—besides the *Phaedo* and the *Parmenides*—*Republic* 402C, 472C–D, 484C–D, 500E–501C, 510A–B, D, 520C, 540A, *Phaedrus* 250A–B, 251A, *Timaeus* 29B–C, 37C–E, 39D–E, 48E–49A, 50C, 52C, 92C, etc.

ideal standard: to be Υ is to resemble this standard—about in the same manner, perhaps, as to be a meter in length is to resemble the standard meter. This view underlies the proof for the doctrine of reminiscence in the *Phaedo:* to perceive the equality of, e.g., two stones is to perceive that they (imperfectly) resemble the Idea of Equality, and hence such perception presupposes a previous acquaintance with that Idea, an acquaintance which must date from the life of the soul before birth.[22]

Although assumption (7) is often presupposed in the dialogues, it is rejected in the *Parmenides*—and on excellent grounds! When proposition (7) is combined with (5), we obtain the conclusion, that there exists an idea I'' which accounts for the resemblance between the X that is Υ and the Idea of Υ-ness, that we may designate I'. According to proposition (4), this Idea I'' is distinct both from X and I'. Now, by virtue of (7), I' resembles I'', and hence, by the same argument, there exists a third Idea I''', and so on in infinitum. Yet, all these Ideas: $I', I'', I''', \ldots$, are nothing but the same Idea of Υ-ness.

> I think the most likely view is [Socrates says] that these Ideas exist in nature as patterns, and the other things resemble them and are imitations of them; their participation in Ideas is assimilation to them, that and nothing else.
>
> Then if anything, he [Parmenides] said, resembles the Idea, can that Idea avoid being like the thing which resembles it, in so far as the thing has been made to resemble it; or is there any possibility that the like be unlike its like?
>
> No, there is none.
>
> And must not necessarily the like partake of the same Idea as its like?
>
> It must.
>
> That by participation in which like things are made like, will be the absolute Idea, will it not?
>
> Certainly.
>
> Then it is impossible that anything be like the Idea, or the Idea like anything; for if they are alike, some further Idea, in addition to the first, will always appear, and if that is like anything, still another, and a new Idea will always be arising, if the Idea is like that which partakes of it.

[22] *Phaedo* 74A–75C.

Very true.

Then it is not by likeness that other things partake of Ideas;
we must seek some other method of participation.[23]

Here, it is clearly pointed out that this form of the infinite regress
depends upon acceptance of (7) and, in view of the regress, (7) is
rejected. Strangely enough, however, Plato apparently did not see
that (7) is in effect equivalent to (6), that the rejection of (7)
logically requires the rejection of (6), too, and that, if (6) is rejected, the previously studied form of the infinite regress is likewise
eschewed.

The basic intuition of the theory of Ideas finds its expression in
the propositions (1)–(5). The conception of the Ideas as archetypes
or ideal standards, of which propositions (6) and (7) are an expression, contradicts the basic intuition and complicates the theory
as a whole. The theory is complicated still further by the following
feature. When speaking of Ideas, Plato often has in mind a type of
attribute which, with a modern terminology, we may describe
thus: the given attribute is determinable (in the sense of the English
logician W. E. Johnson)[24]; those attributes which are determinate
forms of the given attribute are arranged in a series as higher and
lower degrees thereof; among these degrees there is one which is
higher than all the others. Beauty as conceived by Plato is such an
attribute: if something is beautiful, it always has some determinate,
higher or lower degree of beauty; and there is one degree of beauty
which is higher than all other degrees. In so far as Plato's Ideas are
general attributes, thought of in a realist fashion, we would expect
Plato to postulate both an Idea of determinable Beauty and Ideas
of each determinate degree of this determinable. But—as is well
known—Plato does nothing of the sort. Instead he postulates only
one unique Idea of Beauty, but this Idea he associates with the
highest degree of beauty.[25] This highest degree, in Plato's opinion,

[23] *Parmenides* 132D–133A.

[24] Cf. W. E. Johnson: *Logic*, vol. I (Cambridge 1940), ch. 11.

[25] It is especially in the case of the notion of beauty and ethical
notions that Plato seems prone to adopt this line of thought. The
clearest passage is perhaps *Symposium* 209E–212A (on beauty).—On
the other hand, in several passages these Ideas come in pairs: beauty—
ugliness, good—evil, etc. Cf. *Euthyphro* 5C–D, *Republic* 476A, *Phaedrus*
246E, *Sophist* 247A, *Theaetetus* 186E. Perhaps Plato sometimes thought
that there stood Ideas at the opposite poles of a given scale, but that

is never exemplified in the world of the senses.[26] When a sensible object is said to partake of the Idea of Beauty, this, therefore, means that the object possesses some inferior degree of the determinable attribute; the Idea of Beauty itself is either the highest degree of that attribute or the ideal standard exhibiting that degree.

*

The metaphysical status of Ideas is explained by Plato mostly in metaphorical terms, and it is difficult to know in how far his statements in this respect are meant to be taken seriously. One thing, however, stands out clearly, viz. that the Ideas are "eternal".[27] The sense in which, according to Plato's most considered opinion, the Ideas are eternal, is, I believe, explained by the passage on eternity in the *Timaeus*:

> The past and the future are created species of time, which we unconsciously but wrongly transfer to the eternal essence; for we say that it [the eternal being] 'was', it 'is', it 'will be', but the truth is that 'is' alone is properly attributed to it, and that 'was' and 'will be' are only to be spoken of becoming in time, ...[28]

---

there were no Ideas for the intermediate points of it.—In "Eudoxus-Studien V", *Quellen und Studien zur Geschichte der Mathematik, Astronomie und Physik*, Abteilumg B: Studien, vol. 3, O. Becker tries to make a case for the thesis that Plato sometimes conceived the relation between Ideas and participants in analogy to that between pure and mixed colours, and that this conception was further elaborated by Eudoxus.— There are passages where Plato seems inclined to the view that to possess a degree of a quality is to participate to a degree in the Idea. Thus, instead of there being Ideas of various degrees of, say, beauty, there will be only one Idea of beauty but the relation of participation holding between particulars and the Idea will itself be of various degrees. Cf. *Republic* 472B–C. Perhaps also *Phaedo* 101B is to be understood in this sense: the greater number is greater by participating to a higher degree in the Idea of Plurality (or Number), and the greater measure is greater by participating to a higher degree in the Idea of Magnitude.

[26] Cf. *Hippias Major* 289D–292E, *Symposium* 209E–212A, *Phaedo* 74A–75D, *Phaedrus* 250A D.

[27] Cf. *Phaedo* 78D–79A (the Ideas unchangeable), *Republic* 500B–C *Philebus* 59A–C, *Phaedrus* 247D–E.

[28] *Timaeus* 37E–38A.

In the same passage everlasting time is said to be a moving image of eternity, distinct from eternity itself which rests in unity.[29] With reference to these words in the *Timaeus* we may, it seems, state as Plato's opinion:

(8) *The Ideas do not exist in time.*

The statement in the *Phaedrus* that the Ideas are located in "the region above the heaven"[30] is a metaphor which itself seems to indicate that the Ideas do not exist in space. This impression is confirmed by Aristotle's explicit assertion that, according to Plato, there is no body outside the heaven and that the Ideas, being nowhere, are not outside either.[31] Probably Plato believed in proposition:

(9) *The Ideas do not exist in space.*

The eternity of Ideas is for Plato intimately related to another property of Ideas, viz. their simplicity:

(10) *Ideas are not compounded out of parts.*

In the *Phaedo* this proposition is clearly stated. In one of his attempts in that dialogue to prove the immortality of the soul Socrates takes for granted the following principle:

> Now is not that which is compounded and composite naturally liable to be decomposed, in the same way in which it was compounded? And if anything is uncompounded, is not that, if anything, naturally unlikely to be decomposed? . . . Then is it most probable that things which are always the same and unchanging are the uncompounded things and the things that are changing and never the same are the composite things?[32]

Whereas sensible things belong to the class of compounded, changing and perishable entities, the Ideas belong to the class of simple,

---

[29] *Timaeus* 37D–E.
[30] *Phaedrus* 247C.
[31] *Physics* 203A8–9. Cf. 209B33–210A2.
[32] *Phaedo* 78B–C.

unchanging entities.[33] In the *Philebus* the Ideas are called "monads", a term which in Plato's language usually connotes something simple, uncompounded.[34]

In contradistinction to the objects of sense perception the Ideas can be apprehended only by abstract thought: only the eye of the mind can see them. Sense impressions may remind us of Ideas, but an Idea is never a part of the contents of sense impressions. The specific mental faculty through which we apprehend Ideas is designated by various Greek words of which the best English equivalent is "reason".[35]

＊

The science which investigates the realm of Ideas is called Dialectic. In the *Phaedrus* Plato states two principles which are involved in dialectical research. One is that "of perceiving and bringing together in one Idea the scattered particulars", the other is that "of dividing things again by classes, where the natural joints are, and not trying to break any part, after the manner of a bad carver".[36] According to Plato's view, all existing things are eternally distributed into a system of kinds[37] and within this system of kinds he assumes a fixed hierarchy of genera and species. The dialectician who endeavours to become aware of this hierarchical order may start from below, from the particulars, and work his way upwards, classifying the particulars into their lowest species, bringing these species together under their nearest genera and then continuing step-by-step along the species-genus-sequence; or he may start from above and work downwards, at each stage dividing the genus at hand into its proper species. It is to these two possible directions of dialectical inquiry that the two "principles" of the *Phaedrus* refer.

In the *Philebus* the particulars are considered as infinitely many and infinitely varied, whereas the number of species of a given

[33] *Phaedo* 78D–E.

[34] *Philebus* 15A–B. Cf., however, *Philebus* 16D where an Idea is still considered as a monad but is simultaneously said to be "many"—since it stands at the top of some section of the species-genus hierarchy —and "infinite"—since infinitely many particulars are comprised under it.

[35] Cf., e.g., *Phaedo* 78D–79A, *Republic* 507B–C, 511D–E.

[36] *Phaedrus* 265D–E.

[37] Cf. *Sophist* 252A.

genus is thought to be always finite. Also the number of stages in the hierarchy of genera and species between any particular and any genus is there, it seems, assumed to be finite. The first phase of dialectical inquiry is accordingly characterized as a transition from the infinite to the finite, the second as a reverse transition. The classification of speech-sounds which is embodied in the alphabetical transcription of the spoken language is mentioned as an example of the first phase.[38] Some of the examples by which Plato illustrates the second phase are: the division of the genus 'sound' or 'utterance' into its various species, vowels, sonants, mutes; the division of the genus 'musical note' into its species, low, high and level[39]; the division of the genus 'human being' into men and women, or that of number into odd and even.[40]

Intimately related to these two phases of dialectical inquiry is the task of defining each kind, since Plato thinks of definition as being essentially definition by genus proximum and differentia specifica.[41]

The two tasks of Dialectic formulated in the *Phaedrus* are mainly concerned with answering questions of the following types: to what species does this particular belong? what is the genus proximum of this species? which are the species of this genus? To define a given kind involves the further but related problem: what are the differentia specifica of this species?

A third task of Dialectic becomes apparent in the *Sophist*, a task which cannot readily be reduced to that of answering such problems of classification. Given two kinds, or Ideas, *A* and *B*, Dialectic has to investigate also whether *A* can be truly predicated of *B* or *B* of *A*. Taking the notions of Being (Existence, Identity), Motion and Rest as his paradigms, Plato discusses such questions as: does Motion exist? does Rest exist? is Rest in Motion? is Motion at Rest?[42] The same kind of dialectical investigation is abundantly exemplified in the *Parmenides*.

All the tasks of Dialectic so far mentioned are probably alluded to in the following description of that science from the *Sophist*:

---

[38] *Philebus* 18A–D.
[39] *Philebus* 17A–D.
[40] *Statesman* 262C–E.
[41] Cf. *Phaedrus* 265D–266B, 277B–C. Cf. also the definitions in the *Sophist* and the *Statesman*.
[42] *Sophist* 250A–259B.

Stranger. Now since we have agreed that the Ideas are similarly related to each other in respect of their intermixture, must not he possess some science and proceed by means of reason who is to show correctly which of the Ideas harmonize with which, and which reject one another? And also if he is to show whether there are some Ideas extending through all and holding them together so that they can mingle, and again, in divisions, whether there are not other universal principles of the divisions?

Theaetetus. Certainly he needs science, and perhaps even the .greatest of sciences.

Str. Then, Theaetetus, what name shall we give to this science? Or, by Zeus, have we unwittingly stumbled upon the science that belongs to free men and perhaps found the philosopher when we were looking for the sophist?

Th. What do you mean?

Str. Shall we not say that the division according to Ideas and the avoidance of the belief that the same Idea is another, or another the same, belongs to the science of Dialectic?

Th. Yes, we shall.

Str. Then he who can do this has a clear perception of one unique Idea extending over many which are separate from one another, and of many Ideas differing from one another but included under one unique higher Idea, and again of one Idea constituted by the union of many wholes, and of many Ideas entirely apart and separate. This is the knowledge and ability to distinguish in accordance with the Ideas whether, in each case, communion can take place or not.[43]

In the *Republic* Plato brings out another aspect of the two phases —the ascending and the descending—of dialectical inquiry. In the first phase the mind gradually mounts to higher and higher principles. The principles are "hypothetical" only, until the mind has grasped the first principle, which—apparently—is the Idea of the Good. But from this moment on the mind is in possession of a higher kind of knowledge which is non-hypothetical. It now turns downwards again and derives the previous hypotheses from the first principle. Dialectical science treats its hypotheses:

[43] *Sophist* 253B–E.

not as beginnings but really as hypotheses, as steps and springboards so to speak, in order that it may rise to that which is not hypothesized and is the beginning of everything and, having grasped it, may proceed downward to the end, clinging to the things that cling to that, and making no use whatever of any object of sense but only of Ideas themselves through themselves on themselves, and ending with Ideas.[44]

Here, too, the two aspects of Dialectic that were distinguished in the *Phaedrus* and the *Philebus* are probably present to Plato's mind. But, obviously, the scope of Dialectic is here widened so as to embrace also propositions of another kind than the classificatory propositions of those dialogues. The pre-eminence of the Idea of the Good is probably connected with the doctrine of the *Phaedo* that the ultimate explanation of anything must be the showing that it is best for it to be as it is, and the similar principle which the *Timaeus* lays down for the explanation of the physical world.[45] What Dialectic explains in this teleological fashion, can hardly be merely theorems of classification. Actually, Plato envisages the possibility that the theorems of the mathematical sciences may obtain a foundation in Dialectic.[46] Thus, it seems that, in its final stage, Dialectic is here a deductive science which is the logical basis for the entire field of rational knowledge and which derives all its conclusions from a first self-evident principle, expressing the supreme insight into the Idea of the Good.

[44] *Republic* 511B–C.
[45] *Phaedo* 97C–99C, *Timaeus* 29A.
[46] *Republic* 510C–511E, 533A–D.

4

LEARNING AS RECOLLECTION

JULIUS MORAVCSIK

Important philosophic theses often have the disturbing character of falling somewhere between the areas of a priori propositions, empirical theories, and mere metaphors. One such thesis is Plato's proposal, expounded most fully in *Meno* 80D–86C, that learning of a certain kind is recollection. The aim of this paper is to explore both the nature of the problem which this proposal was designed to solve, and the explanatory power of the alleged solution. In what follows no attempt will be made to give a comprehensive interpretation of the passage referred to above; in particular, nothing is said about the relation of this proposal to the Theory of Forms, and about whether the slave boy has knowledge or mere belief at the end of the demonstration of his learning geometry. Attention is given, however, not only to what Plato actually said, but also to what his statements entail. Thus, for example, part of this investigation explores the type of learning model Plato commits himself to, even though no full account of any model is given in the text.

A few preliminary remarks about the concept of learning should help to clarify Plato's problem. Underlying the puzzles discussed below is the assumption that learning can be distinguished from the more generic concept of acquiring intellectual skills. That is to say, learning something is one, but not the only one, possible mode of acquiring it. Not every way of acquiring a skill will count as a way of learning. It is logically possible that the skill of performing simple arithmetical operations could be acquired by submitting to a certain kind of surgery. Even if this were the case, we would not count it as a case of learning. In order to ascribe to someone the acquisition of a skill, it is sufficient to establish that at some time t′ he did not possess that skill, and that at a later time t″ he did possess it. In order to ascribe learning to this person, further assumptions have to be made. The defining conditions for what constitutes learning will differ depending on the nature of the subject to be

This essay has not been previously published.

learned. It is not clear that there are any general conditions other than the condition of acquisition that all kinds of learning must meet. In any case, for the purposes of this paper it is sufficient to assume that such conditions can be spelled out with respect to the learning of intellectual skills such as knowing how to do arithmetic, and how to demonstrate geometrical theorems.

If conceptual difficulties surround the concept of learning, the question may arise: "is learning possible?" to which the obvious reply would be: "why not?" An answer to *this* question leads to our passage in the *Meno*. For the thesis that learning taking the form of inquiry is recollection—proclaimed at 81D4–5—is given as an answer to an argument designed to show the impossibility of such learning. The argument is expounded in 80D5–E5. It is stated twice, first by Meno and then by Socrates. Socrates' version of the argument proceeds as follows. It is not possible for a man to inquire either into what he knows or into what he does not know. He cannot inquire into that which he knows, since if he knows it there is no room for inquiry. On the other hand, he cannot inquire into that which he does not know, since in that case he does not know what it is that he should be seeking.

As stated, this is a paradox of learning taking the form of inquiry, and not a paradox of learning in general, or a paradox of acquiring information, or a paradox of knowledge. The second half of the paradox depends on the assumption that the projected learning must be given direction by the learner himself. It follows from this that the only kind of learning called into question, and thus the only kind of learning that is explained as recollection, is learning taking the form of inquiry. This is brought out by the Greek words used in the passage. The paradox at 80D–E is stated in terms of ζήτησις (inquiry) even though in 81E4–5 μάθησις (learning) is called recollection. Thus the learning of non-intellectual skills such as riding, or learning by being told, or by imitation, are not included either in the paradox or in its intended solution, since these modes of learning do not involve inquiry in the relevant sense.

The relevant sense of inquiry is itself, of course, in need of clarification. There are reasons to suppose that Plato did not want it to include empirical inquiry. One such reason is that in the case of empirical inquiry the paradox can be resolved by invoking the distinctions between sense and denotation, and between understanding a sentence and knowing which truth value to assign to the proposition expressed by it. For example, the answer to the question: "is it cold in Escanaba?" is an empirical proposition. We can describe the inquiry in two stages. The first is the understanding of the sentence "it is cold in Escanaba," the second is the process of verifying the proposition expressed by the sentence, involving the gathering of evidence furnished by the senses that leads to the assignment of a truth value to that proposition. The two stages are not only distinct as the stages of understanding and verification, but they also contrast with each other as an internal (understanding) and external (verification) process. Thus the paradox can be resolved for this case by pointing out that in a sense the learner knows what he seeks; i.e., he understands the proposition the truth value of which he attempts to determine. What he does not know at the beginning of the inquiry is the truth value of the proposition in question. This solution leaves us, however, with the unanalyzed notion of understanding a sentence. The clarification of this notion leads to a consideration of a priori inquiry, since the grasping of meanings of sentences entails knowledge of certain a priori propositions.

The distinction between understanding and verification applies also to a priori inquiries. In the case of this type of inquiry, however, it is far more difficult to draw a sharp line between the two kinds of processes representing the two stages of inquiry. Not only are verification procedures such as proof, calculation, etc. not matters of gathering external evidence, but they are also not clearly separable from processes that make up understanding. In the case of propositions derived from definitions, such as the one expressed by "red is a colour," verification does not involve anything in addition to understanding, and thus the distinction coalesces. We can see from this that even if the first step toward solving Plato's paradox lies in distinguishing between understanding and verification, further explanations are required to illuminate the notion of understanding in the case of empirical inquiry, and in the case of a priori inquiry the processes that make up both understanding and verification.

There are a number of considerations weighing against the hypothesis that Plato understood the paradox within the limits mentioned above. The foremost of these is that he nowhere mentions such a restriction. Another consideration is that the distinction between conditions for truth and conditions for meaning does not emerge in Plato's writings until the *Sophist*, which belongs to the later dialogues. Thirdly, though distinctions like that between the a priori and the empirical are often drawn by Plato (though never exactly in such terms or terms coextensive with these), they are not invoked in the passage under consideration. These considerations seem, however, to be outweighed by the evidence in favor of ascribing to Plato the more limited conception of the paradox. The foremost of these are the philosophical considerations mentioned above. For though admittedly some of the technical distinctions required to explicate the restricted nature of the paradox do not appear in this passage or in any of the dialogues written in the same period as the *Meno*, it is intuitively easy to see that one would not be bothered by the paradox except in cases of a priori inquiry. Even if one did not have at one's disposal technical notions helping to eliminate the paradox for cases of empirical inquiry, one could be intuitively certain that in these cases the paradox can be resolved in ways other than by invoking the recollection theory. Secondly, nowhere in the passage can one find a mention of empirical investigations.[1] Plato's illustration of the recollection thesis, which in turn is an answer to the paradox, involves the science of geometry, a branch of knowledge regarded by Plato as a priori (as evident, e.g., from Bk. VII of the *Republic*). The context of the passage is the search for an answer to the question: "what is excellence?" and Plato would regard any satisfactory answer to this question as an a priori proposition. In 81C7–8 Plato mentions the problem of finding out what excellence is as something falling within the scope of the recollection theory. Further evidence is furnished by the discussion of the recollection theory of learning in *Phaedo* 72E ff., where it is made clear that recollection leads eventually to knowledge and that only a priori knowledge is regarded by Plato as genuine knowledge. To sum up, although Plato places no explicit limitations on the paradox, he discusses it and the recollection thesis only in connection with what he takes to be a priori inquiries. This, in conjunction with our analysis of the nature of the paradox,

[1] Evidence for this as well as a decisive refutation of the claim that the slave boy conducts an empirical investigation can be found in G. Vlastos' "Anamnesis in the *Meno*," *Dialogue*, 4 (1965), pp. 143–167. A bibliography of recent interesting material on this topic is to be found in note 2 of this paper. I am indebted to Professor Vlastos for helpful suggestions concerning this topic, made in personal correspondence.

makes it reasonable to assume that both the paradox and its proposed solution are interpreted by Plato to apply to a priori contexts only.

Having considered the nature and scope of the paradox, it is time to consider the ways in which and the extent to which Plato could have regarded the recollection thesis of learning as an answer to it. Some clues are given in the ways in which Socrates' restatement of the paradox differs from Meno's (80D5–8). In Meno's version the paradox is about inquiry into that of which we are *altogether* ignorant. Socrates' restatement omits this strong qualification ($\pi\alpha\rho\acute{\alpha}\pi\alpha\nu$). The reason for this is presumably that the intended solution covers only those cases in which we in a sense know what we are searching for. The recollection thesis is no answer to a paradox that assumes that the object of inquiry is not known in any way whatsoever at the start of the investigation. The other difference between the two versions is that Meno spells out only the second half of the paradox (we cannot inquire into that which we do not know), and he does this in terms different from those of Socrates. For though Meno too states the difficulty of directing an inquiry toward an unknown object, he adds the question of how one would know that what is found is the information sought initially. This second problem, how does one know that one arrived at the correct solution, is not mentioned by Socrates. The reason for this is presumably that as he interprets the puzzle this question need not arise. If one understands what one investigates, then one will know when an answer is given to the original question. Of course, one might interpret the added question in Meno's version also as raising the problem of how one knows that one knows something. This problem is, however, not dealt with in the *Meno* or in any of the other middle-period dialogues. The difficulty is recognized explicitly only in the *Theaetetus*, which is one of the later dialogues.

These clues confirm our initial suggestion that the recollection thesis is designed to show that in a sense the inquirer does and in a sense does not know that which he is seeking. The distinction between understanding and verification is related to the solution of the paradox in the following way. In the case of inquiries leading to empirical discoveries the initial state of the inquirer is one of knowing (i.e., understanding, which is to be explained by the recollection theory) and of not knowing (i.e., not having evidence to assign the proper truth value to the proposition that serves as the object of inquiry). In the case of inquiries terminating with the knowledge of a priori truths, knowing and not knowing cannot be strictly separated as understanding and verification; the recollection theory is supposed to explain both of these.

At least two features that are logically tied to the concept of remembering have also roles in Plato's characterization of a priori inquiry. One of these is the historical and the other the entitative aspect of remembering. We can explain the historical aspect by saying that if Jones remembers something at time t', then there must have been an earlier time t'' such that at that time Jones knew, believed, experienced, etc. that which he remembers at t'. In short, the claim "Jones remembers p, but at no previous time did he know, believe, experience, etc. p" is self-contradictory. While this historical condition is necessary for remembering, it is not sufficient, else we would have no way of distinguishing between "Jones remembers p" and "Jones at one time knew, believed, etc. p, and now he knows, believes, thinks of, etc. p again." In other words, there is a difference between remembering something from some previous occasion and thinking the same thing twice on two temporally separate occasions. This difference leads us to the entitative feature of remembering. This feature is explained by the statement that there must be an entity or entities contained in a remembering organism, be it mental or physical, such that this or these are related causally both to the event of experience, awareness, etc. at time t' and to the event of remembering at t''; and that the presence of this element or these elements in the organism distinguishes the remembering mind or organism from one that is merely thinking of something twice.

Our review of the relevant passages will show that both of these features of remembering have roles in Plato's analogy. At this point, however, we should note that by itself the historical feature neither answers the paradox nor gives any explanatory power to the analogy. The entitative feature, however, can even perform both of these functions—given certain qualifications—by itself. This is the feature of the analogy that ties Plato's thesis to what later became known as the innate idea theory. The problem about inquiry is, as we noted earlier, that it seems necessary to suppose that the learner in a sense knows and in a sense does not know what he is seeking. The historical feature of recollection does not help with this problem. For the question: "how does he know what he is inquiring about?" cannot be answered by saying that he has seen it before in another life. This answer has significance only if we add: "and he remembers now." Thus we are relying again on the entitative feature. The explanatory force of the analogy with regard to learning is again carried by the entitative feature. For what is crucial to the explanation of learning geometry is not that one has seen the truths of geometry before in a previous existence, but that these truths are somehow within us, and the task of learning is to bring them to consciousness. Thus the entitative feature allows us to reply to the paradox that in a sense what is to be inquired after is in the mind, and yet in a sense it is not known, i.e., not brought to the surface of consciousness. We can see from this that the claim that we have a set of concepts and beliefs given innately to our minds such that given proper stimulation (and stage of maturation) these can be brought to consciousness, is crucial to the recollection thesis if it is to have any explanatory power at all. Evidence that Plato construed his thesis in this manner is provided by 85C4-5, where Socrates says that recollection involves bringing out in people beliefs that were in a sense in them all along. The theory of innate ideas can be derived from the recollection thesis by dropping the historical feature and modifying the entitative aspect.[2] For the theory thus construed can be understood as the claim that the mind is furnished innately with a set of concepts which it contains in a way analogous to the way in which what is remembered is stored in the mind.

Plato's theory as presented contains two parts. First there is a general account of the processes underlying what we observe as learning, and then an illustration is provided by having Socrates help a slave boy discover some elementary truths of geometry. The general account can be summarized in the following way. The soul being immortal, previous to our lives we have seen and learned all "things." What we call learning is simply recollecting what we once possessed. Furthermore, all things that make up nature are related to each other, and thus if one recollected one part, nothing prevents one from discovering all the rest, provided that sufficient effort is made on the part of the learner.

[2]See, e.g., N. Chomsky, *Cartesian Linguistics*, New York, 1966, pp. 63 and 108. For further elaboration see the author's "Linguistic Theory and the Philosophy of Language," *Foundations of Language*, 3 (1967), pp. 209-33.

This account raises several questions. First, what is the force of adding the condition of remembering to the condition of having previously seen all things? Since the latter is equivalent to the historical feature of recollection, we must assume that the addition entails the entitative feature of recollection, else there would be no point in Plato's talking about remembering instead of seeing something twice. Secondly, what are the elements of nature that the soul has "seen and learned" before? The Greek word used here ($\chi\rho\acute{\eta}\mu\alpha\tau\alpha$ 81C7) is so neutral in meaning that it does not settle the issue. Still, it seems reasonable to suppose that the "things" cannot be the facts, empirical and otherwise, that make up the history of the world. For example, it is most implausible to suppose that Plato construed human souls as having seen or learned either in Hades or in any of their previous lives the fact that in A.D. 1966 the Braves would move from Milwaukee to Atlanta. It is far more likely that what Plato supposed to have been seen and learned before are elements of simple a priori propositions. Such an interpretation not only makes sense of the passage under consideration but fits well with our previous considerations about the scope of the paradox. The third question is: what is meant by saying that all things making up nature are related, or "akin"? The phrase "all [things that make up] nature" could not refer, as Bluck seems to have thought,[3] to everything that exists, since that would imply that all particulars that partake of the Forms are related to each other. "Nature" in this context must mean "what is permanent and intelligible," thus having a meaning related to phrases like "the nature of a Form" (see, e.g., *Symposium* 210E5). If Plato thinks primarily of concepts as innate in the human mind, rather than propositions, then the claim can be best construed as stating that these concepts form a "field" of some sort, so that if one has brought one element to consciousness then this will bring with it the ability to bring to consciousness other members of the field as well. In other words, the grasp of one innate idea will facilitate the grasp of the rest, and this is to be accounted for by assuming that these concepts form an interrelated field.

This is not the only possible interpretation. Another interpretation suggests itself according to which recollection and the corresponding sense of "learning" are to be understood as the intuitive

[3] R. D. Bluck, *Plato's Meno*, Cambridge, 1961, p. 288.

grasp of simple concepts and the drawing of deductive inferences. If this view is correct, then Plato must think of the realm of a priori concepts and propositions as constituting a deductive hierarchy. Such a conception of a priori knowledge would be surprisingly congenial to empiricists like Hume and surprisingly unlike the conception of a rationalist like Kant. One of the difficulties of this view is that it gives an implausible interpretation of 81C9–D3, where Plato marks off two stages in recollection. As we saw, the first is to recollect one of the elements in the mind, and the second step is to go on and recover all the rest. According to the deductive interpretation Plato commits himself here to saying that if one succeeds in understanding an a priori proposition about a Form, then he can deduce from this all of the other a priori propositions. Not only is this claim intrinsically implausible, but there is no evidence in the other dialogues that Plato ever held such a view. Another difficulty of this interpretation is that, as we saw, the recollection theory is applicable also to situations in which there is little if any room for deductive arguments such as the discovery of answers to questions like: "what is excellence?" "what is learning?" Finally, if recollection is primarily a deductive activity, why would it be necessary for Plato to say that at a previous stage the soul has "seen all"? There would be no need for this if all a priori propositions were deductively related, and if men had innate reasoning ability. None of these objections is decisive, but it is worth noting that the alternative interpretation better fits Plato's general account of recollection.

One point emerging from this discussion is that on any reasonable interpretation Plato holds that the mind contains not only innate abilities such as the ability to reason deductively, but also concepts such as those of geometry and valuation. The term "innate" does not cause difficulties as long as it is used to characterize abilities. We can contrast innate with acquired abilities by stating that the latter are the result of training or conditioning. It may seem, however, that the notion of an innate idea or concept is less clear. It helps to point out that Plato's claim is not about the slave boy or Meno in particular, but about the human species of which Meno and the slave boy are only instances. To say that a concept is given innately to humans is to say that, given proper stimulation and a required stage of maturation, any human will utilize this concept in the interpretation of experience, and that the concept can be shown not to be acquired from experience by abstraction or by any other known process.

Let us now consider the status of the recollection thesis. Was it intended by Plato as an empirical hypothesis or as an a priori claim? In order to see this matter more clearly, one must realize that "learning" is used by Plato in these passages in two senses. For Plato makes the following claim. i) Learning is, in certain types of cases, recollection. Occasionally this is expressed by ii) what we call "learning" is really recollection (81E4–5). At one point, however, during the illustration of the theory, Socrates asks Meno iii) whether the boy is learning from him or is simply being reminded (82B6–7). It is impossible to assign consistent sense to i)–iii) without invoking two senses of "learn." "Learn*" has the ordinary sense of "learning"; i.e., it has the sense that would allow Plato to use it to cover all cases that would count ordinarily as learning. The sense of "learning**," on the other hand, is to be contrasted with that of "recollecting." "Learning*" carries no such contrast since it has no implications as to what theory could best account for all cases that fall under it. "Learning**" is roughly equivalent to "acquiring knowledge in such a way that what becomes known is qualitatively identical to what the learner has been exposed to by part of the external environment." Making use of this distinction we can express Plato's claim as the statement that learning* a priori matters never involves learning**, but recollection. Thus in i) and ii) "learning" should be interpreted as "learning*" while in iii) "learning**" is used by Plato. There is no evidence to support the claim that the theory of recollection is used to define either "learning*" or "learning**." The only plausible candidate for a definiendum would be "learning* a priori matters," but when Plato claims that this can be accounted for only by the recollection theory, he is not claiming this as a matter of definition, based on the meanings of the relevant phrases, or concept containment. If he thought that this was a matter of definition, then there would have been no point to the inclusion of the conversation with the slave boy.

We might consider the suggestion that Plato intends the thesis as an empirical hypothesis. Some encouragement for this view may be derived from 86B6–7, where some uncertainty is expressed by Socrates with regard to the explanation proposed in the preceding passage. A closer examination of the context shows, however, that

Plato expresses reservations only with regard to some of the details of his theory; he has no doubt about the general claim that learning is recollection. There is further evidence in 81 E3 ff. that tells against this interpretation and supports the claim that for Plato his theory has a priori status. For in this passage Meno asks Socrates to teach him that learning is recollection. In reply Socrates points out that on his own view Meno cannot be taught that learning is recollection, he will have to recollect that fact. Meno concludes this interlude by asking Socrates to help him get clear about this matter in any way he can (82A7–B2). This interlude shows that the point of introducing the conversation with the slave boy is to help Meno to recollect what learning is. Thus recollection takes place on two levels; the slave boy is recollecting geometry, and Meno is recollecting what learning is. The parallel shows that Plato's theory of learning is meant to be an a priori thesis. Since we saw above that the theory is not put forward as something true by definition, its intended status must be that of an a priori non-analytic truth.

There are two grounds for Plato's thesis that the learning of a priori truths must be recollection. One of these is the resolution of the paradox of inquiry. The recollection thesis enables us to give a consistent and intelligible account of how the inquirer at the outset both knows and does not know what he is seeking. The other ground is the set of general characteristics holding for normal conditions of human inquiry into a priori subjects that are illustrated in the conversation with the slave boy. With regard to these conditions Plato's argument seems to take the following form: given that there is successful inquiry into a priori matters, and given the nature of such inquiry (illuminated negatively by the learner's paradox) together with certain general facts about human learning conditions, learning within this restricted scope must be like recollection. This structure is very similar to the structure of Kant's transcendental arguments. In those arguments too, certain propositions are shown to be necessary on the basis of the analysis of all-pervasive human abilities and their typical manifestations.

In this connection it is also illuminating to compare Plato's treatment of the learner's paradox with the so-called paradox of analysis discussed in twentieth-century analytic philosophy. The paradox of analysis arises in connection with the analysis of the meanings of expressions that have an established use. According to the paradox, such an analysis can only be either trivial and unilluminating or incorrect. For if the definiens reflects correctly the established meaning of the definiendum then the analysis should not yield anything new and illuminating. If it does yield something new and illuminating, then how could it reflect correctly the established meaning of the definiendum?

The learner's paradox is wider in scope. It calls into question any inquiry into those subjects for which the senses can furnish no relevant evidence. The paradox of analysis calls into question only those inquiries the object of which is the establishment of analytic propositions that are true by definition. The paradox of analysis arises only in connection with inquiries whose aim is to establish a proposition of identity one side of which stands for expressions whose meanings must be—ex hypothesi—understood at the outset of the inquiry. The recollection theory and the paradox that it resolves carry no such restrictions. The two paradoxes are equivalent only if all a priori propositions are analytic and true by definition. Plato certainly would not have accepted this claim about the a priori, at least in any form that would construe analyticity in terms of logical truth and stipulative or conventional definitions.

These considerations show the recollection thesis to be an a priori non-analytic answer to the question: "how is inquiry into a priori matters possible?" As an answer, the recollection thesis states that inquiry of this type is analogous to recollection. The initial understanding of the object of inquiry is made intelligible by saying that these objects are in our minds in a way analogous to the way in which the content of a recollection is in our minds between the initial experience of what is later remembered and the act of remembering. Finally, the description of recollection suggests that the connections between the concepts given innately are not solely analytic. It is time to test this interpretation on the passage in which the recollection thesis is illustrated.

The illustration (82B–85B) consists of a dialogue between Socrates and a slave boy, at the end of which the slave boy has some understanding of certain procedures by which one can construct squares of areas determined with reference to the size of the sides and diagonals of a given square. At the termination of the conversation Meno and Socrates agree that the slave boy did not acquire his knowledge in the form of information presented by an outside source; he discovered things for himself and his discovery resembled recollection. This agreement cannot rest on empirical grounds, since the inductive basis for the conclusion interpreted as an empirical generalization would be slender indeed. The same consideration shows that the slave boy's knowledge[4] could not be based on empirical evidence, since the group of squares scrawled into the sand by Socrates would hardly furnish adequate grounds for inductive generalization. Nor is there material surrounding the passage in question that would indicate that the conversation is interpreted as a "crucial experiment" either by Meno or by the slave boy.

The demonstration is supposed to show that a slave boy can learn a part of geometry by recollection. The conversation is interrupted twice by Socrates to point out to Meno that the slave boy is not being instructed, he is only being asked questions (82E4–5, 84C11–D2). How are we to understand this contrast between instruction and questioning, especially in view of the fact that many of the questions require only a yes or no answer? (E.g., "doubling the size gives us not a double but a fourfold figure? True." (83B8–C2). There is apparently, according to Plato, a gap between the question and the response. This unobservable gap is *understanding*. The need for this intervening process is brought out partly by the fact that at one point of the discussion Socrates deceives the slave boy by leading him to an incorrect conclusion. Thus the slave boy is forced to see that mere assent to authority will not do. Thus recollection is not the observable event of the slave boy answering a question, but rather something of which the answering is only a sign. In order to understand the contrast between instruction and questioning we must draw the following fourfold distinction: what the slave boy is exposed to, the meaning of what the slave boy is exposed to, the process of understanding, and the response that is the outcome of understanding. Questioning is supposed to serve merely to stimulate the process of understanding. Being instructed would involve information being conveyed to the subject in such a manner that what he comes to know can be identified with what is conveyed to him from the outside source. Under these circumstances understanding could be reduced to simple decoding and would not require the addition of concepts or propositions from within itself.

---

[4] The term "knowledge" is used loosely here, leaving it an open question whether at the end of the conversation the slave boy has knowledge in the Platonic sense, or merely true belief.

We can represent the slave boy as a geometry learning device. The input of this device is what the slave boy is exposed to, while the output, according to Plato, is understanding. The output is unobservable; the observed event of answering provides merely indirect evidence for understanding. Thus input and output do not correspond to what is observable and unobservable. In this respect too, learning is analogous to recollecting, as the diagrams below indicate.

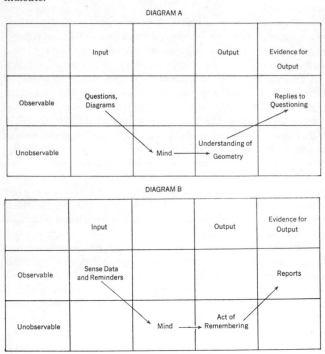

DIAGRAM A

	Input	Output	Evidence for Output
Observable	Questions, Diagrams		Replies to Questioning
Unobservable		Mind → Understanding of Geometry	

DIAGRAM B

	Input	Output	Evidence for Output
Observable	Sense Data and Reminders		Reports
Unobservable		Mind → Act of Remembering	

There is no great difference between the nature of the observable input, Socrates' verbal behaviour, and the observable response, the verbal behaviour of the slave boy. Likewise, there is no great difference in the nature of a reminder and our report of recollection. The difference lies in the nature of the input and the act of understanding as well as between the reminder and the act of remembering. These differences are so great that Plato thinks we must assume, in order to explain the connections, the existence of an independent contribution of the mind that helps to bridge the gaps. The difference between reminder and recollection can be explained only on the assumption that the mind has stored something within it between the time of the experience and the time at which the experience is remembered, and that this element plays a vital role in the act of remembering (this was called above the entitative feature of remembering). According to Plato the difference between the input and the act of understanding can be explained only if we assume that the mind contains elements of what is understood in a way analogous to the way in which it contains what enables us to remember, and that these elements in the mind play a vital role in understanding while the role of the input is merely one of stimulation.

It remains to be shown that the illustration contains the recollection of concepts and the recollection of non-analytic connections between these concepts as well as the understanding of analytic connections. The conversation with the slave boy is divided into three parts: 82B9–E1, 82E14–84A2, and 84D3–85B2. As we saw above, the sections are marked off by brief interludes in which the significance of the illustration is explained by Socrates. The first few lines of the first section (82B9–C5) serve to help the slave boy to grasp the concept of a square. The slave boy comes to understand that the square's four sides are all equal, and that its size is irrelevant to its geometrical properties. This section is also a part of the recollecting process, and it provides evidence in support of the claim that some of what falls under the concept of recollection is non-inferential. For in this section the slave boy recollects what a square is; he is not drawing inferences from proposition to proposition. The remainder of the first section is taken up mainly by the slave boy's reaching the erroneous conclusion that by doubling the sides of a square one doubles the area. Most of the second section is taken up by Socrates' showing that this conclusion is false. This part of recollection is inferential and deductive. That is to say, the slave boy comes to see his error by understanding the logical consequences of his false belief, as they unfold with the aid of Socrates. Thus this section provides evidence for saying that the ability to understand deductive relations between a priori propositions is part of the recollection process. In the third section, however, the boy is helped to understand how to construct a square with an area twice the size of any given square. This method of construction is, of course, quite general. But by itself it does not *prove* deductively any relationship between sides and area. The diagram shows that a given method of construction *must* always yield a square with an area of doubled size. This truth is grasped by the boy intuitively. The construction of an actual diagram and the counting of squares and lines within the diagram only aid his intuition. Thus the third section provides us with an illustration of yet another aspect of recollection; the grasping of non-analytic connections between concepts.

In order to avoid misunderstanding, the conclusion about the third section that is proposed in this paper should be restated in the following way. It is not claimed that Plato distinguished between analytic and synthetic connections among concepts given innately and that he consciously included in the demonstration examples of both types of connection. The claim is, rather, that Plato does not make an explicit distinction between analytic and synthetic, and that both his description and his illustration of recollection are such that not all of it can be characterized adequately as the grasping of simple concepts and the understanding of deductions and analytic truths. It is true, of course, that the state of understanding reached by the slave boy is regarded as in need of further improvement, but this improvement is envisioned as the result of further exercises similar in nature to the ones performed ($85C9$–$D1$). Plato does not suggest that the slave boy will have knowledge only if he has understood geometry in axiomatized form.

Before turning to a final appraisal it is worth while to consider a possible objection to Plato's procedure. It might be argued that the whole discussion is vitiated by Plato's failure to distinguish concepts from propositions. One might argue along these lines that given this distinction Plato's illustration shows only the power of the deductive capacities of the slave boy. This would hardly show anything about innate ideas or the need for the recollection theory of learning. How we form concepts is one question, requiring an empirical answer; how to explain logical relationships between propositions is another. Plato's recollection theory is perhaps merely a mixture of a dim recognition of the nature of deductive reasoning and bad armchair psychology.

In reply it should be said that though there are important differences between concepts and propositions, there are also important similarities, and that the differences are not relevant to Plato's discussion. The most crucial difference between concept and proposition is that only the latter is true or false. There is, however, corresponding to every sentence expressing a proposition, e.g., "the cat is on the mat," a subsentential expression derivable by nominalization e.g., "the cat's being on the mat," and thus a corresponding concept. Thus, as Kant saw, one may talk of necessary connections between concepts (e.g., containment) and necessary links between propositions interchangeably. For Plato's purposes it makes little if any difference whether one admits of concepts or propositions as given innately to the human mind. As for the connections between these, we saw above that not all of them can be construed on Plato's view as analytic.

As a final review, let us return to the point made at the beginning of this paper and ask whether the recollection thesis is best classified as empirical hypothesis, a priori truth, or mere metaphor. We saw already that Plato intended the thesis to be an a priori truth. He is justified in this interpretation, however, only on the assumption that no alternative explanation of the general facts of learning is possible. This assumption is dubious; Plato might have tried to consider several alternatives to "being instructed" and recollection.

As a hypothesis about the structure of the mind the recollection thesis seems to fall between being a very general empirical theory and being a metaphor. The reason for this is the inherent vagueness of the thesis. All that Plato can conclude from his analysis is that *something* in addition to deductive reasoning capacity must be given to the mind innately in order to bridge the gap between input and understanding. Plato's argument does not warrant more specific guesses about the structure of the mind. He has certainly no right to suppose that he has shown a need for assuming that all elements of a priori propositions are given to the mind innately. Thus the recollection thesis shows only that there must be (in some way not yet clearly specified) concepts and propositions given innately to the human mind if the learning of such subjects as geometry under normal conditions is to be accounted for by the most plausible hypothesis available.

This criticism is not so much a rebuke to Plato as encouragement for the present. The path from metaphor to theory is long and arduous in the history of science as well as in the history of philosophy. The product of Plato's fertile imagination needs to be properly understood in order for it to serve as the basis for the theories of the present.

5

KNOWLEDGE, BELIEF AND THE FORMS

R. C. CROSS AND A. D. WOOZLEY

In order to distinguish between the philosopher and the non-philosopher, Plato draws a distinction between knowledge and belief, and in doing this he makes a two-fold distinction between, on the one hand, two different states of mind, and on the other between two different sets of objects corresponding to these different states of mind. The philosopher's state of mind is knowledge and its objects are Beauty itself, Justice itself, and so on (i.e. the Forms); the nonphilosopher's state of mind is belief and its objects are the many particular things, just acts and so on. We ought now to ask ourselves whether there is in fact a distinction to be drawn between knowledge and belief, and if there is, whether Plato's way of representing the distinction is satisfactory.

(1) *The distinction itself.* To say 'I know that such and such' is to say something logically different from 'I believe that such and such'. If I say 'I know that two and two are four', in saying 'I know' I am committing myself to the position that what I know is true, that I can't be wrong, i.e. that two and two cannot but be four. To put it generally, if I say 'I know that p' (where p is any proposition), then the statement 'I know that p' entails 'p is true'. Notice that it does not follow that p is in fact true. It may be that I have been mistaken in claiming to know that p, and thereby committing myself to the position that p is true: p may in fact be false. It is still true, however, that so far as I am concerned, by using the word 'know' I committed myself to the truth of p. If it turns out that p is in fact false, then my claim to knowledge was mistaken. Now contrast this with the use of word 'believe' when for example, I say, 'I believe that the Prime Minister of Great Britain and the President of the United States met last June'. In using the word 'believe' I do not commit myself to the position that I cannot be wrong about such a meeting. I have a certain amount of evidence about it. I seem to remember reading about it in the Press or hearing something about it on the radio, and so I believe that such a meeting took place; but I am

prepared to admit that I may be wrong, that *p* may be false. Notice too, that the strength of my beliefs may vary. I may very strongly believe that there was such a meeting because I clearly remember reading about it in *The Times* and seeing pictures of it on television and noting references to it since, or I may just believe there was such a meeting because I was out of the country at the time but seem to remember reading something about it in a foreign news-paper. In the first case I have good evidence for my belief and hold it strongly, in the second less good evidence, and I hold it less strongly; but in both cases alike, though in different degrees, I am prepared to admit that I may be wrong. Now contrast this with the use of the verb 'to know'. If I say 'I know that the Prime Minister and the President met last June' I am excluding the possibility that I may be wrong, that *p* may turn out to be false. If, in fact, it is subsequently shown that the Prime Minister and the President were each in their own countries at the time in question, and could not have met, my claim to knowledge is seen to have been mistaken and I shall have to withdraw altogether my statement that I knew they had met. If, however, all I said originally was that I believed they had met, there is no need to withdraw my statement that I so believed. What has happened is that my belief has been shown to be false. I believed, falsely as it turns out, that *p*. The position can be brought out in this way. In the first case, looking back on the whole situation, what we would *not* say is, 'so he knew falsely that *p*'. What we have to say is 'so he did not know after all', i.e. he made a mistaken claim to knowledge. In the second case, however, what we do say is 'so he believed falsely that *p*', 'his belief that *p* was false', and we would not say 'so he did not believe after all'. Again, while, as we said above, the notion of degrees makes sense with a belief—a very strong belief that, a belief that, a weak belief that ('I believe there was a meeting though I may be mistaken')—such a notion does not make sense in the case of knowledge: i.e. we could not say 'he knows very strongly or confidently that', 'he knows less strongly or confidently that'. In the case of knowing you either know or you don't know. It is a knock-down business with no degrees in it.

It would thus seem even from these brief considerations that there are logical differences between the verb 'to know' and the verb 'to believe', or to put the matter in a more familiar way, that there is a distinction between knowledge and belief, and that Plato was correct in drawing a distinction between them; and further that, since the verb 'to know' is a powerful word—in Plato's language (*R*.477D) "knowledge is the most powerful of all the faculties"—the distinction is one of importance.

(2) *Plato's development of the distinction.* Granted then that it is important to distinguish between knowledge and belief, we have now to consider whether Plato's way of representing the distinction is satisfactory. As we have already pointed out he draws a twofold distinction: (a) a distinction between the two states of mind, knowledge and belief, and (b) a distinction between two classes of objects, Forms on the one hand, and the many particular things on the other, corresponding to these two states of mind. It will be convenient to consider (a) and (b) separately.

(a) *The distinction between knowledge and belief as states of mind.* It will be remembered that in the important passage 477C Plato described knowledge and belief as powers or faculties, but in other places he seems to be thinking of them rather as conditions or states of mind brought about by the exercise of the respective faculties, and later at 510D he explicitly calls them conditions or states of mind (*pathēmata en tē psychē*). For our immediate purposes, then, we can regard them as states of mind, and as such Plato points out at 477E that they are to be distinguished in that knowledge is infallible, cannot be mistaken, whereas belief is fallible, can make mistakes. In the present context this is all he has to say on the distinction between knowledge and belief as states of mind, and the rest of the passage is devoted to the development of the distinction at (b) above between the two different classes of objects corresponding to these two different states. From other parts of his writings, however, we can add some further points. In the *Timaeus* (51C), where incidentally as in the present passage of the *Republic* Plato is arguing from the difference between knowledge and belief to a difference in their objects, he says that rational understanding or knowledge and true belief differ in that the former is produced by instruction, the latter by persuasion; the former can always give a true account of itself, the latter can give none; and the former cannot be shaken by persuasion whereas the other can be won over. These differences can be illustrated from elsewhere in the dialogues: the "accountability" characteristic of knowledge, for example, is illustrated later in the *Republic* itself at 506C where Plato distinguishes knowledge from true belief on the ground that the latter is "without understanding", cannot, that is, in the language of the *Timaeus*, give an account of itself. Similarly in the *Meno* (98A) it is said that true beliefs are liable to run away out of the mind of a man and thus not to be worth much, until one binds them down "by a reckoning of the cause". When they are so bound down they become knowledge and remain stable. What Plato seems to mean is that unless you understand why a statement *p* is true, then you do not know that *p*, but have only a true belief; and in the *Meno* passage the point is added that the latter is unstable, liable to change. Thus Cornford and Lee are both somewhat misleading in their translation of the passage at *Republic* 506C, since Lee represents Plato as talking of "a true but unthinking opinion", and Cornford translates "a true belief without intelligence", both translations possibly suggesting that there is something silly or stupid about a true belief; but Plato does not mean that. The belief might be quite intelligent in our ordinary sense of that word. Plato's point is that it remains only a belief unless the holder of it has "understanding", i.e. grasps why it is true, is able to give an account of it. Again the influence of persuasion on beliefs is brought out in the *Theaetetus* (201), where knowledge is distinguished from true opinion on the ground that a jury, though they do not have knowledge of some matter, may nevertheless be rightly persuaded to form a true belief about it and so reach a proper verdict. If we put all this together, Plato is then saying that we can distinguish belief from knowledge as states of mind in that (1) (from our present passage 477E) belief is liable to error, knowledge not, and (from elsewhere) (2) belief can be produced and changed by persuasion, knowledge not, and (3) in the case of belief we do not understand why a proposition is true, whereas in knowledge we do. Now there may be points to disagree with here. It might be said, for example, that the approach is too psychological—that if one wants to distinguish between knowledge and belief one should think rather of the logical differences involved in the use of the verbs 'to know' and 'to believe', instead of becoming involved in attempting to discriminate between different states of mind. By and large, however, for our present purposes, we might say that the points Plato makes are not unreasonable. In particular his point in the present passage, which is the one with which we are directly concerned, namely that knowledge excludes error, whereas this is not so in the case of belief, and that they are thus distinguishable, is one that we ought to accept, even though we might want to frame it differently. We could then say that, so far, there is no reason for serious quarrel with the way in which Plato develops the distinction between knowledge and belief.

(b) *The distinction between knowledge and belief in respect to their objects.* It is when we come to this distinction that serious difficulties begin, difficulties moreover which raise points of much general philosophical importance. It is important, therefore, on both counts to spend some time on them. We said [elsewhere[1]] when we were discussing Plato's principle at 477D that different faculties are to be distinguished by the difference in their objects, that it seemed in fact that different faculties could have the same object, that for example one could come to know some thing or object about which one had previously only a true belief, or again that it could be said that the Guardians in Plato's own city had knowledge, and the Auxiliaries true belief, about the same object, namely the maintenance of the ideal state. At the same time we agreed that there was a trickiness in the word 'object' here, and it is time now to say more about this.

(1) If we consider the verb 'to know' there are two familiar uses of the word. (a) We may use it with a noun immediately following which grammatically is the direct object of the verb. In this use we could speak of knowing a person, or a thing, or a place—for example, I know Jones, I know his yacht the *Sally Anne*, and I know the anchorage where he moors her. Here we are using 'know' to mean 'am acquainted with'—I have seen and spoken to Jones often, I've been on the *Sally Anne*, and so on. In this use of the verb 'to know' we can in ordinary speech sensibly talk of knowing things or objects. This notion of direct acquaintance with something, developed in a certain specialised way, has been prominent in many philosophical theories and has been given the label 'knowledge by acquaintance'. For our immediate purposes the important point is that there is a familiar use of the verb 'to know' with a noun or pronoun immediately following which is grammatically the direct object of the verb, such that we can speak of knowing things or objects. (b) There is also, however, a very familiar use where the verb is not followed directly by a noun, but instead by a 'that' clause: for example, 'I know that China is a large country', 'that swallows are migrants', 'that light travels at a speed of 186,000 feet per second', and so on. In this case I may never, for example, have been to

[1] *Plato's Republic: A Philosophical Commentary* (London: Macmillan & Co., 1964), Ch. 7, p. 151.

China, have no direct acquaintance with it, but from reading books on geography, looking at maps and so on, I know that it is a large country. This is clearly a very important use of the verb 'to know', since when we reflect we realise that most of such knowledge as we claim to have takes the form of knowing that something or other is so and so. Again, for this use of the verb 'to know' philosophers have a label—'knowledge by description'. The example just given about China will help in fact to explain the label: I have no direct acquaintance with China but have read descriptions of it, and so know it by description. Now in this case, unlike (a), what immediately follows the verb is not a noun or a pronoun but a 'that' clause. In this case then, what I know is not a thing or object in any ordinary sense; instead, what I know is that something or other is so and so. It would seem, then, that in this use of the verb 'to know' we ought to be very suspicious of talk in terms of 'knowing objects' or of 'the objects of knowledge'. We shall come back to this shortly.

Meantime (2) let us see how the verb 'to believe' behaves in this respect. What strikes us at once here is that there seems to be no use corresponding to the use of the verb 'to know' as at (a) above where the verb is followed by a noun or pronoun which is grammatically its direct object. We must not be misled by a sentence like 'I believe Jones'. This is not at all like 'I know Jones'—Jones is not grammatically the direct object and what we are really saying is 'I believe that Jones is speaking the truth', i.e. the grammatical object of the verb is really a 'that' clause. In fact it seems that there is no use of the verb 'to believe' corresponding to the use of 'know' at (a) above. When we believe, what we believe is expressed as a 'that' clause; that is to say, in this respect the use of the verb 'to believe' follows the use of the verb 'to know' at (b) above. Thus if we were to talk about the 'objects' of belief, again we would be using 'object' in the highly suspect way to which we have already referred. But before we discuss this further there is a third point to notice.

(3) If we consider again the distinction Plato draws at 477C between knowledge and belief—knowledge is infallible, unerring, whereas belief is not so, can make mistakes—two points arise. In the first place, the sense in which knowledge is unerring should be the same as that in which belief is liable to error. We have, however, seen at (2) that in the case of belief, what we believe is expressed in a 'that' clause, and in this case error must arise when the

'that' clause is false. Thus the error here is related to the truth or falsity of the 'that' clause. Similarly then in the case of knowledge, the unerring nature of knowledge should be related to the truth or falsity of the 'that' clause which expresses what we claim to know—in the case of a correct claim to knowledge the 'that' clause must always be true. It is, however, only in the use of the verb 'to know' at (1) (b) above, i.e. where we are talking about knowledge by description, that this arises, and once again this is the use of 'know' where we have already questioned talk about 'objects' of knowledge. Indeed, secondly, even apart from this, the criterion that knowledge cannot be mistaken does not easily fit the use of 'know' at 1(a) above, i.e. knowledge by acquaintance. It seems as though in the case of knowledge by acquaintance you are either acquainted with a thing or are not acquainted with it, and in neither case does the question of truth or error arise. Alternatively, if a place were sought for error by saying that sometimes one might fail to recognise subsequently something one was already acquainted with, then this would be to allow that knowledge by acquaintance could be mistaken. The case is quite different with (1)(b) above, where questions of truth and error are in order, since in (1)(b) what one wants to say is that in claiming to know that something or other is the case, one is claiming that the 'that' clause is true, and thus knowledge is in this way unerring, excludes the possibility of mistake. But this again leads us back to knowledge that, as opposed to knowledge of things or objects.

(4) It is time now to return to the consideration of the use of the notion of 'objects' in connection with knowledge and belief. When Plato asks at the very end of 476 whether a man who knows knows something or nothing we are inclined to agree with Glaucon's answer that he knows something. Similarly Plato's remark (at 478B) that a man cannot believe and yet believe nothing (the 'in' in Lee's translation 'believe in nothing' should be omitted) seems innocuous enough. It looks then as though we would all agree that when a man knows he knows something, and similarly when he believes he believes something. The trouble lies in the ambiguity in the word 'something'. This can be seen in the discussion in the text since Plato there proceeds to argue that in the case of knowledge the something that is known must be something that is real, and that in the case of belief, while the something believed cannot be real, as in the case of knowledge, it must nevertheless have some

sort of reality, cannot be completely unreal—if it were the latter then in belief we would be believing the completely unreal, i.e. nothing. Hence then the subsequent argument by which Plato seeks to show that the objects of belief are the many particular things which occupy a half-way position between the completely real, which is the object of knowledge, and the completely unreal. In both cases, then, Plato is committed to a search for appropriate objects and in both cases the objects must have some sort of reality. Now if we consider knowledge by acquaintance at (1) (a) above, it is plausible to say that if I am acquainted with something, there must be a real something for me to be acquainted with. If I know Jones, i.e. am acquainted with him, then there must be a real person Jones for me to know—I can see him and hear him and touch him. Similarly, if I know his yacht, there must be a yacht which I can see and touch and climb aboard and so on. In this context then it is plausible to talk in terms of real objects or things—if there were no such real objects then there would be nothing to be acquainted with. The situation, however, is quite different, in the case of knowledge by description at (1)(b) above, and with belief at (2) above. In both these cases, as we have already agreed, what we know or believe is that such and such is so and so. The 'object' then, if we were to use that word, that we know or believe in these cases appears in the form of a 'that' clause. But in these cases what are we then to make of Plato's argument that the 'object' must have some sort of reality, that otherwise we would not know or believe at all? Suppose I believe that there is a desk in the next room. Following Plato's line of argument the 'that' clause will be the object of my belief. It seems clear that it is a mistake to raise questions about the reality of this sort of object as we could raise questions about the reality of what we familiarly call objects, such as desks or chairs. To ask whether 'that there is a desk in the next room' is real or unreal or semi-real is to ask a question that is void of application. Whether there really is a desk next door or not, my belief is still the same. Only, if there is no desk next door, the belief is false. For this latter reason it is clear, too, that it is not possible to hold that the 'object' of a belief, meaning by this the 'that' clause, must have some sort of reality in the sense that what I believe to be the case must in some sense be the case; for when I believe that something is the case, as we have already seen at (3) above, nothing follows about the truth or falsity of what I believe: what I believe may be the case, but it may just as well not be the case, i.e. my belief may be false. Our conclusion then from this must be that while it is in order to talk of objects and the reality of objects in the case of knowledge by acquaintance, in the case of knowledge by description and of belief such talk is mistaken or at best highly misleading. Moreover, in the present case it has the very important consequence that Plato uses it in establishing a wide-reaching metaphysical view which distinguishes between two classes of objects, Forms on the one hand and sensible particulars on the other, and two levels of reality or existence, that of the Forms, which are completely real or existent, and that of the sensible particulars, which are semi-real, partly existent and partly non-existent.

(5) Finally, it is worth asking why Plato should have become involved in these difficulties, and here two points suggest themselves. (a) It is true that when Plato is considering knowledge, or belief, or indeed thinking generally, he tends to take as his model sense-awareness, i.e. our apprehension through our sense organs of the world surrounding us, and particularly the model of sight and touch. For example, in the *Republic* itself at 476B the lover of sights and sounds cannot "see" the nature of the Beautiful itself (where the "seeing" is not seeing with the eyes but seeing so to speak with the mind's eye), and so again at 479E; again at 511A the Forms are "seen" by thought (compare 533D 'the eye of the soul'); or again 511B, reason "grasps" the first principle of everything (where the Greek verb means 'to lay hold of', 'grasp', 'touch', and Lee's translation 'reached' somewhat obscures the point). There is a passage in the *Theaetetus*, 188E ff., where Plato is discussing false judgment, which brings this out strikingly. There it is argued that it is not possible for a man to see something and yet see nothing—if he is seeing any one thing he must be seeing a thing which is (i.e. exists) and similarly with hearing and touching. Similarly, then, a man who is judging some one thing is judging something which is (exists). A man who judged something which is not (i.e. falsely) would be judging nothing, and a man judging nothing would not be judging at all. Plato is not content to accept this argument and proceeds to try to account for false judgement in several different ways. None of these accounts, however, is really successful, and the whole section in the *Theaetetus* again shows the influence on Plato of the model of awareness through the senses, i.e. through sight, touch, etc., when he comes to consider knowing, believing, and so

on. Hence it has been said that Plato tends to regard thinking as a sort of ghostly sensing. The influence on Plato of the analogy from sense-awareness, from seeing, touching, and so on, when he is discussing knowledge and belief can be overstressed. For example, so far as language is concerned, we ourselves very frequently use the language of sight and touch in the same context ('he grasped the solution', 'he saw the answer', etc.); and again, there are elements in Plato's thought that point in a different direction. Still, it is true that when he is talking of knowledge and belief the model of seeing or touching does seem to be prominent. Now, of course, in the case of sight and touch, the notions of acquaintance (in the fairly wide sense in which we have been using it), of objects, of the reality of the objects, all have a place. If I am seeing or touching something, then I am immediately aware of, directly acquainted with, a thing or object, and it must be a real thing or object—there must be something there that I am seeing or touching. If then we take sight or touch as our model when we come to discuss knowledge or belief, it is natural to find a parallel in knowledge by acquaintance, and then to suppose that somehow knowledge that and belief can be made to fit into the same pattern and that talk in terms of objects and the reality or non-reality of these objects is in order here too. Enough, however, has perhaps been said, for it to be realised that the analogy with seeing or touching can be fundamentally misleading in the case of knowing that and belief. It may be then that some of the difficulties in Plato arise from his being over-ready to accept this analogy. It is certainly true that he is not clear in his thinking about the difference between acquaintance and knowledge that, and we have pointed out [elsewhere[2]] that it might be said that there is the same ambivalence about his use of the Greek noun δόξα (*doxa*) which we translate as 'belief'—that there are times here too when he seems to mean by belief some sort of immediate awareness, whereas he also clearly uses it elsewhere to mean belief that. (b) It is also probably true that in his theory of knowledge Plato was influenced by his metaphysical views—or perhaps it would be better to say that his theory of knowledge and his metaphysics had a reciprocal influence on each other. He wanted to hold that the familiar world, the world of particulars revealed to us through sense perception, was in various ways an unsatisfactory world, and that there was another permanent unchanging world, the world of Forms which transcended, lay behind the familiar world, and was superior to it in status—it was this latter world alone that was truly real, while the familiar world was only partly real. Certainly one of the reasons which led Plato to the two-world view was that he thought it was demanded by the difference between knowledge and belief: i.e. as in the present arguments in Book V of the *Republic*, his epistemological views led to the two-world view. At the same time Plato had other reasons, some of which should become clear later, for his two-world view. It might be said then that because in any case he believed his metaphysical two-world view to be correct, he was perhaps over-ready to make his arguments from the side of theory of knowledge fit in with his metaphysics.

Two points of warning should be added to conclude this discussion. First, in it the reader has been introduced in a general way to the distinction between knowledge by acquaintance and knowledge by description, and it has been indicated that important use has been made in philosophy of this distinction. It should be noted, however, that while we have talked above about knowing an object by acquaintance, where 'object' could mean an object in the familiar sense, such as a yacht or a desk or a chair, in the specialised sense of knowledge by acquaintance that has been used for example in fairly recent philosophy, it would not be said that we could be acquainted with an object like a desk or chair. Instead it would be said, for example, that we have knowledge by acquaintance only of "sense data", and that our knowledge of a physical object such as a desk is knowledge by description. Clearly, beyond issuing this warning we cannot pursue the matter here. A good place to see the use made of the acquaintance-description distinction is for example in Bertrand Russell's *Problems of Philosophy*, Chapter V. The second warning relates to Plato himself and it is perhaps unnecessary to give it since the point should already be clear; but it is a point of much importance in understanding Plato. We said above that in the case of knowledge by acquaintance it was plausible to hold, as Plato said, that there must be a real object there with which one is acquainted, just as when we touch something, for example, the desk, there must be a real object there to be touched. When, however, Plato says that knowledge is of what is real he means by 'real' something different from what we would mean if we spoke of desks or chairs as real. He would say that the desk as a particular sensible object is only half real. He would also say that there can only be belief about the desk, never knowledge of it. Knowledge can only be of the Forms and the Forms alone are truly real.

This brings us to the second topic of the present essay. [We have discussed elsewhere [3]] something of the use Plato makes in Book V of the notion of 'Forms' and we have just been discussing the role of these Forms in his theory of knowledge. It would seem helpful now at this stage to take a more general look at the theory of Forms, partly by way of amplifying what we have already learnt. . . .

A very great deal has been written over many years about the theory of Forms, and it is quite impossible in a narrow compass to be other than arbitrary in one's way of presenting the theory. What we shall do here is, after one or two preliminary remarks, to collect, mainly from the *Republic* and from the dialogues whose date of composition is recognised to be earlier than that of the *Republic*, some examples of some of the various roles played in Plato's philosophy by the Forms, and then add one or two brief comments.

The first preliminary remark is concerned with the label to be used in English in connection with the theory. When Plato himself wants to refer to Beauty as opposed to the many particular beautiful things or Justice as opposed to the many particular just acts, he very frequently does this by the use of the Greek word for 'itself'. Thus Beauty is *auto to kalon* (literally 'the beautiful itself'), Justice is *auto to dikaion* (literally 'the just itself'), and so on. He also, however, uses the two Greek words εἶδος (*eidos*) and ἰδέα (*idea*) in this connection, apparently completely interchangeably. Thus instead of speaking of 'the Beautiful itself', etc., he will speak instead of 'the *eidos* of the Beautiful' or 'the *idea* of the Beautiful'. The English word 'idea' is an exact transliteration of the Greek ἰδέα, and hence as we [have] noted,[4] English commentators speak of the 'idea' of Beauty, etc., in Plato, and more generally of Plato's Theory of Ideas. This, however, is an unfortunate rendering of the Greek. The English word 'idea' tends to carry with it the notion that ideas exist only in the mind, that they are only thoughts of ours, that questions can be raised about how far they represent reality, that they are only "subjective", what we think, as opposed to what is "objective",

[3] Ibid.,Ch. 7.
[4] Ibid., Ch. 7, p. 140.

what is really the case independently of our thinking, and so on. It should be clear from what we have already seen, and it should be still clearer from what will be said later, that all these notions are quite alien to Plato's intentions when he talks, for example, of the *eidos* or *idea* of Beauty. This is for him another way of referring to Beauty itself and for him it is Beauty itself that is truly real, that is the object of knowledge; and whatever ideas (in the familiar use of that word) we may have about Beauty, there is a real unchanging Beauty there for us to grasp if we can, and which is what it is quite independently of any ideas of ours. If we are still to use the word 'idea' in connection with Plato's theory, then it must be neutralised and these familiar associations it has must be forgotten; and since it is not easy to do this the translation 'idea' is undesirable. In fact, though there has been controversy over the precise reasons which influenced Plato in his choice of the Greek words *eidos* or *idea* in this context, the words themselves meant originally 'visible shape' or 'form', and, more widely, 'form', 'nature', and then 'form', 'type' (as for instance in the phrase 'forms or types of disease'). The English word 'form' keeps near to the meaning of the Greek words, and is also free from the misleading associations of the word 'idea'. For these reasons then it is proposed to keep to the terminology we have already been using and to refer to Plato's theory as the Theory of Forms.

The second preliminary point is concerned with what is known as the 'Socratic problem', i.e. the question whether we are to take the views attributed to Socrates by Plato in the dialogues as having been actually held by Socrates himself or whether Plato attributes to Socrates views which the historical Socrates never expressed and which are in fact Plato's own. In particular, there has been much dispute as to whether the theory of Forms is Socratic or whether it is primarily a theory which Plato himself developed. However, for present purposes it does not seem necessary to go into this question, nor to be over-anxious about distinguishing Socratic and Platonic elements within the theory of Forms. It will be enough for us to look in a general way at the theory as it is exhibited in the *Republic* and the dialogues composed by Plato earlier than the *Republic*, and to this we now turn.

In illustrating some of the roles of the Forms in Plato's theory, we may begin with what we have already learnt from Book V, and for convenience we will tabulate the various functions of the Forms

as we go along, even though some of the tabulations may be mis-
leadingly brief. The list we will produce is not meant to be exhaustive nor to be arranged in any order that would suggest that one
function of the Forms is more important for Plato than another.

(i) *Forms as the objects of knowledge*. This is familiar from the end of
Book V. Knowledge and belief are different powers in that the
former is infallible, the latter not. Their objects then are different
and the objects of knowledge are, as we find in the subsequent discussion, the Forms.

(ii) *Forms as what is real*. For Plato the reality of the Forms follows
from their being the objects of knowledge, and with this again we
are familiar from Book V, cf. 476E–477A, where it is argued that if
a man knows, there must be something that he knows and that
"something" must be real. We have also seen that in Book V Plato
argues that sensible particulars, the many beautiful things and so
on which the lover of sights or sounds sees or hears or touches, are
not perfectly real: they are only semi-real and occupy an intermediate position between what is completely real (the Forms) and
what is completely unreal. They are then appearances of the underlying reality, the objects not of knowledge but of belief.

(iii) *Forms as ideal standards*. This again we have met in discussing
Book V, since in examining the argument there[5] which purported
to show that particulars were only semi-real we suggested that
possibly what Plato had in mind was the notion of the Forms as
ideal standards of perfection to which particulars only approximate.
As we indicated, the best place to see this aspect of the Forms is in
the *Phaedo*, 74–75. It is connected there with the doctrine that
learning is recollection, that we had knowledge of the Forms before
we were born into this world, but lose it at birth and then are reminded of it again by our experience of the sensible world, so that
we are enabled to judge the latter against the standard of the perfect Forms. A short quotation from 75B of the dialogue sums up this
role of the Forms: "I suppose then that we must have acquired
knowledge of the nature of the Equal itself before we began to see
and hear and to use our other senses, if we were going to refer to
that criterion things that appeared to the senses equal, on the
ground that they all do their best to be like it, though they are
inferior". And Plato makes it clear immediately after (75C–D) that

[5] See ibid., Ch. 7, pp. 161 ff.

the same holds also for the Forms generally, for the Beautiful itself, the Good itself, and so on. The doctrine of recollection is in itself an interesting link in Plato's whole attempt to account for *a priori* knowledge. For our immediate purposes, however, what we have to note especially in this section of the *Phaedo* is how the Forms function as criteria or standards—Justice itself (the Form Justice) is the perfect exemplar or instance of justice against which we must measure the imperfection of our own just acts. The latter "do their best to be like" perfect justice but fall short, fail to be themselves perfectly just.

(iv) *Forms as universals*. What we mean by this should become clear as we proceed. Let us illustrate this function of the Forms by two quotations. The first is from Book X of the *Republic*, where at 596A Plato says, "Well then, shall we proceed as usual and begin by assuming the existence of a single essential nature or Form for every set of things which we call by the same name?" The second is from the earlier dialogue, the *Meno*, 72A ff. Meno has been asked to say what he thinks virtue is and has replied by giving a list of particular manifestations of virtue—the virtue of a man is to administer the state, of a woman to order her house, and so on. Socrates then goes on, "How fortunate I am, Meno! When I ask you for one virtue you present me with a swarm of them, which are in your keeping. Suppose that I carry on the figure of the swarm, and ask of you, What is the nature of the bee? and you answer that there are many kinds of bees, and I reply: But do bees differ as bees, because there are many and different kinds of them; or are they not rather to be distinguished by some other quality as for example beauty, size or shape? How would you answer me? *Meno:* I should answer that bees do not differ from one another, as bees. *Soc.:* And if I went on to say: That is what I desire to know, Meno; tell me what is the quality in which they do not differ, but are all alike;— would you be able to answer? *Meno:* I should. *Soc.:* And so of the virtues, however many and different they may be, they have all a common nature [an identical Form] which makes them virtues; and on this he who would answer the question, What is virtue? would do well to have his eye fixed; Do you understand?" (Jowett's translation.) Socrates subsequently illustrates the sort of answer he wants by taking the example of figure or shape. Here again if asked what is figure it will not do to reply, for example, roundness, for roundness is only *a* figure, and there are many other figures, e.g.

squareness, etc., and Socrates goes on, 74D, "And suppose that he were to pursue the matter in my way, he would say: Ever and anon we are landed in particulars, but this is not what I want: tell me then, since you call them by a common name, and say that they are all figures, even when opposed to one another, what is that common nature which you designate as figure—which contains straight as well as round, and is no more one than the other—that would be your mode of speaking?" It will be noted from these passages that the Forms are being used to account for the fact that things in the world go together in groups or kinds, that for example there is a group of particulars which, though they differ from one another individually, e.g. some are bigger, some smaller and so on, nevertheless still form a group such that they are all bees; or, again, to take another example, that there is another group of particulars such that, though again they differ in certain ways from one another, they are all chairs, and so on. Plato is suggesting that in each case there is a group or kind because there is a single characteristic, namely the one Form (e.g. Beeness, Chairness), present in all the many particular instances (of bees, of chairs) within the group. There is, that is, a one over the many in each case. He is also saying that it is because of this that we are able to use general terms, or, as he calls them, 'common names'— e.g. 'bee' is not the name of one particular bee, but has general application to any of the particulars within the group, so that we can say this is a bee, that is a bee, and so on. In philosophy the term 'universal' has been used of that which is common to a group of particulars or again from the side of language as that of which a general term is the name. Hence then our use of the word 'universal' at the beginning of this paragraph.

(v) *Forms as "causes"*. This function of the Forms is best seen at 100C–D of the *Phaedo* where Socrates says "I no longer learn about, and cannot understand . . . these other subtle 'causes', but if anyone tells me that anything is beautiful, as having a bright colour or a special shape or anything of that sort, I dismiss the other 'reasons' —all the others confuse me—and purely and simply and perhaps naïvely keep to this, that the only thing that makes it beautiful is the presence of, or its participation in—or whatever the relationship may be—that 'Beautiful' [the Form of Beauty]. I do not now insist upon any particular relationship, but only that all beautiful things are beautiful simply *because of* the Beautiful" (Bluck's translation).

Here then the Forms are "causes". It is important, however, to recognise that the Greek word αἰτία (*aitia*) which Plato uses here is a tricky word—perhaps even trickier than our own word 'cause'. Without going into the difficulties that surround it, we might say for our present purposes that by 'cause' here is meant something like a necessary condition. This is why we have put the word in quotation marks, letting it take its colouring from the context.

Now when we look at the various jobs of the Forms listed above, it is obvious that the theory of Forms has a very wide range. This is why Professor Cherniss entitled an article which he contributed to the *American Journal of Philology* (*A.J.P.* Vol. LVII, 1936) 'The Philosophical Economy of the Theory of Ideas' (reprinted as Essay 2 in this volume). He argued there that by one single unifying theory, namely the theory of Forms, Plato was able to solve outstanding problems in ontology, in ethics and in epistemology; and he thus commended the theory for its philosophical economy. About the alleged economy of the theory we will say something later. Meantime it may be useful to say a little about the theory under the three heads listed by Professor Cherniss.

(a) First, then, from our list above we can see that the theory of Forms is an ontological theory, i.e. a theory concerned with being or existence. This is clear from (ii), (iii) and (v) above and is also involved in (iv). In its ontological aspect, what the theory of Forms is maintaining is that there is a world of permanent, unchanging and perfect entities which are unaffected by variations in circumstances or conditions and which comprise reality. It is they that are "real" or, as Plato sometimes says, "completely real" or "truly existent". The ordinary, everyday, sensible world, on the other hand, is not completely real: it is only semi-real: it is the world of appearance as opposed to the world of reality, namely the Forms; and further, it owes such reality as it does have to the Forms. The theory of Forms then is a metaphysical theory, in that it claims to be telling us something that is true about what there is independently of human beings and minds. To use a phrase used by Socrates in the later dialogue, the *Parmenides* (132D), the Forms are "as it were patterns fixed in the nature of things", i.e. they are the permanent furniture of the universe. There are various difficulties in this ontological aspect of the theory of Forms, but one word of caution may be relevant. The theory maintains that our ordinary, everyday objects, for example the chair I am sitting in, are not "real" or "really real", but are in a sense only appearances; and the unphilosophical reader may be tempted to reject out of hand a theory which denies the full reality of the chairs he sits in, the houses he sees when he goes out into the street, and so on. Now Plato may be mistaken in what he is saying, but his view cannot be rejected in this out-of-hand way. For one thing, many philosophers besides Plato have held that the everyday world is a world of appearances, and have contrasted it with a reality beyond appearances; and if the unphilosophical reader is unmoved by this consideration, he must be asked why he himself calls the chair he sits in real, as opposed to a hallucinatory or dream chair. In fact he will find that the word 'real' is a very tricky word. It might be suggested that when he calls the chair he is sitting in real, as distinct from a hallucinatory or a dream chair, he is employing certain criteria, not in themselves easy to formulate, which he regards the "real" chair as satisfying. One such criterion, for instance, might be that the real chair is in some sense or other more permanent than the hallucinatory chair. Moreover, the word 'real' seems in addition to have a commendatory or preferring force: because the object satisfies these criteria, he singles it out for preference or commendation by calling it real (cf. the use of the word 'real' in an argument whether or not, for example, Britain is a "real" democracy). Now a philosopher might want to suggest either that the criteria we ordinarily employ in using the word 'real' are too unexacting or that sensible objects when carefully considered do not in fact adequately satisfy even our existing criteria, or he might want to suggest a combination of both. That is, in one way or another he might want to shift the use of the word 'real', so that everyday sensible objects no longer counted as "real" or as "completely real". This is what Plato is doing when he says that only the Forms are completely real whereas the sensible world is a world of appearances, only semi-real. As we have said, this may be a mistaken move. The arguments behind it may not be sound, it may lead to more confusion than it is worth, and so on. The point however is that it cannot be rejected out of hand simply because it denies the "reality" of our everyday world.

(b) Secondly, the theory of Forms figures prominently in Plato's ethical views. Here all five functions of the Forms that we have listed are really involved, but perhaps the third (Forms as ideal standards) has a special relevance. [There were moral problems] that faced Athens at the end of the fifth century.[6] It was in fact a time of much questioning of the traditional morality, and the notion that moral standards were a matter of convention, that there was no absolute right or wrong, gained considerable currency. This was a notion to which Plato was violently opposed, and the theory of Forms in its ethical aspect is an attempt to account for absolute moral standards. The theory holds that there are Forms of moral characteristics (e.g. of goodness, justice, etc.) as well as of non-moral characteristics. Indeed, it seems probable that, at any rate at the beginning, under the influence of Socrates, the former were Plato's primary concern, though mathematical Forms (Equality, etc.) had also already become prominent in certain of the dialogues earlier than the *Republic*. Now granted that there are Forms of moral qualities, when we look at our list of the various jobs the Forms do, we can see how Plato regarded his theory as providing an answer to any relativist view of morals. For example, in our list the Forms again function as objects in the case of our knowledge of moral truths (i); they are real, are what they are quite independently of what we may think of say (ii); and they are perfectly that to which imperfect particulars only approximate (iii). Thus, for example, the Form Justice is a perfect, unchanging pattern or model or standard, there to be known, given that men, or some men at least, can be brought to know it, and just conduct then is no matter of convention, but a matter of conforming to the ideal standard of Justice which like the other Forms is part of the nature of things. It can be seen then that Plato's ethical theory is interlocked with his epistemology and his metaphysics; his is certainly an ethics that has a metaphysical basis. It can also be seen how this political theory in the *Republic* in turn interlocks with these. For Plato absolutely certain knowledge is possible, in morals as elsewhere. As we shall see, it requires men of special ability to reach it, and even they can only do so after a long and arduous training. When they have reached it, however, they have arrived at absolute truth: in the moral-political sphere they just know wherein the good life consists. On Plato's view then they alone are fit to rule and it is plainly to the benefit of the mass of the citizens that the few who have this knowledge should guide their lives for them. It is this interlocking of different facets of his thinking that makes

[6] See ibid., Introduction, pp. xiii–xiv.

Plato's political theory especially important. If we find the political theory repellent, it is not merely enough to dismiss it as a product of anti-democratic bias. If we think it is mistaken, we have to show why it is mistaken; and just because, in Plato's thinking, it is tied in with, amongst other things, his ethical, epistemological and metaphysical views, we have to have them too under consideration if we are criticising his political theory. There is one further point we ought to add. This relates to a development in his thinking which we shall find when we study Books VI and VII of the *Republic*[7]; for in these books a special status is assigned to the Form of the Good as the supreme Form, and Plato suggests that the notion of the reality of the Forms (and this would apply to all Forms) cannot be separated from the notion of their goodness, or that, to use somewhat grandiose terms, reality and value coalesce.

(c) Thirdly, the theory of Forms is very much concerned with epistemological issues, i.e. with questions concerning the nature of knowledge, its distinction from other types of cognition, and the objects of the various types of cognition. Since these issues are particularly prominent in Books VI and VII of the *Republic*, it may be useful to say rather more on this matter than we said on (a) and (b), and here we shall have particularly in mind the role of the Forms at (i) (Forms as objects of knowledge) and at (iv) (Forms as universals) in our list above. Let us begin then with (i). Plato is convinced of the fundamental difference between knowledge and belief. Knowledge is unerring, infallible. What is known remains true always. Beliefs, on the other hand, are always liable to error and subject to alteration. Further, he believes that given the proper training, the philosopher can attain to this infallible knowledge, can attain, that is, to truths that remain true always. But now to use the 'object' talk which we discussed above, it follows that granted the existence of knowledge as described it must have appropriate objects, i.e. just as knowledge itself is stable and unchanging, so its objects, what it knows, must also be stable and unchanging. At the same time Plato is convinced, and in Book V we considered some of his arguments for this, that the many particulars of the sensible world cannot satisfy this requirement. They are in a state of constant change, are now this and now that, are imperfect, and have none of the stability and permanence required if they are to be ob-

[7] Cf. ibid., especially Ch. 10, pp. 260–61.

jects of knowledge. But knowledge does exist and Plato has no
doubt of that. It follows then that its appropriate objects must exist,
namely objects that are permanent and unchanging, i.e. what
Plato calls Forms. This argument for the Forms is implicit in Book
V of the *Republic*. It is put clearly and explicitly in the *Timaeus*
(51D) (the *Timaeus* has usually been regarded as a late dialogue but
may in fact have been the crowning work of the *Republic* group of
dialogues. See G. E. L. Owen, *Classical Quarterly*, N.S., Vol. III).
"My own verdict, then, is this. If intelligence and true belief are
two different kinds, then these things—Forms that we cannot perceive but only think of—certainly exist in themselves; but if, as
some hold, true belief is in no way different from intelligence, then
all the things that we perceive through the bodily senses must be
taken as the most certain reality. Now we must affirm that they are
two different things, for they are distinct in origin and unlike in
nature" (Cornford's translation). Plato then thinks that the existence of knowledge requires that there should be Forms, since they
alone provide the appropriate objects of knowledge. We have already in the earlier part of this essay discussed the difficulties
that arise over this notion of "objects" of knowledge. It is important, however, to recognise that when Plato makes his Forms
perform the role of objects of knowledge, he is attempting to answer
a genuine and serious philosophical problem. There are some propositions which we are all inclined to regard as true, come what may,
that is, as necessarily true. For example, within Euclidean geometry
we would say that we know that triangles on equal bases and between parallels are equal in area, and that this is a truth that holds
always. It is not that we have found this true in some particular
case or even that we have considered many cases and never found a
contrary instance. Rather we know this to be true for any triangles
whatsoever. Triangles on equal bases and between parallels must
be equal in area, and no particular instances in the way of diagrams or models that we can see or touch could ever falsify this.
Contrast a proposition like 'jet engines are noisy'. It may well be
that in our experience this has always so far been true. Yet clearly
this has been a matter of experience and the possibility is open that
on some further occasion we may come across a jet engine that is
not noisy—indeed it might be that some invention would make jet
engines completely silent. Or again the difference between our two
propositions, the triangle case and the jet engine case, can be

brought out by considering how we would verify them. In the case of 'jet engines are noisy', experience is clearly relevant. It would be relevant to the truth of this proposition to go to airfields and listen to jet engines, and it would, up to a point anyhow, be sensible to suggest that even though all the jets on this airfield are noisy, it would be worth going round some other airfields to check that the jets there are noisy too. But clearly in our triangle case there is something entirely wrong with the notion that even though the proposition about the equality of the triangles holds in this particular case and that particular case, it might nevertheless be wise to go on looking at more cases to make sure there was no mistake. Given an understanding of Euclidean geometry, we know that this proposition must always be true of all cases. It is a necessary proposition, could never be false, whereas the jet case is one which may be true for all the instances we have come across, but could in principle be falsified. In contrast with the triangle type of proposition, which is a necessary proposition, it is convenient to call the jet type of proposition a contingent proposition: it happens to be that way but it could be different. Necessary propositions are also often called *a priori* propositions, i.e. propositions such that no experience could falsify them and which in that way come "before" sense experience; and the knowledge involved in knowing them is labelled *a priori* knowledge. Contingent propositions, on the other hand, are often called *a posteriori* propositions, in the sense that their truth or falsehood is dependent on sense experience and thus they come "after" sense experience. Now what account to give of necessary propositions or, if we prefer it, *a priori* knowledge is a philosophical problem which has long exercised the minds of philosophers, and still does. What we must note for our present purposes is that the theory of Forms is an attempt to account for necessary propositions or *a priori* knowledge, and this is why above we said that in his theory Plato is attempting to answer an important problem. What he is saying is that if we are to account for necessary propositions we must look beyond the sensible world. Sensible objects are subject to change—what is true of this particular object now may not be true tomorrow or even the next moment; the features they appear to possess are subject to all sorts of conditions: e.g. colour is subject to the intensity of the light, the observer's eye, etc., the shape of an object to the distance we are from it and so on; in various ways they are imperfect and imprecise—the triangle we draw or model is only an imperfect representation of what a mathematician means by a triangle, and can never be perfectly·triangular. It is impossible then, Plato thinks, to frame a precise statement about any particulars that will hold always; in fact necessary statements cannot be concerned with the sensible world. The objects then that we are thinking about when we do make necessary statements must be different from the objects of the sensible world: they must be permanent and not subject to change, they must retain a fixed nature independently of the conditions under which they are apprehended, and they must be perfect. Only granted such objects can we account for necessary truths and for the possibility of *a priori* knowledge. It would take us too far afield to discuss Plato's argument in any detail here. What has been said earlier in the essay in the discussion on knowledge and belief (cf. particularly pp. 176–179) may suggest to the reader that Plato is over-influenced in all this by the model of knowledge by acquaintance. Nevertheless his solution of the problem of necessary truths has, with various modifications, found support among many philosophers; W. D. Ross, for example, in recent times, in his book *Plato's Theory of Ideas*, p. 225, in expressing approval of the theory of Forms says, "In reason we have a faculty by which we can grasp universals [he is referring here to Plato's Forms] in their pure form and to some extent see the relations that necessarily exist between them".

It will be noticed that in thinking of examples of necessary propositions in what we have just been saying, the example we actually used was a geometrical one; and, in fact, mathematics is the field that we tend to think of when the question of necessary propositions is raised. There does seem to be a difference in kind between mathematical propositions like two and two make four or our triangle case, and most other sorts of proposition that we can think of. Two and two, we think, from the nature of the system of numbers must always be four, and similarly triangles on equal bases and between parallels must always be equal in area from the very nature of our geometrical system. Nothing could possibly upset these propositions, and they thus seem to have a special status. Now Plato was the first philosopher who clearly recognised the special status of mathematical propositions as necessary propositions, though he also believed that the field of necessary propositions extended beyond mathematics. Indeed, as we shall see in detail in the following chapters, he was not prepared to allow that the mathematician has knowledge in the full sense. On the other hand, he was equally clear that there is a certainty about mathematical propositions that is quite absent from the propositions which we merely believe (i.e. the sort of everyday propositions that the lover of sights and sounds of Book V entertains). Thus he describes the mathematician's state as one intermediate between belief and knowledge in the full sense, and gives it the name 'thinking' (*dianoia*). Similarly, on the object side, he is clear that the objects about which the mathematician thinks are not the changing, unstable objects of the world of sense perception, but must belong to the intelligible world. Whether Plato regards them as Forms or as a special class of mathematical object, is again a point [which we discuss elsewhere.[8]] What is clear beyond any doubt is that they belong to the intelligible, not to the sensible, world, and in this allocation Plato is showing that he recognises the special character of mathematical propositions which we have just been discussing. This is why too in the higher education of the Guardians in Books VI and VII it is the various branches of mathematics that are the essential preliminaries to the study of philosophy. In the latter alone, Plato thinks, full knowledge is attained, but mathematics is the essential bridge-study which introduces the mind to the intelligible world, the world of stable, permanent objects about which alone certainty is possible. This recognition by Plato of the special status of mathematical propositions and the emphasis that he puts on mathematics is clearly of great importance in the history of thought, when we consider how fundamental a part mathematics has played in the subsequent development of western civilisation.

The function of the Forms as universals ((iv) on our list) is of course closely connected with what we have been saying. It has an ontological or metaphysical side as well as an epistemological side. (a) On the metaphysical side Plato thinks the Forms are necessary not only to account for such existence as particulars do have, but to account also for the fact that they go in groups or sets, e.g. one group all of which are square in shape, another group circular in shape, another group (of particular acts) all of which are just, another group comprising unjust acts, and so on. He thinks this grouping of particulars by kinds can only be explained by, in each case, a common Form which is somehow present in all the particulars of the group, or which they all somehow share (cf. on this latter point the

[8] Ibid., Ch. 9.

language in the *Phaedo* quotation at (v) in our list). (b) On the epistemological side not only are the Forms necessary if we are to get beyond belief to knowledge—the point we have just been discussing above—but also to account for the experience we do have of the world. There are two connected features of the latter that are relevant here. (i) We experience things in the world as belonging to kinds—we are constantly noting similarities between things and thus classifying them (e.g. these shapes are all similar and we classify them as square—this is square, that is square, etc.). (ii) This is reflected in the language we use, for by far the greatest part of our language is made up of general words, e.g. 'square' is not a word that we use only of the shape of the top of the table in our own dining-room, but of the tops of many other tables which in this respect are similar to our own table. Indeed, the point of using the word 'square' of our own table is to relate it to the many other tables—they are all square tables. Both (i) and (ii) Plato thinks can only be accounted for by the existence of the Forms: we experience things in groups and are able to classify them accordingly because of the presence of a common Form in the group (the metaphysical counterpart noted at (a) of this classifying activity of ours); and the occurrence of general words as a feature of our language is explained by supposing that their reference is to the Form present in the many instances of which they are used: i.e. if for the moment we regard 'square' as a name, then it is not the name of the shape of my table-top nor of yours but the name of the Form common to them, i.e. when we call them square we are referring to the common Form Squareness present in them. This problem of how we are able to use general terms has become known as the problem of universals, and any discussion of it as such lies beyond our present scope. At the moment it must suffice to say that Plato holds what is called a realist view of universals. We have already seen that the Forms are entities that exist in their own right, independently of any thinking of ours, and we have just seen that Plato uses them to account for our classificatory activities and consequent use of general words, i.e. as a solution to what might be described in a very unsatisfactory way as the problem of universals. Plato's, then, is a realist view because he believes that universals are real entities which are what they are quite independent of the existence and nature of human or other minds, and of which general words are the names. For difficulties in this realist view and for other possible views of universals the reader may be referred to A. D. Woozley's *Theory of Knowledge, An Introduction*, pp. 70–101. The whole problem of classification and the use of general terms is one which has recurred constantly in philosophy. Thus this aspect of the theory of Forms, which seeks to provide a solution to this problem, is of the utmost importance; and this is so, even if one finds more difficulties in the solution than W. D. Ross does when he writes (*Plato's Theory of Ideas*, p. 225) "the essence of the theory of Ideas lay in the conscious recognition of the fact that there is a class of entities, for which the best name is probably 'universals', that are entirely different from sensible things. Any use of language involves the recognition, either conscious or unconscious, of the fact that there are such entities; for every word used, except proper names—every abstract noun, every general noun, every adjective, every verb, even every pronoun and every preposition—is a name for something of which there are or may be instances."

Finally, having now looked at the various functions of the Forms in relation to Plato's metaphysical, ethical and epistemological views, let us come back to Professor Cherniss's commendation of the theory for its philosophical economy. Certainly if it worked over all the areas we have mentioned, it would be an extremely economical theory. Indeed, one of the troubles with the theory, one is inclined to think, is that it is too economical, that the Forms are set to perform too many tasks, some of which are incompatible. We can do no more than illustrate this very briefly here. Consider the function of the Forms at (iii) on our list (Forms as ideal standards). Now as an ideal standard the Form is perfectly that to which imperfect particulars in varying degree approximate: for example, no particular act is perfectly just—only Justice itself (the Form) is perfectly just. It follows from this, first, that the Form becomes a sort of ideal particular, i.e. it is the perfect instance of that of which it is the Form, and it then becomes appropriate to predicate a Form of itself, i.e. to say Justice is just, Holiness holy (and Plato does say precisely this at *Protagoras*, 330C–D); and secondly, that the tendency when regarding the Forms as ideal standards, as the perfect exemplars to which things in our world can only approximate, will be to push them right out of our world, to regard them as quite separate and apart from particulars. Now difficulty arises when we consider the first point in relation to the function of the Forms at (iv) (Forms as universals). At (iv) the problem is how we are able to predicate the same general term of a number of particulars, and the answer to it is that we are able to do this because the general term refers to a property or attribute which is common to the particulars (i.e. to a universal). The Form then is the common attribute of a group of particulars and is predicated of the particulars, but, of course, is not itself a particular, but belongs to a totally different logical category. Indeed, one of the great achievements of the theory of Forms in this respect is that it points to the important distinction between attributes (or universals) and substances (particulars) of which the attributes are predicated. On the other hand in (iii), as we have seen, the Form itself becomes a subject of predication in that it becomes an ideal particular of which it is then itself predicated—Justice is just, Holiness holy. It is quite clear that the "economy" of the theory has led here to a very serious difficulty. In answer to this it has been suggested by some commentators that it is incorrect to think of Plato's Forms in the way in which we think of universals—that really the Forms should not be regarded as universals at all. This is a controversy which, unfortunately, we cannot pursue here, but it may be remarked that the reader who does pursue it for himself will find it philosophically interesting and rewarding. Again, the second point we raised above, namely the tendency towards separation of Form and particular which results from the function of the Forms as ideal standards ((iii) in our list), causes difficulty when we consider the functions of the Forms at (iv) and (v). In these latter functions the forms make particulars what they are, and here what seems important is that the Forms should be present in the particulars, and not separate from them. Once more the "economy" of the theory seems to create difficulty. The quotation from the *Phaedo* in (v) of our list may suggest that Plato himself felt some difficulty about the relation, as may the discussion in the first part of the later dialogue, the *Parmenides* (130–135), which everyone who is interested in the theory of Forms ought to read. Again, however, it has been argued that the difficulty arises from misunderstanding the nature of the Forms, and again it is impossible here to pursue the point. The reader, however, should bear in mind this problem of the relation between particulars and Forms when reading Books VI and VII.

Chapter 8 of *Plato's Republic: A Philosophical Commentary* by R. C. Cross and A. D. Woozley (London: Macmillan & Co., 1964). Reproduced by permission of authors and publishers.

6

HYPOTHESIS IN THE *REPUBLIC*

RICHARD ROBINSON

I. A CONFLICT BETWEEN PLATO'S EPISTEMOLOGY AND HIS METHODOLOGY

Plato believed in the possibility of absolute, incorrigible knowledge. Intelligence, he said in the *Timaeus* 51D–E, is not the same as true opinion, for these two came into being separately and are unlike in nature. 'The one comes to be in us through teaching, but the other owing to persuasion; and the one can always give a true account, but the other none; and the one is immovable by persuasion, but the other can be persuaded away; and it must be said that the one can be enjoyed by every man, but intelligence by gods, and by some small race of men.' In the *Theaetetus* he argued elaborately and energetically that knowledge would not be true opinion even if that opinion could give an account of itself. In the *Republic* he was, though brief, most definite of all; he bluntly said that knowledge could not be the same as opinion because the latter is fallible but the former infallible (477E). He rated opinion at a very low value compared with knowledge.

But his hypothetical method, if our analysis of the *Phaedo* has been correct, can never attain to absolute knowledge. It is merely approximative; and, however much work has been done, the possibility that the ruling hypothesis is false must always remain. It thus appears that Plato's methodology in the *Phaedo* is at variance with his epistemology as stated in the *Republic* and later works. The Aristotelian or the Cartesian methodology would have been, it seems, more suitable to this theory of knowledge; for both Aristotle and Descartes believed in absolute incorrigible starting-points, guaranteed by an infallible intuition, from which certain conclusions could be deduced.

We have seen that Plato regarded his hypothetical method as only a second best; but, when we recall that he believed in the possibility of absolute knowledge, we may think that he ought to have regarded it as a tenth best, and we must certainly wonder why he devoted so much space to its elaboration and so little, apparently, to the elaboration of a method for winning the real and not impossible prize, infallible certainty.

There is a passage in the *Cratylus* (436D) that seems to record the kind of dissatisfaction with mere hypothetical consistency that we should expect from a man with Plato's view of knowledge.

> If the giver [of names] made a mistake in the first place and then distorted the rest to meet it and compelled them to accord with him, it would not be at all surprising, just as in diagrams sometimes, when a slight and inconspicuous mistake is made in the first place, all the huge mass of consequences agree with each other. It is about the beginning of every matter that every man must make his big discussion and his big inquiry, to see whether it is rightly laid down or not (ὑπόκειται); and only when that has been adequately examined should he see whether the rest appear to follow from it.

A much stronger statement of dissatisfaction, which the context proves to refer expressly to hypothetical procedure, is to be found in the dialogue we are about to examine (533C): 'For if a man's beginning is something he does not know, and the end and what comes between are constructed out of what he does not know, what contrivance can ever turn such consistency into knowledge?'

2. TRANSLATION OF PASSAGES ON METHOD IN THE 'REPUBLIC'

The 'first-best' method, which seems to be demanded by these complaints and by Plato's epistemology, is indicated in the diagram of the Divided Line in the *Republic;* and to that we must therefore turn.

The main passages concerning hypothesis in the *Republic* appear in the part devoted to the higher education of the rulers, the part whose problem is 'how and through what studies and exercises the saviours of the republic will come to exist in it, and at what age each of them will take up each activity' (502C–541B). Socrates holds that these saviours must pursue 'the greatest study, the idea of the good' (505A). He does not himself know what the good is, except that it seems to be neither pleasure nor knowledge; but he suggests that it is to intelligence and the ideas as the sun is to sight and the visibles. It gives us all the knowledge and truth we have, but is itself superior thereto. And to the things we know it gives all the existence and reality they have, but is itself beyond reality in dignity and power.

Consider then, said I, that, as we say, they are two [namely, the good and the sun], and the one reigns over the intelligible sort and sphere, the other over the visible. . . . You have these two kinds, visible and intelligible?

I have.

Then take them as if they were a line cut into two unequal sections, and cut each section again in the same proportion, both that of the sort that is seen and that of the sort that is thought; and then, in degree of clearness relative to each other, you will have, in the visible, as the one section, images—I mean by images first shadows, next appearances in water and in things of a close and smooth and plain constitution, and everything of the sort, if you understand me.

I understand you.

Let the other section be what this one resembles, the animals about us and the whole class of everything that grows or is made.

Let it be, said he.

Would you be willing to say, said I, that we have divided it so that in degree of truth the likeness is to what it is like as the opined is to the known?

I certainly should, said he.

Now consider how we are to make the section of the intelligible part.

How?

In that the soul, using as images what was previously imitated, is compelled to pursue one section of it from hypothesis, not proceeding to a beginning but to an end; but for the other, which leads to an unhypothesized beginning, the soul goes from hypothesis and without the images of the other, making the inquiry by ideas themselves through themselves.

I do not understand that very well, said he.

Once again, then, said I. You will understand it easier if I say this first. I think you know that those who study geometry and calculation and such matters hypothesize the odd and even and the figures and three kinds of angles and related matters in each inquiry. Assuming that they know these things, and making them hypotheses, they do not expect to give any account (logos) of them either to themselves or to others, as being plain to all; but beginning from them they go through the rest consistently and end with what they set out to examine.

Certainly, he said; I know that much.

And they use the forms that we see and make their arguments about them, although they are thinking not about them but about what they resemble, making their arguments for the sake of the square itself and the diagonal itself, not of that which they draw. And so with the rest. What they model and draw are things of which there are shadows and images in water; but they use these things themselves as images again, their aim being to see those very things that can be seen only by thought.

That is right, he said.

Well, then, I meant that this kind is intelligible, but yet the soul is obliged to use hypotheses in pursuing it, and does not go to a beginning because it cannot get above the hypotheses, and uses as images the very things that are themselves imitated by those below them and honoured and valued as clear in comparison therewith.

I see, he said. You mean the object of geometry and the related sciences.

Then understand that by the other section of the intelligible I mean that which is grasped by pure discussion through the power of dialectic, making the hypotheses not beginnings but really hypotheses, like steps and sallies, in order that, going as far as the unhypothesized to the beginning of everything and grasping it, it may descend again thus to an end, clinging to the things that cling to that, using absolutely nothing sensible but only ideas themselves through themselves on themselves, and ending with ideas.

I see, he said, not indeed sufficiently, for I think you mean a big job. But I see this much, that you want to distinguish the part of intelligible reality which is the object of dialectic as being clearer than that which is the object of what are called the sciences, for which hypotheses are beginnings; and, while those who study them are obliged to do so by thought and not by senses, yet, because they inquire from hypotheses and do not ascend to a beginning, you think they do not have intelligence about them, although they are intelligible with a beginning. And to the state of the geometers and such persons I think you give the name 'thought', as being something between opinion and intelligence.

You have understood me perfectly, said I. And now take it that to the four sections there correspond these four effects in the soul: intelligence to the highest; thought to the second; to the third give conviction, to the last conjecture, and arrange them proportionately, giving to each as much clearness as its correspondent has truth.

I see, he said, and I agree and arrange them as you say. (509D–511E.)

Socrates next illustrates 'our nature regarding education and the lack of it' by the image of the Cave (514A ff.). He supposes men chained from childhood in a cave so that they see only the shadows of themselves and of certain statues and other objects that are being carried along behind them, and hear only their own voices and the echoes of the voices of the men carrying the objects. Such men, he says, would take these shadows and echoes for the truth; and, if they were afterwards unchained and made to look at the reality, they would be dazzled and take it for illusion. Becoming accustomed to the truth would be a long and painful process; and it would have to be repeated at many stages of increasing brightness before they were at last able to look directly at the sun itself. But once it was achieved they would pity the state of their fellow prisoners. If they returned to the cave they would be unable to see in the dimness; and those who had never been released would be confirmed in their belief that it was a bad thing to go upwards. In this image, Socrates says, the upward progress symbolizes the ascent of the soul to the intelligible place. The idea of the good is seen last and hardest among known things; but when we see it we infer that it is the cause of all that is right and fine everywhere. Education is not putting sight into blind eyes, but turning round eyes that are looking in the wrong direction. The question thus arises which studies drag the soul away from that which becomes to that which is. Arithmetic does so, because its object, the one, &c., never appears to sense except along with its opposite. What looks one also looks a multiplicity; and this confusion in the report of the senses compels the reason to intervene. As successive stages in the education of the rulers Socrates appoints plane geometry, solid geometry, astronomy (which he converts into kinematics), and harmonics. The final study, the grasping at the good itself, will be dialectic.

> This at any rate, I said, no one will allege against us, that any other inquiry [than dialectic] attempts methodically and universally to ascertain with regard to each thing what that very thing itself is. All the other sciences are either concerned with men's opinions and desires or with productions and manufactures, or they are aimed at the care of what grows and is manufactured. As to the rest, geometry and those connected therewith, which we said grasped something of reality, we see that they dream about reality, but cannot see it with waking eyes so long as they use hypotheses and do not canvass them, being unable to give an account of them. For if a man's beginning is something he does not know, and the end and what comes between are constructed out of what he does not know, what contrivance can ever turn such consistency into knowledge?
>
> None, said he.
>
> Then, said I, dialectical method alone proceeds in this way, destroying the hypotheses, to the very beginning, in order to obtain confirmation. It gently pulls and draws upwards the eye of the soul that is literally buried in a sort of Philistine filth, using the sciences we have detailed as its assistants in the conversion. 'Knowledge' we often called them owing to custom; but they need another name, clearer than 'opinion' and not so clear as 'knowledge'. I think we previously defined it as 'thought'. But men do not dispute about a word when they have such great matters to examine as we have proposed.
>
> No indeed, said he. [I follow Adam's excision of the next sentence, and keep the MS. ἀρέσκει thereafter.]
>
> We are content, then, said I, as before, to call the first part knowledge, the second thought, the third conviction, and the fourth conjecture; and the last two together opinion, and the

first two together intelligence; and to say that opinion is about becoming but intelligence about being; and that intelligence is to opinion what being is to becoming; and knowledge is to conviction, and thought is to conjecture, what intelligence is to opinion. But let us not go into the proportion and division of their objects, the opinable and the intelligible, Glaucon, in order not to involve ourselves in many more discussions than we have had already.

Anyhow I agree with you about the rest, he said, as far as I can follow it.

And do you call dialectical the man who takes the account of the essence of each thing? And if he cannot give an account to himself and others, then, so far as he cannot, you will not call him intelligent on the matter?

How could I? said he.

And the same with the good? If a man cannot by his account separate and distinguish the idea of the good from all else, and persevere through everything in the battle of refutation, eager to refute in reality and not in appearance, and go through all these things without letting his argument be overthrown, you will not say he knows the good itself or any other good; but, if he is somehow grasping some copy of it, he is grasping it by opinion and not by knowledge, his present life is a dreaming and a dozing, and before he wakes up here he will have gone to Hades and be completely asleep?

Yes, by heaven, said he, I say all that emphatically.

Well, then, your children, whom you are training and educating in the discussion—if you ever trained them in reality, I presume you would not let them govern the city and decide the most important things until they had ceased to be as irrational ($\dot{a}\lambda\acute{o}\gamma o\upsilon\varsigma$) as lines.

No, indeed, said he.

You will legislate for them to lay hold especially of the discipline that will make them capable of asking and answering questions most scientifically?

I shall, said he, along with you.

Then does it seem to you, said I, that dialectic lies on top of the sciences like a coping-stone, so that no other science could properly be placed above it, and the matter of the sciences is concluded?

Yes, he said.

Then the allotment is all you have left, I said; to whom we shall give these sciences and how. (533B–535A.)

Socrates then proceeds to answer this last question.

3. MATHEMATICS

Let us begin our attempt to understand what Plato says about hypothesis in these passages by considering what he says about hypothesis in mathematics. And first let us notice a remarkable feature that seems to contradict our previous account of hypothesis. This is that Plato here treats as hypotheses certain propositions which the mathematicians think they know, which they consider 'plain to all'. Thus every element of provisionality and approximation is removed. The mathematicians' procedure is represented as a single forward march once for all. And so, though the word 'hypothesis' is here, no element of what we thought it meant remains. There is no question of hypothesizing in the sense of deliberately assuming, for the time being, a proposition which you know that you do not know.

The explanation of this anomaly is that Plato is regarding the mathematicians as not treating certain propositions as hypotheses when they ought to, as not using the hypothetical method when they ought to. He thinks they are wrong to take the propositions from which they begin, 'the odd and even and the figures and three kinds of angles and related matters', as evident and known to be true. They should take them as tentative hypotheses. His complaint is that mathematicians do not use the hypothetical method although they should. The word 'hypothesis' is Plato's interpretation of their procedure, and not the word they themselves would use. Contemporary mathematicians did not describe themselves as starting always from hypotheses. This passage is not evidence for that; and the *Meno*, which explicitly borrows from mathematical procedure, surely implies that what they called the 'by hypothesis' method was not their regular procedure but a special method, frequent indeed (πολλάκις *Men*. 86E) but not preponderating.

Plato means, then, that the mathematicians, who usually proceed dogmatically and only occasionally hypothetically, ought to proceed always hypothetically, because in reality they never know their ultimate premises to be true. In the *Meno* he borrowed a special mathematical method for philosophy. This method afterwards came to seem to him very important indeed, as we see in the *Phaedo*. And now that he is writing the *Republic* he has come to think that this procedure should be not a special but the general method of mathematicians. He wants to extend the use of their method far beyond what they themselves would do, because he has come to think that, besides the hypotheses which they themselves recognize as such, all their other starting-points are hypotheses too.

What makes Plato think that the mathematicians do not really know their starting-points? One answer to this has already been rejected in the general discussion of the hypothetical method (see p. 104 of *Plato's Earlier Dialectic*); it was not that he thought he saw that some of them were in fact false. The context seems to suggest that it was his opinion at this time that nothing is really known unless it is deduced from the idea of the Good; and that was perhaps his opinion when he wrote the *Phaedo* too. It might also be that by using his hypothetical method he was led to believe in the merely provisional nature of all ordinary starting-points, including those of mathematics, whereas formerly he had without realizing it assumed that there are plenty of certain starting-points. There is very little in his text by way of a direct answer. When he says that 'they do not expect to give any account (logos) of [these hypotheses] either to themselves or to others' (510C), he seems to think of this as the consequence of their supposing that they know them rather than the cause of their really not knowing them; but his similar language in a later passage ('they use hypotheses and do not canvass them, being unable to give an account (logos) of them' 533B–C) implies rather that the cause and the proof of their not really knowing their starting-points is precisely their inability to give a logos of them. The only other direct statement on the point seems to be this: 'because they inquire from hypotheses and do not ascend to a beginning, you think they do not have intelligence about them, although they are intelligible with a beginning' (511C–D). This would apparently come to the same as the former passage if giving a logos of a proposition were sufficient to turn it from an 'hypothesis' into a 'beginning'. It is noteworthy that the *Phaedo* also speaks of giving a logos of an hypothesis. What this giving a logos would consist in will appear if we can elucidate what Plato understands by dialectic in the Line; for he holds that dialec-

tic does give a logos of everything. First, however, let us consider
one more side of his discussion of mathematics.

What the Divided Line says about mathematics falls into two
distinct parts. Separately from the mathematicians' attitude to
hypothesis, Plato brings out the fact that they use sensible images
in order to deal with the supersensible realities they are talking
about. (To the Greeks this was as true of arithmetic as of geometry.)
The question thus arises whether he thought there was a necessary
connexion between these two marks of mathematics. Did he think
that geometry must use hypotheses as it does because of its employ-
ment of images, or that it must use images because of the way it
treats hypotheses, or both? Or was he merely noting a chance conjunction in contemporary mathematics, an accident of history?

That he thought it merely a chance conjunction is strongly
suggested by the consideration that in the *Phaedo* he declares that
the hypothetical method makes no use of the senses. At the very
least this means that that method *need not* use the senses; and, if so,
surely there cannot be a necessary connexion between the two
marks. Furthermore, according to the Divided Line mathematics
is not alone in using hypotheses. Dialectic uses them too. One of
the curious things about the Line is the way in which Plato says
that mathematics starts from hypotheses, as if he were going to
say that dialectic did not, and then says that dialectic does so too.
'The soul, using as images what was previously imitated, is compelled to pursue *one* section of it *from hypothesis*, not proceeding to a
beginning but to an end; but for the *other*, which leads to an unhypothesized beginning, the soul goes *from hypothesis*', &c. (510B).
But Plato is quite definite in the Line that dialectic does not use the
senses; it follows that the use of hypotheses does not entail the use
of the senses. This impression is strengthened by the fact that the
Republic contains no statement that such a connexion exists, and still
less a statement as to what sort of thing it would be if it did. The
only text that carries even the shadow of an implication that it
exists is this: 'The soul, using as images what was previously
imitated, is compelled to pursue one section of it from hypothesis'
(510B). Here the fact that the use of images is attached as a participle to the use of hypotheses in the main verb perhaps gives a
faint indication that they are necessarily and not merely historically
connected. And that is all. Burnet could only say that the special
sciences 'depend on hypotheses of which they can give no account,

and are therefore obliged to use sensible diagrams' (*Greek Philosophy*, 229); he offered no justification for his 'therefore'.

Yet we should prefer to believe that Plato found some necessary connexion between the two marks, not merely because a philosopher systematizes whenever he can, but further because Plato regards mathematical procedure as the work of a distinct type of mental activity which he calls thought or διάνοια as opposed to intelligence or νόησις. If these two marks were connected only historically, 'thought' would not be a real species of mental activity, but a conjunction of two real species. And he does seem, in a vague and general way, to make Socrates regard what he describes as an organic whole.

Jackson suggested that the hypotheses of the mathematician are still dependent on the particulars or 'many' from which they were originally derived, because they have not been shown to be correct and complete accounts of Ideas. We may perhaps interpret this as saying that an hypothesis, being arbitrary, is not a sure grasp of an Idea, and therefore can be accepted as true only so far as it agrees with the particulars in which the Idea is exemplified. If, however, we came to know the Idea itself and see it face to face, all appeal to the sensibles would be irrelevant, and at the same time our attitude to the Idea would not be an hypothesis but something better.

There is, however, no evidence for Jackson's acute suggestion in the text, and it seems to be gravely damaged by the fact that, according to the *Phaedo*, hypothetical method is independent of the senses. If we are to show any necessary connexion between the two characteristics ascribed to mathematics in the Line, we must do it without violating this fundamental fact that the hypothetical method has nothing to with the senses.

A much more probable suggestion is that Plato is connecting geometry's use of the senses not with its use of hypothetical method but with its *failure to use the hypothetical method*. His view is that geometry treats its starting-points as certainties when it ought to treat them as hypotheses, because that is what they really are, though the geometer does not recognize the fact. Its material only justifies it in being hypothetical; yet it proceeds dogmatically. Plato felt, though without full explicitness, that no one would be as confidently dogmatic as the mathematicians were unless he had sensible experiences to go upon, that what made the mathematicians so convinced of their 'hypotheses' was that they seemed to be

directly given in sensible intuition. They were 'plain to all' or
παντὶ φανερά in the physical sense of being there to see in the
geometer's sand. In geometry the appeal to spatial intuition and
the claim that one's postulates are certainties go together. Plato's
contemporaries accepted both. Plato and the twentieth century
reject both.

4. THE UNHYPOTHESIZED BEGINNING

In contrast to the procedure of mathematics the Divided Line
indicates a method that makes a proper use of hypotheses and a
proper disuse of the senses; and to this let us now turn. Dialectic, in
contrast to mathematics, does not take for certain propositions that
ought to be merely hypothesized. It makes hypotheses 'really
hypotheses'. By that Plato means that dialectic not merely un-
covers and confesses its premisses (mathematics does that much),
but also admits that it does not know those premisses (which
mathematics ought to do but does not). It openly declares, and it
always bears in mind, that its premisses are merely 'hypothesized',
that is, assumed to be true until we learn better.

Plato further explains that dialectic takes its hypotheses οἷον
ἐπιβάσεις τε καὶ ὁρμάς. The odd thing about this phrase is that it
seems to couple an instrument with an action; for ἐπιβάσεις is
apparently passive but ὁρμάς surely active in sense. Most translators seem to have felt that, coupled as they are, these words must
really be either both active or both passive, and have chosen to
make them both passive. They have thus given to ὁρμάς a passive
sense which, if we may argue from Liddell and Scott's silence, it
never bears. If we must accept this dilemma, it would surely be
easier to take ἐπιβάσεις as active for once. But it is better to go
between the horns and say that Plato coupled active and passive
here, or at least did not make up his mind whether he meant
ἐπιβάσεις actively or passively; and so I translate ἐπιβάσεις by an
ambiguous and ὁρμάς by an active word: 'steps and sallies'. In any
case the phrase is merely a metaphor for what Plato has already
told us in saying that dialectic treats its premisses as hypotheses.
They are not laid down as definitive parts of science; they are
merely posited temporarily in the hope that they will lead us
towards science.

So far this sounds like the hypothetical method of the *Phaedo*. But
Plato introduces a most striking addition. He now proposes, by

means of this tentative and hypothetical attack, to reach in the end an absolute certainty. It is not a matter of perpetual improvement and approximation, as in the *Phaedo*, but of attaining incorrigible truth. For he is not merely blaming the mathematicians for thinking they have absolute certainty when they only have hypotheses, as we have remarked. He is furthermore, as we must now observe, declaring that a proper method, while recognizing hypotheses for what they are, can so manipulate them as to reach incorrigible truth. Thus he is making a double criticism of mathematics. On the one hand, it assumes a certainty to which it is not entitled; on the other, it ought to obtain a certainty which it does not possess. The peculiarity of the Line is that, while Plato is trying to get away from the dogmatism of mathematics, he himself hopes to arrive at a dogma, namely the anhypotheton.

Plato expresses dialectic's claim to certainty mainly by denying the term 'knowledge' or ἐπιστήμη to mathematics. "Knowledge" we often called them [i.e. the mathematical sciences], owing to custom; but they need another name, clearer than "opinion" and not so clear as "knowledge". I think we previously defined it as "thought"' (533D). And it is to mathematics that the following applies: 'For if a man's beginning is something he does not know, and the end and what comes between are constructed out of what he does not know, what contrivance can ever turn such consistency into knowledge?' (533C). Plato is not nearly so ready to assert the complement, that dialectic or right manipulation of hypotheses *is* knowledge, although that is here the obvious and inevitable tendency of his thought. He does once name the highest of his four faculties 'knowledge' (533E); and, since his whole description of the faculty is in terms of its use of hypotheses (511B–C, cf. 533C–D), that must really mean that this use of hypotheses can yield certainty. But mostly he prefers to wrap up the conception of certainty in that of the 'unhypothesized', or in the still vaguer conception of a 'beginning' as something opposed to an hypothesis. We must examine these two latter conceptions.

The word 'anhypotheton' or 'unhypothesized' was apparently coined by Plato in the Divided Line. He used it twice in this passage and never again. In view of the context and especially of the passages just quoted about mathematics' not being knowledge, what he understood by 'not hypothesized' must have been something to which the provisionality and arbitrariness of an hypothesis did not attach, something in other words that was known and certain once for all. Shorey wrote that 'Plato, except in mystical passages, has no absolute $\dot{\alpha}\rho\chi\alpha\acute{\iota}$' [beginnings]; and that 'methodologically and in its most important sense for the Platonic dialectic [the anhypotheton] denotes the habit of the flexible disciplined intelligence which is able and willing to revise, correlate, and unify its opinions through a virtually infinite receding series of hypotheses' (*The Idea of Good*, &c., 232, 234). This amounts to making 'anhypotheton' signify the hypothetical method as we have found it in the *Phaedo*, a perpetual approximation based on the exploration of implications. Now the Line certainly does suggest that dialectic is tentative and approximative as mathematics is not. But that is only the one half of what it suggests; and the other is that through this provisionality dialectic finally reaches a certainty that is real and not, like that of mathematics, illusory. It says in effect that mathematics is dogmatic from the start, and unjustifiably; whereas dialectic is dogmatic only at the end, and is then fully justified in being so. We greatly misrepresent Plato's account of dialectic here if we leave out either the preliminary tentativeness or the final certainty.

'Anhypotheton' and 'beginning' seem to be equivalent in Plato's terminology here. One way in which he expresses his criticism of mathematics is by saying that it mistakes hypotheses for beginnings. He speaks of those sciences 'for which hypotheses are beginnings' (511C7); and he tells us that dialectic 'makes the hypotheses not beginnings but really hypotheses' (511B5). This seems to mean that mathematics treats propositions as incorrigible which it ought not to. A beginning, then, is a proposition that we are fully justified in taking for incorrigible, as an hypothesis is one that we must maintain only tentatively. And thus a beginning is the same as an anhypotheton. The root notion of perfect certainty is described as a 'beginning' when it is regarded as the best or the only real basis for deduction, but as an 'anhypotheton' when it is regarded as differing from an hypothesis, which is also in a sense a beginning of deduction, by not being provisional.

Nowhere in the dialogues is any proposition put forward as an anhypotheton or a beginning. Nearest comes the proposition put forward in the *Crito* as 'the beginning of the inquiry' (48E), of which Socrates says that whose who believe it and those who do not have no common ground, and must despise each other when they see each other's decisions (49D). But there is a great difference between the notion implied here and the notion expressed in the *Republic* by 'beginning'. The idea of certainty or incorrigibility is absent from the *Crito*. And there must be some common ground between the supporters and the opponents of a proposition if that proposition can be reached by a method. The general impression left by the dialogues is that no proposition there enunciated is to be taken as more than a corrigible hypothesis. Although a certain manipulation of hypotheses can according to the Line result in an unhypothesized beginning, this kind of manipulation is apparently either not practised or at most never brought to a successful conclusion in the dialogues.

Could there be more than one genuine 'beginning'? Most students of Plato believe that he thought there was really only one, namely, the Idea of the Good. This might be divided into several propositions; but they would form a single, closely knit organic whole. The evidence for this view is indirect; for Plato does not explicitly say that the anhypotheton is the Good. We infer it from the following facts. First, the simile of the Sun has told us that the Good has a unique place in all our knowledge, and now the Line gives a unique place in our knowledge to the 'unhypothesized beginning'. Secondly, while the Line tells us that we reach the 'unhypothesized beginning' at the end of an upward path of reflection, the Cave says that the released prisoner sees the sun last of all, and here the sun probably means the Good as it did in the simile of the Sun. Lastly, there is a passage in Book VII which, while it does not mention the 'beginning', describes dialectic in language reminiscent of the Line as pressing on until at last it reaches—the Good: 'When a man attempts by dialectic without any of the senses through the logos to press on to what each thing itself is, and does not desist until he grasps what Good itself is by means of intelligence itself, he arrives at the end of the intelligible' (532A–B).

This, apparently, is the evidence for our belief that the 'unhypothesized beginning' mentioned in the Line is the Idea of the Good. The value of the last point is diminished by the fact that this passage recalls the Cave far more than it recalls the Line; so that it is perhaps only a form of the second argument. It must also be said on the other side that a later passage suggests that the Good is only one of the crowd of dialectic's objects ('And the same with the good' 534B). But on the whole the evidence seems sufficient.

Plato does not mention the 'beginning' or the 'anhypotheton' again after the *Republic*. But that he always retained the conception of the logical 'beginning' is suggested by its reappearance in Aristotle.

5. THE UPWARD PATH

What was the nature of that 'upward' path by which, according to Plato, we pass from hypotheses to an unhypothesized beginning? The material for an answer is scanty. Socrates four or five times says that dialectic goes *from* hypotheses *to* beginnings; but, if we ask him *how it can*, or even what makes him think that perhaps it might, he hardly seems to answer. There are only two passages that are anything like descriptions. The first is as follows: 'Making the hypotheses not beginnings but really hypotheses, like steps and sallies, in order that, going as far as the unhypothesized to the beginning of everything and grasping it, it may descend again thus to an end' (511B). This really contains no description of the manner at all. It says that we start by real hypothesizing and that we end by grasping the beginning. But as to how the trick is done, no word is said. One might almost suppose that Plato thought it obvious *how* you did it, or that he thought his readers would no more expect an explanation than a cook expects the recipe-book to tell her how to boil water.

The other passage is this. 'The dialectical method alone proceeds in this way, destroying the hypotheses, to the very beginning, in order to obtain confirmation' (533C). Here there does seem to be a mite of description; but it is very hard to interpret. What receives confirmation? And what is 'destroying' hypotheses? The latter question is so difficult that many readers take the text for unsound, and emend. Certainly the phrase cannot have its most obvious meaning of 'refuting'. Plato cannot be thinking of proving an hypothesis to be false (although that is what Aristotle meant by the phrase, *EE* 1222B28); for he implies that dialectic 'destroys' *all*, or at least all relevant, hypotheses, and he surely would not think that every hypothesis mooted would by some strange accident turn out to be false, that we should never hit upon a true one. He cannot have thought it the function of dialectic to disprove all hypotheses whatsoever; some of them must be true.

It seems equally unlikely that all the hypotheses would turn out to be true. Hence 'destroying' hypotheses apparently does not consist necessarily in deducing them from a higher hypothesis, which in turn will be deduced from a still higher hypothesis, and so on up to the 'unhypothesized beginning'.

Thus 'destroying' hypotheses appears to be neither refuting nor establishing them. Plato seems to be telling us of something that the dialectician will do to *all* the hypotheses he deals with, regardless of whether they are in fact true or false propositions. What then could dialectic possibly destroy with regard to *all* hypotheses? Why, precisely their hypothetical character, of course. Plato is not referring to the destruction of the proposition itself, i.e. to its refutation. It may be refuted but it may be established. He is referring to the destruction of our attitude towards it, which consisted in hypothesizing it. To 'destroy hypotheses' is not 'to prove the falsity of certain propositions which we formerly hypothesized' (nor to prove their truth), but 'to cease hypothesizing certain propositions which we formerly hypothesized, and take another attitude towards them'.

Hypothesizing a proposition includes both holding it as the beginning of a train of thought, and holding it tentatively. Which of these attitudes are brought to an end in the dialectician's destruction of hypotheses? The tentativeness will apparently be brought to an end in every case; for, after the dialectician has done his work, every proposition considered is either a certain truth or a certain falsehood. This seems to be implied by Plato's account of the downward path. The other element, the being a beginning of a train of thought, will apparently be brought to an end in nearly every case but not quite all. Nearly every proposition considered will be either rejected as certainly false or deduced from a higher proposition; but one proposition will still be underived, namely the 'unhypothesized beginning'.

If this is the correct interpretation of 'destroying the hypotheses', we have the unfortunate consequence that this passage, which at first raised our hopes, really tells us no more than the other about the *method* by which the dialectician gets from tentativeness to certainty, from hypotheses to the anhypotheton. This 'destroying the hypotheses' turns out to be merely another name for the fact that he *does* start with hypotheses and uncertainty and *does* end with perfect certainty and without hypotheses; but *how* he does so is said no more here than there. But these are the only two passages in which Plato is quite explicitly referring to the upward path in unmetaphorical language. It follows that all interpretations of this path are doubtful; and that they have to be based on the adduction of passages whose relevance is never certain. We will now review the principal kinds of interpretation that have been suggested.

6. THE SYNTHESIS-THEORY OF THE UPWARD PATH

First there is what may be called the synthesis-theory of the upward path. According to one passage in the Line, the work of dialectic consists of two distinct operations, first the upward path towards the 'beginning', and then a downward path away from the 'beginning' (511B). Now Plato's later dialogues also tell us that dialectic consists in two opposed operations. This is very clear in the *Phaedrus* (265–6), hardly less clear in the *Statesman* (285) and the *Philebus* (16–18), and perhaps to be discerned also in the *Sophist* (253). In these passages the two parts of dialectic are (1) synthesis or generalization and (2) division or classification. Now—so interpreters have thought—it is very unlikely that Plato would twice in his life distinguish dialectic into two separate operations and mean different things by the distinction each time. We must suppose that he means by it in the *Republic* what he tells us that he means by it in the later dialogues. It is not as if these processes were totally unknown to the middle dialogues. The lover's ascent towards absolute beauty in the *Banquet* is very similar in tone to the upward movement of dialectic in the *Republic*, and it is a process of generalization. The *Republic* itself mentions generalization at least twice (531, 537) and division at least once (454), and in two of these passages the activity is said to belong to dialectic. These are the considerations that have led to the view that by the upward and downward paths of dialectic in the *Republic* (511B) Plato meant the synthesis and division described in the *Phaedrus* (265–6). They are weighty enough to have convinced Zeller and Heinrich Maier and Rodier. The upward path would thus be, apparently, a gradual assembling of related species under their appropriate genus, and then the treatment of that genus as itself a species to be placed along with its fellow species under an appropriate genus, and so on

repeatedly, always ascending towards a higher genus, always unifying a larger manifold. Thus the metaphor of 'upward' would
here mean towards the more universal, though it does not in
the *Phaedo*.

What should be our judgement on the synthesis-theory of the
upward path? It seems rather doubtful whether Plato would think
of the Idea of the Good as being the *summum genus*, which he would
have to do on this interpretation; and very doubtful that he could
ever think that the process of finding the genus in a group of species
was in any sense 'destroying hypotheses' or 'treating hypotheses as
steps and sallies towards the unhypothesized'. In what sense would
the Good be 'unhypothesized' if it were the result of this procedure? These considerations presuppose a certain community
between Plato's logic and ours; but the following are independent
of that. Although the notions of synthesis and division occur in the
Republic in some sense, the actual nouns that are technical for these
notions in the later dialogues (συναγωγή and διαίρεσις) do not
occur in the *Republic;* nearest to them are συνοπτικός, κοινωνία,
διαιρεῖσθαι. Moreover, neither the words nor the notions occur in
the Divided Line itself, but only in other parts of the dialogue.

If the upward path were generalization, it would surely have to
be empirical. Generalization picks the universal out of the particulars given to sense. *Phaedrus* 249BC, which seems to describe
generalization, mentions 'many sensations'. Rodier saw this
necessity, and accordingly maintained that Plato believed the upward path to be empirical; only when the 'anhypotheton' had been
reached and the downward path begun did the dialectical procedure dispense entirely with the senses. Now, while what Plato
says is not explicit enough to make this interpretation impossible,
it does make it very improbable. The most obvious way to take the
passage that distinguishes the two paths is as meaning that both of
them proceed entirely without the senses. 'By the other section of
the intelligible I mean that which is grasped by pure discussion
through the power of dialectic, making the hypotheses not beginnings but really hypotheses, like steps and sallies, in order that,
going as far as the unhypothesized to the beginning of everything
and grasping it, it may descend again thus to an end, clinging to
the things that cling to that, using absolutely nothing sensible but
only ideas themselves through themselves on themselves, and ending with ideas.' The phrase 'using absolutely nothing sensible' is

contiguous to the description of the downward path, and so might conceivably refer to that alone. But the 'absolutely' or παντάπασιν seems to embrace the whole of dialectic. Certainly the whole is referred to by the initial phase, αὐτὸς ὁ λόγος ἅπτεται τῇ τοῦ διαλέγεσθαι δυνάμει; and my translation of this is based on the belief that it refers to the process of dialectical question and answer which Plato held to be independent of the senses: 'that which is grasped by pure discussion through the power of dialectic.' Moreover, the passages where dialectic is described without distinction of paths as dispensing with the senses (510B6–9, 532A6), and the whole contrast between dialectic and mathematics, seem to tell us definitely that dialectic is beyond experience throughout its course.

Another difficulty for the synthesis-theory is as follows. If the synthesis of the *Phaedrus* is the upward path of the Line, where does the division of the *Phaedrus* come in? We naturally think that it constituted the downward path; but there are reasons for believing that, if synthesis and division were applied to the Line by Plato at all, they both went in the upward path. Proclus seems to have understood division as belonging to the upward path (*in Euclid*. 211 Friedlein). In *Republic* 534B–C division seems to be a process of arriving at the Idea of the Good; and therefore would come in the first part of dialectic. If *Sophist* 253D explains the upward path, as Maier thought, then again division would belong to the upward path. Above all, the following reflection seems to make it impossible for division to come in the downward path: Plato surely conceives of the downward path as a proof, a deduction, a demonstration, in which conclusions are drawn from the anhypotheton as from an axiom; but how could division ever prove anything? If for these reasons we come to think that both synthesis and division must go in the upward path of the Line, we have sawed off the branch we were sitting on; for what originally led us to use these conceptions in the interpretation of the Line was precisely that the later dialogues present them as a dichotomy of dialectic and the Line also makes a dichotomy of dialectic. But it now appears that the dichotomy in the later dialogues is a subdivision of one side of the dichotomy in the *Republic*.

The synthesis-interpretation of the Line consists in reading into the Line what is said in some passages of the later dialogues, because both the Line and those other passages are dichotomies of dialectic. It is thus an argument from analogy: 'since the Line has certain features of these later passages, therefore it has the others too.' But it is not a strong analogy, because the points of difference are weighty and the points of resemblance are not. Here are nine points of difference. Unlike the Line, the later passages do not mention (1) the senses, or (2) hypothesis, or (3) the 'beginning', or (4) the metaphor of up and down, or (5) a fixed temporal order for the two processes. Unlike the later passages, the Line does not mention (6) synthesis, or (7) division, or (8) definition. Above all, (9) the *Republic* belongs to Plato's middle period, whereas the other passages, with the possible exception of the *Phaedrus*, are very much later. The resemblances are merely the following four: both sets of passages (1) refer to Ideas, (2) are about dialectic, (3) divide dialectic into two processes, and (4) use πάλιν [again] or αὖ [once more] or πάλιν αὖ [once again] to pass from one process to the other. I mention the fourth resemblance because Rodier did so; but it is worth nothing at all, for Plato constantly uses those adverbs to mark any sort of transition whatever.

I conclude that it would be very wide of the mark to say that the upward and downward paths mentioned in the Line were thought of by the author as consisting either essentially or mainly in synthesis and division respectively. On the other hand, it is clear from certain passages in the *Republic* that Plato was already thinking of something at least faintly like the synthesis and division of the *Phaedrus* as being activities proper to the dialectician; and it is fairly likely that he would have agreed, if asked, that these activities might sometimes aid the activities of the upward and downward paths.

7. MATHEMATICAL THEORIES OF THE UPWARD PATH

Let us turn to the theories that give dialectic a mathematical tinge. One of the most frequent of these is that the upward path is what the Greek geometers called analysis; and it has sometimes been said, following a tradition that Plato invented analysis, that the Line is the first statement of this method. Cornford is, so far as I know, the latest person to interpret the Line by means of geometrical analysis; but he assumes a heterodox view of analysis which I have argued to be false (*Mind* XLV, 464). According to the ordinary view, which is really as certain as anything in the history of thought, analysis consists in finding a proof of *p* by hypothesizing *p*, observing that *p* entails *q*, inferring *q*, observing that *q* entails *r*, inferring *r*, and so continuing until you reach a proposition, say *s*, which you independently know to be true. Your proof of *p* is then as follows: 'we know *s* to be true, and *s* entails *r* entails *q* entails *p*; therefore *p* is true.' This statement of the proof was called the synthesis, in contrast to the analysis which was the discovery of the proof. The method requires that the implications observed shall be reciprocal; not merely must *p* entail *q* but *q* must entail *p*, and so on; and this condition frequently holds in mathematics.

Once we have realized what geometrical analysis was, there is little incentive to read it into the Divided Line. It would have to mean that dialectic hypothesizes some proposition and goes on deducing its consequences until it arrives at the Idea of the Good, which it independently knows to be true. It then (and this synthesis would be the downward path) asserts the Idea of the Good, and deduces consequences therefrom in the reverse order until it arrives at the original hypothesis, which is thus established. But the Idea of the Good is not antecedently known to be true; it is just the task of the upward path to lead us to our first knowledge of the Good. It would be slightly less absurd to say that the original hypotheses or 'steps and sallies' of the upward path are propositions about the Good itself, proposed definitions of the Good; that the analysis consists in inferring consequences from these until we come to something we know (if we can), and the synthesis in proving our definition of the Good from the known fact. But the Line is equally fatal to this; for the Good does not come at the end of the downward path. It comes at the beginning thereof, and is the presupposition of all categorical proof.

Another of the mathematicizing interpreters of the Line is Milhaud. He holds that if we think of mathematics when we read what Plato has to say about science, everything becomes astonishingly clear. Plato's theory of science was an analysis of rational geometry as he knew it and practised it. The domain of intelligence is distinguished from that of opinion by two things. The first is logical rigour; for in both its parts intelligence forms chains of propositions closely bound to each other, whereas opinion never gives us any necessity. The second is the creative initiative of the soul, making her own hypotheses (*Les Philosophes-Géomètres de la Grèce*, 245).

These and other reflections of Milhaud's can be guaranteed to

stimulate a person interested in Plato's epistemology; but the conclusion must nevertheless be that Milhaud is mistaken. Like many
other readers, he has attributed to Plato something that he himself
admires, but Plato did not think of. His interpretation seems to
leave no place for the unhypothesized beginning, which is the key-
stone of the doctrine. It illuminates particularly clearly the great
fault of most mathematicizing explanations, which is that they ask
us to believe that Plato is here borrowing something from mathematics, although he quite explicitly says that he is producing
something which mathematics lacks. There really can be no doubt
that the Line examines mathematical method and finds it wanting,
that Plato here presents dialectic as a procedure distinct from that
pursued by the geometers, and better. If in the face of this we insist
on saying that nevertheless the dialectical method *is* something
Plato learnt from mathematics, we shall inevitably imply one of
two unpleasant things: either that he was mistaken in supposing he
had a non-mathematical method, or that he was dishonourably
denying the mathematicians a credit he knew to be their due.

The proposition, that Plato did not receive from contemporary
mathematics the notion of the method which he attributes to
dialectic in the Line, does not settle the question whether he
thought his new method would or could be adopted by mathematicians in the future. This problem, whether mathematics
could become dialectical, seems identical or vitally connected with
these others. Could mathematics become knowledge (for only
dialectic really knows, according to the Line)? Could it dispense
with sense? Could it cease to take hypotheses for beginnings?
Could it obtain a real beginning? Are its objects possible objects of
dialectic? What are its objects? These questions are so doubtful and
have been so much argued that we must postpone their discussion
until we have completed our present inquiry into the method of
passing from hypotheses to the anhypotheton.

A more attractive kind of mathematicizing interpretation of the
Line was put forward by Julius Stenzel. He said that the Line 'is
unambiguously the proposal to axiomatize'. By this he seems to
have meant that mathematics starts with a welter of propositions
and proofs, and the upward path consists in gradually reducing
them to the order of a system entirely deducible from a few precise
propositions. The unhypothesized beginning is the unity of the
whole that we thus obtain; and from this unity the logos itself,

reversing its direction, can, without making use of sense, render all the earlier stages evident and intelligible. Thus the important thing is not in the least whether the propositions refer to anything sensible, but only that they shall be logically connected together and made to depend on principles. (*Verhandlungen des internationalen Mathematiker-Kongresses Zürich* 1932, Bd. I, 331.)

This interpretation, which we may call the axiomatization-theory of the Line, is a valuable insight. The word 'axiomatization', as now used in mathematics and logic, evokes a conception of which a seed is to be found in the Line. Plato expresses here the notion of minimizing the number of one's unmediated assertions by deducing as many of them as possible from the rest; this idea bore fruit in Aristotle's theory of science and Euclid's axiomatization of geometry.

It is important, however, to realize the distance and difference between the idea of axiomatization in the Line and that in a mathematician like Hilbert. For one thing, Plato's conception of logical rigour, if he can be said to have one at all, is much less exacting than that of twentieth-century logic (see *Plato's Earlier Dialectic*, pp. 132–33). Its looseness appears, for example, in his habitual assumption that a single axiom might suffice to generate a whole system. Phrases like 'the first hypotheses' (*Phd.* 107B) are unusual in his works. Ordinarily he thinks of a single hypothesis as fertile by itself, ignoring in his methodology the other premises to which he is allying it; and in the Line above all the 'beginning' is invariably referred to in the singular. *Principia Mathematica*, because of the plurality of its primitive propositions, would have been a disappointment to him. Thinkers have been working recently to reduce the number of postulates required for logic; but Plato is not confining himself to logic. He seems to hope for nothing short of deducing the whole of knowledge from his single 'beginning', a goal which now appears infinitely far removed.

So much for the far less rigorous nature of Plato's conception, but there is another important difference between his Divided Line and the present idea of axiomatization. Today axiomatization is an autonomous ideal, at least in mathematics. Perhaps we have ulterior motives for trying to axiomatize chemistry; but we axiomatize mathematics for the sake of the axiomatization itself. We enjoy the elegance of a deductive system as such; the fewer the postulates, and the faster they generate the theorems, the better we like it. Hence we sometimes feel no interest in the question whether the postulates are *true*, or even go so far as to say that the question has no meaning, since 'true', which means 'deducible from a given set of postulates', is a term that can apply only to theorems. Now this attitude is foreign to the Divided Line. To Plato, the question whether the 'unhypothesized beginning' is true is perfectly legitimate and supremely important. To Plato, on the other side, axiomatization has no value as such; and is desirable only because, if we can certify the 'beginning', axiomatization thereby certifies all the rest. Axiomatization, like many other human activities, arose as a means to something else and later became an end in itself. In modern logic it is pursued for its own sake; but Plato valued it only as a means to sure knowledge. It was an instrument in his passionate 'quest for certainty'. He could not feel as certain as he wished about any proposition in mathematics or physical science. He had hopes that he could find a lake of certainty in the mountain of the Good, and could then, by channels of axiomatization, conduct its water down to the shifting deserts of mathematics and physics. The axiomatization-theory, therefore, is an incomplete account of the Line because it ignores Plato's quest for certainty, and does not tell us how he hoped to find certainty. It seems to be an account of the downward rather than of the upward path.

8. THE 'PHAEDO'-THEORY OF THE UPWARD PATH

Let us now consider the suggestion that the upward path of the Line is the hypothetical method described in the *Phaedo*.

The method described in the *Phaedo* was to defend a proposition by deducing it from an hypothesis, and to defend this hypothesis first by drawing all its consequences to see if they were self-consistent, and secondly by deducing the hypothesis from a higher hypothesis, and so on until you came to something adequate. The original defence of a proposition by deducing it from an hypothesis would no doubt be regarded by Plato in the *Republic* as belonging to mathematics and not to dialectic; but were the *Phaedo*'s subsequent operations on the hypothesis itself what Plato had in mind in the Line under his metaphor of the upward path of dialectic?

The first of these subsequent operations (Socrates in the *Phaedo* insisted that it should come first) was to draw the consequences of the hypothesis to see whether they were self-consistent. This, I have argued, was to subject the hypothesis to the Socratic elenchus, for Plato thought of the elenchus as making a thesis lead to self-contradiction. If, then, the upward path of the Line was, or included, the hypothetical method of the *Phaedo*, it was, or included, the Socratic elenchus.

Plato probably did, in the *Republic*, think of his upward path as including the elenchus of hypotheses. To treat hypotheses as 'really hypotheses', which the mathematician fails to do, included making a methodical attempt to show that they led to a self-contradiction. When he wrote that 'by the other section of the intelligible I mean that which is grasped *by pure discussion through the power of dialectic*', τοῦτο οὗ αὐτὸς ὁ λόγος ἅπτεται τῇ τοῦ διαλέγεσθαι δυνάμει, he was referring to the dialogue between two or more persons in which by question and answer and elenchus, without any appeal to the senses, Socratics earnestly and laboriously pursued consistency and enlightenment.

If we turn to the description of dialectic in Book VII, which is universally recognized to be an expression of the same ideas, we find a passage in which the elenchus is prominent:

And do you call dialectical the man who takes the account (*logos*) of the essence of each thing? And if he cannot give an account (*logos*) to himself and others, then, so far as he cannot, you will not call him intelligent on the matter?

How could I?, said he.

And the same with the good? If a man cannot by his account (*logos*) separate and distinguish the idea of the good from all else, and persevere through everything in the battle of refutation (ἐλέγχων), eager to refute (ἐλέγχειν) in reality and not in appearance, and go through all these things without letting his argument be overthrown, you will not say he knows the good itself or any other good? (534B–C.)

A further confirmation of this view, that the upward path in the *Republic* would contain elenchus as the hypothetical method of the *Phaedo* did, may be drawn from the *Republic*'s use of hypothetical method in establishing that the soul has three parts. Socrates there hypothesizes a proposition 'in order that we may not be obliged to waste time examining all such objections and making sure that they are not true' (*R.* 437A). This seems to imply that, if you want to use a proposition as a premiss, the alternative to hypothesizing it is examining and disarming all the objections to it. But the alternative to hypothesizing a premiss should be the upward path of dialectic. That path, therefore, seems to involve attempting to refute the hypotheses.

The other part of hypothetical method according to the *Phaedo* was the deduction of the hypothesis, after it had been tested for self-contradiction, from a higher hypothesis posited for the purpose. Was Plato in the *Republic* envisaging this as also part of the upward path of dialectic? The answer appears to be yes, for the following reasons. First, there appears to be nothing in this part of the *Phaedo*'s method that conflicts with anything said in the Divided Line, and hence it seems more likely than not that on this point Plato's view in the *Republic* does not differ from his view in the *Phaedo*. Secondly, since the downward path sounds like a deduction of theorems from axioms, it is quite likely that the upward path would proceed from as yet unproved theorems to as yet uncertified axioms from which the theorems followed. Thirdly, if we do not count this second part of the *Phaedo*'s method as part of what Plato intended in the upward path of the *Republic*, we have not yet shown any reason for Plato's metaphor of 'upward'. The elenctic procedure, which is all of the content that we have yet given to the upward path, has nothing upward about it. In this procedure an hypothesis is tested by having its consequences drawn, which is a downward path. If no contradiction appears, that is the end of the elenchus. If a contradiction does appear, we proceed to take another hypothesis which, we hope, will not develop the same defect. But this new hypothesis will not necessarily be in any natural sense 'higher' than the discarded one; it is much more likely to be 'on the same level', since it is intended to fulfil the same function. These reasons seem to suggest that we should take the upward path of the *Republic* as including the second element of the *Phaedo*'s hypothetical method as well as the first.

9. THE INTUITION-THEORY OF THE UPWARD PATH

The upward path of the *Republic* includes, then, the hypothetical method of the *Phaedo*. On the other hand, the hypothetical method of the *Phaedo* does not seem to exhaust the upward path as Plato conceived it in the *Republic*, because it cannot give, and does not claim to give, the infallible certainty, the sure grasp of an 'un-hypothesized beginning', which is emphasized in the *Republic*. The characteristic and new element in the *Republic* is the claim to have a method that gives absolute certainty. It will not do to say that the upward path is merely self-criticism that never reaches any absolute at all, merely the readiness to reconsider and go behind any postulate, or 'the habit of the flexible disciplined intelligence which is able and willing to revise, correlate, and verify its opinions through a virtually infinite receding series of hypotheses' (Shorey, *The Idea of Good, &c.*, 234). It is true that Plato in the Line is pointing to a contrast of intellectual temperaments, and that 'the scientific habit of reasoning from unquestioned assumptions does differ from the philosophical readiness and ability to extend indefinitely the analysis of the presuppositions either of science or of common sense' (Shorey, *What Plato Said*, 233). But it is false that that is all he is doing. In the few words of the Line he manages to convey not merely this, but also that the philosopher, just because he leaves no assumption unquestion*ed*, will finally reach one that is unquestion*able*.

The question therefore seems to arise: What method has Plato in the *Republic* in addition to the hypothetical method of the *Phaedo*, through which he thinks the dialectician can escape from the tentativeness of the *Phaedo*'s procedure and reach indubitable certainty? I believe, however, that the true answer to this question is to deny part of what it implies. I believe that Plato in the *Republic* claims the possibility of certainty for the dialectician without having any more method at his command than the *Phaedo* gave him. He merely claims that the man who competently and conscientiously practises this hypothetical and elenctic procedure will, or may, one day find himself in the possession of an unhypothetical certainty. He conceives that the dialectician takes an hypothesis and deduces its consequences, trying his hardest to discover some contradiction in those consequences. If he does discover one, the hypothesis is thereby refuted. He then takes another hypothesis, usually a modification of the first one designed to avoid the contradiction which refuted that. He then deduces the consequences of this second hypothesis, again trying his hardest to make it lead to a contradiction. He continues this process for a long time, making a great effort to be patient and thorough. Some day, after months or years of labour, he reflects that he has now been attempting to refute the same hypothesis for many weeks, and that this last hypothesis has endured every test and stood consistent in all its consequences, which he has deduced on every side as far as it seems possible to go. With this reflection (if he ever gets so far) it dawns on him that this hypothesis is certainly true, that it is no longer an hypothesis but an anhypotheton.

In this process the last event, the 'dawn', is something like what was afterwards meant by the doctrine of intuition, for 'intuition' means certain knowledge not reached by method.

On this 'intuition-theory' of the upward path, that path is not a process of *proof* at all. It does not *demonstrate* the 'beginning' at which it arrives. Socrates never says that it does; he uses only vague language such as 'proceeding' to a beginning. If we get the opposite impression, it is because he compares the path of dialectic to that of mathematics and the latter is a chain of inference; but, because they are both paths, it does not follow that they are both demonstrations. The 'beginning' at which dialectic arrives is the Good; and Plato's view seems to be that the Good, far from being proved, is the presupposition of all proof that is not hypothetical.

But if the path does not prove the beginning, what is its use? What confidence can we have that our beginning is less arbitrary than that of mathematics? Or, if we can be confident of this, why do we need the path at all? Why not begin at the beginning instead of a long way before it! The answer to this is the positive side of the intuition-theory. The prisoner released from the Cave goes through a series of objects graduated in brightness before he can look at the sun, which is the brightest of all. But the series of preliminary objects does not demonstrate the existence of the sun; it only enables him to see it. The prisoner by this process gradually strengthens his eyes. By practising on effects he gains the power to see the cause of those effects. So the dialectician on the upward path is gradually strengthening his mental vision until he can apprehend not merely the effects with which he had to start but also the cause of these effects; but he is not demonstrating the existence of that cause except in the sense in which the raising of the curtain demonstrates the existence of the stage. The upward path is an intellectual discipline that results in knowledge and yet does not prove anything. 'Plato constantly uses metaphorical expressions taken from the senses of sight and touch to denote the immediate character of his highest knowledge' (Lutoslawski, *Origin and Growth of Plato's Logic*, 294; see the references there). What makes the beginning a real beginning and 'unhypothesized' is simply the fact that it is the first thing to be really known. Mathematics is not knowledge. The upward path is not knowledge. We have our first perfect knowledge when at last we apprehend the Idea of the Good; and that is why this Idea is our true 'beginning' although it comes late or never in our lives.

A similar view is implied by the account of the lover's progress in the *Banquet*. The beautiful itself is known through itself; but a long apprenticeship among the many beautifuls is necessary before this direct knowledge can occur. Because this knowledge requires many preliminaries, and yet is direct when it comes, it may suitably be represented by the language of vision and of the sights revealed to the religious after a laborious initiation. A similar view is implied again in the *Seventh Letter*, with the two differences (1) that here Plato does not imply anything about the nature of the object known by this process, and (2) that he describes the illumination when it comes as 'sudden'. 'It cannot anyway be expressed like other learning, but after community of life with much discussion of the matter itself it suddenly appears in the soul like light kindled from leaping fire, and thenceforward sustains itself' (341C). 'Hardly when each of these things is compared with the others, names and definitions, sights and perceptions, and men criticize them in question and answer with benevolent criticisms and without envy, does wisdom and intelligence about each thing flash out, straining human power to the utmost' (344B).

In the downward path we for the first time possess categorical demonstrative knowledge, knowledge obtained by sure inference from a sure premiss. Many of the steps we then take will, no doubt, have been already contemplated during the upward; but at that time they were only hypothetical, because we did not know whether their premisses were true. The downward path distinguishes the true from the false hypotheses of the upward; and it will probably add some entirely new propositions.

If the intuition-theory is right, the Line contains a doctrine similar to Aristotle's. For Aristotle too has an upward and downward movement of thought. In the downward, which he calls apodeixis or syllogism, we are rigorously demonstrating incorrigible conclusions from incorrigible premisses of a universal character;

and in the upward we are obtaining those universal premisses by a process that is not demonstration and yet gives them to us without doubt. His word for this upward path, νοῦς, is closely related to Plato's word for the faculty of dialectic in the Line, νόησις. His word for the basic premisses that νοῦς, or intuition, obtains is Plato's word 'beginning'. If we accept the intuition-theory we ought, in view of these resemblances, to suppose that Aristotle's theory of science was a descendant of the theory recorded in the Line.

On the other hand, we ought not to lose sight of the fact that Aristotle greatly developed and altered the theory. According to him, there is a plurality of these 'beginnings' and each special science has some of its own. And, while the path towards them may be dialectic (*Topics* I 2), it may also be something else, such as habituation (*EN* I 4, 1095B4–8). It may even be 'epagoge', which in this connexion appears to be a kind of abstraction and to start from the senses (*Anal.* IV 19). Plato has none of Aristotle's proof that there must be beginnings, none of his long and varied discussion of the nature of a beginning, none of his discussion of the downward path or his epoch-making division of it into the three figures of syllogism, nor even his surely fundamental point that our grasp of the beginning and our grasp of the demonstration are distinct mental faculties (for according to Plato the upward and the downward paths of dialectic belong to the one faculty of 'intelligence'). Nor would Plato have approved of the slovenly argument by elimination which is all that Aristotle offers to prove the existence of intuition (*Anal.* IV 19 and *EN* VI 6). The doctrine of intuition is present in the Line only to this extent, that Plato there exhorts us to acquire the habit of uncovering the premisses of our arguments and asking how we know them; that he realizes that all certainty obtained by inference presupposes a certainty obtained without inference; and that he has faith that there might be such a thing as valid certainty obtained without inference.

The upward path on this theory is identical with something which in the *Phaedo* was not supposed to lead to final certainty. But that is just the difference between the *Phaedo* and the *Republic;* the former does not maintain that the elenchus could ever establish a proposition with certainty, and the latter does. What has caused our bewilderment about the Divided Line is partly the feeling that, since Plato is now claiming a dogmatic certainty which he did not before, he must have some new method which he did not have before. The disappointing conclusion to which we have come at last is that he has not. The new claim for certainty is made on the ground of the old hypothetical method.

Did Plato think of the 'beginning' as a proposition that would necessarily be seen to be true as soon as it was entertained, or as a proposition that could be entertained indefinitely without being seen to be the ultimate truth? Would the dialectician who finally discovered it have a new proposition before him, or an old one at last known to be true? Probably the question as such did not occur to Plato. But he says that in the ideal city the soldiers would hold as steadfast beliefs certain ethical propositions which the rulers knew to be true. If the definition of the Good were such as to convey any meaning to the common man, then surely the rulers would teach it to the soldiers along with the definitions of courage and the other virtues; and thus the few who finally came to know the Good would have been believing it for a long time. Plato actually envisages the case of a man to whom the lawgiver has taught 'what is the fine' (538D). Apart from these considerations, if the upward path includes a thoroughgoing elenchus before it culminates in intuition, it seems that a man could not actually perceive the truth of the true account of the Good until he had submitted it to a very long and very serious examination. Thus the intuition that is faintly suggested by the Line is not the sort of intuition in which conception and confirmation occur simultaneously. The confirmation, that is, the apprehension that the proposition is true, may be sudden, as it is implied to be in the *Banquet* and the *Seventh Letter;* but it occurs long after the first conceiving of the proposition.

10. COMMENTS

A few remarks may be added in evaluation of Plato's statements about hypothetical method in the *Phaedo* and the *Republic,* so far as they can be evaluated without first pleading a whole system of methodology.

The question how far Plato was bringing something new into human consciousness with his hypothetical method is not one that we can answer with any precision, owing to the scantiness of our evidence for previous thought. The previous forms of methodological consciousness to which he owed most were no doubt those present in Socrates, the mathematicians, and the Eleatics. His dialogues make it probable that he thought he obtained his conception of the elenchus from Socrates; but any statement as to how far he really did so, and how far his own mind had unconsciously remoulded what he found in his teacher, would be worth asserting only at the end of a long study of the evidence for the historical Socrates. Probably, however, it was his own idea to make the elenchus serve positive and constructive ends. In Socrates it had been purely refutative, as its name implies; Plato was responsible for the view that it could serve to suggest more and more improvements in an hypothesis until it became practically unassailable. He was thus reproducing in philosophy the methodical constructiveness that had previously appeared only in mathematics, and paradoxically using for the purpose a method that was essentially destructive. The originality of this would have been much less if, as Burnet suggested, mathematics itself at that time made all its constructions by a destructive method, by reduction to absurdity; but we have rejected this view (*Plato's Earlier Dialectic*, p. 112).

Part of his originality lay, then, in demanding the generalization of certain aspects of mathematical thought, and their extension to all thinking. These aspects were its constructiveness, its deductiveness, its clear distinction between conclusions and premises, and its open confession of its premises. But he not merely borrowed these elements for philosophy. He also made an advance on them, which could be applied with benefit in all fields of thought, including mathematics itself. For he demanded that the premises should be not merely confessed but criticized. He is the first person to show any sign of at once believing and disliking the proposition that every proof has unproved premises; a linked insight and dissatisfaction which are of great importance in methodology. He is really the author of 'the quest for certainty', because he was the first to appreciate the obstacle to certainty. Out of this appreciation arose a seed that grew in Aristotle's mind as the doctrine of intuition, the faculty that gives certainty without proof. Out of it also grew, in Plato's own mind, the hypothetical method, with its emphasis on tentativeness and provisionality, which are now seen to be very necessary until intuition is achieved. The hypothetical method, suggested according to the *Meno* by a device often used by contemporary mathematicians, but perhaps in truth merely crystallized thereby, came to be in Plato's view not an occasional dodge but the sole and universal method of all responsible thinking.

It seems reasonable to ask what it is in the nature of things and the nature of men that makes the hypothetical method desirable. For if a method is suitable, that must surely be because the reality sought to be known is such and such, and the human mind that seeks to know it is such and such. That a method is good ought to be derivable from the situation to which it applies. But Plato's insight did not go so far as that. He does not give us a reasoned derivation. Like most expounders of method, whether in abstract thinking or in aesthetic composition or in physical skill, he writes out of an uncriticized conviction that these are the things that have caused the successes he is conscious of having achieved.

We must evidently accept Plato's provisional and tentative method of using hypotheses, and his call for tentative constructions, for deduction and the confession of premises and the criticism of them. As to the method by which these premises are to be tested, we should all of us today want to make some use of a way that he rejected altogether, the appeal to sense. We believe that in the interpretation of nature the main test of an hypothesis is whether its consequences contradict what is given to sense, or, on the contrary, truly predict sensations that were not expected. Most of us would allow to Plato that there is another test as well; but we should want to reformulate his description of its nature. He supposed that an hypothesis might generate a consequence that contradicted another of its consequences or the hypothesis itself. We should perhaps agree that this might occur; but we should say that the vast majority of the cases Plato thus classified demand another explanation. The contradiction is really generated by the conjunction of the hypothesis with one or more of our standing beliefs. The aim of the hypothetical method thus becomes the establishment of consistency among our standing beliefs; and on occasion the appearance of a contradiction may call for the abandonment not of the hypothesis under consideration but of some other proposition.

With these corrections we should most of us accept the hypothetical method as stated in the *Phaedo*. But few would nowadays agree with the *Republic*'s claim that this process might culminate in intuitive certainty. The above correction makes this claim even more dubious. That Plato vaguely supposed that somehow or other his dialectical procedure would illuminate the premisses, and so make everything as certain as the conclusions are, provided you assume the premisses, was largely because he remained under the impression that an hypothesis can by itself give rise to contradictory consequences. This made it appear that the dialectical examination of a premiss did not itself assume other premisses. Thus an infinite regress did not arise; and if an exhaustive examination of the consequences of the premiss revealed no contradiction, it was possible to feel that the premiss had been established. But what seemed to Plato the gradual forging of an hypothesis to which there were no objections turns out, on this correction, to be merely the gradual forging of a consistent set of beliefs; and it therefore does not escape the stricture passed in the *Cratylus*, that consistency is no guarantee of truth. If an epistemological intuition can ever supervene upon our reflections, it might seem more likely to do so when our reflections took the form of analysis than when they were devoted to the construction of a consistent system. Surely Descartes was nearer the probabilities when he advised us to seek the simplest elements in any field. There seems more chance of intuiting a relation between simple elements in an analysed complex, than of intuiting the truth of a set of propositions ascertained to be consistent.

Chapter X of *Plato's Earlier Dialectic* by Richard Robinson (Clarendon Press, London, 1953). Reprinted by permission of the author and the publisher. [English translations of a few Greek words have been added by the editor.]

7

REASONS AND CAUSES IN THE *PHAEDO*[1]

GREGORY VLASTOS

There is a passage in this dialogue which has led many scholars—
the great majority of those who have translated or discussed it in
detail—to think that Plato's Forms are meant to be causes. This is
the methodological and metaphysical preamble (95E–105C) to the
final argument for the immortality of the soul. The importance of
this passage could hardly be exaggerated: as much is to be learned
from it about Plato's metaphysics, epistemology, and philosophy of
science as from any other text of equal length in his corpus. But it is
also one of the most perplexing. Scholars who have not confessed
its difficulty have evidenced it just the same in the wild diversity of
the interpretations they have put on it. According to Eduard Zeller,
Plato teaches here that the Ideas are meant to be formal, efficient,
and final causes all rolled into one.[2] Paul Shorey, at the other extreme, maintained that when Plato speaks of the Ideas as *aitiai* he is

---

[1] An earlier version of this paper was delivered at Michigan State
University as an Arnold Isenberg lecture and other drafts have been
read elsewhere. I acknowledge with gratitude diverse criticisms which
have helped me improve the paper and most particularly those given
me by Professors Terry Penner and Richard Sorabji, whose detailed
and penetrating queries have prompted revisions which have clarified
and strengthened the argument, though the rewriting may not have
fully met their objections. A debt of another sort I owe to the Center
for Advanced Study in the Behavioral Sciences at Stanford, where the
present draft was completed.

[2] "In dieser ganzen Auseinandersetzung [with the physicists in our
passage] wird nun zwischen der begrifflichen, der wirkenden und der
Endursache nicht bloss nicht unterschieden, sondern alle drei werden
deutlich genug für Ein und dasselbe erklärt," Ed. Zeller, *Philosophie
der Griechen*, II, i, fifth edition (Leipzig, 1922), p. 687, n. 1. I shall not
criticize this statement directly, but my reasons for rejecting it will
become clear as I proceed. I shall follow the same policy with respect
to other views with which I cannot agree. Limitations of space will
prevent me from engaging in controversy except insofar as I find this
essential for the elucidation and support of the interpretations I
propose:

offering "only a tautological logic . . . a consistent and systematic substitution of the logical reason for all other forms of cause."[3] More recently commentators have not hesitated to take their own perplexed reading of this text as evidence of unclear thinking in its writer. Mr. I. A. Crombie tells us there is "a nest of confusions" here, arising from Plato's "jumbl(ing) mathematical and non-mathematical topics together, and fail(ing) into the bargain to distinguish different senses of such notions as 'through' and 'in virtue of'." He says "it would be a useful elementary exercise to make a list of such confusions in this passage."[4]

The interpretation I shall offer here is closer to Shorey's than to Zeller's, and owes no small debt to Crombie's discussion of our passage.[5] But if my analysis is even approximately correct it will show that neither is Shorey's view acceptable *in toto*, and that the "confusions" of which Crombie speaks are not in our text but in misunderstandings of it which he shares with many distinguished scholars. Not that Plato's thought here will turn out to be entirely clear or wholly true. But for all its blemishes, both substantive and expository, it will appear, I trust, to be worthy of a philosopher who was not only a pioneer of unsurpassed audacity but also, when full allowance is made for the difficulties which confronted him, a remarkably sane and clear-headed thinker.

---

[3] *What Plato Said* (Chicago, 1933), p. 179. Zeller's contrary interpretation Shorey had already rejected in "The Interpretation of the *Timaeus*," *American Journal of Philology*, 9 (1888), pp. 395 ff., at p. 406, and still earlier in his Munich dissertation: see his citation from the latter in "The Origin of the Syllogism," *Classical Philology*, 19 (1924), pp. 1 ff., at p. 7, note 2.

[4] *An Examination of Plato's Doctrine*, Vol. II (London, 1963), p. 169. I shall refer to this work hereafter solely by the author's name.

[5] As well as to many other authors, the following most of all: J. Burnet, *Plato's Phaedo* (Oxford, 1911).

F. M. Cornford, *Plato and Parmenides* (London, 1939), pp. 74–80.

J. Moreau, *La Construction de l'Idéalisme Platonicien* (Paris, 1939), pp. 378 ff.

N. R. Murphy, *The Interpretation of Plato's Republic* (Oxford, 1951), pp. 145–48.

A. E. Taylor, *Plato, the Man and his Work*, 4th (Revised) Edition (London, 1937).

To each of these works I shall refer hereafter solely by the author's name.

1. ON THE MEANING OF *Aitia*.

Since so much will turn on the meaning of the word *aitia*,[6] I must begin by calling attention to the fact that its range of significance is far wider than that of the word "cause" as used nowadays both in ordinary speech and in philosophical discussions. I can best do so by recalling some of the things that count as straightforward *aitiai* in Aristotle, whose metaphysical preconceptions did not blunt his sensitiveness to the values of the words he used:

1. Why did the Persians invade Attica? Because the Athenians had raided Sardis.

2. Why is this statue so heavy? Because it is made of bronze.

3. Why is he taking after-dinner walks? Because of his health.

4. Why is the angle at the semicircle a right angle? Because it is equal to the half of two right angles.[7]

I have deliberately avoided the word *aitia* in formulating these examples, so as to bring out the fact that to say that X is the *aitia* of Y comes to precisely the same thing as saying that Y happened, or

[6] Liddell and Scott's *Greek-English Lexicon* lists the following senses for *aitia*: I. *responsibility*; II. *cause*; III. *occasion, motive*; IV. *head, category* under which a thing comes; V. *case in dispute*. In this paper I shall be concerned exclusively with sense II, which the dictionary renders by "cause"—mistakenly so, in my opinion, since, I shall argue, this sense has a much wider signification than that of the English word as commonly used nowadays (the sense in which we speak of a blow as the "cause" of the shattering of a vase or of air pollution as the "cause" of pulmonary irritation), or as employed by philosophers (see, e.g., the article "Causation" by R. Taylor in the Encyclopedia of Philosophy, edited by P. Edwards, New York, 1967; C. G. Hempel on causal explanation in *Aspects of Scientific Explanation*, New York, 1965, pp. 347 ff.; E. Nagel on causal laws in *Structure of Science*, New York, 1961, pp. 73 ff.).

[7] Examples *1*, *3*, and *4* are from the discussion of *aitiai* in the *Posterior Analytics* II, 11; examples *2* and *3* from the chapter on the four *aitiai* in *Physics* II, 3. I have recast the phrasing for obvious reasons, and given a different twist to *2* (Aristotle does not refer to the weight of the statue, and does not think in this connection of bronze specifically as a natural kind, but only as formable matter; but he would not hesitate to recognize the kind of explanation illustrated in *2* as a *bona fide aitia*). I disregard problems of Aristotelian exegesis raised by the fact that not all of the four *aitiai* in the *APo.* are obvious duplicates of the four in the *Physics*. For my purposes it is sufficient to note the prominence of *4* in the *APo.*, which leaves no doubt that Aristotle would recognize it as a star example of a certain kind of *aitia*, even though he finds it hard to squeeze it into the metaphysical mould which dictates the classification in the *Physics* (and also in the corresponding passage in *Metaphysics* V, 2).

happens, or is the case, *because* of X. In proof of this, if proof it needs, I need only refer to the fact that Aristotle speaks of his four *aitiai* as "all the ways of stating τὸ διὰ τί [the *because*]:"[8] Aristotle's so-called four "causes" are his four "*be*causes."

Now not every *because* refers to a cause, though some do, as does the first example: the Athenian raid on Sardis would be a fair example of a temporal antecedent which is the (supposed) sufficient condition of the occurrence of an event, the Persian invasion of Athens. Alternatively, a *because* may refer us to an *aitia* which, while not itself a cause, has definite causal implications. This is brought out well enough in the second example. We could hardly speak of bronze as the "cause" of the weight of a bronze statue: bronze scarcely causes itself to be heavy. What we have here is a natural kind, that is to say, a cluster of properties regularly conjoined, among which is its characteristic specific gravity. Though the laws of the conjunction of these properties are not themselves causal, they have a network of connections with causal laws by means of which we are able to make relevant causal predictions, such as that a bronze statue will outweigh several wooden ones of the same dimensions.

Now consider *3:* Here it would be not just awkward but positively absurd to speak of the *aitia* as the "cause." The health for which the ailing man submits to his peripatetic chores does not now exist and may never come to exist, since his walks may not avail to restore it and he might even die on one of them of a heart attack; how then could this non-existent and perhaps never-to-be-existent thing cause his walks or anything else? To turn the answer to our *why*-question into a statement of a cause we would have to take a detour in full view of the intensional context and make the cause not the health the man expects from his walks but his expectation of getting it from them, backed up by a strong desire to improve his health (stronger than for any of the displaced alternatives). Some philosophers nowadays would deny us even this manoeuvre, holding that it makes no sense to speak of the cause of an action. Into this controversy I do not propose to enter.[9] I need

---

[8] καὶ πάντως ἀποδοτέον τὸ διὰ τί followed by a listing of the four *aitiai*, *Ph.* 198B5 ff. This is one of the countless passages in which τὸ διὰ τί or τὸ διότι = τὸ αἴτιον in Aristotle (for some of them see H, Bonitz, *Index Aristotelicus*, 177A50 ff.).

[9] The best defense of the causal account known to me is by D. Davidson, "Actions, Reasons, and Causes," *Journal of Philosophy*,

not in this inquiry, where all that matters is that if we were talking Greek, then, regardless of our philosophical persuasions, we would not have the slightest hesitation in saying that the man's health *is* the *aitia* of his walks, while in English the most we could do to work the man's health into a causal account of his exertions would be to cite the end in view and his desire to attain it as the cause of these actions.

I have left last the mathematical example, the most striking one for my purposes, for here the gap between *aitia* and *cause* is unbridgeable by any ancillary device that will stand up under examination. We are given *P*, "the angle at the semicircle is the half of two right angles," and *Q*, "the angle at the semicircle is a right angle," where *P* is the penultimate formula in the string of formulae which make up the currently acceptable proof of *Q* in the geometry of the time.[10] This leads Aristotle to take *P* as the *aitia* of *Q*, construing the entailment of *Q* by *P*, already proved a valid consequence of the axiom-set of the science, as an adequate ground of the truth of *Q*. Since this entailment is for Atristotle a relation whose relata are abstract items, he would not dream of saying that one of these propositions *causes* the other. Yet that is the way he is made to talk by G. R. G. Mure in the Oxford translation of the *Posterior Analytics*, by W. D. Ross in his *Commentary*, and by countless textbooks, where he is represented as saying that the premises of demonstrative inference are the "causes" of its conclusions.[11] Such statements have been defended at times by the claim that Aristotle thinks the premises *causae cognoscendi*.[12] But if *causa* in this time-hallowed phrase means no more than "reason" or "principle" the defense is otiose, since reasons and principles have no causal efficacy; while if it does mean *cause*, the claim is false, and may be collapsed by the simple reflection that it is not, in general, true that knowing a given proposition is a sufficient condition of knowing all

---

[10] See T. Heath, *Mathematics in Aristotle* (Oxford, 1949), p. 72.

40 (1963), pp. 685 ff. Cf. also M. White, *Foundations of Historical Knowledge* (New York, 1965,), Chapter V, "Reasons and Causes".

[11] αἰτίων τοῦ συμπεράσματος (71B22, "related to them as effect to cause," Mure in the Oxford translation; "causative of the conclusion," H. Tredennick in the Loeb translation. I have protested elsewhere this venerable mistranslation ("Anamnesis in the *Meno*", *Dialogue*, 4 (1965), pp. 143 ff. note 15). The present paper is an extended version of the protest.

[12] Leibniz speaks of them as causes "de notre jugement" (*Nouveaux Essais*, IV, 17, 3).

of the propositions which it entails:[13] thus one may know the axioms of a system and be ignorant of a whole raft of theorems which a cleverer mathematician would be able to deduce from the same axioms. Aristotle, so far as I know, never made this particular blunder. But even if he had made it, we would still have no good warrant for reading it into the many passages in which he speaks of an entailing premise as the *aitia* of an entailed conclusion, since all such statements make perfect sense if understood to express the simple fact that the premise is a good and sufficient reason for the conclusion.

This brief discussion has shown, I trust, how much more general in signification is the Greek *aitia* than is the current meaning of the word "cause" in English speech. Greek usage would entitle us as a matter of course to speak of something as another's *aitia*, regardless of whether we are referring, as in *1* above, to a straightforward cause, or, as in *2*, to a law-like conjunction of properties or factors such that the instantiation of some of them is a sufficient condition of the concurrent instantiation of others, or, as in *3*, to the end in view of a purposeful agent whose desire to attain it by a certain action we take to be the sufficient condition of his performing the action, or finally, as in *4*, to one proposition as entailing, or implying, another, so that our assurance of the truth of the former warrants equal assurance of the truth of the latter. Here then is the linguistic base from which the whole of the discussion that is to follow will start: the mere fact that Plato speaks of the Forms as *aitiai* in our passage is not of itself the slightest evidence—not even *prima facie* evidence—that he wants them to be causes. There are plenty of other things he may want to express by saying, and with the greatest emphasis, that they are *aitiai*. What he does mean can only be decided from the context. Let us proceed to this.

2. THE "SAFE" BUT "IGNORANT" AITIA

Our passage falls into two divisions. Division One (95E–99C) recounts the youthful infatuation of the Platonic Socrates[14] with the

---

[13] Cf. E. Nagel, *Sovereign Reason* (New York, 1954), pp. 287 ff.

[14] Let me say here once for all that in my opinion the "Socrates" of this whole passage cannot be identified *in toto* with the historical figure, though it may well be that some elements of the account in Division One would fit his intellectual biography, as suggested, e.g., by R. Hackforth, *Plato's Phaedo* (Cambridge, 1955), pp. 127–31 (a book to which I shall refer hereafter solely by the author's name). I shall be using "Socrates" to mean the figure whom Plato makes his mouthpiece in this account.

physical philosophers and the disappointment in which it ended
when he found that all they could offer was material *aitiai* and mechanical causes, while he had become convinced that only teleology
could provide the "true" (98E) or "real" (99B) *aitiai* of natural
phenomena. There is no talk of the Forms as *aitiai*—no mention of
them at all—throughout the whole of this Division, though the
way is prepared for them, by the laying out of a series of perplexities
whose solution would elude Socrates until he had hit upon the
Theory of Forms. This part of Division One I shall discuss at some
length in due course. The rest of it I shall ignore. Though its
historical importance is incalculable—this is one of the great
turning-points in European natural philosophy, the conscious
abandonment of the line of thought which had led, in the systems
of Leucippus and Democritus, to the first rigorously mechanistic
conception of the order of nature—its message is familiar and,
superficially at least, quite clear. I shall, therefore, bypass it in this
paper to concentrate on the far more hazardous task of figuring out
what is going on in Division Two (99C–105C), where Socrates,
frustrated in his search for teleology, falls back on a second-best
method of inquiry of his own.[15]

[15] "Well, I for my part should be delighted to learn from anyone
about this sort of *aitia* [that of 'the good and the fitting,' 99C5]. But
since I have been denied this *aitia* and have failed to either find it
myself or learn it from another, would you like me to show you the
second journey which I have been pursuing in the search for *aitia*?"
(99C–D2). Note that the reference of ταύτης in C8 (the subject of
ἐστερήθην and also, with the implied change of case, of the infinitives
εὑρεῖν, μαθεῖν) is to τοιαύτης αἰτίας in C7; what Socrates has failed to
discover by his own labors or from those of others and is prepared to
do without for the present is the teleological *aitia* itself. This leaves no
room for understanding him to mean (as has been done over and over
again in the literature) that his "second-best journey" is (a) an alternative method of searching for *teleological aitiai* rather than (b) an
alternative method of searching for *aitiai*. The text offers no direct
support for (a), since nothing is said of different methods of looking
for teleological *aitiai* (the natural philosophers were condemned for
failing to look for such *aitiai*, not for looking for them by the wrong
method). There would be indirect support for (a) if we could assume
that the earlier references to teleological *aitiai* as the "true" or "real"
aitiai (98E1, 99B3) mean that these are for Plato not only the pre-
ferred (most fundamental, most illuminating) *explanations of natural
phenomena* (which, of course, they are throughout the Platonic corpus),
but *the only admissible aitiai of anything whatever*. But there is no case for
such as assumption; thus Plato would not hesitate to say with Aristotle

This new method and its distinctive *aitiai* are put forward as the logical pendants of a philosophical "hypothesis,"[16] that of the Theory of Forms or Ideas, which is tersely formulated as follows in the more complete of the two statements in our passage:[17]

each of the Forms exists and it is in virtue of participating in them that other things are named after them [*sc.* for Forms] (102A10–B2).[18]

The formula has in view three sets of items and the relation of "participation":[19]

(1) Forms, that is to say, those of the full-blown theory of Plato's middle period, presented in this dialogue for the first time. The very same terms which he had used to designate the definienda of Socrates' moral inquiries in the earlier dialogues, *eidos, idea,* he now applies to entities endowed with the following set of categorial properties: they are immutable,[20] incorporeal,[21] divine;[22] they can-

---

that the premises of a deductive argument constitute the *aitiai* of its conclusion, without implying the semantic absurdity that the premises are the *teleological aitia* of the conclusion. For the interpretation I have defended here see N. R. Murphy, pp. 145–46; Shorey, *What Plato Said,* p. 534, and the references given there.

[16] 100B; 102A10–B2.

[17] The first one occurs in 100B5–7. It fails to mention "participation."

[18] This formula is practically identical with the one in *Prm.* 130E5–6. For "named after them" cf. note 29 below.

[19] For this trichotomy see Hackforth's notes and commentary on 102A–105B; R. G. Turnbull, "Aristotle's Debt to the 'Natural Philosophy' of the *Phaedo,*" *Philosophical Quarterly,* 8 (1955), pp. 131 ff.; D. Keyt, "The Fallacies in *Phaedo* 102A–107B," *Phronesis,* 8 (1963), pp. 167 ff. I am particularly indebted to Turnbull's discussion and regret that limitations of space deny me the opportunity to explain where and why I disagree with certain features of his interpretation.

[20] 78D (cited in note 44 below); 79D; 80B.

[21] 79B. Though they are not called ἀσώματα here, this is clearly implied. Cf. my comment on this in "The Third Man Argument in the *Parmenides,*" in R. E. Allen, editor, *Studies in Plato's Metaphysics* (London, 1965), pp. 231 ff., at p. 247, n. 2. (This paper appeared originally in the *Philosophical Review,* 63 [1954], pp. 319 ff.)

[22] 84A9 (cf. 80B1).

not be known by means of sense experience,[23] but only by "recollection."[24]

(2) The individual persons and objects of ordinary experience,
designated by proper names and definite descriptions.

(3) The immanent characters of these individuals, designated by
adjectives, abstract nouns, and common nouns. The very same
words *also* name Forms. This becomes strikingly clear on those rare
occasions on which Plato explicitly juxtaposes the Form with the
cognate character to bring out the fact that, though closely connected, they are ontologically distinct. He does so twice in our
passage, contrasting "Greatness itself" with "greatness in us"
(102D),[25] and again "the Opposite itself . . . in the nature of things"
with "the opposite itself . . . in us,"[26] and both with "the opposite

---

[23] 65A9–66A8.

[24] 72E3 ff. With but a single exception, not one of these properties
had ever been ascribed by Socrates to the universals whose definitions
he sought in the early dialogues. The exception (called to my attention by Professor John Malcolm) occurs in the *Hippias Major*, where
Socrates speaks of Beauty as being "always beautiful" (ἀεὶ καλόν,
292E2 and 4; cf. 294D); but his point is saying this in this earlier
dialogue is not metaphysical: he says this only to disqualify an absurdly parochial definiens of beauty.

[25] I capitalize Form-naming words to distinguish them from the
same words used to name characters. Denied this, or any other, in-
scriptional device, Plato had to use identical linguistic tokens to refer
to two distinct entities, distinguishing their reference by context only.

[26] This shows that Plato does not reserve the emphatic use of the
relative pronoun ("Justice *itself*," etc.) for references to the Forms,
though this is his usual practice in his middle period. He may use it
upon occasion, as he does here, to refer to a character; he had so used
it in the earlier dialogues to refer to the Socratic universal, as W. D.
Ross points out (*Plato's Theory of Ideas* [Oxford, 1951], p. 17 and note
1). Commenting on *Phaedo* 103B5, W. J. Verdenius ("*Notes on the
Phaedo*," *Mnemosyne*, S. IV, 11 [1958], pp. 193 ff. at p. 232) says that
here "τὸ ἐν ἡμῖν ἐναντίον is part of αὐτὸ τὸ ἐναντίον"; taking the latter
phrase to designate the Platonic Form, he infers that Plato's Forms
are both "immanent" and "transcendent." This would be unobjec-
tionable, if it were meant to bring out the fact that Plato's theory in
the middle dialogues provides both for immanent characters and
transcendent Forms. But Verdenius appears to mean more than this;
he seems to deny Plato the ontological distinction between "the opposite in us" and "the opposite in nature." On this see the next note.

thing," i.e., the individual that has one of two opposite characters (103B).[27]

It will be convenient to use the following symbols in schematic reference to these items: the English capitals F, G, as character-variables; their phonetic cognates in the Greek alphabet, Φ, Γ, as Form-variables; a, b, c, as stand-ins for names of individuals, and x as a variable whose values are names of individuals.[28]

What the theory asserts then is the following: for any character, F, of any individual, x, there exists a homonymous[29] Form, Φ; and x is F (i.e., x has the character F) if, and only if, x participates in Φ. "Participation" here designates that one-way relation of ontological dependence between temporal things and eternal Forms which is so fundamental a tenet of this philosophy. For Plato nothing

---

[27] Cf. also the contrast between "Similarity itself" and "the similarity which we possess" in *Prm.* 130B. This text brings out explicitly what is implicit in the *Phaedo* texts above, that the word designating a class-(3) item has a referent which is ontologically distinct from the referent of the same word when used of a class-(1) item. It is, therefore, a mistake to deny the ontological distinctness of class-(3) and class-(1) items, as did Shorey in commenting on *Phaedo* 103B: "there are really only two things: the idea, and the particular affected by the 'presence' of or 'participation' in the idea ... (The text) does not justify the duplication of the idea, which [a] is a device employed here only, and [b] with full consciousness, for the purpose of the argument" (*The Unity of Plato's Thought* [Chicago, 1903], note 283; I have interpolated the reference marks). But [a] is false, overlooking 102D and *Prm.* 130B. And [b] is *ignoratio elenchi:* the fact that the "duplication" here does serve the purposes of the immediate argument in no way implies that it is void of ontological significance.

[28] In the paper cited in note 21 above I had noted the necessity of distinguishing systematically between the adjective, *large*, and the Form, Largeness, in analyzing the regress arguments in Plato's *Parmenides*. I there used "*F*-ness" as a Form-variable. In this paper I turn to the Greek alphabet only for reasons of typographical economy. Were it not for this, I would still prefer to write "*F*-ness" for the Form-variable corresponding to the character-variable "*F*": the recurrence of "*F*" in both symbols brings out more forcefully the linguistic link between "Largeness" and "large" and the ontological bond between the entities they denote.

[29] Where x is characterized by F Plato speaks of x as "named" after Φ, its "namesake" (cf. *Phaedo* 78E, *Prm.* 133D, *Ti.* 52A), interpreting the predicative statement, "x is F" as "naming" x "*F*": cf. the formula in *R.* 596A, "we are accustomed to posit a single Form for each plurality to which we apply the same name."

could exist in space and time with a definite character, *F*, if there did not exist a corresponding Φ, while the converse would not be true at all: the existence of a specific Form, say, of a *chiliagon*, would of itself not offer the slightest assurance of its physical instantiation; not only the Form of the Ideal City (*R.* 592AB), but infinitely many other Forms as well exist which have been uninstantiated since time began and may so remain for ever in Plato's universe. So much of his intention is clear enough. But if we probe further, pressing him to tell us just what it is that happens when a particular *F* achieves the required "participation" in a Φ, Plato has no definite answer for us, and he is well aware of this fact. He makes no effort to conceal from the reader that he has yet to reach a clear-cut conception of what "participation" involves, speaking of the relation of Beauty to beautiful things as "presence or association or whatever be the right word for it" (100D5–6).[30] Here is something Plato has not yet cleared up to his satisfaction, though he doubtless expects he will, remaining quite certain for the present that some such relation exists and that, were it not for this, the fact that things have characters would be unintelligible.[31]

Armed with this "hypothesis," Socrates feels empowered to give two complementary answers to the question "Why is *x F*?"[32] Let us

[30] The above translation proceeds on the assumption that Wyttenbach's emendation of προσγενομένη in the MS. to προσαγορευομένη (which appears to have confirmation in a papyrus: cf. Hackforth's note *ad loc.*) is correct. If we stick to the MS. reading (cf. R. S. Bluck, *Plato's Phaedo* [London, 1955], *ad loc.*) or accept Cornford's emendation (p. 77, note 1) to προσγενομένον, the last clause in the above citation would read, "in whatever manner it may come about" or "whatever the relationship may be." The difference will not be great in either case, and will not affect at all the important thing in the citation, *sc.* the avowal of uncertainty in εἴτε ὅπη δὴ καὶ ὅπως. For Plato's use of εἴτε ὅπη (augmented in the third example by εἴτε ὅπως) to avow uncertainty, see *Prm.* 183D, *Ti.* 48C, and *Laws* 899B.

[31] Though the expectation was never adequately fulfilled, Plato retained the confidence that somehow or other things must "participate" in the Forms. In the *Parmenides*, at the end of the second regress argument, Parmenides does not conclude that the notion of participation has been invalidated, but only that "we must look for some other way [i.e., a way other than similitude] by which they participate" (133A5–6).

[32] Also, "Why does *x* come to be *F*?", which is the implied question in 101C2–7: "you would loudly protest that you do not know how else each thing comes to be [*F*] except by coming to participate in the peculiar essence of that [Form] in which it comes to participate and

begin with the first, which he calls the "safe" but "simple-minded" and "ignorant" (100DE; 105C) *aitia*. This is just that x is F because it participates in Φ.[33] What could he mean by that? Two interpretations have been advanced which I take to be mistaken:

In one of them, the Form would be a teleological *aitia*.[34] I fail to see how this could be squared with the following feature of our passage: Socrates makes it abundantly clear that he is still at the time of speaking "deprived" of the teleological *aitia* he had been looking for.[35] But it is no less clear that the alternative line of investigation he is about to explain—the "second journey"—is not something that has popped into his head at just that moment; it is a method of inquiry on which he has been already engaged.[36] This method takes its starting-point from the hypothesis of the Forms. Hence, if Socrates had thought of the Forms as teleological *aitiai*, he would not have said that he is still "deprived" of teleological *aitiai*. He would have said that he does have them, though only on the basis of a hypothesis. On this ground the suggested interpretation must be rejected as not only unsupported by the text—there is

---

so here you have no *aitia* of their coming to be two except their coming to participate in the Dyad—in this all things must come to participate, if they are going to be two—and in the Unit if they are going to be one . . ." (101C2–7). For the translation cf. Cornford *ad Prm.* 129A3 (p. 69, note 1): "As in the *Phaedo*, *metalambanein* means *beginning* to partake when the thing *becomes* like, whereas *metechein* is used of *having* a share and corresponds to *being* like"; however, "beginning" should be corrected to "coming" for obvious reasons (Cornford does not even use it in his own translation!).

[33] Which may be abbreviated to "x is F because of Φ," but only after the context has made it clear this is a contraction of the complete formula: thus "all beautiful things are beautiful in virtue of Beauty" in 100D7–8 is used only after *participating* in Beauty (not Beauty as such) had been said to be the *aitia* in 100B4–6 and again in 100D4–6.

[34] See, e.g., Taylor, p. 203 and note 2; Bluck, *op. cit.*, p. 199; Crombie, pp. 159 ff. The "confusions" which Crombie finds in the passage arise in part from his assumption that "it is apparently taken for granted that wherever this [i.e., a formal *aitia*] is achieved something like a teleological explanation will be forthcoming" (p. 159; "apparently taken for granted" concedes that nothing of the kind is said, or distinctly implied, in the text).

[35] Cf. note 15 above.

[36] Note the preterites: $\pi\epsilon\pi\rho\alpha\gamma\mu\acute{\alpha}\tau\epsilon\nu\mu\alpha\iota$ in 99D1 and 100B4, $\H{\omega}\rho\mu\eta\sigma\alpha$ in 100A3.

no mention of teleology after this point in our passage—but as contrary to the unambiguous implications of our text. It is, there-fore, unnecessary to inquire how Plato could have assigned, with-out grave confusion, to his Forms—entities whose most conspicuous feature is their absolute immutability—the teleological function which, both in this dialogue and in the *Timaeus*, pertains ex-clusively to mind or soul.[37]

A second interpretation deserves a little—if only little—more consideration. This is that the Form is meant to take the place of Aristotle's "efficient cause." So Aristotle himself expounds our passage, imputing to "Socrates in the *Phaedo*" the view that the Forms are "a sufficient *aitia* of generation"—a view which he pro-ceeds to demolish by retorting (a) that eternal Forms could hardly have intermittent efficacy and (b) that the causes of the events we "see" are not Forms, but individual agents—we see the doctor, not "Health itself," causing the patient's recovery.[38] It is hard to be-lieve that so patent a misreading of Plato's doctrine[39] could have

---

[37] The sole pattern of teleological explanation envisaged in the *Phaedo* is that exemplified in the purposeful agency of a mind (the cosmic *nous* of Anaxagoras, 97C1 ff.; the mind of Socrates, 98C2 ff.). In the *Timaeus* those features of the cosmos which admit of teleological explanation are exclusively those which are imputed directly to the activity of divine souls: the Demiurge (46C–E et *passim*) and "his offering" (69C ff.) And cf. note 45 below.

[38] *De Generatione et Corruptione* (which I abbreviate to *GC* hereafter) 335B9–24. The same interpretation and parallel criticisms in the *Metaphysics*: "In the *Phaedo* it is stated that the Forms are *aitiai* both of being and of becoming. But though the Forms exist, their participants do not come into being if there is no mover, while many other things come into being—e.g., a house, a ring—of which we [Platonists] say no Forms exist" (991B3–7).

[39] The only text that could have suggested to Aristotle that the Forms are *aitiai* of generation is 101C2–7 (cited in note 32 above). And there the *aitia* of a thing's coming to be *F* is not (i) the Form but (ii) *the thing's coming to participate in that Form:* Socrates cites, not the Dyad, but "participation in the dyad" as the *aitia* "of the generation of two"; only if Plato had said that the Dyad as such is the *aitia* of, say, a birth of twins, could he have been open to the interpretation that he is counting on the Form to do the job of the "generator" or "mover" or "maker." Contrariwise, there are many passages in the dialogues where Plato not only allows, but argues passionately, for soul as the *aitia* of generation, change, and movement (e.g., the great argument in *Laws* X, whose demonstrand is that soul is "first *aition* of generation and of perishing" [891E]; cf. *Phlb.* 26E ff. and *Sph.* 296B). Aristotle must also

been taken seriously by modern scholars. Yet Hackforth quotes it as paralleling his own claim that the Ideas are meant to be causes of "qualities of concrete things," though not of concrete things themselves:[40] "Beauty itself is not the cause of a beautiful thing, but of a thing's being beautiful" (p. 144). What sense could be made of this Hackforth does not seem to have considered. Had he done so, I doubt that he would have ever committed his interpretation to print. For since all Forms are absolutely free of spatio-temporal limitations, then if any of them were supposed to be acting on a particular spatio-temporal object, *a*, with a determinate property, *P*, we would have to suppose (i) that it is also acting on all other objects in the universe, including those which do *not* have the property *P*, and further (ii) that all other Forms, including Forms corresponding to properties contrary to *P*, are simultaneously acting on *a*. How then (i) could the given Form have that specific causal effect on *a* which would account for its being *P* rather than not-*P*, without having the same effect on all other objects, including those which are not-*P*? And how (ii) could it have any determinate effect on *a* at all, if all those other Forms are simultaneously acting on *a* with contrary effect? The only way to avoid the absurd consequences of the supposition would be to credit Forms with the power

---

have been familiar with the doctrine of the *Timaeus* (57E–58C) that material heterogeneity (*anōmalotēs*) or unevenness (*anisotēs*) is a physical cause of movement (cf. *Ph.* 201B20). Cf. H. Cherniss, *Aristotle's Criticism of Plato and the Early Academy* (Baltimore, 1944), 383 ff.

[40] He quotes with approval *GC* 335B7–24, his only reservation being that he does not think it is entirely clear if Aristotle is saying that the Forms are supposed to be *aitiai* of the generation of substances, which Hackforth would reject, or of the generation of the attributes of substances, which he would endorse: "It is only the latter that Socrates does in fact seek to account for by participation in Forms [observe Hackforth's unawareness of the differences between (i) and (ii) explained in note 39 above: he speaks here as though Plato were being charged with (ii), while he is in fact being charged with (i), a charge which Hackforth proceeds to underwrite]. . . . Aristotle's instances, health and science . . . suggest that he is reporting correctly. . . . In any case, . . . there is no dispute about what his [Aristotle's] criticism is: namely that the Form cannot play the part of 'efficient' or 'moving' causes. It is indeed the weakest point in the theory that he lays his finger. . . . It is not easy to see how Plato could have answered the point about intermittent operation of the Forms in terms of the *Phaedo* doctrine" (145).

to act selectively on different objects in the universe, directing their causal influence to some of them, withholding it from others. And how could Plato have so particularized his Forms as causal agents in the world of space and time without fouling up the most fundamental of his metaphysical principles?[41] Only the most direct and explicit evidence could persuade us that he blundered so grossly. And there is no such evidence. All we have to go on is the fact that he uses the same language of the relation of the Form to a thing which he would have also used if he were speaking of the relation of a cause to its effect: Φ is that "because of which ($\delta\iota'$ $\ddot{o}\tau\iota$, 100D1) x is F;[42] it is that which "makes" ($\pi o\iota\epsilon\hat{\iota}$, 100D5) x to be F; it is the *aitia* of x's being F (e.g., 100C6–7; 101C4–5). Is there no other way of construing these statements that will make better sense?

Consider the following exchange: "Why is this figure a square?" —"*Because* it has four equal sides *and* four equal angles. If it had just the four equal sides that would not *make* it a square; it could have been, for all that, a rhombus."[43] Here it is clear that the "because" which answers our "Why?" is not meant to explain the occurrence of a square-shaped chalkmark on our blackboard. The

---

[41] See Cherniss, *op. cit.*, p. 452 and n. 397 on the proposition that "the ideas themselves are never made productive agents" in Plato's philosophy. In view of this interpretation, which Cherniss maintains forcefully and consistently throughout this work, he might have done better to avoid speaking of the Ideas as "causes" of their "approximations" in the sensible world (p. 218), "of the particular's being" (p. 373), "of that which in particulars is similar whenever and wherever it occurs" (p. 375). He makes it quite clear, of course, that by saying that the Ideas are "causes" he does *not* mean that they have causal efficacy; what then remains unclear is just what *is* meant, when this is not, to justify the use of the term "cause" in this connection.

[42] The "because" can also be expressed by the "instrumental" dative: $\tau\hat{\omega}$ $\kappa\alpha\lambda\hat{\omega}$, 100D7, E2; $\mu\epsilon\gamma\dot{\epsilon}\theta\epsilon\iota$, 100E5, etc.

[43] Compare: "Those characteristics that are indispensable to an act's being just are the characteristics which make the act a just act," Susan Stebbing, *A Modern Introduction to Logic*, 2nd Edition (London, 1933), p. 429. "To teach what makes a member of any class a good member of the class . . . ," R. M. Hare, *The Language of Morals* (Oxford, 1952), p. 102. We find similar uses of "makes" with transparently logical import in Plato's earlier dialogues: Charmides is asked to consider "what sort of man temperance makes you by being present in you" and to answer accordingly the question "What is temperance?" (*Chrm.* 160D6–7). Hippias agrees that "that which is fitting for each thing is what makes each thing beautiful," where "fitting" is being considered as a possible definiens of "beautiful" (*Hp. Ma.* 290D).

occurrence is presupposed and no interest is taken in its cause. Our question is not "What made that chalkmark?", nor yet "What made that chalkmark square?", but rather "What *makes* it square?", which could only mean in this context: Why do we classify it as a square, rather than as a figure of some other shape? Our question is answered when we are shown that the chalkmark *happens to have*—not how or why *it happened to get*—the shape that meets the logical conditions for being square. The *aitia* we are given is a logical one.

At first sight this may seem suspiciously deflationary of what is said in our text. When Socrates maintains with such dogged emphasis that a beautiful thing "is beautiful for no other reason than because it participates in Beauty" (100C9–D), he is certainly putting forward a thesis which could not be reduced with any plausibility to the logical truth that a particular thing instantiates a concept if, and only if, it satisfies the definition. But such a reduction is the last thing I would wish to suggest. To do so I would have to argue that for Plato logic is a metaphysically noncommittal business; and who would want to say such a thing on his behalf? What is his Theory of Forms if not the claim that logical statements presuppose metaphysical ones and would be mumbo-jumbo without them? For Plato the definition of a concept is "the account of the essence" of its Form, Φ.[44] The reason why we can speak significantly and truly of things being square or beautiful, he would insist, is that there exists an incorporeal, immutable, intelligible object, named "Squareness" or "Beauty," in which corporeal, mutable, sensible objects occasionally "participate" and, when they do, are

[44] "That reality itself, of whose essence we give the account when we ask and answer our questions, is it ever invariably the same or does it vary? Equality itself, Beauty itself, each 'what is' in itself, the reality does it ever admit the least alteration?" (*Phaedo* 78D1–5). Burnet rightly remarks *ad. loc.* in his commentary that "we must take λόγον τοῦ εἶναι together as equivalent to λόγον τῆς οὐσίας or 'definition' (comparing *R.* 534B3), and as governing the genitive ῆς." Cf. also *R.* 533A8–B2, and also *Laws* 895D–E, where distinction is drawn between the name, the *ousia* it names, and the *logos* of this *ousia*. It is a mistake to suppose that there is any Form of which there is no *logos*. The view that in *Symp.* 211A it is said or implied that of the Form of Beauty "there is no *logos* nor knowledge" (R. C. Cross, "*Logos* and Forms in Plato," *Mind*, 63 [1954], pp. 433 ff., at p. 443) is not warranted by the text, which says only that Beauty "will not appear" *as logos* or knowledge (since it will appear as that *of* which we have *logos* and knowledge):

rightly called "square" or "beautiful." So what I have called the "logical" *aitia* is at the same time a metaphysical one for Plato; the logical function of Squareness, Beauty, etc., he is convinced, could not be discharged aside from their metaphysical status. But once that is granted, it is the logical function of the metaphysical entity that does the *explanatory* work of the "safe" *aitia*. When I want to know what makes this figure a square rather than a pentagon, what answers my question is not the *existence* as such of the Form, Square—countless other Forms also exist which do not help to answer my question—but the logical content of its definition: this is what marks off the Form, Square, from all these other Forms and, isomorphically, marks off every square in our world from instances of all the other figures. And the fact that this logical function is performed by a celestial Form rather than by a nominalistic *flatus vocis* in no way alters the strictly non-causal import of the formula "*F* in virtue of satisfying the definition." Plato's Squareness has no more causal efficacy than has the nominalist's; it has no power to spawn earthly squares; if it did, so would the Form, Myriagon, and each of the countless others that have had no mundane progeny and never will.[45]

This interpretation of the "*F* in virtue of Φ" formula frees Plato from so much embarrassment and is so consonant with everything else we know of his metaphysical views that it would have a strong

---

[45] Note that when Plato says in the *Timaeus* that the Ideal Model may be "likened" to the "father" of generation, the Receptacle to the "mother," and the things that compose our world to the "offspring," 50D2–4, he makes it very clear that he assigns no causal function to the Ideas in respect of either of the two kinds of causality (teleological and mechanical) which he recognizes in that dialogue (46C7 ff.). The metaphorical remarks in *R*. 506E, 507A, and 508B about the sun as the "offspring" of the Idea of the Good must be interpreted in the light of what Plato means when he says in the *Timaeus* that the whole of the natural universe, not just the sun, is the "offspring" of the Ideas generally, not just of the Idea of the Good. In the *Timaeus* the metaphor is employed in the context of a cosmological scheme which enables us to control the intended meaning in a way that is altogether denied us by the allusive and unexplicated use of the metaphor in Book VI of the *Republic*. When the "father" metaphor is used in the *Timaeus* in a context which makes it clear that the metaphor does express (teleological) causal agency, it is applied not to the Forms, but to the Demiurge (28C3–4), in contradistinction to the Forms.

claim on us even without further confirmation.[46] In point of fact we do get confirmation for it from two distinct data in our passage:

In the first place, it makes good sense of the fact that this formula

[46] A number of commentators entertain and, to all appearances, endorse a substantially identical interpretation, only to shy away from it a page or two later, or even a line or two later. To recount these vagaries in detail would require a special monograph (a rather tedious one). A single illustration must suffice. Cornford (in the work mentioned in note 5, above) begins on p. 77 with an impeccable gloss on 100C4-6: "the fact that this rose is beautiful is the same thing as the fact that this rose partakes of Beauty. We learn nothing about any *cause* which would bring that fact into existence." But see what happens when he proceeds (immediately) to 100D1-8, where Plato, having spoken three lines earlier of Beauty as (a) the reason why (διότι) *x* is beautiful, goes on to speak of it also as (b) what makes (ποιεῖ) *x* beautiful and to say also (c) that *x* is beautiful *because of* (τῷ καλῷ: instrumental dative; cf. note 42, above) Beauty. Cornford becomes greatly exercised over the use of "makes" and wonders: "Does it [the 'makes'] mean that the thing's beauty simply *consists in* the presence either of the Form itself or of the character like that of the Form, as we say that the presence of a gay colour 'makes' the thing gay? Or does it mean that the Form, existing independently, *causes* the thing to be (or to become) beautiful by somehow imparting its own character to the thing? This is precisely the dilemma on which Socrates refuses to pronounce." The language might be expressly designed to leave it unresolved." (The italics are Cornford's.) Now (b), "makes," could not have causal import unless (c), "because of," did, since the latter is used to say the same thing in 100D7 as was said by the use of "makes" at D4-5; and this in turn is the same thing as was expressed by the use of (a), δι' ὅτι, in D1, the very expression used at C5, where Cornford was certain that it had no causal import; how then could he be left uncertain as to the import of "makes" at 100D5? Moreover, any uncertainty on this score could have been resolved by noting that the "makes" is used in Socratic dialogues (cf. note 43) where Cornford would not think of reading causal import into it. That Cornford himself cannot be taking very seriously the "dilemma" on which Socrates supposedly "refuses to pronounce" in 100D1-8 appears on p. 79, where he talks as though the supposed "dilemma" has been firmly resolved in favor of its non-causal horn. He speaks of "Simmias comes to partake of Tallness" as the Platonic analysis of "Simmias becomes tall": "This is a description of the same event in other words. Nothing is said as to any 'cause' in our sense, which would make such an event take place as its effect." But he backslides again on p. 80 in glossing 103D (where, e.g., snow perishes at the approach of heat): "Socrates seems to be unaware that the only efficient cause of change he actually describes is a physical cause of precisely the kind which, in the account of his youthful ex-

is proposed as the "safe" but "ignorant" or "simple-minded"[47] *aitia*. This is what it would obviously be for anyone who has already accepted the metaphysical "hypothesis" on which this *aitia* is so explicitly pegged.[48] On this hypothesis, for all x, x is F if, and only if, x participates in Φ. From this it follows with the "safety" of analytic inference that a, or b, or c, or any other x, is F in virtue of participating in Φ. For just the same reason this *aitia* is "ignorant," i.e., uninformative.[49] Not only does it not profess to give us the slightest help in finding out the cause of any specific happening in the world; it does not even aid us in discovering its correct description: only if we already know that something is F (i.e., if we have already so described it) can we proceed on the strength of this *aitia*

---

periences, he had rejected as unsatisfying." If "coming to partake of Tallness" has no causal import, then Socrates would not have the slightest reason for being "unaware" of the existence of physical causes of becoming tall; why then should he be "unaware" of such causes in the case of a thing ceasing to be snow (i.e., melting) and becoming hot when it comes to partake of Heat?

[47] It is safe: 100D8, E1; 101D1–3; 105B7–C1. It is "simple, artless, and perhaps simple-minded (or stupid)," 100D3–4; "ignorant," 105C.

[48] Plato, of course, would not apply the same description to the "hypothesis," i.e., to the Theory of Ideas. Obviously he would not think of *this* as "simple-minded," nor yet as having the kind of "safety" he is now talking about, since he presents it as a "hypothesis" and refrains from claiming that he has proved it conclusively in this dialogue (which, of course, does not imply that he does not think it susceptible of conclusive proof: in the exchange with Simmias at 107A8–B9 Socrates concedes that the Theory calls for further investigation, but makes no avowal of uncertainty, as was suggested by Jowett's influential and gratuitous rendering of καθ' ὅσον δυνατὸν μάλιστ' ἀνθρώπῳ by "with a sort of hesitating confidence in human reason," now happily corrected to "as far as humanly possible" in the Fourth Revised Edition, Oxford, 1953). The "safety" of the present *aitia* is due to its being so immediate a consequence of the "hypothesis" that once you accepted the latter *you would risk nothing further* in maintaining this *aitia*.

[49] This is no doubt what Shorey had in mind when he spoke of the "tautological logic" of the theory that the Ideas are *aitiai* (cf. the citation in the opening paragraph of this paper and the references in note 3). Unhappily he failed to note that this could only be said of the "safe" *aitia*, and not at all of the "cleverer" one (to be discussed in the next section of this paper), which is conspicuously non-tautological in form, this being the very reason why it is called the "clever" *aitia*. Even in the case of the "safe" *aitia* a certain qualification is necessary (cf. note 78 below), of which Shorey took no notice.

to say that it is F in virtue of Φ, showing that our description matches the definition and thereby clinching the propriety of calling it "F" rather than "G" or something else.

Secondly, the interpretation I have offered makes good sense of another thing in our passage to which I have yet to make reference: the fact that the formula "F in virtue of participating in Φ" is expected to resolve the puzzles about *aitia* which were displayed in Division One of our passage.[50] The first four of these (96D8–E4) are peculiarly mystifying to the modern reader.[51] He is likely to find them not so much puzzles as meta-puzzles: what perplexes him is what there is in any of them that Plato could have thought perplexing. The first pair (98D8–E1) look almost like a spoof. Socrates is supposed to have believed in his benighted youth that if one man overtops another by a head, he does so *because of* a head, and that the same is true of horses: if one horse is taller than another by a head,

[50] They are stated in 96D8–97B3 and resolved in 100E5–B7. I do not lump 96C2–D6 with the puzzles: the belief that a man grows by the intake of food and drink involves no absurdity which needs to be cleared up by the machinery of the "safe" *aitia:* it will be noticed that when the clearing up is done in 100E5 ff. there is no mention of or allusion to the belief that we grow by taking in food and drink. The point of 96C2–D6 is surely to illustrate *another way* in which an infatuation with the methodology of the natural philosophers could do a tyro far more harm than good: it could lead him to "unlearn" (96C6) familiar truths, persuading him that he knew only those causes which he could formulate in the categories of an elaborate physical system and hence to spurn explanations of the usual kind which are cast in homely, everyday language, yet are far more worthy of credence than the windy theorizings which the *physiologoi* would put in their place. (There is no foundation for Burnet's suggestion *ad locum* [apparently swallowed by Hackforth, p. 131] that "Socrates means that his former beliefs were upset by the question of Anaxagoras (fr. 10), 'for how could hair come from that which is not hair and flesh from that which is not flesh?' ". Anaxagoras' highly speculative answer to this question, if true, would not "upset," but only *account for* the belief in 96C8–D5 that a man can increase his bulk by eating and drinking, "when flesh was added to flesh, bone to bone," etc.)

[51] For many years I could not make head or tail of these puzzles, and used to take them as symptomatic of some kind of muddle in Plato's thinking, though without sharing Crombie's confidence that it was the kind of muddle that a tyro in philosophy could diagnose. It was only when I reached the interpretation of the "safe" *aitia* which I present in this paper and saw what kind of solution it would provide to these puzzles that I began to see what gave rise to their perplexities in the first place.

the *aitia* of its superior height is—the head![52] The next pair (E1–4), on the contrary, look like commonplaces: Socrates thought at that time that ten things are more than eight *because* there are two more of them in the ten (than in the eight); and that, given two objects, two and one yards long respectively, the first will be the longer *because* it exceeds the second by half its own length. One wonders how anyone, no matter how young and callow, could have been expected to swallow the absurdities in the first pair, or blamed for countenancing the platitudes in the second.

Light dawns in the following paragraph, where we come upon a fifth and a sixth puzzle: why does one, added to one, make two? (96E6–97A5). Why does one, divided by two, make two [halves]? (97A5–B3). Here the mode of presentation changes:[53] instead of recounting, poker-faced, mistakes incurred in his distant youth when he had been "utterly blinded" (96E5) by his obsessive attachment to mechanistic aetiology, Socrates now refers to similar errors from his present, entirely different, philosophical perspective, and gives us broad hints as to why he can no longer stomach[54] the answers his previous "method"? of thinking had made compelling. Thus, the old answer to the question in the fifth puzzle would have been: the addition of one unit to the other is what makes 2 of them.[55] This, he now says, he no longer accepts, and for the following reason:

> For I would be astounded if, when each of them was apart from the other, each was one and they were not then two, but when they approached each other *this* became the *aitia* of their becoming two: the conjunction involved in their being put close to each other (97A2–5).

[52] On the face of it, this is a low-grade pun: the dative, $\tau\hat{\eta}\ \kappa\epsilon\phi\alpha\lambda\hat{\eta}$ could be used to mean both "by a head" and "because of a head."

[53] The change in tone and perspective is marked by Cebes' question, immediately after the previous puzzles had been laid out: "And how do you think of these things *now?*" (96E5). Thereafter Socrates' verbs change from the past tense in D8–E4 to the present.

[54] "I do not accept," 96E7; "I would be [literally, 'am'] astounded if," 97A2; etc., winding up at B7 with "I will have no truck with this [method of thinking which gives rise to the puzzles]."

[55] 96E8–97A1. To simplify the exposition I abbreviate this puzzle, which in the text (Burnet's, with his expansion) presents the result of adding A to B as a disjunction: either B becomes two, or A becomes two, or A and B taken together become two. The last of the three disjuncts suffices for my purposes above.

Here at last we see the gaffe Socrates had been perpetrating in that period which antedated his discovery of the "safe" *aitia*. He had been confusing the arithmetical operation of addition with a physical process—that of taking things which were "apart" to begin with and putting them "close to each other."[56] And he had been supposing that the feasibility of this material process was the *aitia* of the logico-mathematical truth that the same items which count as units, if taken disjointly, will count as a pair, if taken conjointly. Looking back at this boner from his present philosophical perspective, Socrates says he would be "astounded" if such a thing were true: he would suffer that peculiar sense of intellectual outrage we all feel when asked to believe a proposition which is not just materially false but logically absurd. For obviously the things being talked about are two by hypothesis, and they would still be two regardless of whether they were jammed up together in a cupboard or situated in different galaxies a million light-years apart. How absurd then to offer their propinquity as the reason why they are two![57] So the puzzle can now be solved or, more exactly, dissolved, Plato's solvent being the "*F* in virtue of Φ" formula.[58] If things are

[56] The literal meaning of the verb used for addition, $\pi\rho\sigma\sigma\tau\ell\theta\eta\mu\iota$ A $\tau\hat{\omega}$ B, is "put A next to B." This dead metaphor comes alive in the passage, Socrates shifting back and forth from this verb to variant expressions which refer unmistakably to putting objects close to one another, while he denotes the converse operation not by the usual terms for arithmetical subtraction ($\dot{\alpha}\phi\alpha\ell\rho\epsilon\sigma\iota\varsigma$) or division ($\delta\iota\alpha\ell\rho\epsilon\sigma\iota\varsigma$), but by words which have strong physical evocations: "splitting" ($\sigma\chi\ell\sigma\iota\varsigma$, A7; cf $\delta\iota\alpha\sigma\chi\ell\sigma\epsilon\iota$, A6), "leading apart" ($\dot{\alpha}\pi\dot{\alpha}\gamma\epsilon\tau\alpha\iota$, B3), and "separating" ($\chi\omega\rho\ell\zeta\epsilon\tau\alpha\iota$, B3).

[57] This is reinforced by a further objection: if we were to take twoness as the effect of conjunction we would be faced with the (supposed) paradox that the opposite process of disjunction causes the same effect. Socrates is going on the assumption that if a given process causes a certain effect, the opposite process could not also cause the same effect. There is a fallacy here, but apparently not an obvious one, for I have seen no notice of it in the literature: even if we were to concede the truth of the assumption, the conclusion would follow only if it were true that the disjunction and conjunction *of the same items* produced the same effect. But the latter would *not* be true in the two cases Socrates is discussing: he gets twoness in the first case by conjoining units A and B; he gets it in the second by disjoining, not the same units, but parts inside each of them. However, this fallacy does not invalidate the fundamental insight I expound above; this can dispense entirely with this additional support, which, as it happens, is unsound.

[58] This becomes clear in Division Two of our passage where (100E5–B7) all of the puzzles are resolved seriatim by applying to each the

one in virtue of participating in Unity, two in virtue of participating in the Dyad, then it will be clear that the "Why?" in "Why do one and one make two?" cannot be a physical "Why?" and that its answering "because" must be extracted not from accounts of what happens to objects when they are moved about, but from "accounts of the essence"[59] of the numbers, One and Two.[60]

"F in virtue of Φ" formula. This fundamental point, which should be made the pivot of the interpretation of the puzzles, is not even mentioned by Hackforth (p. 131): he gives no indication that the puzzle laid out in 96E6 ff. is stuffed with hints of the correct solution and that in Plato's opinion the "F in virtue of Φ" formula provides the correct solution. So it is hardly surprising that Hackforth should labor under the misapprehension that Plato is himself taken in by "unreal problems" (cf. the citation from Hackforth and my comment in the concluding paragraph of this section). Crombie too thinks that Plato wallows in the very confusions which the "safe" *aitia* is meant to clear up. Thus he says that "phrases like 'the putting of one alongside one is not the cause of the occurrence of 2' (101B9–C1) are used without any clear indication whether the question is: [a] 'Why are there two things here?' (to which an answer in terms of putting one thing alongside another would be appropriate); or whether the question is: [b] 'How does the number 2 arise?'" (p. 169; I have interpolated the reference marks). Crombie, most surprisingly, fails to take into account the fact that for Plato the number, Two, a Form, could no more "arise" than perish and, hence, could not "arise" from the putting together of two physical objects. Conversely, the fact that, if we did put together two physical objects "here," we would get "two things here," would be as obvious to Plato as to anyone else. Hence Plato could have denounced "because of putting one (object) alongside another" *only* if he thought this an answer to [b]; for he would have seen it as a trivially true answer to [a]. How then could he have failed to distinguish [a] from [b]?

[59] Cf. the citations in notes 32 and 44 above. In the *Republic* Plato says that it is the philosopher's job to ask "what is the essence of the One itself" (524E6) (and by the same token of Two and other numbers). When one had done this one would see that the "accounts of the essence" of One and of Two allow for the participation of the same objects, taken singly, in One, taken jointly, in Two (cf. the preceding note *sub fin.*). Cf. *Hp. Ma.* 301D8–9, where much is made of the fact that Two can be instantiated only by a pair of individuals, each of whom is *one*.

[60] A substantially similar interpretation will be found in Moreau (in the work cited in note 5 above), my only objections to it being (a) that he has to make Plato a neo-Kantian idealist to bring it off ("La cause de la production du 2, c'est à dire d'un objet de représentation double, ce n'est donc pas le rapprochement ou la séparation dans l'espace,

All four of the puzzles in 96D8–E4 will yield to the same treatment on the hypothesis[61] that all of them crop up because in this benighted phase of his philosophical evolution Socrates[62] was confusing physical *aitiai* with logical ones: he was assuming that a

---

mais dans l'esprit. . . . Toutes les difficultés de cette sorte sont donc levées par l'idéalisme mathématique, qui fait de l'unité un act intellectuel indivisible et du nombre une pure relation," p. 382) and (b) that he does not realize how inappropriate "cause" (cf. the start of the citation) becomes when it is clear that (i) this *aitia* is not a physical one and (ii) Plato is not proposing that a psychological cause be substituted for the physical one. In spite of these objections, I must record my heavy debt to Moreau. I have derived greater help from his discussion of the puzzles in the *Phaedo* than from any other single source.

[61] I say "hypothesis," for certainly there is nothing whatever in the wording of these six lines which states or implies that their puzzles arise because physical factors are being confused with logical ones. For this hypothesis I claim no more than indirect verification from the context. We start at 96A8 with the tale of young Socrates' addiction to a methodology which restricts the quest for *aitiai* to physical causes. We are then given a sequence of six puzzles, all of them illustrative of the same perverse line of thought (cf. Cebes' question in 96E6, which concerns the first four, but is answered by the presentation and discussion of the last two; and note that the same solution is offered for all six in 100E8–101C9). The last two puzzles are discussed *in extenso* (twelve lines for these two as against six lines for the first four); and these, as I argued above, turn out to be cases of confusion of physical with logical *aitiai*. It is, therefore, reasonable to assume that the first four are also cases of the same confusion and that this would have come out into the open if they had been discussed, instead of merely mentioned, in the text.

[62] It should be noticed that Plato does not say that *the natural philosophers* had made this confusion, but only that Socrates did so when *he* came under the spell of their teaching. Plato does not hesitate to attack his predecessors sharply for their obnoxious doctrines (see, e.g., *Phlb.* 28D–29A; *Ti.* 48B; *Lg.* 888E–890A and 967A–D). So it is unlikely that he would have hesitated to lambaste them in this passage if such absurdities as those in 96D8 ff. had figured in their writings. And the fact is that no surviving fragment of their original works indulges in this kind of thing. In the light of these considerations we had best refrain from ascribing such logical solecisms to the physical philosophers and mathematicians of the time (as is sometimes done in the literature: e.g., Crombie, pp. 160–61), and understand Plato to mean in our passage no more than he actually says and directly implies, i.e., that since they had failed to clarify the concept of *aitia* and to sort out its categorially different import for categorially different subject matter, they had left their readers defenseless against such confusions as those recounted in our passage.

material factor, like a head, or the material presence of two units, or the material projection of a part of one thing beyond another could account for the respective statements, all of which are true *a priori*, and could only be accounted for by referring to the meaning of the terms they use. Thus, take the most interesting of the puzzles: why are ten things more than eight things? Reflecting on this in Part Two, now that he is well out of that particular fly-bottle, Socrates declares:

> So you would be afraid to say [i.e., you would *not* say] that the ten things are more than the eight in virtue of two things, and that it is because of *this* that they exceed, instead of saying that they exceed in virtue of numerousness and because of numerousness (101B4–6).

What Socrates is telling us, put into modern language, is that the reason why the group of ten is more numerous than the group of eight is simply that it satisfies the logico-metaphysical[63] conditions of (greater) numerousness. If this were to strike us as uninformative, Plato would agree (this is an "ignorant" *aitiai*), but insist that it is not useless on that account, for it would save us from misdirecting our search for *aitiai* to irrelevant factors, such as—in his own formulation of this puzzle—the presence in one group of two units which are not in the other. This would be the reddest of red herrings, unless it were logically related to the relative numerousness of the two groups, e.g., by showing that the first has as many units as does the second *and* more units besides—not necessarily *these* two units, nor necessarily *two* units: *any* number of units in the first group over and above those in it which match, unit for unit, the ones in the second group would fulfil the logical requirements of greater numerousness, and thus enable us to say precisely why there are more in the first than there are in the second.[64] If the

---

[63] I say "logico-metaphysical" rather than just "logical," in deference to the point I made earlier, that for Plato the logical relation of a term to the concept under which it falls is at the same time the metaphysical relation of a sensible to an eternal Form. To say that something is the case "in virtue of numerousness and because of numerousness" (the same thing said twice over again for emphasis, first by the instrumental dative, πλήθει, and then by an accusative with a preposition, διὰ τὸ πλῆθος) is expansible into "in virtue of participating in the Form, Numerousness."

[64] In this discussion I have deliberately gone beyond what we get in the text, in order to bring out the further implications of Plato's basic

insight. If he had had at his disposal techniques of analysis such as are available nowadays to beginners, he could have offered a general formula to cover all four of the puzzles in 96D8–E4, laying down the contextual definition, "where A, B, C are (positive) magnitudes or cardinals, A is greater than B if, and only if, there exists a C such that A = B + C," and then showing that this definition is satisfied in all four cases: in puzzles *1* and *2*, A = the height of the first (man or horse); B = the height of the second; C = the length of a head. In puzzle *3* (the one discussed in the text above), A = 10 units; B = 8 units; C = 2 units. In puzzle *4*, A = 2 yards; B = 1 yard; C = A/2 yards (= 1 yard). Had Plato been able to clean up the problem in this way, he would have spared his readers two blemishes in his present account which help explain why his sound insight may be so easily missed:

(a) he says "numerousness" ($\pi\lambda\acute{\eta}\theta\epsilon\iota$, $\pi\lambda\hat{\eta}\theta$os) in 101B6, instead of "*greater* numerousness," and "magnitude" ($\mu\epsilon\gamma\acute{\epsilon}\theta\epsilon\iota$) in 101B7, instead of "*greater* magnitude," thereby failing to bring out that both are special cases of the "greater than" relation, and that the absolute numerousness or bigness of the things he is talking about is irrelevant to the reasoning;

(b) he gives spurious reasons for rejecting "a head" (i.e., the presence of a physical magnitude the length of a head) as the cause of A's being bigger than B in the first of the two puzzles, saying (101A5–B2) that this would lead to a two-fold contradiction:

(i) the same cause would produce contrary effects (the presence in A of a magnitude equalling a head would result in A being *bigger*, B *smaller*) and

(ii) a cause with a given character would produce an effect of a contrary character (the head, a *small* magnitude, would make A *big*).

The appearance of contradiction arises only because the supposed effect of the alleged cause has been misstated in both cases:

In (i) the supposed effect, correctly stated is (*P*), "A is bigger *than B*" and (*Q*), "B is smaller *than A*"—not (*P'*), "A is *bigger*," and (*Q'*), "B is *smaller*" [*sc.*, than each would otherwise be]. *P* and *Q*, so far from being contraries (as are *P'* and *Q'*), are logically equivalent propositions.

In (ii) the supposed effect, correctly stated, is not (*P''*), "A is big," but only *P* above; and *P''*, of course, does *not* follow from *P*: there is no reason why a man or a horse has to be a big man or horse in order to be bigger than another man or horse (for other examples of this fallacy in Plato see my "Degrees of Reality in Plato," in *New Essays in Plato and Aristotle*, edited by R. Bambrough, London, 1965, p. 14). I submit that here, as in the case of the fallacy I pointed out in note 57 above, Plato's residual confusions and fallacies (which are entirely understandable in a thinker who lacked the rudiments of the logic of relations) do not cancel the validity of the fundamental insight expressed in the "*F* in virtue of participating in Φ" formula. To see the traps into which Plato falls is to admire all the more the tenacity with which, in spite of these mishaps, he pursued the truth he saw.

"safe" and "ignorant" *aitia* did this kind of work for Plato one can see why he could find it so enlightening while ascribing to it no causal agency whatever.

It is sad then to see him charged by serious scholars with having made the very error which, if I am right, he was the first to spot. Thus Hackforth takes him to task for posing a pseudo-problem in asking for the *aitia* of ten being more than eight:

> The question whether the addition of two is the cause of ten being greater than eight is meaningless, because there is no more a cause of ten being greater than eight than there is of Thursday coming after Wednesday [p. 131].

Certainly there is no *cause* here, and who should know this better than does Plato, who gives us, as one showpiece of cockeyed thinking about *aitia*, the puzzle generated by assuming that there is a (physical) cause for the truth that $1 + 1 = 2$? But though there are no causes for such truths, there are most certainly reasons for them, and it was a mark of genius to see that where one type of *aitia*, with its peculiar methodological commitments (those of physical inquiry), is inapplicable, another type of *aitia*, with its entirely different (logico-mathematical) methodology, *is* applicable, and to make his metaphysical theory the vehicle of this insight.

3. THE "CLEVER" AITIA

We can now consider Socrates' second answer to the "Why is x F?" question. Instead of mentioning just the one Form, Φ, he now refers us also to another, Γ, so related to Φ, that whatever is "named" (i.e., characterized)[65] after Γ, will also be "named" after Φ ($103E2-104B4$). The first example given of the Γ-Φ relation is the pair, Three-Odd: whatever is a trio will also be odd-numbered. From this and other examples it is clear that he has in view a transitive, non-symmetrical[66] relation. He has no technical name for it

[65] Cf. note 29 above.

[66] Plato's relation has to cover both cases such as those of the Three-Odd, Snow-Cold couplings, where the relation is clearly antisymmetric, and also others in which, for all we know to the contrary, Plato perhaps thought of the relation as symmetrical, as in the case of the Fire-Hot coupling. What is certain (from examples like Three-Odd, Two-Even, etc.) is that Plato thinks of participating in Γ as a sufficient, but not also a necessary, condition of participating in Φ.

and is content to use a metaphor: he speaks of Γ "bringing on" Φ.[67] I shall speak of it as "entailment," extending this term beyond its normal use as a propositional connective and allowing it to connect concepts, as we sometimes do in informal contexts.[68] The formula then for this *aitia* could be put as follows: "*x is F because it participates in Γ and Γ entails Φ*"; or, more elaborately: "*x is F because, being G, it must participate in Γ; and since Γ entails Φ, x must also participate in Φ, and hence x must be F.*" Plato does not spell out any such formula as this. But an examination of his text will show, I believe, that this is what the sketchier phrasings there imply. For what he understands by them we must rely on his examples. There is a flock of them. First, he gives additional arithmetical cases of Γ-Φ linkages: Five-Odd, Two-Even, Four-Even, Ten-Even.[69] Then, without any apparent shifting of gears, still talking about precisely the same relation, explaining precisely the same *aitia*, he brings in physical, biological, and other examples of Form Γ, entailing Form Φ: Fire-Heat, Snow-Cold, Fever-Sickness, Soul-Life.[70] Does this answer to the "Why is *x Γ*?" question give us more reason than did the preceding to think that his Forms are meant to be causes?

Let me press one of his examples, where Fever is the *aitia* of a sickness. We may assume the following background: a man dis-

[67] Having started off at 103E2 ff. using still more cumbersome language to express the Γ-Φ relation (which I have abbreviated above to "whatever is 'named' by Γ will also be 'named' by Φ"), he shifts casually to *epipherein* at 104E10 and uses it frequently thereafter (I surmise: simply because it is shorter), varying it with the expression discussed in the preceding note, where the Γ-Φ relation is indicated *via* the isomorphic *G-F* relation: if *G* comes to be present in *x*, then *x* will be *F*. As Shorey points out (p. 11 and note 3 of the second paper mentioned in note 3 above; for more examples see Bonitz, *Index Aristotelicus*), the terms *epipherein* and *synepipherein* as well as some of the other terms used here by Plato to express relations between Forms are also used by Aristotle to express entailment relations between general terms.

[68] If we were to convert Plato's talk about Forms into set-theoretical language, taking Φ, Γ, etc. to name sets, the "bringing-on" relation would denote the *inclusion* of the "bringer-on" in the "brought-on," *not* the membership of the former in the latter: Plato clearly has no interest in saying that the Form, Fever, is sick, or that the Form, Fire, is hot.

[69] 104A4–B2; 105A6–7; 105G9 ff.

[70] He had already introduced the Forms Hot, Cold, Snow, Fire, to illustrate the relation of incompatibility between Forms (103C10 ff.) —a relation which I leave out of my discussion in this paper to avoid burdening still further its already overburdened exposition.

plays the cluster of symptoms which would have justified us in classifying him as sick before diagnosing his particular ailment:[71] he suffers from weakness, loss of appetite, pain, and other psychological registers of physical distress. We examine him and see he is very hot.[72] We infer that he is sick *because* of this.[73] Socrates steps in at this point to tell us we are entitled to make this inference only because the man participates in the two Forms, Fever, Sickness, the first of which entails the second. When this is abbreviated to "the Form, Fever, is what makes him sick," it has an alarming ring. It sounds as though the Form were a ghostly stand-in for bacteria. But we need only recall the foregoing argument, which, I trust, cleared the Form of imputation of causal agency in the case of the "safe" *aitia*, to assure ourselves that the same clearance can be given it in the case of the present *aitia* as well. If Φ is not expected to be a cause when it is said to "make" x to be F, then by the same token Γ cannot be expected to be a cause when *it* is said to "make" x to be F.[74]

May we then conclude that here too the "makes" in the Platonic formula has a strictly logico-metaphysical force—that no greater causal significance is to be read into "the Form, Fever, makes the man sick" than into "the Form, Sickness, is what makes him sick"? Such had been Shorey's claim when he maintained against Zeller that in the whole of this passage Plato is concerned with logic, not

---

[71] These symptoms must be sufficient to warrant the classification "sick," but not sufficient to warrant the narrower one, "feverish," else we would lose the "cleverness" of the present *aitia*: we would be back in the formally tautologous, "safe" and "ignorant" *aitia*. And cf. the next note.

[72] This is how we must understand "fever" here (taking *pyretos* in its literal sense, "burning heat, fiery heat," Liddell and Scott, Greek-English Lexicon, *s.v.*, I—i.e., as that "excess of heat" in the body which Plato takes to be a *cause* of a variety of ailments in all of which the patient is feverish: *Ti.* 86A2–3) if Fever-Sickness is to parallel the Fire-Heat, Snow-Cold couplings, as it is surely meant to do: if "fever" were understood here to *mean* a species of sickness in the first place, the coupling would not constitute an example of the "clever," i.e., informative, *aitia*.

[73] A very substantial inference: if valid, it empowers us to infer that he is sick just from knowing that he suffers from "excess of heat," as of course we could not if we were not justified in moving from "he is sick *and* suffers from excess of heat" to "he is sick *because* he suffers from excess of heat" in the first place.

[74] Cf. my critique in note 46 above of the last of the citations from Cornford in that note.

physics, adumbrating a theory of syllogistic inference, not of causal explanation.[75] This is an attractive interpretation: one could wish it were true. And nothing would have stood in the way of our taking it as true if Plato had given only logical and mathematical examples of the Γ-Φ relation. If we had only Three, Odd, Two, Even, and the like among the examples, then certainly the Γ-Φ coupling could be strictly non-causal. That Jones's family must be odd-numbered because it happens to be a threesome is indeed austerely irrelevant to the causal order of the world. Not so when we are told that Jones is sick because he has a fever, that a burning log is hot because it is on fire, that the white stuff on the ground is cold because it is snow. To be sure, none of the entailments holding between the relevant Forms are being credited with causal agency. But they are certainly expected *to have causal implications*. That the occurrence of fever is the cause of the occurrence of sickness would be a textbook example of a cause in Greek medicine.[76] And since the Γ-Φ entailment is being offered as the justification of the causal inference, how could it be empty of causal significance? The same would be true of the Fire-Heat and Snow-Cold couplings.[77] Fire and snow, like bronze in the second example in Section I above, are natural kinds, and the invariance of the concomitance of the characteristic properties in each of them signifies a multitude of causal interconnections with other kinds of matter in the universe. Thus when Socrates maintains that the Form, Snow, is the *aitia* of cold, he is asserting neither the metaphysical absurdity that the Form, Snow, chills selected regions of the universe, nor the semantic absurdity that snow causes itself to be chilly; but what he does assert is nevertheless tied firmly to the causal structure of the world, e.g., to the fact that if we raise the temperature beyond a certain point snow must change to water. This "must" is a causal one. And since in Plato's theory it is grounded in relations of entailment between Forms, it would have to be a fantastically strong "must": it would have to express a *physical* law that has *logical* necessity.

[75] On pp. 7–8 of the second paper mentioned in note 3 above. And this is the less extreme of Shorey's claims: cf. the stronger one (which I cited in my opening paragraph and to which I alluded in note 49 above) that Plato is offering "only a tautological logic". And cf. note 78 below.

[76] Cf. note 72 above.

[77] I ignore the Life-Soul coupling, which raises other problems that cannot be discussed in this paper.

Since Plato claims that the snow of our experience is cold because the Form, Snow, entails the Form, Cold, and since all Forms—those of physical stuffs and processes no less than those of logic and mathematics—are eternal and sustain only immutable relations to each other, he is implying that the laws of nature, could we but know them, would have the same necessity as do the truths of arithmetic and logic.[78]

A theory such as this is not likely to get a sympathetic hearing from philosophers nowadays. Most of us have been brought up to think that the laws of nature are in the last analysis radical contingencies—*de facto* uniformities which we must either exhibit as special cases of still more general *de facto* uniformities or else accept as things for which no further reason can be given. Coming upon Plato's reduction of physical to logical necessity in the *Phaedo*, we may then be tempted to think of it as not only false but unreasonable, wrong-headed, indeed light-headed, a kind of whimsy. We would do well then to reflect that in the modern period too a substantially similar view has been propounded by philosophers—by Leibniz, for example, who held that synthetic, contingent, truths about our world represent necessary, analytic truths, imperfectly comprehended by our finite minds; that the neo-Hegelians, from F. H. Bradley to Professor Brand Blanshard, find in Hume's alternative to Leibniz a dissolution of causality into casuality and insist that "being causally connected involve(s) being connected by a relation of logical *necessity*";[79] and finally that, to speak from the

---

[78] We could have reached the same conclusion in Section I above, if Plato had used examples like Snow and Fire in illustrating the "safe" *aitia*, instead of sticking to logico-mathematical ones (Numerousness, Greatness, One, Two) and to that tantalizing abstraction, Beauty. To simplify the exposition I played his game, using "square" as my own example. Had I shifted to, say, "*x* is bronze because it participates in the Form, Bronze," it would have become apparent that even the "safe" *aitia*, though expressed in a tautological formula, has far-reaching substantive implications for the causal order of the universe: for as I remarked above, the regular concomitance of the properties which make up that natural kind has causal implications; to say that the relevant causal laws are instantiated in *x* because *x* participates in a Platonic Form Bronze, is to credit those laws with absolute immutability and to imply that they may be known *a priori*.

[79] *The Nature of Thought*, Vol. II (London, 1939), p. 515: the italics are Blanshard's. Cf. A. C. Ewing, *Idealism* (London, 1934), p. 171: there is an "intrinsic" or "inherent" bond between cause and effect of which, he says, he can only think of "cause and effect as connected by a

other, far more populous side of the fence, while it is generally admitted that causal laws must support counter-factuals, the problems of explaining counter-factuals on a regularity-theory of the laws of nature is a troublesome one and its solution is still under debate.

There had been no Hume in Plato's past. The physical philosophers had proceeded on the faith that, as Leucippus had expressed it, "nothing happens at random, but everything by reason and by necessity."[80] But when they looked critically at this axiom, as Democritus, the last in the succession, was the first to do, all they could find in nature on which to base their faith in rational necessity was *de facto* regularity. He taught, we are informed, that natural explanation reduces to the principle that "things always are or happen thus" and that "there is no sense in looking for a reason for that which always happens."[81] We cannot tell from surviving fragments or reports what conclusions he drew from this remarkable reflection. But regardless of what Democritus may have made of it, we can see with what force Plato could have retorted: "If you must have rational necessity in nature, you cannot get it from regularities which are matters of brute fact. The only kind of rational necessity known to me is that I find in mathematics[82] and dialectic. Do you know of any others? If so, explain yourself. Until you do, I will continue to believe that nature could exhibit rational necessity

---

relation of logical entailment"; and *Proc. of Aristot. Society*, Supp. Vol. 14 (1935), p. 66: "The cause logically entails the effect in such a way that it would be in principle possible, with sufficient insight, to see what kind of effect must follow from examination of the cause alone without having learnt by previous experience what were the effects of similar causes" (quoted from Ewing by E. Nagel, *The Structure of Science*, New York, 1961, p. 53).

[80] H. Diels and W. Kranz, *Die Fragmente der Vorsokratiker*[5], (Berlin, 1934–37), Frag. B 1.

[81] *Phys.* 252A32–B1 (=frag. A65 in Diels and Krantz).

[82] Plato's criticism of contemporary mathematics in *R.* 510C–511D does not imply (or even suggest) lack of confidence in the absolute certitude of mathematics, whose subject matter is eternal (527B7–8) and, therefore, "draws" or "leads" the soul away from the flux to eternal being (524E–525B). (It should be noted that Plato does *not* impute to the mathematicians the absurd assumption that their subject matter consists of visible figures, he says explicitly [510D6–7] that they are *not* reasoning about these.)

only if its laws mirrored the interrelations of the Forms we explore in logico-mathematical reasoning."

To say this is not, of course, to suggest that Plato's view is un-objectionable. Its most glaring fault is its methodological sterility for natural science. What knowledge of the laws of nature could one hope to secure *a priori* by following out lines of entailment from terms like *fire*, *snow*, and *fever?* The entailments in our passage are depressing commonplaces. But even so, it is not clear that they would warrant the certitude with which they would be credited on this view. How could we know that the Form, Fire, really entails the Form, Heat? It would be no use telling us that we would know this if we had "recollected" the two concepts correctly. For how could we be sure of that? What guarantee would we have that what we learned about fire from our sense experience, sadly limited by the parochial contingencies of our time and place, would not have led us astray? If there were stuffs which burn with a cool flame else-where in the universe, and we had known of them, our notion of fire would have been different, and then we would not have thought of claiming that the eternal Fire is eternally linked to Heat. It is im-possible to tell from our passage to what extent Plato was assailed at this time by such doubts. Here, as elsewhere, he has a way of keeping the spotlight of his discourse on just those areas where he is most confident of the answers, content to leave much else in ob-scurity. This artful chiaroscuro makes life difficult for anyone who tries to expound his thought systematically. Time and again we come across gaps in his thought, not knowing how he would expect us to fill them. This way of writing philosophy is not to be excused, and I have no desire to excuse it. But this much can at least be said for Plato: his silences are themselves suggestive not of confusion but of a canny, self-critical awareness of the limitations of his theory. The problems he persistently declines to discuss in the middle dialogues are those whose solution eludes him.

This is conspicuously true in the present case. If Plato had really thought we could syllogize our way into the secrets of the natural universe, his confidence in such a fantasy would have been pathetic. But the fact is that he offers us no such pseudo-science of nature in this dialogue.[83] His ideas on geography and astronomy he presents

---

[83] He appears to be disclaiming it by emphasizing Socrates' ig-norance of natural cause (99C6–9; 100D3; 101C9–D1).

only in the framework of a myth.[84] If not already in this dialogue, then soon after he must have drawn the only conclusion open to a sensible and honest man who had to live with Plato's metaphysical theory: that there can be, strictly speaking, no such thing as *knowledge* of nature—only educated guesses, verisimilitudes, plausibilities. Such a conclusion is clearly implied in the *Republic*. When he drops empirical sciences like physics, biology, and medicine from the curriculum of higher studies, there is no suggestion that their subject matter will be reclaimed at a higher level by dialectic. Forms like Fire, Snow, and Fever never darken the pages of Book VII of the *Republic*. His point of view remains the same in this respect when he comes to deal directly and at length with empirical topics, as he does in the *Timaeus*. There the Forms of Fire, Water, and the like are accorded a curious and revealing treatment. Their existence is formally proved,[85] and they are placed ceremoniously on their metaphysical pedestals, only to be left there and quietly ignored in the rest of the treatise, where the workings of nature are explored. The plethora of ingenious explanations of natural phenomena displayed in the sequel is spun out of the theory of the geometrical configuration of matter. We are not told that fire causes water to evaporate, melts metals, cuts up foodstuffs into digestible and assimilable particles because the Forms of Fire, Water, etc. entail the Forms of the corresponding processes. The *aitiai* of physical, chemical, and biological phenomena are not deduced from "accounts of the essence" of the Forms, but are derived synthetically from the structure of the atom. And what is claimed for them is not certainty, but verisimilitude,[86] the atomic theory itself being presented as no more than a plausible hypothesis,[87] having no more than aesthetic elegance[88] and the saving of the phenomena to recommend it.

I implied at the start of this paper that our passage in the *Phaedo*, rightly understood, is not unworthy of Plato's philosophical stature.

---

[84] Including some important scientific doctrines, such as the sphericity of the earth, its stability "at the center of the heavens" (108E4–109A6), and the implied repudiation of the ancient notion of an absolute "up" and "down" (112C1–2).

[85] 5B71–52A4.

[86] Cf. my "Disorderly Motion in the *Timaeus*," in R. E. Allen, *op. cit.*, pp. 238–83 and notes.

[87] 53D4–6.

[88] 53D7–E8.

The reader can now see why I made this claim and may assess its merits for himself. If my interpretation is correct, Plato has not only distinguished here mechanical from teleological causes—this part of his contribution I have not attempted to discuss—but has also come within sight of the still more radical distinction between both of these and the logical *aitia* of classification and entailment. Had he availed himself, as Aristotle was to do, of the expository device of philosophical lexicography, this achievement would have been more perspicuous and also, no doubt, more complete, for in making his thought more explicit he would have attained greater lucidity himself. However, we should not be put off by the fact that at no point does he say in the style of his great pupil and critic, "*aitia* has many different senses." There are other ways of exhibiting distinctions, and one way of doing so is to use them. This, I have argued, is what Plato does in our passage, most successfully of all in the part which has been least understood in the scholarly literature, where he uses the "safe" *aitia* to explode pseudo-problems which arise when the categorial difference between logical and physical *aitiai* is ignored.[89] If it were then suggested that Plato cannot be after all so clear on this point, else he would not have used indiscriminately arithmetical, physical, and medical concepts when illustrating the "clever" *aitia*, I trust the answer is now apparent from what I have said in the concluding part of the paper. There is no confusion here, but the expression of his firm conviction that all intelligible necessity, physical no less than mathematical, must be grounded on logical necessity, since it represents the interrelations of eternal Forms, be these articulated in discourse or imaged in the physical world. This conviction could easily have set him started in pursuit of a will o'-the-wisp, a physical science which deduces the laws of nature *a priori*. It is a mark of good sense, no less than of clear thinking, that in his subsequent writings he claimed the certitude of logical necessity only for propositions of mathematics and dialectic, and was content with a physical theory which, he conceded, was no more than a beautiful guess.

[89] I.e., in 96C6–97B3, where he discusses the last two of the six puzzles; and, if my hypothesis concerning the point of the first four is accepted, in 96D8–E4 as well.

Originally published in *The Philosophical Review* 78 (1969), 291–325. Reprinted (with a few corrections) by permission of *The Philosophical Review*.

8

PARTICIPATION AND PREDICATION IN PLATO'S MIDDLE DIALOGUES

R. E. ALLEN

I propose in this paper to examine three closely related issues in the interpretation of Plato's middle dialogues: the nature of Forms, of participation, and of predication. The familiar problem of self-predication will serve as introduction to the inquiry.

I. SELF-PREDICATION

The significance—or lack of significance—of Plato's self-predicative statements has recently become a crux of scholarship. Briefly, the problem is this: the dialogues often use language which suggests that the Form is a universal which has itself as an attribute and is thus a member of its own class, and, by implication, that it is the one perfect member of that class. The language suggests that the Form *has* what it *is*: it is self-referential, self-predicable.

Now such a view is, to say the least, peculiar. Proper universals are not instantiations of themselves, perfect or otherwise. Oddness is not odd; Justice is not just; Equality is equal to nothing at all. No one can curl up for a nap in the Divine Bedsteadity; not even God can scratch Doghood behind the Ears.

The view is more than peculiar; it is absurd. As Plato knew, it implies an infinite regress, one which he doubtless regarded as vicious. Indeed, if a recent critic, Professor Gregory Vlastos, has analysed the Third Man correctly,[1] it implies still more. We must suppose that Plato could swallow, without gagging, a flat self-

[1] Gregory Vlastos, 'The Third Man Argument in the *Parmenides*,' *Phil. Rev.* LXIII (1954), 319–49. For further discussion, see: Wilfrid Sellars, *Phil. Rev.* LXIV (1955), 405–37; Vlastos; ibid., 438–48; P. T. Geach, *Phil. Rev.* LXV (1956), 72–82; Vlastos, ibid., 83–94; R. S. Bluck, *Class. Quart.* N. S. VI (1956), 29–37, and *Phronesis II* (1957), 115–21.

contradiction;[2] that the reason for this, presumably, was that the author of the Third Man—one of the more brilliant of philosophical demonstrations—lacked the wit, or perhaps the diligence, to identify the premisses of his argument; that the man who first explicitly distinguished between universals and particulars confused them; and, finally, that a central thesis of his ontology, the doctrine of degrees of being and reality, rests on this elementary mistake.

Such thorough confusion is not lightly to be imputed to any man, let alone to Plato. Common sense and the common law agree that a man is innocent until proved guilty; and common charity dictates that philosophers be not excepted. The amount of evidence required to convict Plato of so puerile a confusion must be immense indeed. I propose in this paper to show that it has not yet been produced, and in the very nature of the case cannot be produced.

Let us be quite clear on what is to be proved. Plato obviously accepts the following thesis: some (perhaps all) entities which may be designated by a phrase of the form 'the *F* Itself', or any synonyms thereof, may be called *F*. So the Beautiful Itself will be beautiful, the Just Itself just, Equality equal.[3] But this thesis does not, *by itself*, imply self-predication; for that, an auxiliary premiss is required.

This premiss is that a predicate of the type '. . . is *F*' may be applied univocally to *F* particulars and to the *F* Itself, so that when (for example) we say that a given act is just, and that Justice is just, we are asserting that both have identically the same character. But this premiss would be false if the predicate were systematically equivocal, according as the subject of the sentence was a Form or a particular. In that case, to say that Justice is just and that any given act is just would be to say two quite different (though perhaps related) things, and the difficulties inherent in self-predication could not possibly arise. That is, the character of Forms would not be assimilated to that of particulars.

I propose to show that predicates involving the names of Forms

---

[2] The guilty premisses, in Vlastos' formulation of the argument, are (A3) Self-Predication and (A4) Non-Identity; these are so stated, however, that their incompatibility is not immediately apparent.

[3] Cf. *Prt.*, 330C, 331B; *Phd.*, 74B, D, 100C ; *Hp. Ma.*, 289C, 291E, 292E, 294A–B; *Ly.*, 217A; *Symp.*, 210E–211D.

exhibit just this kind of ambiguity. The evidence for this conclusion will be drawn from the theory of predication put forward in the *Phaedo* and from the ontology which underlies it.

II. PLATO'S THEORY OF PREDICATION

Plato has no word for 'predication'. Rather he says that particulars are 'called by the same name' (ὁμώνυμον) as their Form.[4] But this is surely a loose way of describing the use of common terms; 'ὁμώνυμον' is Aristotle's usual term for 'ambiguous'; things called by the same name may have nothing in common but their name. But later in the *Phaedo* this terminology is repeated and made more precise:[5]

Each of the Forms exists, and the other things which come to have a share in them are *named after* them.

The reason for naming particulars after Forms is that they have in them an immanent character defined by their Form:[6]

Not only is the Form itself always entitled to its own name, but also what is not the Form, but always has, when it exists, its immanent character (μορφή).

Significantly, Aristotle chose to emphasise precisely this feature in his summary of the theory of Forms in the *Metaphysics:*[7]

Sensible things, [Plato] said, were all *named after* [Ideas], and in virtue of a relation to them; for the many existed by participation in the Ideas that *have the same name* as they.

These passages imply that '*F*' is a *name*, a name whose *prime* designate is a Form: '*F*' names *the F*. But this name is also applied, through what we may call derivative designation, to particulars, which are *named after* the Form in much the way that a boy may be named after his father. The reason for this, the justification for derivative designation, is that particulars have in them the immanent character defined by their Form; or, to put the matter in a

[4] *Phd.*, 78E2; cf. *R.*, 596A7; *Sph.*, 240A.
[5] *Phd.*, 102B2: cf. *Prm.*, 130E5; italics here, as elsewhere, mine.
[6] *Phd.*, 103E; cf. 103B7 ff.   [7] 987B9 ff., trans. by Ross.

slightly different way, they are named after the Form because of their peculiarly intimate relation to it—they depend upon it for their character and their existence.

We have, then, a theory of predication without predicates. What appear to be attributive statements are in fact *relational* or *identifying* statements, depending on the designation of their predicates. In derivative designation, to say of something that it is *F* is to say that it is causally dependent upon *the F*. Notice that '*F*' is here not strictly a univocal term, but a common name, applied in virtue of a relationship to an individual, the Form.

On the other hand, when '*F*' is used in primary designation, it is a synonym of 'the *F* itself' and '*F*-ness'; therefore, to say that *F*-ness is *F* is to state an identity. It follows that it is invalid to infer self-predication from Plato's apparently self-predicative language. In the first place, '*F*-ness if *F*' is not a predicative statement. Second, we cannot mean by it what we mean when we say that a particular is *F*. The function '. . . is *F*' is systematically ambiguous; its meaning depends upon the context in which it is used, the type of object to which it is applied.[8]

If this is true, it follows that Plato's self-predicative language is both intelligible and logically innocuous. Grammatical predicates are names which exhibit a systematic ambiguity according as they designate Forms or particulars; Forms themselves are proper nameables; what appear to be self-predicative statements are identity statements; and what appear to be attributive statements are relational statements.

We have a reasonably close analogue to this in English: our own use of predicates where standards of weight and measure are in-

---

[8] Note that this view of the way words mean is consistent with a well-known feature of Greek syntax. One may always, in Greek, form an abstract noun by using the article with the neuter singular adjective. 'τὸ ἴσον' ("the equal"), for example, is equivalent to the abstract 'ἡ ἰσότης'; both mean 'equality'. But this usage is quite ambiguous, since 'τὸ ἴσον' may also mean 'the equal thing' or 'that which is equal'; in other words, it is normal usage, in Greek, to use 'the *F* thing' to refer to *F*-ness, particular *F*s, and even the class of *F* things. It has sometimes been supposed that this ambiguity was a source of confusion to Plato; I suggest that it rather confirmed a theory of the way words mean, which, in conformity with normal usage, preserved that ambiguity and rendered it intelligible. The use of 'αὐτό' will always make it clear, should need arise, which type of *F* is in question. 'αὐτὸ τὸ *F*' (the *F* itself) is an identifying phrase.

volved. To say of something that it weighs a pound, or measures exactly one yard, is to say that it bears a specific relation—equality in weight or length—to an individual locked in a vault of the Bureau of Standards, an individual arbitrarily selected to define a unit of measurement. Like '. . . is F', in derivative designation, the function '. . .weighs a pound' covertly mentions an individual of a type from its argument.

The parallel may be made more exact. We may say of other things that they weigh a pound, but if we assert this of *the* pound, we cannot assert it in the same sense. We can measure other things against a standard; we cannot measure a standard against itself. The predicate '. . . weighs a pound' is capable of exhibiting just the kind of ambiguity that Plato's theory requires. It may be systematically ambiguous; on the one hand it mentions a relation; on the other it may be an identifying phrase, designating an individual.

There is no reason in principle why this analysis should not be extended to other types of statement. Why should we not, for example, read statements like 'this desk is brown' or 'that figure is triangular' as asserting that the desk or figure stands in the relation of colour or shape resemblance to *the* brown and *the* triangle, individuals selected to define standards of colour and shape? There is no internal reason why predicates should not be analysed in this way. If they are, attributive statements will then one and all be translated into relation-to-standard statements.

The analogy of relation-to-standard statements to statements involving names of Forms was drawn advisedly;[9] for Forms clearly function, in the early and middle dialogues, as standards and paradigms. Plato's theory of predication admirably supplements a fundamental thesis of his ontology.

III. IMITATION AND DEGREES OF REALITY

The theory of Forms involves two fundamental doctrines: (*a*) that the relation between particulars and Forms is that of imitation, of copy to original, and (*b*) that Forms and particulars differ in

[9] It must be remembered that this *is* an analogy, not a basis for literal explication of the theory of Forms. Forms resemble standards in that they are of a different epistemic order from the class of things they define; but Forms are, as standards are not, also of a different ontological order. This leads to fundamental difficulties if the analogy is pressed; cf. 'Forms and Standards', *Phil. Quart.* VIII (1959), 164–7.

degree of reality. These theses, the proponents of self-predication maintain, obscured in Plato's mind the distinction between characters and things characterised, a confusion which leads directly to the absurdities of self-predication; and the regress arguments of the *Parmenides*, resting as they do on this mistake, reflect not verbal confusion but a radical and deep-seated incoherence in the theory of Forms.

It is clear that Plato's theory of predication does not entail this incoherence; but it is equally clear that it can do nothing, of itself, to prevent it. Indeed, the theory could have contributed indirectly to produce it, for it provides no clear way either to affirm or to deny that the *F has F*-ness. The very language in which the theory of Forms is expressed makes the issue of self-predicability peculiarly difficult to isolate and analyse. This would account for the fact (if it is a fact) that Plato was unable to identify the premisses of the Third Man and therefore could not mend the flaw in his theory.

But is it true that the degrees of reality and copy theories imply self-predication? In fact, they imply nothing of the sort.

(a) *The Copy Theory*. Plato characteristically describes particulars as copying or imitating Forms, and this seems to imply that particulars resemble Forms. The proponents of self-predication maintain that it implies still more: that if *F* particulars and the *F* Itself resemble each other, they must do so in virtue of being *F*.

This conclusion is one of almost breathtaking eccentricity. My hands resemble each other in being hands. Do they also resemble the Hand Itself in this respect? Clearly not. For the relation of hands to the Hand is analogous, on Plato's account, to the relation between pictures or reflections of hands and hands. Therefore, if 'the logic of Plato's metaphor' implies that *the* Hand is *a* hand, it also implies that the picture of a hand is a hand; which is absurd.

Pictures of hands are not hands, though they may resemble hands in colour, shape, and so on. We must, then, distinguish between substantial resemblance (to use Aristotelian language) and accidental resemblance, between the resemblance of things of the same sort, and the resemblance of things which are merely similar in quality. And when this is done, the argument for self-predication from the copy theory is exposed for what it is: a muddle. The reason for that muddle is not far to seek. When the self-predicationists discuss imitation, they have a peculiar type in mind: one thing may be used as a model on which to fashion something else of the same kind––a shuttle, say, as a model for shuttles. But it is clear that this is not what Plato had in mind; in fact, he may well have denied that this type of imitation *is* imitation.[10]

But even if it is granted that the resemblance metaphor does not imply self-predication, it continues to generate familiar difficulties; for if we grant even so much as accidental resemblance between particulars and Forms, there will be a sense, though a weak one, in which the absurdity inherent in self-predication will recur.

Resemblance is an indirect relation, that is, a relation which holds only in virtue of some common term: if *x* and *y* resemble each other, they do so in respect of some common character *C*. But if the relation of any *x* to its *C* is one of resemblance— if particulars resemble Forms—two things follow immediately: there will be an infinite regress of Forms, or third terms in relations of resemblance;[11] and Forms (though, to be sure, not strictly self-predicable) will share classes with particulars and by so much be assimilated to their character.

But does Plato's metaphor commit him even to this? The answer, surely, is No. The objection turns on assuming that particulars resemble Forms, and this assumption is false.

Consider the reflection of a red scarf in a mirror—a good example of what Plato understands by an imitation. It is clearly false that the reflection is a scarf. Is it true that it is red? Or is it only the reflection of a red thing?[12]

The reflection is not similar in *kind* to the original. Is it then similar in quality? If we say that it is, we face an evident embarrassment; for to say this is to say that we can predicate of reflections, which are essentially adjectival, in just the way we predicate of

---

[10] Cf. *Cra.*, 389A ff.; *Sph.*, 239D ff. *Ti.*, 28B, appears to entertain this type of imitation as possible. But notice that the hypothesis that the creator could use a generated model in his work implies an infinite regress, though Plato does not explicitly mention this.

[11] This regress could terminate in a *C* which was self-predicable; but then we would only have laid the foundation of a new regress, resting on a different base.

[12] I do not maintain that the analysis of reflection which follows is the only, or perhaps even the correct, analysis. I do maintain that it is consistent and reasonable, and that, as a matter of historical fact, it is presupposed by the Theory of Forms

their originals, things which exist in their own right. Scarves can be bought and sold, lost or stolen, wrapped around the neck in winter; but I would gladly give you every image that has crossed the surface of my mirror, and count myself no poorer for the loss.[13]

The very being of a reflection is relational, wholly dependent upon what is other than itself: the original, and the reflecting medium.[14] It is for this reason that, though you may call the reflection of a red scarf red if you so please, you cannot mean the *same* thing you mean when you call its original red. The function '. . . is red' is, in this case, systematically ambiguous. It follows that you cannot say that the reflection stands in the relation of colour resemblance to its original, since this implies the univocal exemplification of a common quality, presupposed by an assertion of resemblance. The reflection does not *resemble* the original; rather, it is a *resemblance of* the original.[15] This is its nature, and the whole of its nature. 'Resemblances of' are quasi-substantial; relational entities, not relations.[16] They stand to their originals as the dependent to

[13] This argument may be made more precise. We see reflections in the mirror, and we see the mirror in the room. But 'in' here is ambiguous. Mirrors are physical objects which may be located relatively to other physical objects. But we can locate reflections only relatively to the reflecting medium; otherwise, we would be forced to claim that two things, the reflection and the surface of the medium, may be in the same place at the same time. But given this as a lemma, the following argument seems sound; whatever is red is extended; whatever is extended is locatable with respect to any other thing which is extended; mirror images are not so locatable; therefore, they are neither extended nor red. Rather, they are reflections of an extended red thing.

[14] The mirror of the Forms is of course three-dimensional: the Receptacle. Notice that the fundamental distinction between the Aristotelian and Platonic views of space is explained by their differing evaluation of extended entities. For Aristotle the extended is substantial, real in its own right; and therefore it is for him feasible to adopt a relational view of space, with substances as relata. But for Plato extended entities are reflections, images; space, the medium of reflection, is a precondition of their existence, the receptacle in which Forms are mirrored. It is therefore absolute, not a consequence of the mirroring. Cf. *Ti.*, 50D ff.

[15] The 'is' here is, of course, that of identity.

[16] This distinction between resemblance and resemblances, between relations and relational entities, will no doubt seem strange to those whose imaginations are set in the cast of *Principia Mathematica;* but it has a long and honourable history. It has been the root metaphor for most Western degrees-of-reality philosophies which reject the literal inconsistency of the lower orders of being; and medieval exemplarism is unintelligible without it.

the independent, as the less real to the more real. Plato's metaphor of imitation brilliantly expresses a community between different orders of objects, different levels of reality; it does not, as his recent critics have maintained, collapse that order.[17] Their reading of the metaphor can be sustained only by assuming the very thing that must be proved—that Plato viewed imitation as they do.

(b) *Degrees of Reality*. Plato's metaphor of imitation expresses a fundamental thesis of his ontology, that particulars differ from Forms, as resemblances differ from originals, in degree of reality.[18] For particulars 'fall short' of their Forms, and are 'deficient' with respect to them.[19]

In what sense can a particular be deficient with respect to a Form? Only, the proponents of self-predication have urged, by possessing in merely approximate or comparative degree a character that the Form, which *is* the character, *has* fully. But this assimilates the Form categorically to the class of things it defines; it must possess in pre-eminent degree a character which particulars own only deficiently, and it is therefore itself a particular, albeit, no doubt, a perfect one.

If this interpretation is accepted, it is quite fatal. But it turns on construing the deficiency of particulars as one of quality, rather than of type; they are deficiently something else *of the same sort*, as a blind eye is deficiently an eye, or as one shuttle, modelled on another, may be a defective copy. Yet surely the force of the metaphor of imitation, and of the χωρισμός (separation), is to indicate that

---

[17] It will be objected that Plato compares particulars with reflections and pictures indiscriminately; that pictures are not merely resemblances of, but stand in the relation of resemblance to, their originals; and that, therefore, the above interpretation cannot be attributed to Plato. But this objection overlooks the nature of his theory of art. The analogy is drawn, not to the picture *as* a picture, but to the art object— a 'man-made dream for waking eyes'. The picture does not differ in type or degree of reality from its original; it is an artifact, an object of πίστις (opinion); to apprehend it so is to apprehend it *as* a picture; and to be able to compare it, we cannot confuse it with that original. But the artist holds a mirror up to nature; it is essential to apprehending a picture as an art object that we may take it to be, not a resemblance, but the very thing it resembles, as we may mistake a reflection in a mirror for the thing reflected. Viewed as an art object, the picture no longer retains its independent character: it is assimilated to that of a reflection, which is to say that its full meaning is relational, dependent upon the nature of its original.

[18] Cf. *Sph.*, 240A–C; images are not real, but really are images.

[19] *Phd.*, 74D5–7, E1–4, 75A2–3, B4–8.

the deficiency in question is that of one *type* of thing with respect to
something of another type: 'deficiency' is here a category distinction, not a distinction within categories. Particulars are deficient
not because they have the characters they have but because they
are the kind of things they are—because they are qualified by
opposites, because they change, because they are in some degree
unintelligible, because they depend for their existence upon Forms
and are themselves *not* Forms—because, in a word, they are images.
The interpretation of the self-predicationists, though it gains an
initial plausibility by interpreting 'deficiently' in the way most
obvious *to us*, is impossible, for it assumes (and does nothing to
prove) that Forms and particulars are of the same type.[20] But Plato
does not say that they are; and he does say that they are not.[21]

If the foregoing analysis has been sound, the arguments offered
to show that Forms are self-predicable beg the question: in each
case the conclusion is proved only because, implicitly, it has been
assumed.

IV. FORMS AND UNIVERSALS

The case for self-predicability rests, in the final analysis, not on
Plato's apparently self-predicative language, nor on the logic of his
imitation metaphor, nor on supposed systematic presuppositions
of the degrees of reality theory; it rests on a false assumption about
the nature of Forms, imported bodily into his text by his interpreters. It is to the credit of the proponents of self-predication that
they have seen the implications of that assumption far more clearly
than the majority of their critics.

[20] Note the further difficulty that certain Forms define characters
which admit of no logical extreme. There is no largest, or smallest,
possible thing, a fact which Plato, who was familiar with the Zenonian
treatment of infinity, must surely have known. But if the self-predicationists are correct in their interpretation of 'deficiency', Largeness
must be the largest thing possible, Smallness smaller than any small
thing; at this point, the imagination boggles.

[21] It will doubtless be urged that the Good of the *Republic* (and
analogously, the Beauty of the *Symposium*) is 'the best', and better than
any good thing. But the question is whether it is 'better' in the *same*
sense in which one good thing is better than another. Can we compare
things of different ontological status in the way we compare things of
the same ontological status? The answer implied to this question by
Plato's theory of predication, the imitation metaphor, and the degrees
of reality theory, is No; and that answer, as I shall show, is sustained
and made intelligible by Plato's theory of participation.

It is generally agreed that Forms are universals, and in some sense that is surely true: 'One over Many' is the nub of the argument for their existence. In *some* sense, then; but in *what* sense?

On this question, the verdict of recent scholarship has been almost unanimous. The Form is a *commutative* universal, a character or attribute, a nuclear identity capable of instantiation in diverse material contexts, a pure 'what' which in some mysterious way inheres in and qualifies 'thats'. On this commonly accepted view, Platonism differs from other theories of the commutative universal only in that it is realistic and extreme; the universal exists 'alone by itself', independent of any mind and any instantiation. No one need think of it; nothing need have it. Its existence is intrinsic to itself.

Now commutative universals or attributes clearly cannot be identified with standards and paradigms; for the latter are things characterised, not characters; and if there is confusion on this point, self-predication follows immediately. But Forms clearly function in Plato's ontology as standards and paradigms; therefore, if he also thought of them as common characters or attributes, the result is shipwreck.

But did he? I submit that he did not, that this is an assumption of Plato's critics, not of Plato. For consider its consequences.

To begin with, it wrecks dialectic. With the commutative universal, the relation of genus to species is always that of the more abstract to the more concrete: the genus is essentially poorer than its species, having less content, and this diminution continues as one proceeds upward in the abstractive hierarchy, so that the highest genera are most barren of all. But such a view as this clearly cannot provide a ground for the synoptic vision of all time and all existence, or account for the fact that dialectic ends in an unhypothetical first principle, or provide a basis for the deduction of lower from higher which the downward path of dialectic requires.

Second, this assumption destroys the main point of the χωρισμός. It is of course trivially true that attributes and their instantiations are ἕτερα ὄντα, different sorts of things. It may even be true, granted a few assumptions, that attributes are causes of their instantiations, since they are that by which things are what they are; and also true that attributes may exist 'alone by themselves', independently of instantiation. But is it *not* true—though this is at the heart of the χωρισμός—that an attribute may be instantiated imperfectly or in deficient degree. A crooked line is not an imperfect instantiation of straight linearity; on the contrary, it is a full and complete instantiation of the *kind* of crooked line that it is, and the kind is repeatable, though the line itself is not. In general, things exhibit the characters they exhibit and none other; so far as commutative universals are concerned, to say that something is deficient with respect to one character is merely an awkward way of saying that it quite fully has another. But with paradigms and standards, the language of approximation and deficiency makes perfect sense.

This point is related to a further one. Particulars, unlike Forms, are qualified by opposites. We can form no stable conception of them, 'either as being or as not being, or as both being and not being, or as neither'.[22] The plain meaning of this statement, in its context, is that particulars are both *F* and not-*F*, either *F* or not-*F*, and neither *F* nor not-*F*. If Plato understood *F* to be an attribute or commutative universal, then he must have believed that particulars are (quite literally) self-contradictory, and supported that absurdity by arguments which are a fortiori equally absurd; whereas, I suggest (though I will not here attempt to prove), if we interpret the negation here involved as that of deficiency or privation, implied by approximation to an entity which stands on a different level of reality, it is possible to construe this discussion in a way that does not make Plato both a skeptic and a fool.

Instantiations do not pursue, or fall short of, or imitate, attributes; they simply have them or fail to have them. Nor are they of a lower degree of reality. On the contrary, the major objection to extreme realism is that it posits a domain of reality so drained of actuality that it is shadow-thin, a ghostly wraith hovering about the verges of existence, powerless even to gibber.

Forms are not commutative universals.[23] What, then, are they?

---

[22] *R.*, 479C, trans. by F. M. Cornford.

[23] I have not troubled to criticise this view in greater detail simply because it has never, to my knowledge, received explicit defence. At times it is accepted on the basis of an undistributed middle: Forms are clearly universals; by a universal we commonly mean a commutative universal or attribute; therefore, Forms are commutative universals or attributes. But there are hints in the literature of another motive. It seems sometimes to be assumed that every philosophy must (ought to?) hold a theory of commutative universals; therefore Plato must have

A thorough attempt to answer that question would far outrun the limits of this paper. But Plato has provided us with an analogy, and that analogy is worthy of attention. Forms are like originals; particulars are like images or reflections. The comparison is significant.

To begin with, it places the One over the Many; there may be many reflections of a single thing, and those reflections gain their community of character from that thing. Second, the analogy expresses degrees of reality; reflections depend upon their original both for their character and their existence; it depends upon them for neither. Third, the analogy illustrates how particulars may approximate to Forms and yet be categorically distinct: reflections may differ in the degree to which they are true to their original, but no matter how faithful they are to it, they can never become it, for it is of a different order than they. Finally, the analogy helps to make clear in what sense Forms are standards and paradigms; in order to know that anything is a reflection, still more to know of what it is a reflection, one must know its original. But the original, then, is a standard or criterion, by which we judge of images and their degree of adequacy.

The metaphor of resemblance is not, of course, fully adequate. Most notably, it sheds no direct light (unlike the imitation metaphor) on the teleological side of Plato's thought, nor on the question of how the reflection of an unchanging object may be in flux. But it brilliantly conveys features essential to Plato's view of Forms and their relation to particulars; and by appealing to what is close at hand and familiar, it provides us with at least an intuitive grasp of how a Many can be unified by a One which is not a commutative universal. Finally, it suggests that Forms stand to particulars, not as attributes to instantiations, but as exemplars to exemplifications, and that participation, $\mu \acute{\epsilon} \theta \epsilon \xi \iota \varsigma$, is not nearly so mysterious as it has sometimes seemed.

V. PARTICIPATION

The objects of our changing world of sense, though each is different from every other, are in certain fundamental—though

---

held such a theory. I find it odd, in the light of the past five hundred years of philosophy, and especially of the last fifty, that anyone should blithely assume the premiss to be true. But true or false, the conclusion is a *non sequitur*.

varying—respects, the same. In difference we find community of character; in diversity we find unity. How is this to be explained?

The theory of Forms is intended as an answer to this question, and the solution it offers is this. The particular objects of sense are unified by a One which stands on a different level of reality from theirs; their community of character is to be explained by the introduction of Forms. Unity and diversity are reconciled if we posit the existence of two domains, Being and Becoming, a world of particulars, of things unified, and a world of Forms, their unity. To understand the One and the Many, we must understand that the One is *over* the Many.

But if this solves one problem of community, it leads directly to another. In placing the One over the Many, we unify the Many; the next task, clearly, is to unify the Many and the One. The community of particulars is to be explained by the introduction of Forms; but how are we to explain the community of particulars and Forms?

This is the problem of participation: given a diversity of domains, of worlds, to account for their community. It clearly cannot be met by positing a One over the original Many and their One; for this merely supplies us with another Many demanding unification, and with a vicious regress. Being and Becoming must either then be collapsed or infinitely fragmented; but in either case, the problem of community, to which this ontology had addressed itself, remains unsolved.

Paradoxically, we cannot assert that Forms and particulars are related or that they share any common character. For the relation between a Form and a particular must be either a Form or a particular or some third kind of thing. If it is either a Form or a particular, the original question is unanswered, since our problem is to account for the community between Forms and particulars, and that problem cannot be solved by multiplication. But if the putative relation is some other type of thing, a member of some third domain, we must ask what accounts for the community of three domains, not merely of two. Therefore, any attempt to relate Forms and particulars will lead, no matter how that relation is construed, to an infinite regress. It follows that Forms and particulars are not related. But in that case they cannot share common predicates; for if two things share a common predicate they are similar, and similarity is a relation. But here no relation is possible.

Being and Becoming must be distinct and yet together, and their nexus of connection can belong to neither, nor can it be anything distinct. We have here one of the fundamental problems of Plato's ontology. His solution is to be found in the doctrine of degrees of reality.

Particulars and Forms are not merely different types of things; they are types of things which differ in degree of reality, for the one is wholly dependent upon the other. Particulars have no independent ontological status; they are purely relational entities, entities which derive their *whole* character and existence from Forms. Because their being is relational, adjectival, dependent, relations to bind them to Forms are neither possible nor required. To understand the community of Being and Becoming, we need only understand the dependent nature of Becoming.

But this leads to a further difficulty. We must say that particulars are, that they have a kind of existence, though in the same breath we must go on to affirm that they do not have existence in the way that Forms, things which are fully real, do. This is the problem of εἴδωλα (images): images are not real—yet they really are images. We talk about them, predicate of them, and act with respect to them, for they form the substance of our world. But they are wholly dependent upon their transcendent source, and of immensely less reality; and therefore, though we must say that they *are*, we must also say they *are not*.

We cannot say that particulars and Forms exist in the *same* sense, for that is what the degrees of reality theory denies. Can we then assert their existence in a different sense? But if 'existence' is simply ambiguous, if to say that a Form exists and that a particular exists is to say something wholly different about each, then the community which is fundamental to degrees of reality is abandoned, and we are left with a domain which in no proper sense exists at all. We are committed, not only to maintaining *degrees* of reality, but to maintaining degrees of *reality*.

The solution to this difficulty has already been hinted at in our examination of Plato's theory of predication. Particulars are named after Forms because Forms are their causes. To say of anything that it is *F* is to say that it depends for its existence upon *the F*, that in virtue of which *F*-things are *F*. But the *F* is not merely a cause; it is an *exemplary* cause. Particulars not only depend upon it; they are resemblances of it, as reflections are resemblances of their originals.

Like reflections, they differ in type from their originals; they share no common attribute; and yet they exhibit a fundamental community of character. From this analysis it follows·that the names of Forms cannot be applied univocally to Forms and particulars, exemplars and exemplifications; diversity of type implies a distinction between primary and derivative designation. But it also follows that the names of Forms are not simply ambiguous; community of character implies that the meaning of a term in derivative designation is defined in terms of its meaning in primary designation.[24]

It also implies that statements such as 'the *F* is *F*', though their form is that of a mere statement of identity or synonymy, play an important function in explicating the theory of Forms; in asserting that the *F* is *F*, we are asserting, not only that it is the cause of *F*-things, but also the peculiar manner in which it is the cause. It is an exemplary cause and, as such, exhibits a community of character with its exemplifications.

---

[24] There is an interesting type of ambiguity involved here, something intermediate between univocity and full equivocity. Aristotle calls it πρὸς ἕν ambiguity, or equivocity by reference. (Cf. *Metaph.*, 1003A33 ff.; *E. N.* 1096B27; *Topics*, 106A9 ff.; W. D. Ross, *Aristotle's Metaphysics*, vol. I, p. 256; J. Owens, *Doctrine of Being in the Aristotelian Metaphysics*, ch. iii et seq.) It is the peculiar merit of equivocity by reference that it expresses the community of different orders of things without assuming the diverse instantiation of a common universal. It requires no more than some form of the dependence-relation in order to be applicable. It is for this reason that this type of equivocity plays so important a role in Aristotle's *Metaphysics*. First Philosophy or Theology has as its object being qua being, and the characteristics which essentially pertain to it. But to speak of the being of a substance and of an accident is to speak of two very different things. τὸ ὂν λέγεται πολλαχῶς; 'being' is said in many ways. A substance 'is' in the full sense; its being is its own. But the being of an accident is adjectival, attributive, in some sense borrowed from that of the substance to which it belongs. It holds its existence, not in its own right, but by virtue of its relation to what is self-existent; and its being is defined by that relation.

It is important to note what this denies: it denies that being is a genus, that is, a universal or common term. (Cf. *Metaph.*, 1003A 33 ff.; 1053B22; 1045B6; *E. N.*, 1096B27.) Being is not a genus because it can be predicated of everything, whereas a genus cannot be predicated of its differentiae. (See *Metaph.*, 998B23; 1059B31; and Ross, op. cit., ad hoc.) To say that substance and accident both exist is not to say that they share a common character, but that they stand in a certain relation: the one is dependent upon the other. 'Being' is a πρὸς ἕν equivocal; so too are the names of Forms.

VI. THE THIRD MAN

It is easy to show that the regress arguments of the *Parmenides* are powerless against this position. The first (131C–132B) assumes that the Form and its particulars are called by the same name and that that name is applied univocally; the second (132C–133A) assumes that particulars resemble Forms. Both are fallacious. Let 'F_1' be substituted for 'F' when 'F' is used in primary designation, and 'F_2' in derivative designation. Then it is false to say that F-things and the F are called by the same name, equally false to say that they resemble each other either in respect of being F_1 or F_2. These arguments, because they neglect the systematic ambiguity of the names of Forms, are, it would seem, the results of mere confusion—may be viewed, indeed, as *reductiones ad absurdum* of that confusion.[25]

We may go further. The fundamental difficulty underlying the Third Man is ontological, not linguistic. Not only the regress arguments but all of the objections to participation in the *Parmenides* posit an identity of character between Forms and particulars; the Many and the One are to be unified, in effect, by a further One. These arguments demonstrate conclusively that this supposition is absurd.

Yet they point to a difficulty which is crucial in any exemplaristic ontology. For though there can be no identity between exemplars and exemplifications, there must be community of character; and how is this community to be explained? It can be explained by treating exemplifications not as substances in which qualities inhere but as relational entities, entities in which resemblance and dependence so combine as to destroy the possibility of substantiality. Plato's use of the metaphors of imitation and reflection, and his characterisation of particulars and Forms, indirectly indicate that he accepted this solution.

[25] It should be noted that the Third Man does not presuppose the distinction between commutative universals and instances. The argument rests on a categorical or type confusion: it can be generated by confusing exemplars with exemplifications, goals with the things which have them, or standards with the things they measure. This list is not exhaustive.

Orginally published in *The Philosophical Review* LXIX (1960), 147–64. Reprinted by permission of the author and the editor of *Philosophical Review*.

9

PLATO AND THE THIRD MAN

COLIN STRANG

Having been asked to dispense with footnotes I have cut my references to a minimum so as not to clutter up the text. This means that
my indebtedness to others has not been properly acknowledged.
I owe most to Vlastos, Sellars, Geach, Owen, Cross and Plato, and
much to others; the writings I have consulted, though not all are
referred to in the text, are listed in a bibliography at the end.

THE *TMA* AND ITS LOGIC

The TMA, *first version*

"I take it that what makes you believe in unitary Forms [*or*, that
there is one Form in each case] is something like this: (1) whenever
you think 'Here is a plurality of large things', (2) perhaps you
think, as you survey them all, that there is one Form which is the
same [for them all]; (3) whence you conclude that the Large is one
[*or*, that there is one (the) Large].

True.

(4) Then taking the Large itself together with the others, the
large things, (5) when in turn you survey them all, won't there
appear once again a one Large in virtue of which they all appear
large?

Evidently.

(6) Then a second Form of Largeness will have turned up, in
addition to Largeness itself and its participants; (7) and over all
these there will be yet another, in virtue of which all these will be
large; (9) and now you will have on your hands not one Form in
each case (8) but an infinite number of them" (*Parmenides* 132A1–
B2).

I shall not be discussing the second version of the *TMA* (132D1–
133A3) in any detail; although it gives prominence to different
features of the argument, it comes essentially to the same thing.

Formalisation of Version 1

   1. *Let there be several (a set of)* A*'s; call them Set 1.*

OM Given a set of A's, they participate in one and the same $F(A)$.

   2.   By *OM, the* A*'s of Set 1 participate in one and the same* $F(A)$; *call it* $F_1(A)$.

   3.   *There is one and only one* $F(A)$. (The Uniqueness Thesis, *U* for short.)

SP $F_1(A)$ is an A.

NI $F_1(A)$ is not a member of Set 1.

   4.   By *SP* and *NI, the* A*'s of Set 1 together with* $F_1(A)$ *form a new set of* A*'s; call it Set 2.*

   5.   By *OM, the* A*'s of Set 2 participate in one and the same* $F(A)$; *call it* $F_2(A)$.

SP $F_2(A)$ is an A.

NI $F_2(A)$ is not a member of Set 2.

   6.   By *NI*, $F_2(A)$ *is another* $F(A)$ [*i.e.*, it is not identical with $F_1(A)$].

   7.   *Moves* 4–6 *may be repeated again*, and indeed indefinitely.

   8.   *Therefore there are an infinite number of* $F(A)$*'s.*

   9.   *Therefore not-*U.

The numbered and italicised sentences are paraphrases of the corresponding sections of my translation; the rest shows what must be assumed, and where, if the argument is to be formally valid.

The Uniqueness Thesis (U) *and the* reductio ad absurdum

U is no more a premiss to the argument as it stands than a parenthetical remark about the weather would be. It is the contradictory of the conclusion; and since it is one of the less dispensable theses of the theory of Forms, we are to infer that the conclusion cannot be accepted and that one of the premisses must be rejected in consequence. By putting *U* where it really belongs we can begin to expand the argument into a *reductio ad absurdum* and thereby exhibit its real point:

10.   But *U* (*i.e.*, not-not-*U*).

11.   Therefore *either* not-*OM or* not-*SP or* not-*NI*.

For a full expansion we should need to specify which premiss was for rejection, *e.g.*, *SP*, and give it the proper *reductio* prominence:

To prove not-*SP*—suppose *SP*, then if so-and-so then not-*U*; but *U*; therefore not-*SP*, *Q.E.D.* Now version one of the *TMA* nowhere suggests this expansion, since *SP* remains concealed throughout. But version two not only brings it to the surface, in the guise of the Form-particular resemblance thesis, but also gives it the required prominence and the death by *reductio*: "Then it follows that a thing can't be like the Form, nor the Form like something else; otherwise alongside the Form a second Form will turn up, etc." (132E6); "So it is not by likeness that other things participate in the Forms, and some other way of participation will have to be found" (133A5).

The One over Many Thesis (OM)

Two logical points about *OM* need making. The first and most crucial is that the argument relies on nothing stronger than the thesis (weak *OM*) that for any set of *A*'s there is *at least one* F(*A*). Secondly, the thesis (strong *OM*) that for any set of *A*'s there is at least one *and also only one* F(*A*) is not identical with *U*, which says that there is only one F(*A*) *simpliciter*. Not-*OM* (strong) entails, but does not follow from, not-*U* (the *TMA* conclusion); but it does follow from the *TMA* premisses, thus: the *A*'s of Set 1 participate in $F_1(A)$ (by prop. 2); and being also members of Set 2 (by prop. 4) they participate in $F_2(A)$ (by prop. 5); therefore (by prop. 6) they participate in more than one F(*A*), *Q.E.D.* However, the fact that not-*OM* (strong) follows from the *TMA* premisses does not invalidate the argument, since it is only the weak *OM* that is relied on as a premiss.

The next point about *OM* as used by Parmenides in the *TMA* is a tactical one. Had he begun unambiguously with the strong version he might have given the argument a (false) appearance of inconsistency. Had he begun unambiguously with the weak one, the dialogue might have run like this:

Parm.   Your reason for holding *U* is that there is at least one F(*A*) over a set of *A*'s, isn't that right?

Soc.   No, No! How could it be? *Only one* F(*A*).

Parm.   Very well, then: at least one and also only one.

Soc.   If you like.

Parm.   Then what I shall show is that if there is at least one there cannot be only one.

What is here gained in logical clarity is lost in elegance and conciseness. As it is, Parmenides formulates *OM* ambiguously and so contrives to extract from young Socrates an admission which is at once the target of his attack and one of the premises from which his attack is launched. Socrates, for whom Set 1 of *A*'s is the only set and $F_1(A)$ the only $F(A)$, is thus easily led from *OM* as applied to Set 1 (prop. 2) to *U*(prop. 3); indeed, since he takes *OM* in the strong sense, the two propositions are for him equivalent.

However, *OM* as given by Parmenides need not be so taken. My wife and I share one and the same house, but we also share a cottage, one and the same cottage. Peter and Paul are co-heirs in virtue of being heirs of one and the same man, James; but they, and possibly James as well, may also be co-heirs of John, one and the same man, but another man. I take *mia tis . . . hē autē* to have the same force as "one and the same" in these contexts.

THE *TMA* AND ITS CONSEQUENCES

I take my formalisation of the *TMA* to represent what Plato intended. It seems obvious to me that it relies on the Self-Predication Assumption (*SP*) and the Non-Identity Assumption (*NI*), and that Plato knew perfectly well that it did. To the objection that if this is so it is odd that scholars have only recently spotted these assumptions the reply is that until recently Plato has greatly excelled his commentators in logical acumen.[1] And it would take someone his equal in logical acumen to convince me that the *TMA* is invalid. It has been said that the *TMA* is "a record of honest perplexity" (Vlastos, *A*, p. 343). I cannot see that Plato was at all perplexed, unless it was over the decision as to which of the premises was to be jettisoned; and I doubt whether he remained perplexed for very long even about this.

Self-Predication, Paradigmatism and the Standard Yard

I take it for granted that the Self-Predication Assumption, that $F(A)$ is A, is presupposed by the central theses of Plato's middle-

Originally published in *Aristotelian Society Supplementary Volume* XXXVII (1963) 147–64. Reprinted by permission of the author. For an explanation of references see bibliography, p. 199.

[1] In any case, Aristotle spotted them; Alexander in *Metaph.*, 84, 27ff., following the *Peri Ideon*, reads "If the man which is predicated is other than the men of which it is predicated . . . . and if man is predicated both of the particulars and of the idea, there will be a third man over and above the particulars and the idea."

period paradigmatic theory: the theses (1) that the relation of particular to Form is that of copy to original, and (2) that knowledge of Forms, and in particular of timeless truths about Forms, is acquired in this life by recollection of what was already known by the discarnate soul before birth. (2) presupposes a consequence of (1), namely that Form and particular resemble each other (1a); and (1a) entails, or is equivalent to, *SP*. Therefore if *SP* goes the paradigmatic theory collapses. That Plato was aware of presupposing *SP* is shown by a number of by now familiar passages, especially *Phaedo* 103E3–5: "Not only is the Form itself for ever entitled to its own name, but so is something else entitled to the Form's name which is not the Form but always has the Form's *morphē* (character) so long as it exists."

Geach has fruitfully compared Plato's conception of the paradigmatic Form with the Standard Pound. I shall pursue this comparison further, taking the Standard Yard as my example; and what a close investigation of the Standard Yard should reveal is just what is wrong with the Form as paradigm, and why this defect should lie so well concealed. The facts on which I rely, and my quotations, are drawn from *Mass, Length and Time* by Norman Feather, F.R.S.

The Weights and Measures Act of 1824 constituted as the legal British standard yard a standard made in 1760 by John Bird. This was damaged in 1834, and the commission set up to replace it decided to reconstruct the damaged standard as accurately as possible in terms of its certified copies. They thereby ignored the provisions of the 1824 Act that restoration should be in terms of the length of the pendulum which, swinging in a vacuum in the latitude of London, should have a periodic time of two mean solar seconds exactly. (Compare *Cratylus* 389B: "And now suppose he breaks the shuttle he is making: will he look to the broken one when making the replacement, or will he look to the same Form he looked to when making the one that broke?")

The work was done in 1844/45. "Five bronze bars were machined as nearly as possible alike . . . one of the five bars was chosen as the 'imperial' standard and the other four were designated 'parliamentary' copies. Use of the new standard was legalised by the Weights and Measures Act, 1856, and a precise definition of the unit, the Imperial Standard Yard, was given by the Act of 1878, of the same title. According to this Act, unit length is the distance between the axes of the central grooves on the two gold plugs, when the temperature of the bronze bar is 62°F and it is supported horizontally on eight interconnected rollers so arranged (at intervals of 4.78 in.) as to bear equally the weight of the bar" (p. 12).

Is the standard unchanging? Bronze bars vary in length with temperature. Still, isn't it true that (to adapt Geach's dictum, p. 81) the standard yard is a yard long whatever its length? No, it is not a yard long at 32°F, nor if only supported at its ends, nor if it becomes twisted or bent. In fact it is only a yard long if it satisfies the conditions, both explicit and implied, specified by the definition of unit length given in the Act. Since it is never possible to say categorically that these conditions are exactly fulfilled, it follows that the standard bar can never be known to be exactly a yard long, even by definition. (But it is certainly as much entitled, if not more so, to the description "a yard long" as any other object which may be measured against it, and in the same sense. What is predicated of the standard and its copies is predicated of them unequivocally. This was normal Academic doctrine (see Owen, *B*, pp. 104–5), and in this respect the paradigmatic theory was not in error.)

So the standard bar, not being unchanging, is an unpromising candidate for Formhood (though I shall be reconsidering it). A far likelier candidate is suggested by the 1878 Act, namely the unit length it defines, the Imperial Standard Yard (I.S.Y.), not to be confused with (though often not distinguished from) the standard bar in terms of which it is defined. The I.S.Y. is not liable to change in the ways I have mentioned. Also it is invisible. Nor can it be said itself to have a length: it *is* the length the standard bar *has* under the conditions specified. But if we make the I.S.Y. the Form, paradigmatism collapses; for neither the standard bar nor anything else is a copy of it or resembles it in any way. And the makers of the bar never 'looked to' the I.S.Y., as defined, when making it, since the I.S.Y. was not defined until thirty years later. It is only when copies of the standard bar are made that the I.S.Y. is 'looked to'; but it is the standard bar, also 'looked to', which is the paradigm. The attempt to turn the I.S.Y. itself into a paradigm, a kind of invisible analogue of the standard bar, is what invites the *TMA*.

But even the I.S.Y. would hardly satisfy a Plato who had dropped paradigmatism and retained the rest. For (1) it is man-made, coming into existence at a particular time and always liable to redefinition. And (2) it is liable to change in another rather odd way. Bronze bars tend to contract slightly during the first few decades after fabrication: "the standard yard ... shortened by some 200 millionths of an inch after the standard was made legal in 1856" (p. 17). If the standard bar shortened, the I.S.Y. changed (though hardly in length, or at any rate not the kind of length predicable of a bar, for though the unit 'yard' is shorter than the unit 'metre' it is not shorter than any bar; in fact length is predicated of unit and bar equivocally, which is as much as to say that the former is not a paradigm of the latter). But I do not think these two features of the I.S.Y. spoil the analogy between it and the non-paradigmatic Form. Of the kinds of Form Plato had particularly in mind some were not subject to alteration in this kind of way, *e.g.*, the mathematical ones; while if others might on a Protagorean type of view be thought of as changeable, *e.g.*, justice, it was part of Plato's absolutist doctrine that they were not, simply.

Is the standard unique? The 1878 Act might have designated as standards all the five bars made, since when made they were all indistinguishable in length. The only embarrassment would have been ambiguity of the definition had they later become distinguishable. Provided this danger can be ruled out there is nothing logically suspect in a multiplicity of standards. Unit length might be defined in terms of the wave-length of sodium light; and its infinite instances, deemed to be identical at all times and places, would be the standards. "If a method of using them for the definition of our units of measurement can be found, the problem of accurate copying of arbitrary standards will in principle no longer arise; nature will have provided completely interchangeable natural standards in over-abundance" (p. 27).

Earthly standards may be multiple in another way also: there may be hierarchies of derivative standards, *e.g.*, from the 'imperial' standard down to the wooden ruler and the cheap steel tape.

If more than one, why not less than one? For the purpose of making things a yard long it is not in fact necessary for there to be any paradigmatic standard at all. Though it would be inconvenient, one could work directly from a definition of the yard in terms of, *e.g.*, periodic time of swing—and I shall call a definition of this kind an Analytical or A-*logos*. The *logos* defining the I.S.Y. in the 1878 Act was not of this kind, since it defined the I.S.Y. in terms of a standard object—and I shall call a definition of this kind a Paradigmatic or P-*logos*. (Of course any object satisfying an

A-*logos* may be treated as a paradigm; it would have to be designated as such by means of a *derivative* P-*logos*, and so long as the designated object continued to satisfy the A-*logos* the two *logoi* would remain materially equivalent.)

Is the standard visible? It is. But of course the whole point of comparing standard bar and paradigmatic Form is to treat the latter as an invisible analogue of the former.

Because the Form is invisible and an object of thought only, one can safely invest it with any consistent set of properties one chooses, unrestricted by any considerations of empirical fact. (Some scholars appear to think that the Forms, *qua* objects of thought, are entitled to an *inconsistent* set of properties, any awkward property being predicated of them metaphorically.) Plato gave them stability and uniqueness. But although the analogy with the standard bar is thereby weakened it can still throw light on the *TMA*. For the *TMA* nowhere concerns itself with stability or invisibility, but only with uniqueness and the property of being a paradigm; and just as the *TMA* shows that Forms cannot have both these properties, so an analogous argument will show that standards cannot either:

> If there are standards, and if *all* standards are paradigms, there must be an infinite number of them. For there will be a standard which is a yard long, and it will be so either in virtue of a higher standard which is also a yard long or in virtue of something else which is not. It is easily seen that there is *either* an infinite regress of standards a yard long *or* there is a standard which is not a yard long. But not the former; therefore the latter, and this will be the (unique) standard proper.

This argument does not exclude the possibility that the standard proper may co-exist with a finite number of paradigmatic standards.

The standard proper, which is not a yard long, may be thought of either as the unit length or as the *logos* specifying unit length (standards of the latter kind are to be found in the publications of the British Standards Institution). It seems clear enough that without a *logos* specifying unit length no object can have unit length and *a fortiori* no object can be a standard of unit length, *i.e.*, a paradigm. Note that my argument began "If there are standards". There need not be any. The *OM* may be taken as asserting that there are.

I have been at pains to distinguish between unit length and the bronze bar. If they are both called 'The Imperial Standard Yard' it is easy to confuse them and to think that there is something which is *both* the unique, invisible and unchanging length which things a yard long have *and* exactly a yard long, all other things a yard long being copies or reproductions of it. (Notice that the 'is' before 'both' is called on to do duty both as the 'is' of identity and as the 'is' of predication; the *esti* in the phrase *ho esti X* also has this dual function.) Feather shows that he misses the distinction when he says "it is necessary to define an arbitrary length which can be accurately reproduced" (p. 19), and "a natural standard would be one which . . . occurs in nature lavishly reproduced in a multitude of exact copies" (p. 27). Plato was particularly liable to miss it since his paradigms, unlike Feather's, were themselves unique, invisible and unchanging; and the argument of his which I go on to consider in the following section is a symptom of this confusion.

The Uniqueness Thesis and the Third Bed Argument

Would he have been willing to sacrifice the Uniqueness Thesis? Apart from the fact that it is still being insisted on in the *Philebus* (15A, B) he had already explicitly supported it with a puzzling argument in the *Republic* (597C), which we may call the Third Bed Argument (*TBA*). This runs as follows:

> Whether from choice or because some necessity was upon him not to make more than one bed in nature, the fact remains that God made only one, that one Which is Bed (*ho esti klinē*); two such, or more, never did nor ever will come from the hand of God. For if He were to make as many as two a further one would crop up *whose form* (*eidos*) *they, in turn, would both have;* and this one, and not those two, would be What is Bed. I take it God saw this, and since he wanted to really be maker of Really Being Bed, not a maker among others of beds among others, he produced one only in nature.

(The two proposed Forms are the First and Second Beds; the one that supervenes is the Third Bed.) The argument is in the form of a *reductio ad absurdum:* There cannot be two Forms; for suppose there were two, they would not be Forms at all, but something else would be the Form. It relies clearly enough on the weak version of *OM:* the first two Beds, simply *qua* a plurality, require a further Bed above them. But why are we obliged to deny that the first two Beds are Forms? The only reason offered is that they both have the *eidos* of the Third Bed. The assumption behind this must be that anything which has the *eidos* of *A* cannot itself be the Form of *A;* and it follows from this that F(*A*) cannot itself be *A*. So it appears that one of the premisses of the *TBA* is the denial of Self-Predication.

· Cherniss (*B*, pp. 259–60) properly emphasises this point; and if this were all there was to be found in the passage he would be entitled to see it as a clear enunciation of the doctrine that the Form *is*, but does not also have, what other things *have* as a character. Now whereas this doctrine is certainly adopted in the *Parmenides* (see 158A, which Cherniss quotes) and maintained thereafter, it is far from being single-mindedly asserted here. The context of the *TBA* is thoroughly paradigmatic: the products of the painter, the carpenter and God are called straightforwardly 'three beds' (597B5) and 'three kinds (*eide*) of beds' (B14); and the carpenter is said to work with his eye on the Form (596B7) in the usual way (B6).

If the denial of *SP* is a premiss of the *TBA*, then the Form's uniqueness depends precisely upon its *not* being a paradigm. Now it would be reasonable to assert the Form's uniqueness on these terms; for while any substance can be readily enough duplicated in thought (*e.g.*, the two Cratyluses), it seems impossible to do the same for a character or predicate—which seems to be Aristotle's point (*Metaph.* 1038B34) that it is the Form's status as substance that makes it vulnerable to the *TMA*. If, as I think, Plato failed to see, or glimpsed only momentarily, the point of his own argument, then one cannot quote it, as Cherniss does, to show that he had a clear insight into the fallacy of the *TMA*. On the contrary, this passage is itself ripe for the *TMA* treatment, for it sees the Form at once as a character which things have and as a paradigm of that character.

The Non-Identity Assumption

The *NI*, as Vlastos formulates it, is inconsistent with *SP;* but this is surely an odd way of writing in an assumption. In my own version *NI* appears only in its special application to each stage of the regress. Generalised, it would read "$F_n(A)$ is not a member of Set *n*", or in words "The Form over any set is not a member of that set". It follows from this that no F(*A*) is over itself and *a fortiori* that no F(*A*) is *A* in virtue of being over itself. But since any F(*A*) is *A* it must be so in virtue of some other F(*A*)—whence the regress.

Since in the heyday of the paradigmatic theory Plato had in mind Set 1 as the only set and $F_1(A)$ as the only Form, the *NI* would have meant for him only that the Form, $F_1(A)$, was not over itself. The *OM* thesis seems to me to be as clear a statement of this as could be expected from one for whom the question had not yet arisen. When he later came to realise that $F(A)$'s being A invited the *TMA*, it was open to him to save his theory by denying *NI*. His single $F(A)$ would then have been an A, the paradigmatic A, either (i) in virtue of being over itself or (ii) not in virtue of anything.

Against option (i) I offer the following argument. If particular A's are A by participation in $F(A)$ *only because* $F(A)$ *is itself an* A, then by analogy $F(A)$ will be an A by participation in itself only because it itself is already an A: and this is circular. On the other hand, if the thesis that particular A's are A's by participation in $F(A)$ and the thesis that $F(A)$ is itself an A are independent of each other, so that the former could hold even if the latter did not, then paradigmatism collapses. For since the particular A's are already A's in virtue of something other than resemblance to $F(A)$, A-ness cannot be conferred on them by $F(A)$ *qua* paradigm. The force of this argument comes out more clearly if it is reconstructed in terms of the standard bar being a yard long in virtue of itself as paradigm.

Against option (ii) I can only say that if the A-ness of particular A's is in need of explanation, then the A-ness of $F(A)$ needs it too. A bronze bar, whether a standard or not, is a yard long in virtue of *something:* either of a standard bar (which is not itself) or of a *logos*-standard, *i.e.*, ultimately of a *logos*-standard.

These objections to (i) and (ii) may be thought either to lack cogency or to be too tortuous to have suggested themselves to Plato. It may be thought that they are both simple devices for saving the paradigm theory of Forms. However that may be, I am inclined to think that by the time of the *Parmenides* Plato did not see in this theory much that was, from an epistemological point of view, worth saving. The rest of my paper is an elaboration of this point.

THE COMING TO BE AND PASSING AWAY OF A PARADIGM

Dispute and Agreement

The *OM* is, if anything, a logical reason for generating Forms; but it has no tendency to generate them as paradigms. Plato's motive for postulating paradigmatic Forms was epistemological. They offered a neat solution to a problem which is never far below the surface throughout the dialogues and is frequently hauled up for display and study. The problem is the intractability of the sorts of question raised in the Socratic dialogues as compared with other sorts of question. The things (or terms or concepts—it doesn't matter which for the moment) these questions are about are disputed (I shall call them *D*-things); others, by contrast, are agreed or straightforward (I shall call them *S*-things).

Alcibiades I (111B ff.) distinguishes between *D*-things such as justice and injustice, those *S*-things on which the relevant experts agree, such as arithmetic, spelling and health, and those *S*-things on which all those who speak the same language agree, such as sticks, stones, men and horses. The *Euthyphro* (7B–D) distinguishes between disputes (about *S*-things) which can be resolved by counting, measuring or weighing, and disputes about just, unjust, beautiful, ugly, good and bad (*D*-things) which cannot be resolved in any such way. The *Phaedrus* (263A–C) distinguishes the *amphisbētēsima* (the Greek for *D*-things), which include justice, goodness and love, from the things we are all in one mind about (*S*-things), such as iron and silver. The *Republic* (523–4) distinguishes between those things (*S*-things) on which the unaided senses can adjudicate without trouble, *e.g.*, fingers, and those things (*D*-things) which invite the scrutiny of, and puzzle, the intellect, *e.g.*, large, small, hard, soft, thick, thin, heavy, light, one, many. The *Statesman* (285D ff.) distinguishes between those things (*S*-things) which have easily recognisable 'sensible images' and the most important things (*D*-things), which have none.

The *Euthyphro* (6E) says, what is obvious, that the reason for asking the Socratic question 'What is *X*-ness?' is that the answer will provide a criterion for deciding what things are or are not *X*. In other words it would turn a *D*-thing into an *S*-thing. The reason why philosophers do not ask this question about *S*-things is two-fold: first, such things have 'sensible images' so that we can learn what they are ostensively, as the *Statesman* points out; and secondly, it is not specially difficult to answer the question and so provide an agreed *logos*. (The *Meno* gives specimen definitions of figure and colour (74B ff.), the *Theaetetus* of mud and a couple of mathematical terms (147C ff.), the *Statesman* of weaving (279B ff.), the *Sophist* of angling (219A ff.), and there are others.) The procedure involves a survey of undisputed examples of the thing to be defined. But any attempt to define *D*-things in this way is blocked at the start, since what is in dispute is, precisely, what is or is not an example of the thing to be defined; in the absence of 'sensible images', the *Statesman* says, we must show what the thing is in a *logos* unaided by any of the senses (285E4 ff.)

What an *S*-thing is can be shown as well as stated. But even showing it will involve saying something, so that the thing will have two distinct *logoi*: a Paradigmatic or *P-logos* of the form 'A thing is an *X* if and only if it is like this and this', and an Analytical or *A-logos* of the form 'A thing is an *X* if and only if it is a *Y*' or '*X*-ness is *Y*-ness'. (To repeat something I said earlier, the two *logoi* will be materially equivalent on condition that the standard object or objects referred to in the *P-logos* satisfy the *A-logos*.)

With regard to *D*-things, the position at the end of the first act (the Socratic dialogues) is that *P-logoi* are not available and agreed *A-logoi* have proved impossible to catch. This lack of sign-posts to the truth would be no embarrassment to Protagoras, since it is a direct consequence of his key doctrine. But for Plato it was a very serious embarrassment indeed, calling for desperate measures. For one thing, he had passionately held convictions on ethical matters; for another, he thought they were not merely true for him but objectively true, which adds up to a claim to knowledge; and finally, he never seems to have abandoned the principle that a claim to knowledge must be backed by a *logos*.

When the curtain rises on the *Phaedo* we see at once that the insignificant *eidos* or *idea* of the first act has been promoted to the rôle of protagonist and given the task of rescuing Plato from his dilemma. The plot is ingenious: the *eidos* is dressed up as the paradigm to be named in a special kind of *P-logos*: 'A thing is an *X* if and only if it resembles the Form *X*'. Then provided one has some sort of access to the Form, the *logos* will serve as the required criterion. A claim that something is just can be backed by the statement that it resembles the Form of Justice. Access to the Form is by recollection, otherwise one would not recognise it for what it was when one 'saw' it (to borrow an argument from *Meno* 80D5 ff.).

The terminology, but not the thought, of the paradigmatic theory is already familiar from *Euthyphro* 6E: 'Tell me what the *idea* is so that by looking to it and using it as a *paradeigma* I may be able to pronounce as holy any act . . . which is of that kind (*toiouton*).' To be told what the *idea* is here means being given an *A-logos* of it

('Holiness is *X*-ness'); and it is clearly the *idea* as defined, *i.e.*, the whole *logos* or its predicate, that we look to as *paradeigma* and that enables us to identify as holy anything which is *X* (*toiouton*). (This passage alone should make us cautious of supposing that the paradigmatic language of *Statesman* 285D–6A is to be taken at its face value, as Cherniss (*B*, p. 248) takes it.)

Disputes and Relatives

The line of argument developed in the last section generates Forms of *D*-things only, not of *S*-things. One of the 'more exact' Academic arguments for the Forms, alluded to by Aristotle in the *Metaphysics* (990B15–17) and extracted by Alexander from the *Peri Ideōn*, is also selective in this way, being an argument for Forms specifically of relatives (*tōn pros ti*). The argument itself, its interpretation and its sources in the dialogues have been exhaustively discussed by Owen (*B*), and I refer readers to his article for the details. 'Relatives' here is used in a wide sense to cover all predicates which require completion if they are to be applied unambiguously to things in this world: large *for* a *W*, equal *to X*, good *for Y*, unjust *to Z*. Non-relatives like 'man' and 'mud' are predicable without qualification, so that paradigm-cases of their application are to be met with in abundance here below.

Now with some minor exceptions which need not concern us, the classes of *D*-things and *S*-things coincide with those of relatives and non-relatives respectively. And the reason why relative predicates should give rise to disputes is not far to seek. What is good for *X* is bad for *Y*: and quite generally, in things of this world relatives are always found in company with their opposites (Plato, *passim*). But if 'good for *X*' and 'bad for *Y*' are not contradictories, as Plato was well aware (*R.* 436B–7A), whence the dispute? First, most people do not realise that these terms *are* relatives; and secondly, even those who do realise it often find it necessary to argue from 'good for *X*' to 'good' *simpliciter* since 'good for *X*' is often not a sufficient reason for choice or action. (This holds of relatives generally, *e.g.*, "This *X* is heavier than most *X*'s, so it is heavy, so I mustn't carry it, because I was told not to carry heavy things.") It is in fact about the (improper) unqualified predication of relatives to things in this world that men dispute most violently. Plato thought that if there were one thing to which a relative predicate really and truly and properly applied without qualification (and hence to which the opposite predicate never applied, however qualified), then there would be one indisputable instantiation of the predicate in question to which reference could be made for the resolution of disputes and the extraction of *A-logoi:* this was the paradigmatic Form, and reference to it was by recollection.

Recollection versus *Dialectic*

The *TMA* may seem too remote and formal a reason for abandoning "one of the richest and boldest metaphysical theories ever invented in Western thought" (Vlastos, *A*, p. 334): a little inconsistency would be a small price to pay for retaining it. But the inconsistency of paradigmatism was, taken by itself, the least of its defects; what Plato had finally to face up to was a consequence of its inconsistency, namely its epistemological sterility.

In the interval between the second act and the third, which begins with the *Parmenides*, the paradigmatic *eidos* and its brother, recollection, have been unmasked as impostors and quietly buried. The *TMA* is offered by way of justifying the action taken as technically correct. I shall now enlarge on what I have already suggested as the real reason behind it. The *Symposium* and *Phaedrus* have splendid things to say about beauty, but unlike the *Hippias* they do not begin to tell us what it is or is not. What paradigmatism has to tell us about any one Form, *e.g.*, justice, differs hardly at all from what it has to tell us about any other, *e.g.*, mud. Even the *Phaedo* concedes the simple naivety of the theory (100D4). If it is its richness and boldness that attract readers of Plato in the first instance, it is this essential simplicity that leads them to cling to it, on Plato's behalf as well as their own, in face of the more troublesome offerings of the later dialogues. Doing dialectic for your knowledge looks far more arduous than simply recollecting.

To say this is not to be unfair to the recollection theory. A participant in a definition hunt whose soul had in its divine journey seen the Form of the definiendum and who now suddenly recollects what it then saw (like a dish aerial catching and holding a satellite), if he were to break in with the cry "I've got it, I see it and it's lovely, but I can't tell you anything about it" or "A thing is *X* if and only if it resembles the Form I now see" (*P-logos*), would rightly be silenced for irrelevance. And even if he were able, on the strength of his vision, to produce an *A-logos*, it would be as critically examined as any other hypothesis and remain a candidate for rejection for all the clarity he claimed for his recollection. To say with Gulley (p. 44) that "recollection affords that recognition of truth which will guide the steps of analysis and ensure the correctness of its results", or with Cherniss (*A*, p. 47) that "*diaeresis* appears to be only an aid to reminiscence of the idea", is, if anything, to put the cart before the horse.

In the *Phaedrus* (249B6–C4) Plato identifies recollection with dialectic, but this is a passage chiefly about recollection and hardly at all about dialectic. Thereafter when he is doing or talking about dialectic or anything else Plato says no more about recollection, for which his admirers may be thankful. For to identify the two is to behave like the man who builds a wireless set, saying at each step exactly what he is doing and why, and then adds by way of explanation, "Of course, I do it all by magic" or "What I am doing *is* magic" or "Technology is magic".

The more you become aware of, and enthralled by, the peculiar anatomy of individual Forms, the fewer and the less important become the things that can be said about Forms in general. They remain unchanging (*Prm.* 135C1), if only to be the subject matter of timeless truths; they remain single (*Phlb.* 14E5 ff.); but what they do not remain is paradigms.

BIBLIOGRAPHY

R. S. Bluck: "Forms as Standards", *Phronesis* II, 2 (1957).

H. Cherniss: *A, Aristotle's Criticism of Plato and the Academy* (Baltimore, 1944).

——*B*, "The Relation of the *Timaeus* to Plato's Later Dialogues", *American Journal of Philology* LXXVIII, 3 (1957).

R. C. Cross: "*Logos* and Forms in Plato", *Mind*, October 1954.

N. Feather: *Mass, Length and Time* (Edinburgh, 1959 and Penguin Books, 1961).

P. T. Geach: "The Third Man Again", *Philosophical Review* LXV, January 1956.

N. Gulley: *Plato's Theory of Knowledge* (London, 1962).

G. E. L. Owen: *A*, "The Place of the *Timaeus* in Plato's Dialogues", *Classical Quarterly* N.S., 3 (1953).

——*B*, "A Proof in the *Peri Ideon*", *Journal of Hellenic Studies* LXXVII (1957).

W. Sellars: "Vlastos and the Third Man", *P.R.* LXIV, July 1955.

G. Vlastos: *A*, "The Third Man Argument in the *Parmenides*", *P.R.* LXIII, July 1954.

———*B*, "Addenda to the Third Man Argument: a Reply to Mr. Sellars", *P.R.* LXIV, July 1955.

———*C*, "Postscript to the Third Man Argument: a Reply to Mr. Geach", *P.R.* LXV, January 1956.

Originally published *Proceedings of the Aristotelian Society*, Supplementary Volume No. 37 (1963), pp. 147–64.
Reprinted by permission of the author and the Aristotelian Society.

10

ΣΥΜΠΛΟΚΗ ΕΙΔΩΝ

J. L. ACKRILL

It is the purpose of this short paper[1] to consider the meaning and implications of a sentence in Plato's *Sophist*. At the end of the section on κοινωνία γενῶν (the combination of kinds) the Eleatic visitor is made to speak as follows (259E4–6): τελεωτάτη πάντων λόγων ἐστὶν ἀφάνισις τὸ διαλύειν ἕκαστον ἀπὸ πάντων, διὰ γὰρ τὴν ἀλλήλων τῶν εἰδῶν συμπλοκὴν ὁ λόγος γέγονεν ἡμῖν (the isolation of everything from everything else is the total annihilation of all statements; for it is because of the interweaving of Forms with one another that we come to have discourse). I shall be mainly concerned with the second half of this remark, and shall refer to it, for brevity, as sentence or statement S.

Cornford (in *Plato's Theory of Knowledge*) translates sentence S thus: 'any discourse we can have owes its existence to the weaving together of Forms' (p. 300). In his commentary he writes: 'All discourse depends on the "weaving together of Forms." . . . It is not meant that Forms are the only elements in the meaning of all discourse. We can also make statements about individual things. But it is true that every such statement must contain at least one Form.' A few lines later Cornford says that the point made by Plato in S is 'that every statement or judgement involves the use of at least one Form'; and later (p. 314) he remarks that Plato 'has said that "all discourse depends on the weaving together of Forms," *i.e.* at least one Form enters into the meaning of any statement'.

Cornford seems to take it for granted that Plato is saying something about Forms being 'contained in' or 'used in' statements. But he notices that not every statement does 'contain' a plurality of Forms—Plato's own examples a few pages later, the statements about Theaetetus, do not do so. So, to avoid attributing to Plato an

[1] This is a shortened version of a paper read to a colloquium at the Classical Institute on March 14, 1955. The paper was designed to provoke discussion: this fact may help to excuse some oversimplification and some overstatement.

obvious howler, he construes S as meaning not that every statement
uses or contains or is about a συμπλοκή εἰδῶν (interweaving of
Forms) but that it necessarily contains at least one Form. But this of
course is just what τὴν τῶν εἰδῶν συμπλοκήν does not mean, as is
particularly evident when we take account of the word ἀλλήλων
(one another), which Cornford omits in his translation. 'Discourse
depends on the weaving together of Forms *with one another.*' Who
could suppose that this meant merely that at least one Form enters
into the meaning of any statement? *If* S says something about
Forms being contained in any *logos*, then what it says must be that
a συμπλοκή εἰδῶν is contained in any *logos*. If this last is evidently
false, as shown by Plato's examples a moment later, we must question the assumption that S does say something about Forms being
contained in *logoi*.

It is worth noticing briefly how Ross (in *Plato's Theory of Ideas*,
p. 115) deals with our passage. The Eleatic visitor, he says, asserts
'that all discourse depends on the weaving together of Forms by the
speaker or thinker. This is in fact an over-statement, since a
sentence may have a proper name for subject, and a proper name
does not stand for a Form or universal. But the *predicate* of a sentence
normally stands for a Form, and all subjects of statements except
proper names stand either for Forms or for things described by
means of Forms.' Ross does not pretend that S is true; he takes it to
mean that every statement involves at least two Forms and shows
this to be false. But notice how he proceeds. He does not say: since
on our interpretation of S it is blatantly false perhaps our interpretation is wrong. Instead Ross glosses over the falsity of S (on his
interpretation) by calling it an overstatement. But of course Plato is
claiming to say something true of *all logoi* (259E4, 260A9). So S, on
Ross's interpretation, is just false, and glaringly false. Misleading
smoothness shows itself again a moment later: talking of the examples 'Theaetetus is sitting', 'Theaetetus is flying', Ross says not
that they refute S (on his interpretation of S) but that they 'do not
illustrate Plato's thesis'. If I asserted, rather solemnly, that all
philosophers are good-tempered, and immediately went on to chat
about the bad-tempered philosophers I know, you would hardly
say that my examples were 'not illustrating my thesis'.

Surely then something has gone wrong with the interpretation
of S. Surely it must not be understood in such a way that the statements about Theaetetus are clear refutations of it. Surely it must

not be taken to imply that every statement asserts or is about a relation between Forms (or even 'things described by means of Forms'). How then is it to be understood?

Let us look back at what Plato has said before about the συμπλοκὴ εἰδῶν; not at the section in which he investigated connections among various chosen Forms—this is, comparatively, a matter of detail—but at the passage 251D–252E, which seeks to show that there *must be* a συμπλοκὴ εἰδῶν. Statement S says something about the necessity of συμπλοκὴ εἰδῶν for all *logoi:* it is reasonable to try to elucidate this by considering the arguments by which in the first place Plato sought to demonstrate that there must be such a συμπλοκή.

Plato lists, in this earlier passage, three possibilities: (1) that every Form combines with every other, (2) that no Form combines with any other; (3) that while some pairs of Forms do, others do not, combine with one another. By ruling out the first two possibilities he establishes the third; and it is this limited intercommunion of Forms that is subsequently spoken of as the συμπλοκὴ εἰδῶν. The argument for this last consists in effect of the arguments which disprove the other two possibilities.

The first possibility is ruled out on the ground that if it were true such statements as κίνησις ἵσταται (motion rests) would follow. These we can see to be self-contradictory, logically impossible— ταῖς μεγίσταις ἀνάγκαις ἀδύνατον (to the last degree impossible). So if they are entailed by (1) then (1) must be false. To generalise: if a statement in which A is asserted of B is self-contradictory, logically impossible, then it follows that Form A does not combine with Form B. Since we are trying to understand what Plato means by his talk of 'combination' there can be no question of challenging the validity of his argument here; we have to take the argument as a clue to what 'combination' means. What emerges so far is that some restriction on the intercommunion of Forms is implied by the fact that some sentences express statements which are self-contradictory.

Plato's refutation of the second possibility—μηδεμία σύμμειξις (no intermixture)—has two parts. Firstly, if this were true all the theories put forward by philosophers about reality, change, the constitution and behaviour of the world, would be null and void. Pluralists, monists, Eleatics, Heracliteans, all of them λέγοιεν ἂν οὐδέν, εἴπερ μηδεμία ἔστι σύμμειξις (would be saying nothing, if there were no intermixture). Secondly, the very statement of (2) involves a contradiction. Its exponents, in stating it, must combine words into sentences—συνάπτειν ἐν τοῖς λόγοις—and in so doing they contradict their own thesis. It does not need others to refute them: οἴκοθεν τὸν πολέμιον καὶ ἐναντιωσόμενον ἔχουσιν (they will be opposed by a foe within their own household).

Taking this point first, we must notice exactly how the exponents of (2) are refuted out of their own mouths. It is not of course that they straightforwardly both assert and deny σύμμειξις; it is that the statement of (2) necessarily presupposes the falsity of (2). Arguments of a somewhat similar kind are used by Plato elsewhere. In 249C he mocks at those who claim to know for certain the truth of a thesis whose truth would in fact make it impossible for anyone to know anything. Or compare *Sophist* 244. The theory that only one thing exists must be false, or at any rate it cannot be true. The statement 'only one thing exists' would have no meaning at all unless there were several different words with different meanings. The meaningfulness of the statement therefore presupposes, as a necessary condition, its own falsity.

The thesis 'no Forms combine with one another' is held to be self-refuting because its meaningfulness presupposes that some Forms do combine. Here then is another clue to an understanding of Plato's talk about Forms combining. That some statements are self-contradictory was taken as proof that some pairs of Forms are irreconcilable; now the fact that a certain statement is meaningful is taken to prove that some Forms do combine with others. Plato's conclusion, that there are connections between Forms, but not between every pair of Forms, rests upon the simple fact that some sentences are meaningful and some are not. The former presuppose the existence of concept-friendships or -compatibilities, the latter the existence of concept-enmities or -incompatibilities.

To return to the first part of Plato's refutation of (2): if there were no σύμμειξις (intermixture) all the philosophers' accounts of things would be empty, they would not be saying anything at all, nothing significant. This last is how I want to translate λέγοιεν οὐδέν. This expression can of course mean simply 'to say what is false' or 'to say what is silly'; but it can also mean 'to make no genuine statement at all', 'not to succeed in saying anything'. It seems to me that the argument here demands this last sense: if there were no σύμμειξις then no statement of any theory could be even significant. For suppose λέγειν οὐδέν here meant just 'to say what is false.' Then (a) the argument would be evidently inconclusive. For granted that alternative (2) did entail that all those philosophers' theories were false—well, perhaps they are false. Plato himself remarks that it is hard to decide about the truth of such theories (243A2–3). To point out that (2) entailed the falsity of the theories listed would convince nobody that (2) was false unless he chanced to be a firm believer in one of those theories. (b) Again, on this interpretation of λέγειν οὐδέν, it is completely mysterious why (2)—the thesis that no Forms combine—should entail that the theories are false. For they are certainly not all theories *about* Forms. Empedocles talked about the world and its processes, he did not assert that certain Forms combined. So how would the assumption that no Forms combine make his theory necessarily false? (c) If, however, it were claimed that the philosophical theories mentioned did in fact *assert* that Forms combined, the result would be that Plato's argument was not indeed invalid but utterly pointless. For it would amount to this: some Forms must combine; for if none did then all philosophers who said they did would be wrong.

Taking λέγειν οὐδέν to mean 'to speak falsely' we find Plato's argument weak, obscure or pointless. It is surrounded by arguments that are cogent, clear and highly relevant. This is a good reason to suspect that interpretation. If we take the expression to mean 'to make no genuine statement, to convey no *logos* whatso ever' the argument falls properly into place. If there were no liaisons among concepts the philosophers' statements (indeed all statements) would be just meaningless. Just as it is a presupposition of there being self-contradictory statements that some pairs of concepts will not go together, so it is a necessary condition of there being significant, non-self-contradictory statements (whether true or false) that some concepts will go together. These, I suggest, are the points Plato is making in his proof that there is a συμπλοκὴ εἰδῶν. Human discourse is possible only because the meanings of general words are related in definite ways; it is essential to language that there be definite rules determining which combinations of words do, and which do not, constitute significant sentences. To map out the interrelations of concepts (inclusion, incompatibility and so on) is the task of dialectic (cp. *Sph.* 253B–E).

I am obviously under an obligation to show that with my interpretation of S—as opposed to that of Cornford and Ross—there is no difficulty over the specimen *logoi* about Theaetetus. I must show that the dictum 'without a συμπλοκὴ εἰδῶν no *logos* would be possible' is *not* invalidated by the fact that many *logoi* contain only one general word, together with, for instance, a proper name. A quotation from a recent book on logical theory will help to make this clear (P. F. Strawson, *Introduction to Logical Theory*, 1952, p. 5):

> One of the main purposes for which we use language is to report events and to describe things and persons. Such reports and descriptions are like answers to questions of the form: what was it like? what is it (he, she) like? We describe something, say what it is like by applying to it words that we are also prepared to apply to other things. But not to all other things. A word that we are prepared to apply to everything without exception (such as certain words in current use in popular, and especially military, speech) would be useless for the purposes of description. For when we say what a thing is like, we not only compare it with other things, we also distinguish it from other things. (These are not two activities, but two aspects of the same activity.) Somewhere, then, a boundary must be drawn, limiting the applicability of a word used in describing things.

Substantially the same point is made by Aristotle in *Metaphysics* Γ. 4, where he argues for the Principle of Contradiction. He admits that it cannot be proved; for any proof would necessarily make use of the principle in question. But he says that you can explain to someone the necessity of this principle—provided he will say something significant, with a definite meaning; for you can then show him that he must intend his statement to rule out something or other, to be incompatible with at least one other statement. A statement compatible with every other statement would tell one nothing. ἀρχὴ . . . τὸ ἀξιοῦν . . . σημαίνειν γέ τι καὶ αὐτῷ καὶ ἄλλῳ. τοῦτο γὰρ ἀνάγκη, εἴπερ λέγοι τι. εἰ γὰρ μή, οὐκ ἂν εἴη τῷ τοιούτῳ λόγος, οὔτ' αὐτῷ πρὸς αὐτὸν οὔτε πρὸς ἄλλον. ἂν δέ τις τοῦτο διδῷ, ἔσται ἀπόδειξις. ἤδη γάρ τι ἔσται ὡρισμένον.[2] To return to Plato: the statement 'Theaetetus is sitting' is a genuine informative statement only because it rules something out ('Theaetetus is not sitting' or, more determinately, 'Theaetetus is standing').To say that it rules something out is to say that there is an incompatibility (μηδεμία κοινωνία) between two concepts ('sitting' and 'not-sitting' or, more determinately, 'sitting' and 'standing'). In studying the relations among concepts a philosopher elicits the rules governing the use of language; that there are some such relations, some such rules, is a necessary condition of there being a language at all: διὰ τὴν ἀλλήλων τῶν εἰδῶν συμπλοκὴν ὁ λόγος γέγονεν ἡμῖν.

These few remarks must suffice to indicate how a συμπλοκὴ εἰδῶν is presupposed by any and every statement, including those about Theaetetus. Plato admittedly does not argue the point in connection with the Theaetetus examples, which are used in the discussion of a different topic. Still it is a related topic since it does involve the incompatibility of two predicates. And I think that if we had asked Plato to reconcile S with these examples he would have done so in the way suggested in outline above. This at any rate seems more plausible than to suppose that he follows up S by using examples of *logoi* which he would have been totally unable to reconcile with S.

I have gradually passed from talking about Forms to talking about concepts, and I have taken these to be, in effect, the meanings of general words. Correspondingly, I have implied that the task assigned in Plato's later dialogues to the dialectician or philosopher is the investigation and plotting of the relations among concepts, a task to be pursued through a patient study of language by noticing which combinations of words in sentences do, and which do not, make sense, by eliciting ambiguities and drawing distinctions, by stating explicitly facts about the interrelations of word meanings which we normally do not trouble to state, though we all have some latent knowledge of them insofar as we know how to talk correctly. To justify all this, and to add the many sober

[2] "The starting point . . . is the demand . . . that he shall say something which is significant both for himself and for another; for this is necessary, if he really is to *say* something. Otherwise there will be no discourse' either with himself or with another. But if this is granted, there can be demonstration; for we shall already have something definite" (1006A18–25).

qualifications which it evidently demands, would take a volume. I can mention, here in conclusion, only two small points.

There is a section of the *Sophist* (254B ff.) where Plato is undoubtedly *practising* the dialectic he has previously described. He first distinguishes certain εἴδη (cp. 253D1–3) and then determines their interrelations (cp. 253D9–E2). It is important to notice that what Plato does in this section is to appeal to truths too obvious to be disputed, in particular truths which anyone who knows the language must immediately admit. For instance, Being is proved to be different from Sameness by a simple substitution-argument (255B8–C4): if they were *not* different then to say of two things that they both existed would be to say that they were both the same. But this is not so. In particular, we have agreed that κίνησις (motion) and στάσις (rest) both *exist;* but it would be different, and indeed absurd, to say that they are both *the same*. The dialectician's statement that Being is different from Sameness merely makes us see clearly (or at a new level) a fact about the meanings of words which we already in a way know. The dialectician makes explicit the rules in accordance with which we all already talk.

Finally, a reference to the *Parmenides*. After his searching criticisms of Socrates Parmenides goes on to imply that the theory of Ideas *is* capable of being salvaged, but that great skill and subtlety will be required for this. He adds (135B): 'if in view of all these and similar objections a man refuses to admit that Forms of things exist, or to distinguish (ὁρίζεσθαι) a definite Form in each case, he will have nothing on which to fix his thought, so long as he will not allow that each real thing has a character which is always the same; and thus he will completely destroy the possibility of significant talk (τὴν τοῦ διαλέγεσθαι δύναμιν)'. This passage may be taken to show that, in spite of the powerful criticisms voiced by Parmenides, Plato did not propose to abandon completely his theory of Ideas. It may be that he thought of himself as maintaining a revised version of the theory whereas we might find it more natural to say that he jettisoned the theory. Anyway the passage quoted strongly suggests that what he is now sure of is *not* that there must be Forms as conceived in the middle dialogues, Forms as ethical ideals and as the metaphysical objects of intuitive and perhaps mystical insight; what he is now sure of is that there must be fixed things to guarantee the meaningfulness of talk, fixed concepts —the meanings of general words—whose role is to ensure τὴν τοῦ διαλέγεσθαι δύναμιν. The *Sophist* explains further that these concepts must stand in certain definite relations to one another, and gives the dialectician the task of investigating the boundaries and interrelations of concepts.

Originally published in the *Bulletin of the Institute of Classical Studies*, No. 2 (1955), 31–35. Reprinted by permission of the author.

11

PLATO AND THE COPULA:
Sophist 251–59

J. L. ACKRILL

My purpose is not to give a full interpretation of this difficult and important passage, but to discuss one particular problem, taking up some remarks made by F. M. Cornford (in *Plato's Theory of Knowledge*) and by Mr. R. Robinson (in his paper on Plato's *Parmenides, Classical Philology,* 1942).[1] First it may be useful to give a very brief and unargued outline of the passage. Plato seeks to prove that concepts[2] are related in certain definite ways, that there is a συμπλοκὴ εἰδῶν (an interweaving of Forms) (251D–252E). Next (253) he assigns to philosophy the task of discovering what these relations are: the philosopher must try to get a clear view of the whole range of concepts and of how they are interconnected, whether in genus-species pyramids or in other ways. Plato now gives a sample of such philosophising. Choosing some concepts highly relevant to problems already broached in the *Sophist* he first (254–55) establishes that they are all different one from the other, and then (255E–258) elicits the relationships in which they stand to one another. The attempt to discover and state these relationships throws light on the puzzling notions ὄν (being) and μὴ ὄν (not being) and enables Plato to set aside with contempt certain puzzles and paradoxes propounded by superficial thinkers (259). He refers finally (259E) to the absolute necessity there is for concepts to be in definite relations to one another if there is to be discourse at all: διὰ γὰρ τὴν ἀλλήλων τῶν εἰδῶν συμπλοκὴν ὁ λόγος γέγονεν ἡμῖν (it is because of the interweaving of the Forms with one another that we come to have discourse.)[3] So the section ends with a re-

---

[1] I shall refer to these two works by page numbers, without repeating their titles.

[2] The use of this term may seem provocative. But whether or not the εἴδη (Forms) and γένη (kinds) of the *Sophist* are something more than 'mere' concepts, a good deal of interpretation of 251–59 can satisfactorily proceed on the assumption that they are *at least* concepts.

[3] It will be convenient to give here, once for all, the translation of a

assertion of the point with which it began (251D–252E): that there is and must be a συμπλοκὴ εἰδῶν (an interweaving of Forms).

The question I wish to discuss is this. Is it true to say that one of Plato's achievements in this passage is 'the discovery of the copula' or 'the recognition of the ambiguity of ἔστιν' as used on the one hand in statements of identity and on the other hand in attributive statements? The question is whether Plato made a philosophical advance which we might describe in such phrases as those just quoted, but no great stress is to be laid on these particular phrases. Thus it is no doubt odd to say that Plato (or anyone else) *discovered* the copula. But did he draw attention to it? Did he expound or expose the various roles of the verb ἔστιν? Many of his predecessors and contemporaries reached bizarre conclusions by confusing different uses of the word; did Plato respond by elucidating these different uses? These are the real questions. Again, it would be a pedantic misunderstanding to deny that Plato recognised the ambiguity of ἔστιν merely on the ground that he used no word meaning 'ambiguity', or on the ground that he nowhere says 'the word ἔστιν sometimes means . . . and sometimes means . . .'. If he in fact glosses or explains or analyses the meaning of a word in one way in some contexts and in another way in others, and if this occurs in a serious philosophical exposition, then it may well be right to credit him with 'recognising an ambiguity'. I mention these trivial points only to indicate, by contrast, what the substantial question at issue is.

It is generally agreed (e.g. Cornford, p. 296) that Plato marks off the existential use of ἔστιν from at least some other use. How he does this can be seen from his remark about κίνησις (change) at 256A1: ἔστι δέ γε διὰ τὸ μετέχειν τοῦ ὄντος (it is because it shares in being). This διά (because) does not introduce a *proof* that κίνησις ἔστιν (change is): this was already agreed without question before and used to establish a connection between κίνησις and τὸ ὄν (between change and being) (254D10). Nor, obviously, does it introduce the *cause* why κίνησις ἔστιν: it does not refer to some event or state which resulted in the further state described by κίνησις ἔστιν. The words introduced by διά give an expansion or

---

few Greek expressions that occur often in this paper. ἔστι (or ἔστιν) means 'is'; οὐκ ἔστι (or οὐκ ἔστιν) means 'is not'; μετέχει means 'shares in' or 'partakes of'; μετέχειν (infinitive) and μέθεξις (noun) mean 'sharing in'; εἶδος (plural εἴδη) means 'Form'.

analysis of ἔστιν as this word is used in κίνησις ἔστιν, i.e. as used existentially. μετέχει τοῦ ὄντος (shares in being) is the philosopher's equivalent of the existential ἔστιν; but, as will be seen, it is not his analysis of ἔστιν in its other uses. So the existential meaning is marked off.

The philosopher's formulation (κίνησις μετέχει τοῦ ὄντος [change shares in being]) both elucidates the sense of ἔστιν in κίνησις ἔστιν and also makes clear—what is not clear in the compressed colloquial formulation—the structure of the fact being stated; makes clear that a certain connection is being asserted between two concepts. The philosopher's formulation contains not only the names of two concepts but also a word indicating their coherence, μετέχει, which is not itself the name of an εἶδος but signifies the connection between the named εἴδη.

There remain two other meanings of ἔστιν, as copula and as identity-sign. The assimilation of these had led to a denial of the possibility of any true non-tautological statements. What is needed in order to deprive this paradox of its power is a clear demonstration of how the two uses of ἔστι differ. By 'demonstration' I do not mean 'proof' but 'exhibition' or 'display'. The way to sterilise a paradox is to expose and lay bare the confusion from which it arises. One can draw attention to the two different uses of ἔστι, point out how they are related, perhaps provide alternative modes of expression so as to remove even the slightest temptation to confuse the two.

Consider how Plato deals, in 256A10–B4, with the pair of statements κίνησίς ἐστι ταὐτόν, κίνησις οὐκ ἔστι ταὐτόν (change is the same, change is not the same). These look like contradictories yet we want to assert both. We need not really be worried (οὐ δυσχεραντέον); for we are not in both statements speaking ὁμοίως (in the same way). Analysis of the statements (introduced again by διά [because of]) will show exactly what is being asserted in each and enable us to see that there is no contradiction between them when properly understood. The first statement means κίνησις μετέχει ταὐτοῦ (change shares in sameness). The second means κίνησις μετέχει θατέρου πρὸς ταὐτόν (motion shares in difference with respect to the same).

The essential points in Plato's analysis of the two statements are these: (1) where ἔστιν is being used as copula it gets replaced in the philosopher's version by μετέχει; (2) the philosopher's version of οὐκ ἔστιν, when the ἔστιν is not the copula but the identity-sign, is (not οὐ μετέχει, but) μετέχει θατέρου πρός . . . (shares in difference from). By his reformulation of the two statements Plato shows up the difference between the ἔστιν which serves merely to connect two named concepts (copula) and the ἔστιν (or οὐκ ἔστιν) which expresses the concept of Identity (or Difference) and at the same time indicates that something *falls under* the concept of Identity (or Difference).

With Plato's procedure here one may compare a passage in Frege's paper *Über Begriff und Gegenstand*.[4] One can just as well assert of a thing that it is Alexander the Great, or is the number four, or is the planet Venus, as that it is green or is a mammal. But, Frege points out, one must distinguish two different usages of 'is'.

> In the last two examples it serves as a copula, as a mere verbal sign of predication. (In this sense the German *ist* can sometimes be replaced by the mere personal suffix: cf. *dies Blatt ist grün* and *dies Blatt grünt*.)[5] We are here saying that something falls under a concept, and the grammatical predicate stands for this concept. In the first three examples, on the other hand, 'is' is used like the 'equals' sign in arithmetic, to express an equation. . . . In the sentence 'the morning star is Venus' 'is' is obviously not the mere copula; its content is an essential part of the predicate, so that the word 'Venus' does not constitute the whole of the predicate. One might say instead: 'the morning star is no other than Venus'; what was previously implicit in the single word 'is' is here set forth in four separate words, and in 'is no other than' the word 'is' now really is the mere copula. What is predicated here is thus not *Venus* but *no other than Venus*. These words stand for a concept.

Frege explains the copula by talking of something's *falling under* a concept: Plato uses for this the term μετέχειν. Frege expands the 'is' of identity into 'is no other than . . .', in which phrase the 'is' is simply the copula ('falls under the concept . . .') and 'no other than . . .' stands for a concept. Plato expands the ἔστιν of identity

---

[4] I quote Mr. Geach's translation, in *Translation from the Philosophical Writings of Gottlob Frege*, edited by Peter Geach and Max Black, pp. 43-44.

[5] One is reminded of Aristotle, *Physics* 185B28.

into μετέχει ταὐτοῦ ... (shares in sameness) (and οὐκ ἔστιν into μετέχει θατέρου ... [shares in difference]) where μετέχει does the copula's job ('falls under') and ταὐτόν (or θάτερον) names a concept (sameness [or difference]). In offering the analyses that he does it seems to me that Plato, no less clearly than Frege, is engaged in distinguishing and elucidating senses of 'is'.

The claim that one of the things Plato does in *Sophist* 251–59 is to distinguish between the copula and the identity-sign would seem to be supported by the following consideration: that this distinction is just what is required to immunise us against the paradoxes of the ὀψιμαθεῖς (the late learners) (251B), and Plato does suppose that his discussion puts these gentlemen in their place. Robinson, however, denies that this consideration has any force (p. 174): 'Plato certainly thought of his Communion as refuting the "late learners". But it does not follow that he thought the manner of refutation was to show that they confused attribution with identity. Nor is there anything in the text to show that he thought this.' Robinson is certainly right to say that it does not *follow*. Still we are surely entitled—or, rather, obliged—to make some reasonable suggestion as to how exactly Plato did suppose himself to have 'refuted' the late learners. If the above interpretation of 256A10–B10 is sound, that passage exposes the error of the late learners, who construed every 'is' as an identity-sign; and it would be natural to infer that Plato himself regarded the distinction drawn in that passage (and elsewhere) as the decisive counter-move against the late learners. Moreover, if no *other* reasonable suggestion can be made as to how exactly Plato thought he had disposed of the late learners and their paradox, this fact will be an argument in favour of the interpretation of 256A–B which finds in it an important point which is directly relevant to, and destructive of, the paradox.

Now it might be suggested that it is by his proof that there is Communion among εἴδη (251D–252E) that Plato refutes the view that only identical statements are possible; that it is here, and not in later talk about ὄν (being) and μὴ ὄν (not being), that he supposes himself to be refuting the late learners. But what are the arguments by which he proves there is Communion?[6] The first (251E7–252B7) is this: if there were no Communion then philoso-

---

[6] I have discussed these arguments, in another connection, in a short paper in the *Bulletin of the Institute of Classical Studies of the University of London*, No. 2 (1955), pp. 31–35. [Reprinted above as Essay 10].

phers and 'physicists' in propounding their various views would in fact be 'saying nothing' (λέγοιεν ἂν οὐδέν). It is simply *assumed* that this apodosis is false and that Empedocles and the rest were talking sense. But, of course, this assumption is exactly what the late learners, maintaining their paradox, will deny; and an argument based on it is obviously no good against them. Plato's second argument for Communion (252B8–D1) is that the theory that there is no Communion cannot be stated without implying its own falsity. As applied to the later learners the argument would be: you say only identity-statements can be true; but this statement—'only identity-statements can be true'—is not an identity-statement; so on your own theory your theory is false. Now this argument is certainly formidable and might easily put a late learner to silence; he could hardly be expected to distinguish between first- and second-order statements. Yet as a refutation of the thesis itself it is surely superficial and unsatisfactory. For the thesis was put forward not only by elderly jokers but also by serious thinkers who felt themselves obliged to maintain it for what seemed to them compelling theoretical reasons. Robinson writes as follows (p. 175):

> To such more responsible thinkers it is folly to say: 'But you obviously can say "man is good"; and if you could not, all discourse whatever would be impossible, including the paradox that you cannot say "man is good".' For these thinkers already know that you can say that 'man is good', and that the supposition that you cannot immediately destroys all thought and speech. Their trouble is that, nevertheless, they seem to see a good reason for denying that you can say that 'man is good'. What they want is to be shown the fallacy in the argument which troubles them. They know it must be a fallacy; but they want to see what it is. Now for such thinkers Plato's exposition of his doctrine of Communion is no help whatever. For he merely points to the fact that we *must* be able to say 'man is good,' because otherwise no thought or communication would be possible. He does not even notice any argument to the contrary, much less show us where they go wrong.

I agree with Robinson that, for the reason he gives, Plato's proof of Communion cannot be said to dispose satisfactorily of the paradoxical thesis (even though the second argument in the proof is valid against the thesis); for nothing is done to expose the error or confusion which led quite serious persons to embrace the paradox. Surely this passage (*251D–252E*) cannot be the whole of what Plato has to say in rebuttal of the late learners and their paradox. Surely he somewhere exposes the underlying error, the rotten foundations on which the paradox was built. And he does this, I suggest, for instance in the passage previously discussed, by clearly distinguishing two different uses of ἔστιν, as copula and as identity-sign, and by showing how the two uses are related.

Let us turn now to Cornford. He says that the copula 'has no place anywhere in Plato's scheme of the relations of Forms' (p. 279). The relation between Forms that combine—'blending'—is a symmetrical relation; so it cannot be the same as the relation of subject to predicate in an attributive statement, i.e. the relation indicated by the copula (pp. 256–57, 266).

First a very general point. The relation 'being connected with' or 'being associated with' is a symmetrical relation. But there are, of course, many different *ways* in which things or persons may be associated or connected; and many of these ways involve non-symmetrical relationships. One may say of a group of people, members of one family, that they are all connected. But if one wishes to say *how* they are connected each with the other, one must employ such expressions as 'father of', 'niece of', which do not stand for symmetrical relationships. Now it is agreed by Cornford that the philosopher's task, according to Plato, is to 'discern clearly the hierarchy of Forms . . . and make out its articulate structure' (pp. 263–64). Every statement the philosopher makes in performing this task may be expected to assert some connection or association between Forms. And 'association' is indeed a symmetrical relation. But surely the philosopher could not possibly achieve his purpose without specifying the *kind* of association there is in each case. And he could not do this without bringing in some non-symmetrical relations. Consider the following small extract from a possible 'map of the Forms':

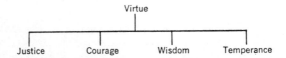

Virtue

Justice   Courage   Wisdom   Temperance

The structure exhibited here must be described by the philosopher; and to do this he *must* advert to a non-symmetrical relationship. In the above diagram the words 'Virtue' and 'Justice' are not merely close together; one is *under* the other. Similarly, Virtue and Justice are not merely connected; they are connected in a particular way: Justice is *a species of* Virtue.

Non-symmetrical relations must then be invoked if the complex structure of the 'world of Forms' is to be described; nor is this something Plato could easily have overlooked. Certainly the analogy he draws with letters and musical notes (*253A–B*) does not support the idea that the dialectician would, according to him, be satisfied with asserting *symmetrical* relations between εἴδη. If we are to say whether 'f' and 'g' fit together, with the aid of 'i', to make an English word we must obviously specify the *order* in which the letters are to be taken: 'gif' is not a word, 'fig' is. The scale of C major is not just such-and-such notes, but these notes in a certain order. Whatever terminology one uses to state the facts about spelling or scales or Forms, some non-symmetrical relation must come in. But if Cornford's view were right and every philosopher's statement told of a symmetrical 'blending' of Forms, the philosopher would never be able to express irreducibly non-symmetrical truths, such as that Justice is a species of Virtue. So we may suspect that Cornford's view is not right.

To this it will be objected that the *Sophist*, though it implies that the philosopher will have to study relations between genera and species, does not itself explore such relations; so a proper interpretation of the *Sophist* should leave them aside and concentrate on how Plato proceeds in exhibiting the relations which he does in fact consider. Let us then look at some of the statements of Communion which Plato makes.

Firstly, 'Motion exists' (I retain Cornford's translation; 'Change' would be better). Cornford says (p. 256): ' "Motion exists" means that the Form Motion blends with the Form Existence'; and (p. 279): ' "Motion blends with Existence" is taken as equivalent to "Motion exists".' He also says (p. 278): 'The relation intended (*sc.* by "blending") is not the meaning of the "copula" . . .; for we can equally say "Existence blends with Motion".' Taken together these remarks lead to absurdity. For if 'Motion blends with Existence' means 'Motion exists', then 'Existence blends with Motion' must mean 'Existence moves'. And then, if 'Motion blends with

Existence' is equivalent to 'Existence blends with Motion', 'Motion exists' must be equivalent to 'Existence moves'. Plato obviously did not intend this. The trouble lies in Cornford's insistence on the 'blending' metaphor, which suggests a symmetrical relation, to the exclusion of others which do not. What 'Motion exists' is equivalent to is not 'Motion blends with Existence' ('blending' being symmetrical), but 'Motion shares in, partakes of Existence' ('partaking of' being non-symmetrical). Cornford's remarks lead to absurdity because he will not let into his exposition any non-symmetrical expression like 'partakes of' (even though Plato's exposition bristles with this metaphor).

Secondly, 'Motion is different from Rest'. Now this is indeed equivalent to 'Rest is different from Motion'. But before drawing any inference concerning 'Communion' we must put the statement into its 'analysed' form, into dialectician's terminology. We get: 'Motion communicates with Difference from Rest'. The question is whether 'communicates with' in this formulation can be taken to stand for a symmetrical relation. But if it is so taken we must be prepared to say that 'Motion communicates with Difference from Rest' is equivalent to 'Difference from Rest communicates with Motion'; for the 'Communion' asserted in the first statement is evidently between Motion on the one hand and Difference from Rest on the other. But then, since 'Motion communicates with Difference from Rest' is the technical way of saying that Motion is different from Rest, we must suppose that 'Difference from Rest communicates with Motion' is the technical way of saying that Difference from Rest moves. So we shall find ourselves claiming that 'Motion is different from Rest' means the same as 'Difference from Rest moves'. As before, the absurdity results from taking 'communicates with' as standing for a symmetrical relation. If 'Motion communicates with Difference from Rest' means that Motion is different from Rest (as it clearly does), then 'communicates with' must here stand not for 'blending' but for a non-symmetrical relation ('partaking of', 'falling under').

These considerations, it may be said, are still very general and involve too much extrapolation and 'interpretation'. I am not sure how much weight to attach to this criticism. For one must suppose that Plato had something reasonable and consistent in his mind when writing the very taut piece of exposition in *Sophist* 251–59; and if Cornford's account leads, on reflection, to grave difficulties or absurdities this is a sound *prima facie* argument against it. (Even if in the end Cornford's account were to be accepted it would be desirable that the defects in Plato's discussion—as interpreted by Cornford—should be candidly exposed.) However, it is certainly necessary to turn to a closer examination of Plato's actual terminology.

Plato uses a great variety of terms in speaking of relations among εἴδη. While some of them (e.g. συμμείγνυσθαι) seem naturally to stand for the rather indeterminate symmetrical relation 'being connected with', there are others, like μετέχειν, which we expect to be standing for some more determinate, non-symmetrical relation. Cornford denies that this expectation is fulfilled and says that Plato does not distinguish 'partaking' from the mutual relation called 'blending' or 'combining' (pp. 296–97). He does not support this by a detailed study of all the relevant passages. His explicit argument that 'participation' as between Forms is a symmetrical relation (like 'blending'; hence nothing to do with the copula) rests on the one passage *255D*, in which Existence is said to *partake of* both τὸ καθ' αὑτό and τὸ πρὸς ἄλλο (roughly: *the absolute* and *the relative*). Cornford writes (p. 256): 'So the generic Form partakes of (blends with) the specific Form no less than the specific partakes of the generic'. And in his footnote on *255D4* he says: 'Note that Existence, which *includes* both these Forms (*sc.* τὸ καθ' αὑτό and τὸ πρὸς ἄλλο), is said to *partake of* both. This is one of the places which show that "partaking" is symmetrical in the case of Forms.' I do not know which are the other places Cornford here alludes to; yet the reference to *255D* is by itself a very inadequate justification of Cornford's sweeping remarks about 'participation', and of his insistence on symmetrical 'blending' as the one and only relation holding between Forms.

Professor Karl Dürr, in his paper *Moderne Darstellung der platonischen Logik*,[7] assigned precise and distinct meanings to various terms used by Plato in *Sophist* 251–59, but did not attempt anything like a full justification. More useful for us is the following observation by Sir David Ross:[8] 'Plato uses κοινωνία, κοινωνεῖν, ἐπικοινωνία, προσκοινωνεῖν in two different constructions—with the genitive (*250B9, 252A2, B9, 254C5, 256B2, 260E2*) and with the

---

[7] In *Museum Helveticum*, 1945, especially pp. 171–75.
[8] In *Plato's Theory of Ideas*, p. 111, n. 6.

dative (*251D9, E8, 252D3, 253A8, 254B8, C1, 257A9, 260E5*). In the former usage the verbs mean "share in"; in the latter they mean "combine with" or "communicate with".' I do not think Ross should have added that 'though Plato uses the two different constructions, he does not seem to attach any importance to the difference between them'. For Plato does not use the two constructions indiscriminately or interchangeably. A comparison between the two groups of passages yields a clear result (I leave out of account *250B9* and *260E2* and *E5*, which are not in the main section on κοινωνία γενῶν [the combination of kinds]). κοινωνεῖν followed by the genitive (e.g. θατέρου) is used where the fact being asserted is that some εἶδος is (copula) such-and-such (e.g. different from . . .); that is, it is used to express the fact that one concept *falls under* another. The dative construction, on the other hand, occurs in highly general remarks about the connectedness of εἴδη, where no definite fact as to any particular pair of εἴδη is being stated. Surely this confirms—what ordinary Greek usage would suggest—that Plato consciously uses κοινωνεῖν in two different ways. Sometimes it stands for the general symmetrical notion of 'connectedness', sometimes it stands for a determinate non-symmetrical notion, 'sharing in'.

There are thirteen occurrences of the verb μετέχειν or noun μέθεξις in *Sophist* 251–59. One of these is at *255D4*, in the passage used by Cornford in his argument quoted above. But in all the other twelve cases it is clear that the truth expressed by 'A-ness μετέχει B-ness' is that A-ness is (copula) B, and never that B-ness is (copula) A. For instance, τὸ ὂν μετέχει θατέρου (*being shares in Difference*) . . . formulates the fact that Existence is different from . . .; it does not serve equally to express the fact that Difference exists—that is expressed by τὸ ἕτερον μετέχει τοῦ ὄντος (*Difference shares in being*). The way Plato uses μετέχειν in all these cases makes it very hard to believe that he intended by it a symmetrical relation.

It is worth attending specially to the passage officially devoted to the statement of certain relations among the five chosen γένη (kinds), *255E8–257A11*. Here the objective is to state definite truths in careful, philosophical terminology; not merely to allude to the fact that there are connections among γένη, but to say precisely what some of them are. Now in this passage Cornford's favourite metaphor occurs once (*256B9*), in a purely general reference to the connectedness of concepts (εἴπερ τῶν γενῶν συγχωρησόμεθα τὰ μὲν ἀλλήλοις ἐθέλειν μείγνυσθαι, τὰ δὲ μή [if we are to agree that some of the kinds will blend with one another, some will not]). And κοινωνία with the dative occurs once (*257A9*), in an equally unspecific context (εἴπερ ἔχει κοινωνίαν ἀλλήλοις ἡ τῶν γενῶν φύσις [if kinds are of a nature to admit combination with one another]). The other terms used are as follows. κοινωνία with the genitive occurs once (*256B2*) and is used to state the definite relation holding between two named εἴδη (κίνησις and θάτερον); the fact stated is that Motion is different from . . ., not that Difference moves. μεταλαμβάνειν occurs once (*256B6*) in a passage whose interpretation is controversial. But the significance of the verb is clear. If it were true to say κίνησις μεταλαμβάνει στάσεως (change participates in unchangingness) then one could rightly say κίνησίς ἐστι στάσιμος (change is unchanging). μετέχειν (or μέθεξις) occurs five times (*256A1, A7, B1, D9, E3*), in each case expressing the relation between two named εἴδη the first of which falls under the second. Thus all the real work of the section *255E8–257A11*, all the exposition of actual connections between particular εἴδη, is done by the terms μετέχειν, μεταλαμβάνειν, and κοινωνεῖν (with genitive), that is, by the non-symmetrical metaphor 'partaking of' which Cornford is so determined to exclude. And the role of 'partakes of' in Plato's terminology is clear: 'partakes of' followed by an abstract noun, the name of a concept, is equivalent to the ordinary language expression consisting of 'is' (copula) followed by the adjective corresponding to that abstract noun.

This examination of Plato's use of some terms, though far from exhaustive, is, I think, sufficient to discredit Cornford's claim that the 'blending' metaphor is the one safe clue to Plato's meaning, and to establish that μετέχειν and its variants, μεταλαμβάνειν and κοινωνεῖν (with genitive), are not used by Plato as mere alternatives for μείγνυσθαι (blending). It may be admitted that in *255D*, the passage Cornford exploits, μετέχειν is used in an exceptional way; but one passage cannot be allowed to outweigh a dozen others.[9]

[9] This is rather a cavalier dismissal of the passage on which Cornford relies so heavily. But it is not possible in the space available to attempt a full study of the perplexing argument of 255C12–E1, and without such a study no statement as to the exact force of μετέχειν in 255D4 is worth much. My own conviction is that even in this passage μετέχειν does not stand for the symmetrical relation 'blending'; but it is certainly not used in quite the same way as in the other places where it occurs in 251–259.

To sum up: I have tried to argue firstly, that the verb μετέχειν, with its variants, has a role in Plato's philosophical language corresponding to the role of the copula in ordinary language; and secondly, that by his analysis of various statements Plato brings out —and means to bring out—the difference between the copula (μετέχει [shares in] . . .), the identity-sign (μετέχει ταὐτοῦ [shares in sameness] . . .) and the existential ἔστιν (μετέχει τοῦ ὄντος [shares in being]). ·

Originally published in *Journal of Hellenic Studies* 77 (Part I) (1957), 1–6. Reprinted by permission of the editors and the author.

12

PLATO ON NOT-BEING[1]

G. E. L. OWEN

Platonists who doubt that they are Spectators of Being must settle for the knowledge that they are investigators of the verb "to be". Their investigations make them familiar with certain commonplaces of the subject for which, among Plato's dialogues, the *Sophist* is held to contain the chief evidence. But the evidence is not there, and the attempt to find it has obstructed the interpretation of that hard and powerful dialogue. The commonplaces that I mean are these:

In Greek, but only vestigially in English, the verb "to be" has two syntactically distinct uses, a *complete* or *substantive* use in which it determines a one-place predicate ("X is", "X is not") and an *incomplete* use in which it determines a two-place predicate ("X is Y", "X is not Y"). To this difference there answers a semantic distinction. The verb in its first use signifies "to exist" (for which Greek in

---

[1] Delivered in shortened form as an Arnold Isenberg Lecture in Philosophy at Michigan State University in March, 1967. The lecture took up an older promissory note (*New Essays on Plato and Aristotle*, ed. Bambrough [London, 1965], p. 71 n. 1) which was accepted in its original form by G. Vlastos ("A Metaphysical Paradox", *Proc. Am. Philos. Ass.* xxxix [1965–66], pp. 8–9). The bones of the argument were taken from a larger stew of many years' standing, familiar to seminars at Oxford and Harvard; I wish I could now distinguish the many cooks. But mention must be made not only of clarifications already published by members of those seminars but of unpublished benefactions. In the first class fall J. M. E. Moravcsik, "Being and Meaning in the *Sophist*", *Acta Philosophica Fennica* xiv (1962), pp. 23–78; W. G. Runciman, *Plato's Later Epistemology* (Cambridge, 1962); and most recently M. Frede, "Prädikation und Existenzaussage", *Hypomnemata* xviii (1967), pp. 1–99, and J. Malcolm, "Plato's Analysis of τὸ ὄν and τὸ μὴ ὄν in the *Sophist*", *Phronesis* xii (1967), pp. 130–46: the last two came too late for me to do more than signal agreement in these notes. In the second class, the treatment of καθ' αὑτό—πρὸς ἕτερον on pp. 22–24 was, I think, first suggested by a conversation with R. G. Albritton; it was reached independently by Frede.

Plato's day had no separate word) or else, in Greek but only in translators' English, "to be real" or "to be the case" or "to be true", these senses being all reducible to the notion of the existence of some object or state of affairs; while in its second use it is demoted to a subject-predicate copula (under which we can here include the verbal auxiliary) or to an identity-sign.[2] Plato's major explorations of being and not-being are exercises in the complete or "existential" use of the verb. And, lest his arguments should seem liable to confusion by this versatile word, in the *Sophist* he marks off the first use from the verb's other use or uses and draws a corresponding distinction within the negative constructions represented by τὸ μὴ ὄν, "not-being" or "what is not".[3] For the problems which dominate the central argument of the *Sophist* are existence-problems, so disentangling the different functions of the verb "to be" is a proper step to identifying and resolving them.

Since the following arguments were put together most of these commonplaces have come under fire.[4] Consequently here the fire

[2] For the broad treatment of the verb see LSJ s.v. εἶναι and recent versions of the Oxford and Webster dictionaries s.v. "be"; for the application to Plato see e.g. I. M. Crombie, *An Examination of Plato's Doctrines* (London, 1962), vol. ii, pp. 498–99.

[3] P. Shorey, *What Plato Said* (Chicago, 1933), p. 298, asserted that in the *Sophist* Plato "laid the foundation of logic" by, inter alia, "explicitly distinguishing the copula from the substantive *is*"; A. E. Taylor, *Plato, the 'Sophist' and the 'Statesman'*, ed. Klibansky-Anscombe (London, 1961), pp. 81–82, claimed that Plato "has definitely distinguished the 'is' of the copula from the 'is' which asserts 'actual existence'" and further that "he has . . . discriminated the existential sense of the 'is' from the sense in which 'is' means 'is the same as', 'is identical with'". So, with variations, F. M. Cornford, *Plato's Theory of Knowledge* (London, 1935), p. 296; J. L. Ackrill, "Plato and the Copula", *J.H.S.* lxxvii (1957), p. 2; Crombie, op. cit., p. 499; Moravcsik, op. cit., p. 51.

[4] On the general account of the verb see C. Kahn, "The Greek Verb 'To Be' and the Concept of Being", *Foundations of Language* ii (1966), pp. 245–65, who notes the difficulty of making a firm syntactical distinction between the "absolute" and "predicative" constructions and then argues against taking the first as "existential". Vlastos, in "A Metaphysical Paradox" (n. 1, *supra*) and "Degrees of Reality in Plato", *New Essays on Plato and Aristotle*, pp. 1–19, holds that Plato's theory of ὄντως ὄντα is concerned with grades not of existence but of reality, and explores a sense of ". . . is real" which reduces it to the two-place predicate ". . . is really (sc. unqualifiedly or undeceptively) . . .". That the *Sophist* marks off an existential sense of εἶναι has been queried by Runciman, op. cit., ch. iii; Kahn, op. cit., p. 261; and now Frede and Malcolm, op. cit.

can be confined to one arc, the interpretation of Plato and particularly of the *Sophist*. The general syntactic claims will not come into question: we can accept a distinction between the verb's complete and incomplete uses provided we are wary of confusing the first with elliptical occurrences of the second—and this is no longer a matter of syntax (p. 255, below). The *Sophist* will turn out to be primarily an essay in problems of reference and predication and in the incomplete uses of the verb associated with these. The argument neither contains nor compels any isolation of an existential verb. Yet the problems about falsehood and unreality which it takes over from earlier dialogues do seem to be rooted in what we should call existence-puzzles, so it will need to be explained why they present themselves here in such a way as to lead to a study of "... is ..." and "... is not ...".

The argument from nothing

Let us begin, as Plato begins his own discussion of not-being, with Parmenides. That philosopher had written (B2.7-8): "You could not distinguish, nor could you express, *what is not*." Which of its roles is the verb "to be" playing here? Given the conventional choice it was natural to plump for the existential role. Not because the verb carries no complement—it is noteworthy that scholars have been ready here to detect an unmarked lacuna after the verb. The better reason was that Parmenides goes on to equate "what is not" with "nothing".[5] It would be absurd to think that because a thing is not such-and-such—not blue, for example—it is therefore nothing at all; but it is natural enough to equate what does not exist with nothing. No mermaid exists: nothing is a mermaid. Hence no doubt the pleasing entry in my desk copy of Webster's Dictionary: "Nothing: something that does not exist".

Discontent about the philosophical interpretation of the verb "to be" has often focussed on this reading of Parmenides. How can he be pinned to one use of his favourite verb when he slides so unwarily between different uses? For he argues first that a thing cannot be at one time but not at another (B8.6-21), and then takes himself to have shown that it cannot change at all, i.e. cannot be *anything* at one time which it is not at another (B8.26-28). The objection can be met in this form,[6] but it returns in others.[7] We need

[5] Diels-Kranz, *Vors.*[13] 28B8.7-13, cf. 6.2 with 7.1.
[6] As perhaps in "Eleatic Questions", *C.Q.* n.s. x (1960), p. 94 n. 1.
[7] Thus Kahn, op. cit., p. 251, represents the verb as in effect an assertion sign, engrossing the "existential" and "predicative" uses;

not pursue it: our interest in Parmenides is just that the equation of
what is not with *nothing* has often seemed to settle the matter. For
when Plato takes over Parmenides' topic he adopts this equation,
so here too the question has seemed, by default, to be settled. The
Republic echoes the familiar argument, "How could anything that
is not be known?" (477A1), and adds a little later: "Properly
speaking, that which is not must be called not one thing but
nothing" (478B12–C1). It seems only to be emphasising Parmenides' equation when it speaks of "what is not *in any way*" and "what
utterly is not" (477A3–4, 478D7). And the equation with its atten-
dant phraseology is repeated when Plato returns to the topic in the
Theaetetus (189A6–10) and the *Sophist* (237C7–E2).[8] So it seems that

---

and M. Furth, in "Elements of Eleatic Ontology", *J.H.P.* vi (1968),
pp. 111–32, argues ably that such a "fused" use of the verb would not
itself commit Parmenides to fallacy. Many points in Furth's paper
bear on my contentions here.

[8] Notice that in *Tht.* 188E–89A the move from "what is not" to
"nothing" is argued, not assumed: F(something) → ∼F(nothing)
→ F(one thing) → F(a thing that is), hence F(a thing that is not) →
F(nothing). In the manipulation of the same counters at *R.* 478B–C it is
assumed: F(something) → ∼F(nothing) → F(one thing), but F(a thing
that is not) → F(nothing) → ∼F(one thing), hence F(something) → ∼
F(a thing that is not). Whether it is argued or assumed in the *Sophist*'s
opening puzzle depends on the sense of 237C–E and ultimately
237D6–7. Tht. has just agreed that, since "what is not" cannot be said
of *what is*, it cannot be said of *something* (237C10–D5); and the ES
[Eleatic Stranger] then says, *either* "Do you agree to this because you
look at it in this way, that a man who speaks of *something* must speak of
one thing?" (so e.g. Heindorf, Apelt, Cornford); *or* "Looking at it in this
way, do you agree that a man who speaks of *something* must speak of *one
thing?*" (so e.g. Diès, Fraccaroli, Taylor). The second is attractive
because it takes the argument forward from a proposition already
agreed, that what is not cannot be something: it deduces from this
that what is not cannot be even one thing and hence is nothing, and the
latter proposition thus becomes a corollary and not an assumption of
the argument. But the reading assumes a deviant ὅτι-construction with
(συμ)φάναι, which has no parallel in Plato (*Phd.* 64B3–4, wrongly ad-
duced by Ast et al. as the single exception, is not one: the verb governs
not ὅτι ... but εὖ εἰρῆσθαι ... ὅτι ...). Back then to the first construction: the ES asks why Tht. agrees that what is not cannot be something,
and offers an elliptical argument for it which uses our proposition as an
assumption: F(something) → F(one or more things) {but F(nothing)
→ ∼F(one or more things)}, hence F(nothing) → ∼F(something);
{*but* F(*what is not*) → F(*nothing*)} hence F(what is not) → ∼
F(something).

in these contexts he is expressly concerned with the possibility of speaking and thinking about what does not exist. Peipers, listing what he took to be the occurrences of the "existential" verb in Plato, remarked: "haec nota communis est: in omnibus animo obversatur oppositio *eius quod est* et *nihili* (τοῦ ὄντος et τοῦ μηδενός)."[9]

This conclusion in turn lends a sense to another step in Plato's argument. He contends, in the *Theaetetus* (189A10–12) and the *Sophist* (237E1–6), that thinking or speaking of what is not is simply not speaking or thinking at all, and then in the *Sophist* (238D–39A) he turns this contention on itself and brands the very expressions "what is not" and "what are not" as ill-formed inasmuch as they pretend to pick out one or more subjects of discourse. What can this mean but that he now denies sense to any attempt to speak of what does not exist? Thus Cornford contrasted later attempts to find "non-existent things like Chimaeras" an entrée into discourse, and summed up: "This is all (Plato) has to say about a problem that has troubled modern logicians who have discussed the thesis that 'whatever is thought of must in some sense be' ".[10]

As it stands, this is an ambiguous thesis. I may tell you (a′) "The elves interrupt my typing", when there are no such creatures, or (a″) "De Gaulle means to bribe Britain into the Common Market", when there is no such project; I may warn you (b′) "The creatures named in (a′) don't exist" or (b″) "The project reported in (a″) doesn't exist", and thus in different ways challenge the truth of (a′) and (a″); and in turn I may comment on the sense but not the truth of these last sentences and say (c) "Any one uttering (b′) or (b″) is speaking of what does not exist". All these sorts of utterances, and others too, will fall under the rubric "speaking of what does not exist". Faced with such a division a defender of the established view would probably say that the *Theaetetus* professes to discredit utterances of the (a)-type (and especially (a″)) without noticing the others, while the *Sophist* aims rather at discrediting the other two. For the *Theaetetus* is content to leave the problem of falsehood in its traditional form: it assimilates the falsehood in (a″) to the failure of reference in (a′), but it assumes without question the significance of such expressions as "what is not"; whereas the *Sophist* turns to challenge the very use of these expressions. So it seems that in the *Sophist*, if not before, Plato expressly discounts negations of existence as unintelligible.

This reading of the argument is generally coupled with the assurance that the *Sophist* represents *assertions* of existence as wholly respectable. Cornford has his own version of this conjunction: "Every Form exists; consequently 'the non-existent' has no place in the scheme, and we have ruled out that sense of 'is not' ".[11] This suggests that it was a decision to talk about nothing but Forms which induced Plato to find a discussion of the status of Chimaeras unintelligible. Whether or not Cornford meant this travesty of the argument, he can at least be counted as subscribing to the common view that Plato divides positive statements of existence from their negative counterparts and welcomes the first but disbars the second.[12] There is still room for dissension within this common view: some of its adherents offer Plato the hospitable thesis that "existence is a predicate of everything whatever" or "is necessarily

[11] Ibid., p. 296.

[12] But there is a striking incoherence in Cornford's account. After saying that the existential sense of "is not" has been "ruled out" (p. 296) he goes on to write as though this sense had been not excluded but positively vindicated: he speaks of "the preceding demonstration that 'is not' has two senses—'does not exist' and 'is different from' ", and even of Plato's showing that " 'the thing that is not' does not *always* [my italics] mean 'the non-existent' " (pp. 298–99). Thereafter in translating and explaining 262C3 he reimports the sense "does not exist" without caveat (p. 305 and ibid. n. 1: see p. 262, *infra*). On p. 295 n. 1 (cf. p. 208) he concedes that at 238C "τὸ μηδαμῶς ὄν, 'the simply non-existent', was dismissed as not to be spoken or thought of"; yet he at once dilutes this to the claim that "there are no *true* statements saying that any *Form* does not exist" (my italics again). What is said in 238C is that τὸ μὴ ὄν as there construed is flatly unintelligible; what is said in 257B is that *whenever* (not, as Cornford, "when") we speak of what is not we do not mean a contrary of what is (ὁπόταν τὸ μὴ ὄν λέγωμεν . . . οὐκ ἐναντίον τι λέγομεν τοῦ ὄντος)—this latter phrase representing, by Cornford's own admission, the μηδαμῶς ὄν of 238C (locc. citt.). This unfounded reading of the *Sophist* he subsequently applied to the interpretation of the *Timaeus* 38B2–3 (*Plato's Cosmology* [London, 1937], p. 98 n. 4), and a rejoinder of mine (*C.Q.* n.s. iii [1953], p. 89) which resumed the objections here set out was dismissed by an American scholar as "brushing aside Cornford's attempt" (H. F. Cherniss, *J.H.S.* lxxvii [1957], p. 18), although the scholar neither quoted nor apparently grasped the objection. He then felt able to retrieve "is non-existent" as a "more probable" interpretation of τὸ μὴ ὄν at *Ti.* 38B and yet claim that this agreed with the *Sophist*.

all-inclusive", in a sense which will readmit Cornford's Chimaeras.[13] Still the foundation holds firm. Plato in the *Sophist* has isolated a complete use of the verb "to be", that in which it determines a one-place predicate and signifies "to exist", and within this use he rejects negative constructions with the verb as breeding intolerable paradox. Whether Chimaeras benefit from the distinction is a matter for scholarly debate. They and their like rear no head in the dialogue from start to finish.

This familiar reading of the *Sophist* runs into such troubles that no amount of ingenious patching now seems to me able to save it. I shelve other considerations for the moment and mention two drawn from Plato's own account of his strategy.

The prospect of joint illumination

First, Plato nowhere suggests, and by implication he consistently denies, that he has found a use of the verb "to be" in which only its positive occurrences have significance.

At the end of the long review of perplexities in 236D–50E, the Eleatic Stranger says: "Now that both being and not-being have turned out equally puzzling, this in itself (ἤδη) offers the hope that if one of them can be made out to a greater or less degree of clarity the other can be made out to the same degree" (250E5–51A1). Being and not-being have been steadily coupled in this way in the preceding arguments (241D6–7, 243B7–C5, 245E8–46A2) and they are similarly coupled in what follows (254C5–6, 256E2–3, 258A11–B7, and 262C3, of which more on p. 262 below). After volunteering this prospect of joint illumination it would obviously be perverse to represent a positive use of the verb as luminous but reject the negative as wholly dark. Nor would the perversity be lessened if Plato had argued, as some of his interpreters do, that although the complete or "existential" use of the verb makes sense only in its positive form there is a *different* use or uses marked out in the dialogue in which negation comes into its own.[14] The hope

---

[13] Cf. Runciman, op. cit., pp. 65–66; Moravcsik, op. cit., p. 41; *contra*, W. Kamlah, "Platons Selbstkritik im Sophistes", *Zetemata* xxxiii (1963), p. 23 n. 1.

[14] Thus it will not do to suggest, as Moravcsik does (op. cit., pp. 27–28), that when Plato says that we are now in as much confusion about being as about not-being (250D5–E7) he means that the confusion about not-being is a puzzle about *existence* whereas the confusion about being is due to conflating the *other* uses of "is" (p. 27 n. 1). It is in the lines immediately following those quoted by Moravcsik that Plato

offered by the ES is that any light thrown on either being or not-being will equally illuminate the other. And since he then sets himself to justify expressions of the form "A is not" only when they can be completed into "A is not B",[15] it is an incomplete use of the verb that we can expect to find vindicated in positive constructions too.

Let us call this assumption, that the one cannot be illuminated without the other, the "Parity Assumption" or, for short, "PA". It has obvious affinities with the recommendation at *Parmenides* 135E8–36A2. And it governs the ES's next proposal. "Suppose on the other hand that we can get sight of neither: then we shall at any rate push the argument through, as creditably as we may, between both of them at once" (251A1–3). Since Campbell there has been general agreement on the sense of the words,[16] and no one is likely to explain the talk of pushing between being and not-being as a proposal to hold them apart and save only one. What is envisaged is that both may remain incomprehensible, and then the argument

---

suggests that light thrown on the one will bring corresponding light to the other (250E7–51A3). Moravcsik thinks that the perplexity about being is introduced in 250A–E and not in the preceding 242B–49E because he takes the latter passage to be proving important theorems about existence. Yet one line of argument which would be integral to these "proofs" (243C–44B) is represented by the ES as identical with that which generates the puzzle in 250 (249E7–50A2). As for the ES's supposed interest in proving existence to be indefinable, what he proposes however tentatively at 247E3–4 is a *definition* of εἶναι, and not, as Cornford said (op. cit., p. 238) and many have repeated, a "mark" (*aliter* "symptom", "attempt to characterize", etc.). What he says, on the most natural interpretation, is "I lay it down, as a ὅρον ὁρίζειν the things-that-are, that they are *nothing but* power". Moreover the context (247D2–E6) shows that he is improving on the materialists' attempt to ὁρίζεσθαι οὐσίαν (246B1), where Cornford rightly renders the verb as "define". For ὅρος = "definition" see e.g. *Phdr.* 237D1 (cf. C2–3), *Plt.* 266E1, 293E2; and of course the ὅροι, esp. 414D.

[15] This at least is common ground to those divided by the issue in pp. 236–41, this chapter.

[16] L. Campbell, *The 'Sophistes' and 'Politicus' of Plato* (Oxford, 1867), p. 136. Cornford (op. cit., p. 251) objects that on this reading ἅμα is redundant (251A3), and proposes to understand ἀμφοῖν quite otherwise: "we will force a passage through the argument *with both elbows at once*", a curiously irrelevant appeal to violence which leaves the ἅμα far more nakedly redundant. The ἅμα reinforces Plato's point: if both being and not-being stay intractable we must get clear of both at once.

must get clear of both Scylla and Charybdis. (The project of dispensing with the verb "to be" was after all an occupational temptation in Greek philosophy: witness *Tht.* 157B1–3 and Aristotle, *Ph.* 185B27–28.) So the PA is maintained. Logically it is the proper assumption, historically it is the appropriate reply to Parmenides.[17] It tells directly against the common view of Plato's strategy. Some holders of that view have thought to see a way round it, but this can be blocked in the course of setting out another difficulty.

Negation and contrariety

A second trouble for the received view is that Plato does not say that his problems about not-being come from understanding "being" in a certain way; he says that they come from understanding "not" in a certain way. On his showing, they are to be resolved, not by giving up a particular sense of the verb in negative constructions, but by giving up a confusion about negation.

Twice in setting his puzzles about not-being—once in each of the lines of argument projected in 236E1–2 and followed in the subsequent pages—the ES gets his respondent to agree that what is not is the *contrary* of what is.[18] The sophist's teaching has been branded counterfeit and false. So, in the Greek idiom which is under scrutiny, he professes to deal in what is, but instead he retails and speaks of what is not (or of "things that are not", by contrast with "things that are") ; and this is innocently equated with the contrary of what is. When the ES comes to solve the paradoxes he picks on

---

[17] Whose project was, after all, to discount "is-not" and retain "is"; and his arguments are not to be met by distributing different senses of the verb between the two expressions, cf. nn. 6–7 *supra*.

[18] 240B5, 240D6–8: the puzzles are those of deceptive semblances and of falsehood, respectively. In the first statement of the puzzles (236E1–2), ἀληθές does duty for ὄν in the problem of falsehood but not in that of semblances; in the development of the puzzles (cf. 240B5, 240D6–8) it is vice versa. Plato tries to assimilate the two lines of argument (pp. 249–50, *infra*), so both appeals to a "contrary of what is" are met by the reply in 257B3–C4, 258E6–59A1. Campbell, (op. cit., p. 96) rightly saw τἀναντία τοῖς οὖσι as anticipating τοὐναντίον τοῦ ὄντος of 256E6; Cornford (op. cit., p. 212 n. 1) wanted to distinguish them and thereby to allow Plato's final account of falsehood to recognize "things which are *contrary* to the facts". But Plato's account (263B7–12) insists on the formula ὄντων ἕτερα and defends it by harking back to the argument of 256E–57A, which heralded the contrast between difference and contrariety.

this as a cardinal mistake. When a negation-sign is affixed to the verb "to be" the expression no more signifies some contrary of being than the negation-sign in "not large" compels that expression to mean the contrary of large, i.e. small (257B1–C4). He returns to the point in his summing-up (258E6–7). So—and I shall accumulate more evidence for this later, for it is often tacitly denied— his argument is one from analogy. (In fact it is of the pattern subsequently explained in *Statesman* 277D–78E under the title of "example", *paradeigma*.) It illuminates a troublesome case by a tractable parallel: it draws a comparison between affixing a negative to the verb "to be" and affixing one to a predicate such as "large".[19] Within the comparison the sense of the negated terms is not called in question. What it is designed to explain is the role of the negation-sign itself.

Here again, then, Plato's diagnosis of his perplexity does not square with the usual view. But we have only the skeleton of an argument until we have explained the diagnosis, and this calls for two preliminary points to be made clear. First, I have represented Plato as concerned with affixing negatives to parts of sentences and not, as later logic accustoms us to expect, to whole sentences. This is clear from the text and needs no argument. But I have also spoken of negating the verb "to be" and not only, as in Plato's illustration, of attaching a negative to the expression ὄν, "being"; and this needs explanation. "Being" catches much of the Greek word's variety of use: it shifts between participle and collective noun and abstract noun in a way disheartening to philosophers. But in this context it is a participle. Plato is discussing the negating of predicates: he is comparing what it is to describe something as "not large" with what it is to describe it as "not-being". And the preceding lines 256D11–57A6 show that this participial or predicative use can be taken to represent other uses of the verb in which

---

[19] "Whenever we speak of *not* being we don't mean some *contrary of* being; we just mean *different*. —How? —Just as whenever we call something not large: do you think then we mean *small* by our words, any more than we mean *middling?* —Surely not." Need it be pointed out that this passage does *not* say that "not large" means "*either* middling *or* small", and hence does not introduce a new account of "not", and of "different", in terms of incompatibility? It says that "small" has no more claim to be what "not large" means than "middling" has. Incompatibility has no place in Plato's explanation of falsehood either: see n. 31 *infra*.

"not" can be attached to it: to describe any thing or things as "not-being" is just to say that it "is not" or they "are not".[20] After all, the point of Plato's comparison is to clarify the perplexity about speaking of *what is not* or of *things that are not*. The verb is put in participial form here because Plato wants to draw a clear analogy with the negating of another predicate "large", but it is the negating of "is" and "are" that he is out to explain.

Moreover it is the incomplete ". . . is . . ." whose negation interests him. For the same preceding lines show that "is/are not" and "not-being" are being treated as fragments of predicates drawn from sentences of the form "A is/are not B" or phrases of the form "not being B".[21]

[20] For the purpose of this and later notes it will be useful to set out the relevant passage 256D11–E6. "So it must be possible (a) for not-being to be, (b) in the case of change and moreover (c) in respect of all the kinds. For in respect of all of them the nature-of-difference renders each one (d) different from being, and so leaves it not-being; and thus we shall be right to describe them all, on the same terms, (e) as not-being and (f) on the other hand—since they partake in being—as being, and to say that they are. . . Consequently, (g) for each of the forms *being* is multiple and *not-being* is countless in number." The "not-being" which appears in the singular in (d) is put into the plural in (e) and answered by the plural "being" in (f), which is itself explained by "that they are".(in *cratio obliqua*); so in these phrases "being" is the participle going proxy for finite uses of the verb. Moreover, since "not-being" has been explained in the preceding lines 256D5–8 as equivalent to "different from being", and (d) takes up this equation, "different from being" must also be understood as applying to any subject that is said *not to be*. There is a crux here. In the preceding argument change has been shown to be different from *rest*, from *the different*, and finally from *being* (255E11–14, 256A3–5, 256D5–8); and in these proofs of non-identity it is natural to take "being" and the other terms as nouns, the names of abstract entities. Yet 256D–E is introduced as the immediate corollary of this passage, and the key-expressions can hardly have shifted their roles so profoundly. I shall not pursue this problem beyond pointing out that the proofs of non-identity have consisted in showing the non-substitutability of *predicates* (252D6–10; 255A4–5; 255B8–C3; and on the interpretation given below, 256C8–D7), and that what "being" must be in 256D–E is a *predicate*. Notice too that the conclusions in 256D–57A are said to apply to *all* forms, including "being."

[21] See n. 20 When the *not-being* of (a) reappears in (g) it is said to be countless in number in the case of each form, and this is evidently to say that each form *is not* indefinitely many others. But (g) is presented as a conclusion of the preceding argument, in which change was expressly differentiated from just four other forms; so where has the ES pointed

This being so, it will make for better understanding of Plato's
comparison if it is reformulated by way of a distinction which
Aristotle took up in his logic (*Int.* 19B19–29, *APr.* 51B5–10). It must
be remembered that in Greek the negation-sign is commonly prefixed to the verb, but that it can be shifted to precede and modify
other parts of the sentence. Aristotle accordingly distinguishes (I)
"this not-is white" from (II) "this is not-white". The moral he
draws from his distinction is unclear,[22] but Plato's point can be
clarified by it. For, as applied to Aristotle's examples, I take his
comparison to come to this: that in (I) the negative modifies the
verb and so imports the notion of not-being, while in (II) it modifies the adjective and so imports the notion of not-white; and that
just as in (II) the effect of the negative is not to produce an expression meaning the contrary of the negated term—calling a thing
"not white" does not relegate it to the other extreme, black—so in
(I) saying that it "not is" does not relegate it to another extreme
from being. Thereby he clears the way for his stronger conclusion.
"Not large" does not *mean* "small" any more than it *means* "middling", "not white" does not mean "black" any more than it means
"grey"; but of course things that are not large or not white may be
small or black just as they may be middling or grey. The conclusion
he is leading to is that in one case this latter option is not open.
With the verb "to be" the negative construction not only does not
mean the contrary (which is what the analogy was designed to
show) but cannot even be applied to anything in the contrary
state. For Plato, or his speakers in the dialogue, can find no intelligible contrary to being or to what is (258E6–59A1). But, he
insists, this breeds no confusion in the notion of speaking of what is

---

out the availability of this vast range of fillings for "not-being . . ." or
"is not . . ."? In (c), I think. Commonly (b) and (c) are rendered "in
the case not only of change but of all the other kinds". But one would
then expect the same preposition ἐπί to cover (b) and (c); more im-
portantly, the preposition used in (c) is repeated a few lines later
(255A4–5) to introduce not the subject of "is not" but the various
complements for which it is true of the subject. So the argument is this:
it has just been shown that change *is not* certain other kinds, and this
can be generalized for the complement "all other kinds", since the
difference between *any* kind (ἕκαστον, σύμπαντα) and any other can be
established. Any "differs from being, in respect of any other".

[22] Cf. J. L. Ackrill, *Aristotle's Categories and De Interpretatione* (Oxford,
1963), pp. 143–44.

not. Those who try to justify the notion by searching for such a contrary, and equally those who make capital of the failure to find one, have just mistaken the sense of the negation.

This, then, is what remains to be explained in his diagnosis: the claim that there cannot be anything in a contrary state to being. His meaning is not hard to see, but one clue to it fails. Earlier in the dialogue change and rest were described as "contrary" and "most contrary" to each other (250A8, 255A12, B1), but it is debatable what relationship he means to hold between them. Most commentators have taken him to be denying just that the two are identical and that either is predicable of the other.[23] But these negative conditions seem to be satisfied not only by the pair large and small, which are his examples of contraries in 257B6–7, but by large and middling, and middling is his example of what is not large without being the contrary of large.

More light can be found in the treatment of large, middling and small at *Prm.* 161D1–2. Here he exploits the familiar Greek idea of a middle state between contraries as containing something of both extremes.[24] What is middle-sized is not large, but it avoids smallness by having in it something, in a broad sense some proportion, of both large and small. And this is his point in the *Sophist:* to ascribe not-being to any subject—that is, in this context, to use "is not" or some negative construction with the verb "to be" in describing it —does not preclude ascribing some proportion of being to it—that is, saying that it "is" so-and-so. Indeed, in the case of being, the negation turns out to be applicable only to subjects in the middle state. For Plato's analogy does no more than resume his previous arguments. The attempt to speak of what is not as *nothing*, a subject which is not anything at all, has broken down (237B 39B). Thereafter it has been shown, for some specimen "kinds" of the highest rank, that there must be many things that each of them is as well as a still larger number that each is not (256E2–7),[25] and this is later assumed to hold good of all subjects of discourse (263B11–12). So those who take the negation of "is" to import some contrary of being are those who try, hopefully or polemically, to construct a subject which for every predicate F is not F. This gives the correct

[23] Thus Grote, *Plato*[3] (London, 1875), vol. ii. p. 444; Taylor, op. cit., p. 53; *contra*, Moravcsik, op. cit., pp. 43–47.

[24] Cf. e.g. *R.* 478E1–5.

[25] On this difference in number cf. pp. 254, 260.

sense to the expression "is not *in any way*" which we noticed (Cornford's "the totally non-existent" seems unintelligible), and relevance to the ES's reply that any subject "is in many ways as well as not being in many others" (259B5–6, cf. 237B7–8, 260D3).[26] What he has shown, in short, is that a subject must be identified and characterized as well as differentiated; and for Plato this presents itself as an exercise in the incomplete use or uses of "is."[27]

The reductive thesis

Before interim conclusions are drawn, there is an objection to be met. Perhaps Plato does not wish to exploit an analogy between the variant elements in the sentences (I) and (II) which we borrowed from Aristotle. Perhaps his whole object in 257B1–C4 is to reduce (I) to (II) without remainder.

This reduction appears, unargued and at full strength, in Mr. Crombie. "The view that negation signifies not 'the opposite' but 'the different' is the view that all statements assert that their subject partakes in existence, the function of negation being to locate the subject in some region of existence other than that part of it specified by the negated term. We might put this by saying that· 'not' is logically hyphenated, not to the copula, but to the rest of the predicate; and that is what Plato almost does say in 257C when he speaks of 'not' signifying the opposite of the words to which it is prefixed and then goes on to take examples such as 'not large'."[28] A footnote tries to make amends: "One cannot say that Plato actually makes the point which I say he almost makes, for the copula commonly is one of the words to which the 'not' is prefixed."[29] Commonly indeed: the point is that it is so prefixed in *this* passage, both to the copula and to its proxy the participle. But let us shelve difficulties for the moment and notice how this reading of Plato's argument offers a way round the Parity Assumption.

[26] "But if 'X not-is' is elliptical in this way, surely a subject can exhibit the contrary of being: a black thing unqualifiedly-not-is white for instance." In respect of white the black thing has the partial not-being which marks the lack of some attribute, to whatever degree; it cannot, in virtue of its relation to any predicate, have the total not-being which marks the lack of all attributes.

[27] Or in the vowel-form "being," one of the connectives which bring other forms into combination (253C1–2).

[28] Op. cit., vol. ii. p. 512.

[29] Ibid., n. 1.

Those who think that Plato is preoccupied with an existential sense of "to be" in which the verb cannot be intelligibly negated might well claim, on these terms, to acknowledge the PA. They might agree that, when we are led to expect a joint illumination (or joint eclipse) of being and not-being, it is the same concept of being that we can expect Plato to illuminate in positive and negative statements; but then, with one proviso, they might claim this to be just the concept represented by their non-negatable verb. The proviso is that in negative statements the negation-sign is to be understood as detached from the verb and attached to one of its complements. Rewrite "A isn't (sc. not-is) a greengrocer" as "A exists as a non-greengrocer", and both assumptions seem to be saved. True, so far as Plato's argument is concerned the verb must now give up its connection with a one-place predicate. It must be read as ". . . exists as . . ." in negative statements and so, if even lip-service is to be paid to the PA, in positive statements too. But then we shall find that the one-place predicate was always a red herring. And in settling for the syntactically incomplete use as the existential verb this interpretation does avoid the absurdity (which I believe no commentator has entertained) of suggesting that A's failure to be a greengrocer is a sort of *non*-existence for A.

This reductive thesis will not do. Plato means his analogy and is ready to leave the negation-sign annexed to the verb but, as he hopes, disarmed. But before seeing the thesis founder we must salvage what is true in it. It is true and important that, in the pages before Plato introduces his analogy, he has been showing on what terms something can be described as "not-being" and has done so by proving the thing *different from*, and so *not*, various other things. He has confined his operations to certain "greatest kinds" or, in practice, to the predicate-expressions representing these kinds, and he has proved their non-identity mainly by the experiment of substituting the predicate-expressions in context.[30] Subsequently, when he moves on from such negations of identity to considering falsehood in predicative statements, he builds on this earlier account of "not-being" as grounded in difference-from-some-X. "Theaetetus flies" says what-is-not about Theaetetus because what it says of him, viz. ... *flies*, is *different from* all the predicates he does have—or, in the locution that 263B echoes from 256E, different from "the

[30] Cf. n. 20, *supra*.

many things that are with respect to him" [31] So difference-from-some-X always is, or is contained in, the grounds on which Plato admits any subject as "not-being".

But it is never a ground on which he proposes to transfer the negative construction from the verb. The subject "must be described as different from other things and consequently, in respect of all those other things, it *not-is*. For in *not-being* them it is its own single self but at the same time *not-is* all those countless others" (257A1–6, taken up more emphatically in 259B1–6: the subject, treated as representative of all the others, is Being or What-is). By such arguments he tries to show that "not-is" calls for a completion, and on what terms the completion is to be supplied. But he never professes to cut his knots by relieving his key-verb of its negation-sign. Otherwise his argument would be over by 257A instead of culminating, as it does, in the carefully-worked analogy of 257B–59B. And its conclusion would be different and, considered as a device for saving existence-propositions and disarming their negations, a distinct anticlimax.

Before mounting some larger objections to the reductive thesis it is worth noticing how it gets illicit help from Cornford's version. He renders the ES's warning at 257B9–C3 correctly enough: "So, when it is asserted that a negative signifies a contrary, we shall not agree, but admit no more than this: that the prefix 'not' indicates something different from the words that *follow*—or rather from the things designated by the words pronounced *after* the negative" (my italics). Yet throughout the context he translates τὸ μὴ ὄν by "what is not", reversing Plato's ordering of the last two words. So the innocent reader is led to suppose that Plato is concerned not at all with the negation-sign as preceding and hence modifying the verb but only with its role in such sentences as (II).

But Plato's interest in his analogy is proved by more than the text that Cornford misdepicts. For we have seen, first, that he has a

---

[31] This remains the simplest interpretation, requiring no shift in the sense of "different" such as is sometimes found in 257B (cf. n. 19, *supra*). To be sure, if it were taken as a rule for verifying or falsifying statements it would make falsification an interminable business, but this is not its function. If X is not beautiful, all X's predicates fall into the class different-from-beautiful introduced at 257D4–E11. (For "nature-of-the-beautiful" in this passage as equivalent to the predicate "(the) beautiful" and not to the abstraction "beauty" cf. 257A9 "the nature of the kinds" = "the kinds" and similar periphrases at *R.* 429D, *Phdr.* 248C, etc.)

stronger conclusion in view: "not-X" not only does not *mean* "contrary-of-X" but in one case, that of the verb "to be", cannot even be applied to a contrary, since no subject can be intelligibly relegated to a state contrary to being. But if "not-being" is always to be recast in the form "being not-X" there will be plenty of contraries to being. Finding them will be merely a matter of finding a contrary to the negated term. When *not-being* is *being not-large*, *being small* is the desiderated contrary.

Further, it is the analogy between negating "being" and negating such terms as "large" and "beautiful" that governs the next stretch of the argument (257C5–58C5). The ES observes that "not beautiful" and "not large" each mark off a real class on the basis of a particular difference: the first marks off what is other than beautiful, the second what is other than large.[32] He generalizes this for an indefinite range of values of "not X" (258A4–10); and then he applies the generalization to the case of "not-being" (258A11–B3).[33]

[32] At 257E2–4 ἄλλο τι is often construed as the interrogative *nonne*, but a question answering another question does not need such a prefix (e.g. 257D6–7) and the sentence does not then lead directly to the conclusion in 257E6–7, that "not beautiful" represents a contrast between two things-that-are: on the antithesis must be ἄλλο τι τῶν ὄντων—πρός τι τῶν ὄντων. Again, it is often assumed that what not-beautiful is "marked off from" (ἀφορισθέν) is the same as what it is "contrasted with" (ἀντιτεθέν), which leaves a pointless repetition; what it is marked off from is the whole class *different* under which it falls (cf. 229C1–3, 231B3–4, 268D1–2; so too 257C11); what it is contrasted with is *beautiful*. Thus: "One of the things that are, marked off from a given class (the different) and moreover contrasted with one of the things that are (the beautiful)—is this what the not-beautiful turns out to be? . . . So the not-beautiful turns out to be a contrast between one thing that is and another thing that is," I have shifted between the predicate-expression "beautiful" and the class-description "the beautiful": for the not-beautiful to be is for it to be marked out by a particular difference, viz. from the beautiful, and this comes to more than saying (though it certainly includes saying) that the sense of the predicate "not beautiful" is given by this difference: Plato is also assuming that the predicate has application (cf. p. 259, *infra*).

[33] Since he is still concerned with the effect of negating the verb we are not to supply μόριον with Campbell at 258B1: that is the reductive thesis. Similarly at 258E2 ἕκαστον is better taken with μόριον (cf. 257C11: so Diès et al.) than with ὄν (Campbell), but interposing ἕκαστον between article and noun is poor practice. Accordingly I accept the ἑκάστου of all MSS. (Stallbaum's often-repeated claim that Simplicius "preserved the correct reading, ἕκαστον" is quite misleading: *Ph.* 238.26 reads ἕκαστον but the first transcription at 135.26

The pattern of argument is brought out clearly in his conclusion (258B9–C3): "We must have the nerve then to say that not-being certainly is something with its own nature, just as we agreed that large is large and beautiful is beautiful, and the same with not-large and not-beautiful: *in just the same way*, not-being *too* has turned out to be, and is, not-being—*one* sort of thing to be counted among the many sorts of things that are" (cf. 260B7). The being or reality ascribed here to sorts and classes will be taken up later. Our present business with the argument is that it shows Plato still pursuing his parallel. It is the effect of attaching a negation-sign to the verb "to be" that he wants to explain, and he is still explaining it by analogy with, and not by reduction to, the negating of any grammatical complements the verb may carry.

So the non-negatable use of "to be" is nowhere in view, and the Parity Assumption is not diluted to accommodate such a use. Our interim conclusion stands firm: Plato's account of his strategy tells directly against two theses basic to current views of the dialogue. The one is that he wants to signal a sense of the verb in which it cannot be straightforwardly and intelligibly negated; the other is that he represents his troubles about not-being as due to taking the verb in a certain sense rather than (as in fact he does) to taking the negation in a certain sense. In short, there is no hint that any sense of the key-verb must be dropped or modified between positive and negative constructions, or between the opening puzzles and the subsequent explanations. What then of the commentators' existential verb? Plato's clarifications of "not-being" are a study in the syntactically incomplete "is", and so long as the reductive treatment of the negation-sign was taken to be part of his strategy it was possible to read the "is" as "exists". But it is not part of his strategy; he does not offer to detach the negative from the verb it modifies, only to show grounds for its attachment and bring out its sense by parallels. And I assume without more argument that no one will read these exercises in "not-being" as an attempt to explain the *non*-existence of motion and rest and the other kinds. So the concept of being that he takes himself to be elucidating here is

---

has ἑκάστου). The sense here is: "that part of the different which is contrasted with the being of any subject is not-being": "X is . . ." expresses X's being, and the negation of this imports that part of the different which is contrasted with X's being. For some complement, X is different-from-being . . . .

not that of existence. By Parity, it cannot be an existential sense of "to be" that he means to isolate and explain in positive constructions either. If the Chimaera rears its head in the dialogue, it is in the shape of the familiar interpretation from which we set out. It is time to reconsider our original reason for accepting that interpretation: the equation of "what is not" with "nothing" in Plato's puzzles, which persuaded us that by "what is not" he here meant "what does not exist".

The subject Nothing

(a) Plato equates "what is not" with "nothing"; (b) "nothing" is equivalent to "what does not exist". Can either claim be upset? 1. Perhaps too much weight was put on (a). The ES sets out his puzzles about not-being in five stages, and of these only the first makes any play with "nothing". But the first is the puzzle of falsehood in its old form, using "what is not" without suggesting that its very use is logically incoherent. That suggestion is argued through the second and third stages, but by that time "nothing" has left the scene. So the equation plays no part in the argument it was used to interpret.

This objection fails, but it is prompted by a distinction of the first importance. I discuss it by way of making that distinction clear.

Briefly and provisionally, the stages of the ES's puzzle are as follows; I shall come back to the assumptions which control them later. (i) 237B7–E7 is a version of the familiar paradox.[34] "What is not" stands for nothing, hence speaking of what is not = speaking of nothing = not speaking at all. (So, if speaking falsely is speaking of what is not, there is no such speaking as false speaking; but the application is not made here.) (ii) 238A1–C11 tries for conclusions that have *what is not* as their express subject. Since what is not cannot have any actual attributes, it cannot have any number nor therefore be one or many of anything, yet to speak or think of it we have to refer to it in the singular or the plural; so it eludes our references and cannot be spoken or thought of. But by this reliance on the material mode (ii) undermines itself. (iii) 238D1–239C8 points out that according to (ii) the argument and conclusion of (ii) cannot be consistently formulated. If it proves anything, it

---

[34] But the version already contains the seeds of a transformation, cf. p. 244.

proves that no subject of discourse can be introduced under the description "what is not" or "what are not". So the ES's inquiry has no subject and threatens to vanish without trace.

The remaining two stages (239C9–240C6, 240C7–241B3) bring no new arguments for the incoherence of "what is not". With them the strategy shifts, in a way reminiscent of the second part of the *Parmenides*, from negative arguments terminating in philosophical frustrations and silence to a positive display of contradictions which must somehow be swallowed if sense is to be made of counterfeits and falsehoods.[35] These are not our present business.

What is the connexion between (i) and the two stages which follow it? First, it is obviously not the job of (ii) to challenge (i) in the way that (iii) upsets (ii). No doubt (i) deserves challenge: it interprets its thesis, that "what is not" stands for nothing, simply as allowing the substitution of "nothing" for "what is not" while keeping both expressions in use.[36] So it seems open to the charge of attempting what it claims to be impossible—speaking of what is not. But (ii) also keeps "what is not" in use and indeed makes its role as a referring expression central. Its claim to deal with the "very basis of the argument"[37] means that it picks out *what is not* as its formal subject, where (i) had framed its conclusion in terms of *speaking of what is not*. About this subject it seems to argue for much the same conclusion as that which (i) had reached by its equation between "what is not" and "nothing".

But if (ii) does not challenge (i), it does not seem to build on it either: and this is what suggests that (i) is merely superseded in the argument. (ii) leaves the important equation in silence, and (iii) follows suit: it makes no play with "nothing" and concentrates its attack on (ii). The effect is to make (ii) and (iii) appear a self-contained pair, providing between them all the material for the *Sophist*'s new problem: the problem, namely, whether sense can be made of those expressions "what is not" and "what are not" which

[35] In the *Sophist*, unlike the *Parmenides*, these stages lead to the positive proposal to disarm the paradoxes (241D1–242B5). This seems the correct moral to draw for the *Parmenides* too.

[36] 237E4–6 is not of course a recommendation to drop the expression "nothing", but a claim that speaking of nothing is not speaking at all.

[37] περὶ αὐτὴν αὑτοῦ τὴν ἀρχήν, sc. τοῦ λόγου (cf. 237E7): at 233E1–3 Theaetetus fails to understand τὴν ἀρχὴν τοῦ ῥηθέντος because he does not understand the subject of discussion, πάντα.

had been so artlessly used in describing and debating falsehood. (ii) introduces them as carrying a reference, (iii) replies that on (ii)'s interpretation of them no reference has been made. This is what prompts the notion that the treatment of the key-verb which leads to the impasse in (iii) is not to be explained by drawing on (i). "To be", as any account of the dialogue shows, is a versatile source of mischief; in (i) the ES pays respect to one veteran puzzle which can be got from negating the verb, and it is common opinion that this is a puzzle about non-existent subjects of discourse. But if it is quietly shelved in stating the new paradox, we need not assume this or its solution to turn on an existential use of the verb. And if such a switch of sense seems violent, the objector has a defence. After all, the conventional interpretation requires Plato to drop the existential sense of "what is not" between the puzzles and the solution. It is only an improvement on this to suggest that the sense is dropped in the course of the puzzles and before the substantial problem is set at all.

I said that this objection would serve to introduce a major distinction. What it grasps or half-grasps is that the argument which culminates in (iii) has transformed the old perplexity about speaking of what is not: that it is an anachronism to read the *Sophist* as answering the *Theaetetus*' problem in the *Theaetetus*' terms. Even the *Euthydemus* and the *Cratylus*, which debate the possibility of falsehood expressly in terms of fitting words to the world, use such locutions as "what is not" without ever asking whether *these* are capable of coherent use.[38] The *Sophist* by contrast proceeds on the view that if and only if we can understand the proper use of "what is not" and some related expressions, we shall understand—understand philosophically—the situations those expressions are commonly invoked to explain. When it turns to query the tools which had been taken for granted in constructing the old puzzles, it carries the mark of Plato's maturity. It ranks with, and because it offers solutions it goes beyond, the study of "participation" in the *Parmenides*.

It is also true that the first stage of its argument reads in part (237E1–6) like a mere echo of the old puzzle. If speaking of what is not is speaking of nothing, it is not speaking at all: why? The *Theaetetus* has already supplied one analogy (188E3–89A14): seeing

---

[38] The *Cratylus* at 429D, unlike the *Euthydemus*, uses μὴ τὸ ὂν (and not τὸ μὴ ὂν) λέγειν, but the other expression is implied by 385B10.

nothing is not seeing, hearing and touching nothing are not hearing or touching (188E2–89A14).

Beyond this the objection miscarries. No doubt (i) ends by settling for a version of the old paradox, with the key-expressions still unassailed; but it begins by asking the *Sophist*'s question, and the answer it gives controls the following stages. "Suppose one of this company had to give a serious and studied answer to the question, *what is the proper application of the name 'what is not'*? Of what thing and what sort of thing should we expect him to use it, and what would he point out to his questioner?" (237B10–C4, recalled at 250D7–8).[39] And the answer, that "what is not" = "nothing," is only verbally absent thereafter. It is surely this equation that (ii) is designed to reinforce by its independent proof that what is not cannot be one or more of anything (238A5–B5). The puzzle is converted into one about reference when (ii) deduces that, since what is not (i.q. nothing) does not give us even one thing to mention, it is unmentionable (238B6–C10). And it is the incoherence of this conclusion, and therewith of the original answer, that is shown by (iii).

So the first of the two claims stands firm. The equation with "nothing" cannot be dislodged from the puzzles. We must shift to the second: the claim that "nothing" is equivalent to "what does not exist" or, more exactly, that Plato could not set and solve puzzles about the former without supposing that his puzzles were about the latter. We have a distinction in hand now that will defeat this second conjunct.

2. Let us try adapting a Platonic argument to show that the non-existent is not the same as nothing. If I talk or think of centaurs I am not talking or thinking of nothing, for then I should not be talking or thinking at all. If I tell Theaetetus he has taken wing I speak of a non-existent flight, but not of nothing. Plato's discussion of "is not" in the *Parmenides* (160B6–161A5, countered at 163C2–D1) suggests that he has an approximation to this distinction in view. But as a help to grasping his intentions in the *Sophist* it is open to objection, and it is worth distinguishing objections from two different points of view. One, to put it broadly, is that of the *Theaetetus*, the other is that of the *Sophist*.

The form of the puzzle which is found in the *Theaetetus* seems to depend on obliterating just this distinction. Speaking of something

[39] A syntactically confused text; but the sense is not in question.

is not distinguished from saying something, and the speaking is compared to seeing or touching, as though the words had content to the extent that they made contact with the actual situation (189A3–10). In falsehood the speaker does not touch anything: where there should be the flight ascribed to Theaetetus,[40] there is no such object for the words to hit. There are primitive assumptions about language in Plato which reinforce this view from a consideration of words rather than of speakers. Words are given their purchase on the world by being used to name parts of it, and names, or the basic names to which others are variously reducible, are simple proxies for their nominees.[41] Thus falsehood at its simplest, for instance in the presence of the falsifying situation, becomes as vacuous as calling "Stetson!" when Stetson is not there, or pointing at vacancy.[42] These assumptions have been too often studied in Plato to need expansion here, and I take them to be modified at an essential point in the *Sophist*. In due course I shall argue.(pp. 262–66) that the modification does not make use of an existential sense of "to be": it does not need an existential sign. But there is no blinking the fact that for us Plato's puzzle in the *Theaetetus* seems to consist just in the non-existence of what falsehoods speak of, and that this is apparently what he expresses there by the phrase "speaking of nothing".

Now the *Sophist*. Is it true that if I talk or think of nothing I do not think or talk at all? I seem to be able to do the first without

---

[40] Or perhaps the flying-Theaetetus or the fact-that-Theaetetus-flies: the original puzzle notices no such distinctions, but the suggestion that the false statement says what-is-not *about* something (*Tht.* 188D3, 9–10) implies that what is missing is the flight. This squares with the implication of *Tht.* 190B2–4 that if X is beautiful and I call it ugly what I do is misidentify the *beautiful*, what misfires is the predicate-word "ugly". For an interesting attempt to reimport Theaetetus-flying, on the strength of a construction with some verbs of perceiving (though not with "touching", and not with verbs for saying or believing), see D. R. P. Wiggins' paper in this volume. See too Furth's discussion, op. cit., pp. 123–24.

[41] Thus e.g. *Tht.* 201E1–202B5 and the thesis pursued in *Cra.* 391A–428E.

[42] At *Cra.* 429E ff. Socrates accepts the "Stetson" analogy and offers to vindicate falsehood on these terms, but in effect he does so by distinguishing the conditions for making a reference·(looking towards, pointing, etc.) from the actual use of the name; I shall argue that the *Sophist*'s final account of falsehood is a more sophisticated version of this distinction (pp. 263–64, infra).

ceasing to talk, for I have just done it: I have been asking whether *nothing* is to be identified with *what does not exist*. To meet the *Theaetetus* puzzle we needed a distinction between the case in which there isn't anything being talked about and that in which what is talked about is a fictitious animal or an imaginary situation; now we seem to need a distinction between the case in which there isn't anything being talked about and that in which there is something that is talked about, viz. nothing. Let us for the moment, with Plato's leave, assume these distinctions: let us say that we can speak of mythical centaurs or chimerical flights (which I think Plato does not wish to deny), and that we can also speak of nothing without ceasing to speak (which I take him to be denying). How shall we show that these do not come to the same thing?

Well, we can describe our centaurs. They have hooves, not fish-tails; they are made of flesh and blood, not tin; and they are fictitious, not found in Whipsnade Zoo. Similarly with the flying done by Theaetetus: it can be described, and indeed must be if we are to know what we are rejecting as false. But suppose we are asked to describe the *nothing* that we have been talking about: then there seems to be no description at all available for it. It is not (to put an instance) a horse, for it can't be added to another horse to make two of them. In discourse the function of "nothing", like that of "nobody" and "nowhere" and "never", is just to indicate that there isn't as much as one of whatever it may be. This is a point that Plato drums home for his *what is not* when he equates it with *nothing* in the *Republic* (478B) and in stage (i) of the *Sophist*'s perplexity, and (ii) reinforces it. It can seem an unremarkable point or, as Plato makes it seem in the *Sophist*, astonishing and indeed unintelligible. It is unsurprising if we reflect that expressions such as "nothing" were coined to block gaps that would otherwise be filled by references to one or more of whatever sort of thing is in question. It becomes baffling if we insist that if Nothing can be spoken of it must conform to the rules for those subjects of discourse that it is designed to displace: that is, if we ask Plato's question, "What is the application of this name, 'what is not'? Of what and of what sort of thing should we expect a man to use it?", and then identify What is not with Nothing. For this is to require that if Nothing is to be mentionable it must establish its credentials as a logical subject, identifiable and describable: we must be able to say that it is a so-and-so, and which so-and-so it is. Yet the more we miscast Nothing as such a subject and ignore its role as a subject-excluder, the more we run into those paradoxes flagged by Plato and after him by Frege and Quine.[43] We find ourselves unable to say, not only that it is one or more of anything, but what it *is* at all (238E5–39A2).

Plato's question, then, sets strong conditions for reference. Naturally it produces (anyhow temporary) bafflement when it is applied to Nothing. The word seems to flout the basic requirements of accidence: a singular term, framed to exclude singular reference. But if this were the sole claim of the paradox on philosophers' interest it could long ago have been stored with the other phlogiston of the subject. "Nothing", we could say, is only parasitically singular, taking the size of the gap it blocks; it dissolves into "not even: one thing". If in consequence its role in the language cannot be explained as a name or description under which references can be made, so much the more reason for seeking other models of explanation. But in fact the paradox has no independent importance in Plato's argument. His aim is to show that when "what is not" is correctly understood the *Sophist*'s question *can* be answered. The impression that it cannot is produced by identifying, as the sophist tries to, "what is not" with "nothing"; and I have argued that Plato's subsequent diagnosis makes it certain, for the *Sophist* at least, how he wants to understand this identification. It introduces not a special sense of the verb but a special mistake about negating it. It comes to equating "what is not" not with "what does not exist" but with "what is not anything, what not-in-any-way is": a subject with all the being knocked out of it and so unidentifiable, no subject. As the scope of the negation is cleared up, so it becomes clear that anything can and must "be many things as well as not being many others". The answer to the *Sophist*'s question—the original question, let me insist: not an impostor smuggled in by switching the sense of the verb—is not "nothing" but "anything whatever, considered as differentiable from other things". And the answer (or part of the answer) to the sophist's puzzle about falsehood is that his diagnosis imports an unintelligible term: but not the term on which the commentators pitched.

How much or little do these considerations prove? They prove, I

[43] *Frege: Translations*, Geach and Black (Oxford, 1955), p. 83: "The answers 'never', 'nowhere', 'nothing' . . . to the questions 'when?', 'where?', 'what?' . . . are not proper answers but refusals to answer, which have the form of an answer". They are not of course refusals either; merely designed to show that there is no answer.

think, that it is possible to raise puzzles about Nothing without confusing them with puzzles about non-existence. They show that the *Sophist*'s question brings these puzzles to the fore of the discussion so as to lead naturally to that study of subject-predicate syntax and of the connective ". . . is . . ." which Plato does undertake. They leave the way open to the sole interpretation I can find which squares with the evidence already canvassed and does not accuse Plato of grossly missing or misrepresenting his own strategy.

And they leave Plato's argument a piece of successful pioneering in its chosen territory and not a lame attempt to evade a problem about non-existence by, in Cornford's phrase, "ruling out" an accepted sense of a word in one construction. Teachers of logic generally spend time explaining how substitution-instances are supplied for the constituents of the formulae (Fa) and (Ra,b) before they introduce $((\exists x)Fx)$ or $((\exists G)Ga)$ or any expressions for individual existence. Nor do they mention existence among the requirements for the terms of such elementary propositions. Plato's study is earlier than formal logic and concerned with far more than the construction of formulae, but it can be read as the earliest exercise at the level of those initial explanations. It is essentially preliminary to, and not based on, the isolation or construction of the difficult notion "exist".

Before following out this suggestion it may be as well to make one disclaimer. I am not arguing that Plato never, or never in the *Sophist*, uses the verb *einai* in such a way that "exist" is a natural English translation. No doubt he does. What I hope to show is that the central arguments and explanations become broken-backed if they are read as containing an implicit or explicit separation of such a sense of "is" from others. But so far the interpretation leaves a good deal of unfinished business. I proceed to detail what seem the main difficulties it faces and then, as best I can, to meet them.

Existence reimported

(1) It can be argued on the following grounds that the problem set in the central section of the dialogue can be solved only by isolating an existential use of the verb.

The sophist, unless he is that mere sophist whom Dr. Peck regarded as deserving only treatment in kind,[44] might well feel that a

---

[44] A. L. Peck, "Plato and the μέγιστα γένη of the *Sophist:* a reinterpretation", *C.Q.* n.s. ii (1952), pp. 32–56: my "sophist" is no doubt a fiction but represents positions that (*pace* Dr. Peck) Plato takes seriously and tries to meet.

substantial child has gone with the bath-water. Given greater articulateness he might complain that it is all very well to save the locution "speaking of what is not" by proving it capable of carrying an intelligible reference at the point where the sophist's translation of it is not. But how was he ever induced to suppose, or to try to say, that false speaking is speaking about a non-subject? Surely because what it speaks about does not exist, because there just is not the correlate in the world for the false words to express?

And the ES's puzzles recognize this existential concern. They have been under-described until all the assumptions and problems are set out. In particular, consider the assumption on which (ii) relies to prove that what is not is nothing, i.e. not one or more of anything. It lays it down (238A7–9, C5–6, cf. 241B1–3) that something that is cannot be attached to what is not, and interprets this to mean that what is not cannot have any of the attributes that are, such as number. What is this but the hatstand model of predication: actual hats cannot be hung on non-existent pegs?

Again, stages (iv) and (v) await description. The sophist has been denounced for offering only semblances of the things he claims to purvey, and making false claims in doing so (cf. 236E1–3). So he both purveys, and states, what is not instead of what is. But in both cases this contrast between what is and what is not can be made problematic. (iv) (239C9–40C6) discusses semblances, and its language (esp. the recurrent ἀληθινόν in 240A7–B8) makes it natural to interpret the verb "to be" here as "to be real". What distinguishes a semblance of A from A itself? Well, A is real, the semblance is not (in fact "in no way real, the *contrary* of real"). Yet surely it really is what it is, a semblance? A real unreal, then, which upsets the incompatibility of what is and what is not which we seemed to assume in denouncing the sophist. (v) (240C7–241B3) discusses falsehoods. False thinking is thinking that what is, is not (in fact is "the contrary of what is"), and vice versa; but this diagnosis has to mention what is not as though it had being (241B1–2). Or, to supply the usual interpretation, it professes to refer to just that non-existent state of affairs which the man with false belief supposes to exist.

"To be real", "to exist": such a confusion is one which Plato has the terminology to avoid, for "real" can be turned by the word ἀληθινόν as it is in (iv), and this word does not naturally go proxy for other uses of the verb "to be". Instead Plato seems to do what he can to strengthen the confusion, stretching the same formula to cover the paradoxes of both (iv) and (v) (240C3–5, 241B1–2, D6–7) and ultimately reducing the problem of unreality to that of falsehood (264C10–D5). The conflation can be left as a puzzle to those who believe that in his metaphysics Plato must and can readily divide reality from existence.[45] It does not weaken the point I have to meet. The picture of the argument just given seems to show that its assumptions and problems do not hinge on the connective ". . . is . . ." which carries no expressly existential sense but serves as copula or identity-sign. The senses of the verb that seem to be required are those conventionally associated with the one-place predicate ". . . is". So it is surely this use of the verb, in which it signifies existence or reality, that Plato must pick out for scrutiny if he is to dissolve his puzzles about not-being.

The same moral can be drawn from the puzzles about being which succeed them (242B–250E); for now an enquiry is broached into the number and nature of real things (242C5–6). We have seen that the two lines of perplexity are linked in 250E5–6. So it is the same use of the verb that asks to be picked out and clarified here.

(2) Next, it will be argued that not only Plato's problems but his positive conclusions compel him to distinguish this use of the verb. For (a) it is surely the existence (or else the reality) of change for which he is contending in 248E6–249B3, and which he thereafter assumes (250A11–12, B9, 254D10, 256A1). And (b) it is surely the existence (or reality), first of the not-beautiful and not-large, and then of what-is-not itself, which is the burden of the argument in 257D12–258E5. And finally (c) there is the explanation of falsehood itself (261D–263D). It seems common doctrine that here he "assumes that, whatever statements are about, if they are about anything they are about something that exists".[46] Is not this, after all, the moral of the exercise: that to speak falsely is not to make the vain attempt to mention what does not exist, but rather to mention something that does exist and ascribe to it real properties which are however different from the real properties it possesses? Is not this his way of satisfying the "hatstand" assumption which controls stage (ii) of the first puzzles?

[45] Vlastos, in the papers named in nn. 1 and 4, supra. Since Plato here conflates "to be" with "to be real" and since Vlastos takes the second in Plato to mark a two-place predicate distinct from existence, the interpretation I shall propose can be read as a corollary of his thesis.

[46] Moravcsik, op. cit., p. 41.

(3) That Plato does expressly mark off the existential use of the verb which his reasoning should force him to recognize has been argued in this way.[47]

First, he seems prepared to distinguish two *incomplete* uses of the verb, that in which it couples subject and predicate ("this is fragile") and that in which it marks an identity ("that is Socrates"). The section of the dialogue in which the distinction is drawn is introduced by a puzzle to which it is directly relevant (251A5–C2). Some opsimaths have failed to understand how one thing can have various appellations, for instance how anything can be called not only a man but good; and the common and plausible diagnosis of their confusion is that they have mistaken the different predications for different and competing statements of identity.[48] The appropriate distinction is then made in 256A7–B4. The ES proposes to explain how we can say that a thing is F and yet is not F, when by the first arm of the statement we mean to ascribe an attribute to it and by the second we mean to deny that it is identical with the attribute ascribed. His explanation is that in the first case the thing "partakes of F" whereas in the second it "shares in (i.q. partakes of) difference which severs it from F". These formulae are not expressly proffered as analyses of the verb "to be"; still it seems reasonable to infer that Plato regards the verb in its copulative use as requiring the analysis "partaking of . . .", but in its identifying use as requiring the analysis "partaking of identity relatively to . . ." (or, in the negative form discussed by the ES, "partaking of difference relatively to . . .").

If this is so the context seems to give us yet a third way of analys-

[47] Most explicitly by J. L. Ackrill, op. cit., p. 1. Disagreement with Ackrill's express conclusion, that Plato wants to mark off different senses of "is", does not at all carry disagreement on his substantial issue, that Plato succeeds in distinguishing predications from statements of identity.

[48] To this it is irrelevant whether "man is man" and "good is good" are the sole legitimate forms of statement in their object-language or whether these are the sole forms admitted in their meta-language to justify some analysis (e.g. atomistic) of their object-language. It is irrelevant too (though important for other issues) whether they had any grasp of such distinctions (cf. G. Prauss, *Platon und der logische Eleatismus* [Berlin, 1966], p. 184). What they reject, wittingly or unwittingly and on some level of discourse, is predication: "they do not allow anything to be called another thing by sharing in the other's character" (252B9–10).

ing or paraphrasing out the verb. At 256A1, for instance, the ES remarks that "change is, by *partaking in being*" ($\xi\sigma\tau\iota$ $\delta\iota\grave{\alpha}$ $\tau\grave{o}$ $\mu\epsilon\tau\acute{\epsilon}\chi\epsilon\iota\nu$ $\tau o\hat{\upsilon}$ $\check{o}\nu\tau o\varsigma$). Since this formula did not occur in the previous analyses and since unlike the others it seems to make ". . . is" a one-place predicate, it arguably should represent a third sense of "to be". What can this be but the existential sense?

(4) Finally, the existential meaning appears to be marked off once more at 255C8–D8, where the ES is distinguishing being from difference. "I think you agree that there are two ways in which we speak of 'things that are': in some cases we call them so in their own right ($\alpha\check{\upsilon}\tau\grave{\alpha}$ $\kappa\alpha\theta$' $\alpha\check{\upsilon}\tau\acute{\alpha}$), in some cases we call them so with reference to other things ($\pi\rho\grave{o}\varsigma$ $\check{\alpha}\lambda\lambda\alpha$); but 'the different' is only ever so called with reference to something different ($\pi\rho\grave{o}\varsigma$ $\check{\epsilon}\tau\epsilon\rho o\nu$). This would not be the case if being and difference were not quite distinct things; if difference partook of both characters as being does, the class of different things would sometimes contain a thing that was different but not relatively to something different from it." It is commonly said that here Plato is representing being as both "absolute" and "relative", while difference is only "relative";[49] and that what he means is just that, while the description of a thing as "different" is always an incomplete description, awaiting some further reference to complete it, the description of something as "being" or as "what is" does not in one use of that expression call for any completion. And this latter use, the use in which one can say of something that *it is* and leave it there, is surely the existential use.

So far as I know, and as forcefully as I can put them, these are the considerations which have led scholars to ignore the troubles attending any version of the established interpretation. I must try now to show that they are misleading. Of the four heads of argument, (1) and (2) profess to prove that Plato could not help but notice the importance to his discussion of picking out an existential sense of the verb "to be". (3) and (4) profess to show that he ex-

---

[49] For the list of those who have said so, from Wilamowitz on, see now Frede, op. cit., p. 22; he could have gone back to Campbell op. cit., p. 152. An old comment of mine to the same effect (*J.H.S* lxxxvii (1957), p. 107 n. 25) has been taken as supporting evidence by Moravcsik and Runciman *inter alios* and pp. 255–58, infra, are addressed to them by way of apology. The comment was retracted in the paper mentioned in n. 1, *supra*.

pressly made this distinction. So (3) and (4) make the stronger claim, and I take them first.[50]

The explicit distinction

(*3) The appeal to the expression "partaking in being" can properly be met by the reminder that Plato also uses "partaking in not-being" (μετέχειν τοῦ μὴ ὄντος, 260D7; κοινωνεῖν τοῦ μὴ ὄντος, 260E2–261A1) and plainly does not mean this to signify non-existence or mark a one-place predicate.[51] But without reliance on Parity the same point can be proved of the positive expression. When it occurs in the *Parmenides*, for instance, it is evidently not pre-empted for existential being.[52] And (lest this be set down as another chicanerie of the *Parmenides*) we can bring it home to the *Sophist*. That the phrase can be used of that connective ". . . is . . ." which I have alleged to be at the heart of Plato's investigation is proved by 259A6–8. The ES sums up his argument about the Different: it "partakes in being, and is by virtue of that partaking —but not the thing of which it partakes but something different". The verb in the last clause must be supplied from its predecessor, and the verb supplied is the incomplete "is". (To be sure, the reductivists hoped to save an existential sense for the incomplete "is" without engaging Plato in a study of denials of existence. But their thesis depended on displacing the negative, and that is a past issue.)

Now consider the formula "partaking in being" as it occurs at 256A1. It is embedded in a stretch of reasoning (255E8–256E6) whose results are summarized, with the help of the same formula, at 256D11–E6. The reasoning was sketched under (3): it consists in showing, for various general terms P, that with a certain proviso a specimen subject (in this case, Change) can be said both to be P

---

[50] They have now been ably debated by Frede, op. cit., pp. 55–59 and 12–29, but I retain my own replies as making a few different points of controversial interest.

[51] What it does mean to say that λόγος partakes in not-being is obscure until λόγος is replaced by τὸ λεγόμενον (much as κίνησις and στάσις had to be replaced in the non-identity proofs by κινεῖται and ἔστηκε or κινούμενον and ἑστός, 250C6–D2, 252D6–10). *What is said*, in a falsehood, *is not*: that is, about some subject one says what is not in the sense explained above (p. 237, and n. 31, *supra*).

[52] Among many occurrences note 141E7–14, 161E3–62B8, 163B6–D1, E6–64A1.

and not to be P. The proviso is that the pattern of analysis of "This is P" varies in the two cases: in Plato's examples, the positive statement is predicative and the negative is a denial of identity. The ES concludes: "So not-being necessarily *is* in the case of change, and with respect to all the kinds;[53] for with respect to them all difference makes each one different from what is, and so makes it what is not. Hence it is in just the same way that we can correctly describe them all as 'not being' and on the other hand (since they partake of being) say that they 'are' and describe them as 'being'. . . . So," the ES goes on, "in the case of each of the forms, the being is multiple and the not-being is countless in number."

"The being is multiple, the not-being is countless": I shall come back to this distinction in number, but a little must be said of it now. Briefly, the ES has been arguing concerning a specimen subject that it is, predicatively, many things, but that it is not identical with these things. So it *is not*, as a matter of identity, all those things which it *is* predicatively. But in addition to this it is not, as a matter of identity, countless things which it is also *not* predicatively. (Greed is one of the things which change is not identical with, but neither is it a possible attribute of change.) So if "This is P" is understood predicatively and "This is not P" is understood as a denial of identity, there are countless more things that anything is not than that it is. That the ES has been dividing the positive and negative occurrences of the verb in this way seems clear enough, and I shall suggest a reason later. Meantime the distinction does not affect our argument. The use of the verb "to be" on which the ES rests his conclusion is the connective use, distributed between identity and predication. So he can fairly claim that "it is in just the same way (κατὰ ταὐτά, i.e. by finding an appropriate complement) that we can correctly describe them all as 'not-being' and—since they partake of being—as 'being' ". And to clinch his meaning the ES at once refers to the multiple being and countless not-being of any of the forms he has been discussing. He means that (as Cornford's version paraphrases it) "there is much that each *is* and an indefinite number of things that it *is not*".

So to extract any express recognition of a substantive or existential use of "is" from this passage would not square with the argument. The formula "partaking of being" is not used to mark this distinction in the summary of the discussion at 256E3 (or therefore

in the preceding lines 256D8–9). Nor, as we saw, is it so used in
259A6–8. It cannot therefore have this task in the argument's
opening move at 256A1. Whether the words "change is" are read
as a fragment of the preceding "change is different from rest"
(255E11–12)[54] or as elliptical for "change is with respect to something" (i.e. is instantiated, the converse of participation: 256E5,
263B11–12, and p. 259 below), fragmentary or elliptical they surely
are in Plato's view.

"Partaking in being", then, is not pre-empted for ascribing unqualified being to any subject. But once it is put in this way no
reader of Plato should cavil. Participation was shaped as a technical device to meet just those cases in which a thing is qualifiedly P
but also qualifiedly not P.[55] Consider the uses of "partaking" in
our context: each thing is different, by partaking in the form of
difference (255E4–6); each is identical, by partaking in identity
(256A7–8); and each thing is, by partaking in being. The question
remains what something differs from, what it can be identified
with, and, quite generally, what it is.

A particularly illuminating parallel is the treatment of unity in
the *Parmenides*. There (129C4–D2) Socrates explains how he can
be both one and many: he is many parts, and in this way partakes
in plurality; he is one man, and thus partakes in unity. It would be
absurd to suggest that Plato views these partakings as endowing
Socrates with some kind of unqualified unity and plurality: on these
terms, Socrates would still be the subject of a contradiction and
Zeno's paradoxes could never be cleared up. In other words, Plato
does not represent the situation as analysable into "Socrates is one
& Socrates is many & Socrates is human & Socrates has parts". To
say that Socrates is one and many is to say something elliptical, not
to isolate two independent conjuncts from a longer conjunction:
"one" and "many" are completed by specifying "in what respect
and in what relation" (*R.* 436D).[56] Similarly, then, with participation in being and not-being.

(*4) The second argument for presenting Plato with the explicit
distinction of existence from other sorts of being can be more

---

[54] Cf. Frede, op. cit., pp. 56–57.

[55] See *J.H.S.* lxxvii (1957), pp. 107–11.

[56] This gives added point to Parmenides' query whether Socrates
wants a Form of Man, and to Socrates' hesitation (*Prm.* 130C1–4): for
to admit this *would* seem to commit him to analysing "I am one man"
as "I partake in unity and I partake in humanity". In fact it does not:

quickly met.[57] In 255C12–D7 he does indeed draw a distinction between different uses of the verb "to be"; but these are almost certainly its incomplete uses, in statements of identity and of predication.

First, when the ES marks off difference from being he does not say, as the commentators make out, that to call X "different" is to give a *relative* or *incomplete* description of X (πρός τι). He says that it is to give a description which must always be filled out by reference to something *different from X* (255D1, 7). By contrast, when we describe things as "being" (i.e. say that they are) it is only in some instances that what we say must be completed by reference to something other than the subject (πρὸς ἄλλα, 255C13);[58] in other instances things can be said to be "themselves in their own right" (αὐτὰ καθ᾿ αὑτά, 255C12–13). Now it is in predication that the complement of the verb "to be" imports something different from the subject: on this the ES hangs a major argument at 256A3–C10, and it was of course a thesis basic to the theory of Ideas.[59] In identity-statements, on the other hand, the expressions which flank the verb cannot designate different things; indeed in this context they seem to be regarded as typically of the form "A is A" (254D15, 257A5, 259B3–4).

Secondly, the language with which the ES makes his contrast at 255C–D (καθ᾿ αὑτό . . . ἕτερον, ἄλλο) has already been introduced, at the start of this section of the argument, to mark the distinction between identity-statements and predications. The opsimaths whose theory commits them, wittingly or unwittingly,[60] to leaving only the first sort of statement standing, are said to "debar anything from sharing in the condition of another and so being called that other" (μηδὲν ἐῶντες κοινωνίᾳ παθήματος ἑτέρου θάτερον

---

the essential incompleteness of "one" and "many" and "same" and "different" and "is" and "is not" is well brought out by paradoxes in the *Parmenides* (e.g. 146D5–E4, 147A3–8, 161E3–162B8), and for them the original model of participation holds good.

[57] Cf. Frede, op. cit., pp. 12–29. See also "Additional Note" at the end of this selection, p. 266.

[58] That Plato does not mean to distinguish between ἕτερον and ἄλλο here (Deichgräber *apud* Frede, p. 12 n. 1) is proved by 256C5–6, 257A1, 257B4 and 10, and in the essential anticipation at 252B10, C3.

[59] It is a premise of the Third Man paradox, Alex., *Metaph.* 84.21–85.12.

[60] Cf. n. 48, *supra*.

προσαγορεύειν, 252B9–10); and then in producing the identity-statements that are essential to stating their case they are said to couple the expressions εἶναι . . . χωρὶς . . . τῶν ἄλλων . . . καθ᾽ αὑτό (252C2–5). So the commentators who gloss our passage by the distinction between καθ᾽ αὑτό and πρός τι or τινί in the *Philebus* (51C) or the *Theaetetus* (157Λ–B) have looked too far afield and brought back the wrong dichotomy.[61]

Thirdly, it is this interpretation that explains, as the older one cannot, why the ES needs a different argument (255B8–C7) to distinguish being from *identity*. For "same" is a grammatically incomplete predicate, no less than "different"; what makes the argument inapplicable to it is just that it cannot be supposed to mark a relation between different things (cf. 256B1).

Fourthly, the ES at 255C10 introduces his distinction between uses of "to be" with the words "I think you agree" (and not, as translators on the received interpretation generally feel impelled to turn it, "I think you will agree"). Why assume that he already has Theaetetus' assent? Simply because he has just followed his review of the opsimaths' theory with an argument to show their mistake (252D–254D): predications are possible and necessary, even though in abstract contexts it takes philosophical expertise to determine what can be predicated of what. And Theaetetus has agreed: predication is as necessary as identification.

This plea, that the distinction be read as arising from its context, can be made broader. Just as it is the division of identification from predication that the ES needs to settle the opsimaths' confusion, so it is this that he requires to explain the general paradox about being which precedes it (249C10–250E4: see p. 261 below) and to disarm the paradoxes which follow (255E8–256C10, cf. 259B8–D7). The division that is not made, and not relevant to these problems, is one between a complete or existential use of "to be" and an undifferentiated parcel of incomplete uses.

There is another moral to be drawn from these answers. Even in performing the valuable and essential task of disentangling predicative and identity-statements which carry the verb "to be",[62] Plato can hardly have seen his project as that of displaying different

---

[61] The distinction as here interpreted also leads naturally to Aristotle's division between τὸ καθ᾽ αὑτὸ λεγόμενον and τὸ ἕτερον καθ᾽ ἑτέρου λεγόμενον.

[62] The brunt of Ackrill's argument, op. cit.

senses of the verb. His comments upon its syntax are taken to mark out the different tasks, or different possibilities of combination, of a single undifferentiated form, being. For if (*3) shows that the expression "partaking in being" is not used to identify a special sense of the verb it becomes the less likely that the other expressions quoted in (3) are meant to paraphrase the verb in other senses; no such role is claimed for them in the text (256A10–B4).[63] And the matter seems to be clinched by the argument just discussed. If Plato took himself to be distinguishing senses of "being" he would surely have to conclude, from his reasoning in 255C8–D7, that he had managed to distinguish difference from only one of the concepts falling under that name, i.e. from the sort of being which is *not πρὸς ἄλλο* (or, on the older interpretation, *πρός τι*). One proof that being remains for him a unitary concept is that he concludes directly to his distinction between being and difference.[64]

In the *Sophist*, then, Plato does not (in Shorey's words) "explicitly distinguish the copula from the substantive *is*". Does his argument nevertheless compel him to set apart an existential use of the verb?

The paradoxes

(*1) Consider again the assumptions which govern Plato's puzzles about not-being (236D–241B), and his treatment of those assumptions. The paradoxes are represented as all in various ways dependent on one veteran and protean hypothesis, that *being can have no connexion with not-being* or, more at length, that what-is-not cannot be in any way and what-is cannot not be in any way (cf. 241B1–2, D6–7). Understandably, in view of its ambiguity, the hypothesis takes various forms: in (i), that "what is not" cannot designate anything that is (237C1–7); in (ii)–(iii), that an attribute that is cannot be attached to a subject that is not (238A7–9, C5–6); in (iv), that it is paradoxical that what really is not (or is not real)

---

[63] Indeed, 256A11–B4 (where the supposedly central verb "to be" is merely left to be understood from the previous sentence) is more easily read as offering different analyses of "the same": in "change (is) the same" it signifies "partaking in the form Identical", in "change (is) not the same" it signifies "the form Identical". If οὐχ ὁμοίως εἰρήκαμεν (256A11–12) promises paraphrases these are the readier candidates, but a phrase that often promises paraphrases in Aristotle must not be assumed to in Plato (cf. p. 266 *infra*).

[64] It remains the vowel-form, being (n. 27, *supra*); but I cannot here pursue the conceptual distinctions embodied in the "communion of forms" or the role of μέθεξις.

should really be (or be a real) anything at all (240B12–C3, Bad-
ham's text); in (v), that it is paradoxical, in the case of believing
what is not, that what is believed should also have being (241A3–
B3). In addition, (i) assumes the identity of what is not with
nothing,[65] and (iv) and (v) take what is not to be the contrary of
what is (240B5, D6–9).

I believe it will be agreed that Plato's understanding of these
skeletal assumptions must be gathered from his subsequent treatment of them. On this point the traditional interpretations seem
curiously ambivalent. There is an evident wish to retain the second
assumption, construed as meaning that only existent subjects can
have actual attributes (see (2c) on p. 250). Otherwise the assumptions are regarded as an intractable set of dicta about non-existence
which Plato drops in favour of some innocuous ones exploiting a
different sense of the verb "to be". But neither of these reactions is
Plato's. He offers to *contradict* them all, to refute them and prove
their negations (cf. τὸν ἔλεγχον τοῦτον καὶ τὴν ἀπόδειξιν, 242A7–
B5). He takes them (though he cannot yet allow himself the luxury
of the word) to be, straightforwardly and sense unchallenged, false.

Thus the first is contradicted by showing that, given the appropriate complements, "what is not" and "what is" must be applicable to the same things (256E2–7) and indeed to any subject of
discourse (263B11–12). The third, i.e. the claim that "real" and
"unreal" do not cohabit, can evidently be rebutted in the same
manner, and the ES's formulation of the reality-puzzle (240B9–13)
seems tailored to this solution: the semblance is not the real original
but it certainly is the real semblance.[66] But in the end he simply
reduces the problem of unreality to that of falsehood (264C10–D5).

Nor, of course, is the second assumption smuggled out of this
general rebuttal. It is contradicted by the same passages which
prove the contradictory of the first. What is not (sc. not so-and-so)
must nevertheless have attributes that are—viz. "are with respect
to it", are its attributes (256E5–6, 263B11–12). On these terms an
attribute can evidently be said both to be and not to be, belonging
to some subjects but not others: the incomplete "is" in one more
role, introduced (but not paraphrased) to mark a relation just the
converse of participation.

[65] Cf. n. 8, *supra.*
[66] On this as an element in Plato's standard view of reality see
Vlastos, op. cit. (n. 4 and 45, *supra*).

Here, however, there is a complication which helps to explain the course of Plato's argument. Some forms—being, identity and difference *imprimis*—can be attributed to anything whatever. So how can these be said "not to be" with respect to any subject? Well: they can, provided this is understood as a denial of identity. This I take it is why Plato, discussing these all-pervasive concepts, is ready to explain the "multiple being" which belongs to a subject in terms of the predicates which are true of it, but turns to non-identity to explain its "countless not-being" (cf. p. 254, *supra*). And it is why, when he shifts to such unpervasive attributes as flying and sitting, this asymmetry seems to be quietly given up: the not-being of these attributes is extended to the case in which they are not truly predicable of some subject (263B11–12). But the tacit extension is not a slip: no doubt Plato feels entitled to adapt his analysis to these cases on the ground that non-identity is still central to it. If flying "is not with respect to Theaetetus", the non-identity holds now between flying and any and all of the attributes which do belong to Theaetetus, which "are" for him (p. 237, *supra*). And thus he prepares his ground for contradicting the assumption used in (v) to extract contradictions from falsehood. The man who speaks or thinks falsely does after all and without paradox ascribe being to what is not, or not-being to what is: he counts among X's attributes one which "is not with respect to X", i.e. which differs from any of X's attributes; or he counts among attributes of the second class one which "is with respect to X". The distinction seems to be that between positive and negative falsehoods, and Plato deals expressly only with a falsehood of the first class (263A1–D5); but his language implies that he is ready for the others (240E10–241A1; cf. ἀπραξίαν [non-action] 262C3).

There is no need for more words on the remaining assumptions, that what is not is *nothing* and is *contrary to what is*. The sophist is nowhere advised that his puzzles over not-being and falsehood employ a special concept of being or a sense of the key-verb which will not stand negation. He is instructed in the proper scope of, and safeguards on, the "is" and "not-is" that he mismanaged. He will look in vain for any recognition here of the baffling unavailability of what false statements try but fail to mention.

Let us leave him unassuaged for the moment and notice that the subsequent paradox about being (242B6–250E4) is equally ill-adapted to forcing a recognition of "exists" as a distinct sense of "is". As the ES forecast, the accounts of "is" and "is not" go hand in hand.

This section of the dialogue is designed to culminate in a paradox (the *aporia* of 250E1–2) whose diagnosis is generally agreed.[67] It depends on confusing identity-statements with predications. This is why the ES moves at once to the opsimaths (251A5–C6) and proposes to give one answer to both difficulties (251C8–D2). On the way to his problem he has shown that previous attempts to characterize being (or "what is" and "what are") were unduly restrictive: those who say that being is a plurality or else that it is only one thing, that it is corporeal or that it is immutable and non-perceptible, are all rebuked for leaving something out of the inventory (242C4–249D8). Thus he reaches a proposal (A) that seems to leave nothing out: "being is whatever is changed and (whatever is) unchanged" (249D3–4). He comments that the disjunction "changed-unchanged" is surely exhaustive (250C12–D3), and in fact any other exhaustive dichotomy would serve the paradox equally well. For now he repeats an argument which saw service earlier against the pluralists: being is neither change nor rest—it is this different thing, being (250C3–4). And this is at once restated (B) in the form: "by its own nature being neither rests nor changes" (250C6–7). So (A) seems to be in conflict with (B).

It is commonly agreed that (B) is proved by an illicit move from "X is not identical with either Y or Z" to "X is not characterized by either Y or Z"; and that subsequently the ES blocks this move by distinguishing identity-statements from predications and showing, for some ubiquitous predicates (being, identity, difference), that a subject which is not identical with one of these still cannot help being characterized by it. So this problem is set and solved as an exercise in the logic of identity and predication, not of existence. True, commentators have hoped to find Plato arguing positive truths about existence in his prefatory review of older theories of being.[68] Given his general strategy in the section, such truths could be no more than parenthetical. For my part I doubt that Plato is

---

[67] Even when existence is thought to be the topic of the introductory pages: n. 14, *supra*.

[68] On this see J. Malcolm, op. cit., who finds no existential sense of the verb distinguished in it; and notice that Plato takes no care in these pages to restrict the verb in its critical appearances to one grammatical role. It varies from adverb to connective and from these to roles in which no explicit complement is supplied.

pressing even such parenthetical doctrine on the reader: it is
enough to read this study of "things that are (or are not)" against
the *Parmenides'* study of "things that are one (or not one)" for the
essentially elliptical character of these descriptions to be clear.
Plato's arguments about being are, what he represents them to be,
prefatory to a paradox. What they show (at best) is the incoherence
of certain claims that, for some favoured value of F, *to be* is just
to be F. They lead to the proposal that *to be* is *to be either or both F and
not-F;* and thus they set the scene for the puzzle described above.

The approach to falsehood

(*2) In the ES's scheme, the being of an attribute such as change
or not-being carries at least the requirements that it be un-
problematically identifiable and instantiated. That is, to say that
"it is" promises two sorts of completion: that it is A, "having a
nature of its own", and not B (cf. 258B8–C3); and that it is "with
respect to" other things C, D . . . (p. 259, *supra*). Similarly with any
subject of attributes: to say that "it is" is to face the *Sophist's*
question "Is what and what sort of thing?" What then of the requirement, supposedly fundamental to Plato's final analysis of true
and false statement (261C6–263D4), that the subject of any statement must exist?[69]

Evidently the requirement can no longer be defended as satisfying the "hatstand" assumption discerned in stage (ii) of the
puzzles. The ES has contradicted the assumption governing that
stage, and in such a way as to show that it was not understood as
existential. But consider the analysis itself.

What is striking is that, while Plato insists that a statement must
be *about* (or *of*, or must *name* or *belong to*) something, he does not use
the verb "to be" in any existential sense to bring out the nature of
this thing. He says that a statement must be about *something* (262E5)
and not *nothing* (263C9–11), and he has spent a long argument explaining the terms on which the first but not the second can be
made a subject of discourse; but when he uses the verb in this connexion he speaks of the subject as "what is or what is not" (262C3).
This last phrase has understandably troubled the defenders of the
received view: they have tried to deny that it applies to the subject
of a statement, and even construed it as making a broad distinction
between positive and negative assertions.[70] But the context defeats

[69] Moravcsik, op. cit., p. 41.
[70] Ibid., p. 63 n. 1; cf. Campbell, op. cit., p. 173 ad loc.

them. Plato is arguing that any statement requires the coupling of a subject- and predicate-expression. Without marrying some such expression as "a lion" to one of a different family such as "runs", it is not possible to declare "the action or non-action or being of what is or what is not" (οὐδεμίαν πρᾶξιν οὐδ᾽ ἀπραξίαν οὐδὲ οὐσίαν ὄντος οὐδὲ μὴ ὄντος, 262C2–3). Just as "action or non-action or being" characterizes what the predicate-expression contributes,[71] so "what is or what is not" picks out the contribution of the subject-phrase.[72] Plato wants to provide for such subjects as "the not-beautiful" (or "what is not beautiful") as well as for "the beautiful" ("what is beautiful"). Otherwise he would have disallowed some of his own conclusions as candidates for a truth-value. As it is, when it is most important for the received interpretation that he should pick out the subject by an existential use of the verb, it is the connective "is" and its negation that he leaves centrally entrenched.[73]

It remains to show how the sophist's puzzle is finally diagnosed within this scheme of concepts, which lacks or ignores an expression for "exist" and makes no attempt to isolate such a "kind" or "form" as existence. The *Theaetetus'* analogy between speaking and seeing or touching is not recalled: that was only a symptom.[74] What is taken up is the premise from which the *Euthydemus* started its paradoxes about falsehood, that things (πράγματα) can be spoken of only by expressions which belong to them. The ES accepts this— too hospitably—in the form that any statement having a truth-value must belong to something, viz. to what it is "of" or "about," the πρᾶγμα that it "names" (cf. 263A4–5, 262E12–13). Let me call this relation between a statement and what it is about the

---

[71] And the "being" cannot be represented by the traditional interpretation as existence without committing Plato to explaining in the sequel how existential statements can be false but significant. On the whole phrase, Apelt, *Sophista*, ad loc.; on οὐσία, n. 73, *infra*.

[72] So Diès, "ni action, ni inaction, ni être, soit d'un être, soit d'un non-être", and Taylor, "the action, inaction, or being of anything that is or is not".

[73] The οὐσία of 261E5 is of course the "being" studied in the preceding arguments: the texts cited in n. 52, *supra*, prove that it is not confined to existential contexts, and the other occurrences in the *Sophist* can be explained on the same terms.

[74] Such non-intensionally transitive verbs as "hitting" and "kicking" seem equally appropriate to conveying the sophist's demand for a verbal contact between statement and situation. On one view that (some) verbs of perception are especially important to the analogy, see n. 40, *supra*.

"A-relation", and notice two points in Plato's treatment of it. First, he illustrates but does not offer to analyse it: evidently he assumes that it has been elucidated by the whole study of subject-predicate relations which he now recalls in the dictum "There is much that is with respect to each thing and much that is not" (263A11–12). Secondly, it becomes clear from 262E12–263A10(esp. 263A4–10) and C5–D1 that he takes the intuitively plausible view of the relation: he holds that "Theaetetus sits" and "Theaetetus flies" are both about just one thing, Theaetetus. There is no suggestion that they are about (or name, or belong to) *sitting* or *flying*. Of course statements about sitting and flying are possible, including some which are equivalent to those just quoted: "Sitting is with respect to Theaetetus", for example. But from what Plato says it seems that these are not the same statements: they would not be characterized as being about the same subject (262E5–6).[75]

It is this A-relation, then, that gives the sophist the connexion he demands between the words and the actual situation described: the verbal contact, or the verbal "belonging". (It is what Austin called the demonstrative component in the statement; what is often called the reference.) The sophist is allowed his claim that if this relation does not hold, no truth or falsehood has been uttered. But then it is explained that he has exaggerated the scope of the relation. It is a necessary condition of both truth and falsehood, but it is not a sufficient condition of truth. The mere naming—even the stringing together of names (262A9–10)—does not "complete the business" ($\pi\epsilon\rho\alpha\acute{\iota}\nu\epsilon\iota\nu$ $\tau\iota$) or achieve a truth-value (262B9–C7): that comes only when something is *said about* what the statement is about,[76] and for this one needs to import an expression with quite another function, such as ". . . sits" or ". . . flies". Once the place of "what is not" in the diagnosis has been vindicated, it is in the

---

[75] This brings out the irrelevance of representing Plato as meeting the sophist's puzzle by the explanation that "Theaetetus flies" mentions (= belongs to, is of or about) two things, the falsehood consisting in mentioning together things not found together in fact; or of looking for some "correlate" with which the false sentence as a whole makes verbal contact. The expressions used at 261E4–6 and 262E10–11 are innocuous preliminaries to the point insisted on in 262E5–6, 262E10–263A10, C5–11.

[76] That the $\pi\epsilon\rho\acute{\iota}$ in 263B4–5 is to be coupled with the $\lambda\acute{\epsilon}\gamma\epsilon\iota$ and not merely with the $\check{o}\nu\tau\alpha$ $\dot{\omega}s$ $\check{\epsilon}\sigma\tau\iota\nu$ is certified by 263D1 and generally by the requirement that the $\lambda\acute{o}\gamma os$ must be $\tau\iota\nu\acute{o}s$ or $\pi\epsilon\rho\grave{\iota}$ $\tau\iota\nu\acute{o}s$ (262E5–6, 263A4).

A-relation that Plato seems to locate the residual mistake in the sophist's picture of falsehood. Falsehood had appeared an abortive attempt to mention something, like an unsuccessful effort to touch or to hear; and this confused the conditions for naming with the conditions for truth.

I need not dwell on this familiar and, I think, satisfactory account of Plato's reply.[77] My argument concerns the way in which the relation of aboutness is introduced. Doubtless it needs (and is currently receiving) harder analysis before it will carry any more ambitious study of statement-structure; but Plato's exploration of the ways in which something can be unparadoxically differentiated, assigned and denied attributes, is a necessary and for his purpose an adequate introduction. The requirement that the subject should exist is neither: witness the insoluble and irrelevant query whether he wants to make room for centaurs.

"But the requirement that the statement should be about *something* and not *nothing* just is the requirement that the subject should exist; for Plato, *to be* is *to be something*,[78] and surely this is an account of existence." Two last remarks on this.

I have tried to characterize the scheme of concepts within which Plato studies "nothing" and its twin, 'something', as possible subjects of discourse. For such a study of subject-predicate structure an account of existence is neither a presupposition nor a part; but it might well be a further outcome, much as a logic without existen-

---

[77] But since I have implied that it is novel with the *Sophist* I must notice the unitarian suggestion that the solution is already recognized in the *Euthydemus* (284C) and *Cratylus* (385B), which characterize true speaking as speaking of things that are, as they are, and false speaking as speaking of things that are, as they are not. The first half of the conjunction is echoed in the *Sophist* (263D4-5). But (i) the description of falsehood is not echoed in the *Sophist*—understandably, since it is at least ambiguous and its ambiguity is used to generate unresolved paradoxes at *Euthd.* 284C-E, 285E-286B. (ii) The echo of the truth-description in the *Sophist* has a quite different sense: the *Euthd.* makes it clear that the "things that are" are subjects of the statement (see examples in 284D-E) whereas in *Sph.* 263B4-5 they are equally clearly predicates; and the sense in which a predicate "is (or is not) with respect to" a subject has had to be established earlier (256E5-6, recalled here at 263B11-12).

[78] In the earlier passage cited in n. 1, *supra*, I used the expression "*to be* is *to be something or other*" in describing Plato's theory, and now think this unperspicuous for reasons given here. The familiar idiom εἶναι τι is of course used in the *Sophist* (e.g. 246E5) as elsewhere in Plato.

tial presuppositions can be made to yield a formula for individual existence.[79] This is, I think, what it became in Aristotle's metaphysics. But notoriously Aristotle complains of Plato for not taking this step, for ignoring the consequent distinction of senses in "is" and remaining content with his unitary concept, being.

As for the equation "*to be* is *to be something*", the negation of "to be something" is "not to be anything" or "to be nothing", which Plato holds to be unintelligible; and then it would follow from the equation that "not to be" makes no sense. But Plato recognizes no use of the verb in which it cannot be directly negated. He holds indeed that *to be in no way at all* is a merely paradoxical notion; but he argues with all possible emphasis that this is not the legitimate negation of *to be*. To discount this is to fall into the embarrassments of the traditional account: to saddle Plato with an argument which first sets puzzles about non-existence, then offers to refute the assumptions on which the puzzles depend, and finally backs down

---

[79] J. Hintikka, "Studies in the Logic of Existence and Necessity, I: Existence", *Monist* 1 (1966) pp. 55–76.

Additional Note (see p. 256, n. 57 *supra*).

The preceding argument (255B8–C7) distinguishes being from identity, and since it discusses being without specifying any complement for the verb 'to be' it is often understood as dealing expressly with existence. But it follows the argument of 255A4–B6, in which change and rest (C and R) are distinguished from identity and difference on the ground that, while both C and R can be called either identical or different, C cannot be said to rest nor R to change. Thereafter being is distinguished from identity on the ground that C and R can both alike be said to be, but not said to be identical (ταὐτόν). Throughout both arguments the complements to "identical" and "different" are left unspecified. So in the first argument the ascription of identity to C and R is tacitly understood as meaning that C is identical *with* C, and R *with* R, while in the second it is tacitly understood as meaning that they are the same *as each other*. (The use of the singular ταὐτόν as a joint predicate in 255C1 helps the shift, but is itself illegitimate: the counterpart predicate from the verb "to be" would be ὄν, which cannot be a joint predicate at all.) What the arguments show, if anything, is that for some subject in whose description "the same" and "different" can properly occur (sc. with some undeclared complement), neither expression can be replaced in the description by "changing" or (in the alternative case) by "at rest"; and that, for some subjects in whose joint description "being" can properly occur, that expression cannot be replaced by "identical" (again with some undeclared complement). Patently the argument loses none of its force if we write: "for some subject in whose description 'being' can properly occur (*with some undeclared complement*)"; the argument systematically discounts complements.

and recommends that direct negation be prudently reserved for other uses of the verb "to be".

This essay has not been previously published.

13

SENTENCE MEANING, NEGATION, AND PLATO'S PROBLEM OF NON-BEING

DAVID WIGGINS

SYNOPSIS

I. An analysis of *Sophist* 236E ff. The sentential variant of the problem of non-being in dialogues earlier than *Theaetetus* and *Sophist*. II. The *display theory* of sentence meaning as an escape from Plato's problem of false judgement. The theory's inability to accommodate negation. III. Plato's analytical approach to the problem of sentence-sense in *Sophist*, and anticipations of this in *Cratylus* and *Theaetetus*. IV. Relevant points from the discussion of Being in *Sophist*. V. The *Sophist* explanation of negation. Preliminary criticism and a suggested amendment of the explanation. VI. The analysis of true and false judgement at *Sophist* 263B4 ff. and Plato's return from negation to falsity. VII. Crucial inadequacy of *Sophist* account of negation to sustain Plato's theory of false judgement. VIII. Positive achievements of the analysis.

I

At *Sophist* 236E the Eleatic stranger interrupts a discussion of the nature of a sophist and his particular style of mimesis to introduce a problem which leads into the central theme of the dialogue. It is given in a passage which one might condense and render like this:

This appearing and seeming which we have been talking about and contrasted with being, and this saying things—but things which are not true (*legein men atta alēthē de mē*—), is and has always been a matter of great difficulty and perplexity. It is very difficult to see how without involving oneself in a contradiction one can really affirm that it is possible to say or think anything false. (236E) . . . For [1] such an affirmation involves positing the being of that which is not (*to mē on einai*). Unless there were that which is not there could be no such thing as falsity. (237A) . . .

The stranger continues:

> [But] to what is one to apply the designation (*poi chrē tounom'
> epipherein*) *that which is not?* (237C2) . . . [2] It is clear that *that
> which is not* cannot be applied to anything among things which
> are. (237C6) . . . In which case it can't be applied to *anything.*
> (237C10) . . . [But all the same] [3] anyone who says anything
> must say *something* (*anagkē ton ti legonta hen ge ti legein*, 237D6–7)
> . . . [4] and it is quite undeniable that one who says what is not
> *something* says nothing at all (*ton . . . mē ti legonta pantapasi
> mēden legein*, 237C12). . . . We cannot allow that such a person
> does some saying but says nothing (*legein mengeil en de mēden*).
> [5] We must even deny that someone who attempts to say that
> which is not succeeds in doing any saying at all (*oude legein
> phateon hos g' an epicheirēi mē on phtheggesthai*, 237E3–6).

The puzzle figures here in its most refined form but the genus to
which it belongs is very familiar in Plato's dialogues and has a long
history in the development of his thought.[1] I shall call the particular argument which I shall derive from this text of the *Sophist*
and from *Theaetetus* 189 the sentential variant of the problem of
non-being, calling it a *variant* to indicate that it is merely a single
strand of the much more heterogeneous knot of problems which result from complete generalization of the arguments of Parmenides.
Since it is highly dubious that Plato had the logical apparatus to
disentangle all these perplexities in exactly the way we now should,
a certain risk inheres in this procedure of singling out one variant—

---

[1] See *Euthydemus* 283E7–284C6 (a very crude version with an un-
talented sophist for a mouthpiece, no indication of the depth of Plato's
future interest). For related questions see *Republic* Book V, esp. 487B6–
487C9. The *Cratylus* expresses something nearer to the final version
which I shall attempt to analyse. See 429 ff. and cp. 385. See also
Parmenides 161E. But it is not until the *Theaetetus* and the *Sophist* that the
puzzle really takes on the interesting and special form which I shall
attempt to treat. Even between the *Theaetetus* and the *Sophist* versions
there are differences. But I think that the continuity of the puzzle itself
in these two versions, and the intimate linkage of the two dialogues
(which goes well beyond the continuity of time and place explicitly
signalled by Plato at *Tht.* 210D, *Soph.* 216A), entitle me to concentrate,
as I shall, on their resemblance. If the *Sophist* is to resolve any of the
perplexities of the *Theaetetus* there is a limit to the extent to which the
Sophist can modify the problems of the *Theaetetus*, except in so far as
such modification is made into a relatively explicit part of their eventual solution.

the risk of cutting across Plato's own view of the organization of the problem of non-being.[2] But Plato himself attacks the problem in a piecemeal fashion, and there can be no objection to seeing matters from a particular perspective. What is important is that the perspective should not induce distortion. But I believe, and hope I may make the idea somewhat plausible, that Plato really does recognize the interesting and special problem which he appears to recognize in the passage I have cited, and that his method of exposition is to use it as a way of leading into other Parmenidean questions which are equally important in their own right and which require to be answered before the solution of the sentential puzzle can be completed. I do not number the analysis of "exists" among these other questions. (The only respect in which the sentential variant of the problem of non-being is an existential problem is that it is a particular problem about the 'being' of a certain particular kind of thing.) But I shall argue that it does require e.g. a theory about how there can be any such thing as Flying, as predicated of Theaetetus, to explain in Plato's style how there can be anything I say if I falsely say that Theaetetus is flying. Since the solution of the sentential variant is a solution by dissolution the only mark it leaves on Plato's finished doctrine of judgement or assertion is that the doctrine has been carefully fashioned to leave no room for the question on which the puzzle depended. I see it as my main task to show how.

On the view which I shall take of the puzzle it seems to break down into the following steps.

A. (Compiled from [3] above.) For there to be any saying the saying must be saying *something*. The sentence *Theaetetus is flying* cannot be used for judgement or speech at all unless it says *something*. I shall call this the *saying → saying something* doctrine and I shall call the something in each case *what is annexed* to the sentence. To designate what is annexed to a sentence I shall write either a nominalization of the sentence or the sentence itself in angle brackets. Thus: ⟨flying Theaetetus⟩ or ⟨Theaetetus is flying⟩.

B. (Compiled from [1] above.) If a sentence is true then

---

[2] For some of the doubts one might raise on this score see G.E.L. Owen, "Aristotle on the Snares of Ontology" *New Essays on Plato and Aristotle*, ed. Bambrough (London, 1965), p. 71.

what is annexed to it *is*.[3] So what is annexed to *Theaetetus is sitting*, a specimen true sentence, viz. ⟨Theaetetus is sitting⟩, *is*. On the other hand what is annexed to *Theaetetus is flying*, viz. ⟨Theaetetus is flying⟩, is *not*. For there is no such thing as flying Theaetetus. I shall call this the *Truth = Being (of what is annexed)* doctrine.

C. (Compiled from [4].) If Socrates says *Theaetetus is flying* and ⟨Theaetetus is flying⟩ is not, then what Socrates says in fact is not. Socrates says something which is not. I shall call this the *harmlessly transparent description of the object of saying*[4].

D. (Compiled from [2].). (a) There is not (nor exists) anything which is not. Nothing which is not is. One might call this the *strictly first-order doctrine of first-level existents*. (Russell called something similar a "robust sense of reality".) So, (b) if what is annexed to *Theaetetus is flying* is not, then there in no way is (nor exists) any such thing as ⟨Theaetetus is flying⟩. ⟨Theaetetus is flying⟩ is nothing and nothing is ⟨Theaetetus is flying⟩.

E. (Compiled from [4] and [5] and using the earlier steps.) If Socrates says *Theaetetus is flying* and there is no ⟨flying Theaetetus⟩ then Socrates says what in fact is not. He says what is in fact nothing, and so (new step) he *says nothing*. But we had maintained that all saying was saying something. I shall call this new step *the fallaciously opaque reading of the transparent description of the object of saying*.

It may be guessed from my articulation and labels what I think is *prima facie* wrong with the way in which Plato contrives that E shall contradict A, but each step calls for much more comment and I believe that something of substantial philosophical interest is still

---

[3] *Is* in a sense which we ourselves should analyze as *exists*. It is not to be assumed without argument that Plato himself distinguishes it so. (See note 2 and reference to Owen, *New Essays*, and see section IV below.) For Plato's argument here it is not in the least necessary that he should be in a position to *distinguish* this *esti* from other senses of the verb. It is only necessary that it should have in this argument the force which *in fact* attaches to the use of the verb *is* in the context *X is* where *is* might be properly analyzed by us as *exists*.

[4] *Transparent* in the sense that it disregards the obliquity or "opacity" generated by pure indirect speech reports of direct speech and that extraneous elements are introduced into the description which do not belong inside the direct speech. They could not be admitted to an uncommented report of it. *Harmless* because there are ways (e.g. "in fact" above) of making it clear that this is what is being done.

shown by Plato's reasoning even when certain mistakes are removed. But before I try to show what these are, a word about one
doctrine on which, even if it is mistaken, I shall not comment
further. This is the assumption common to Plato and many others
(e.g. Frege) that the something p said by a man who says p is something, as it were ,"acted upon" by that man. He does not produce
it. It is there, whether or not he chooses to say it. He finds it, so to
speak, and then says it. The puzzle of false opinion in Plato depends on a radically different account of the nature of this something from that offered by Frege (*a thought*), or by the traditional
doctrine of propositions, but the idea that "say" is a transitive verb
is common to all. I think this idea cannot be usefully questioned at
the level of analysis which is required to understand Plato's discussion, whose principal achievement, I shall argue, is to make
plain what this something *exactly is not*, viz. a fact or state of affairs
⟨p⟩. Perhaps it is merely one of several possible options to go on
from here to try to put matters right by distinguishing the proposition from a fact or state of affairs; but a critique of Plato's argument
can relatively safely play along with the assumption (which may
persist after Plato's puzzle is resolved) that *A said that p* has at least
the surface form *subject + verb + object*. For this representation
leaves open the possibility that the accusative may be shown at a
deeper level to be cognate, or that the object may be shown to be
internal.[5] I now take the steps A to E in order.

  The *saying → saying something* doctrine can be misunderstood—

---

[5] There are considerable variations in the way in which intensional
verbs, stating, doubting, inquiring, analyzing, pretending, simplifying,
understanding . . ., relate to their object. But in any deeper analysis
perhaps we could unpack all this from the contribution of the particular intensional verb in any particular sentence of the form *subject + intensional verb + object*. I would add that there is more than one kind of
internal accusative and that if the relevant type of internal analysis
suggests that the intensional action "produces" an internal object
rather than "operates upon" an object, this does not decisively settle
all the existential and ontological questions which have vexed the
philosophy of logic in this area. (Platonizing questions about which the
real Plato does not hasten to commit himself.) Does not an adverbial or
cognate accusative analysis have to avail itself of a store of common
structures objectively identifiable and reidentifiable as the structures of
different speech acts by different speakers at different times? But the
non-metaphorical residue of objective doctrines of propositions or of
Frege's doctrine of thoughts was hardly very much more than this in
any case.

indeed the puzzle can only arise if we misunderstand it—but in it-self it is both correct and correctly enough stated by Plato. If some-one claims to have done some saying (talking) there must be an answer to the question "*what* did he say (talk about)?". Contrast shooting (and missing, or shooting without aiming and hitting nothing), and compare hoping or thinking. But a doubt arises. Surely there is thinking or talking about *nothing*—and this is a sort of thinking or talking. I am about to do some. But how is it com-patible with D that there should be? And if there is thinking about nothing then why should there not also be a saying (talking) which was saying nothing?

I suppose that one sort of thing one thinks about when one tries to think about nothing is how exactly it can be that *nothing* is the largest prime number, or that *nothing* or *nobody* is the present King of France. Logical orthodoxy finds a way of removing the ap-parently referential status of "nothing" within these propositions by parsing them into the form *not*-$(\exists x)(x$ is the highest prime) or *not*-$(\exists x)($King of France $(x))$. And by explaining the frame $(\exists x)(\ldots (x))$ in $(\exists x)(F(x))$ in terms of some sentence or other of the form $(F(\_))$ being true, where $(\_)$ holds a place for an individual name and F is a predicate (like "greatest prime") of individuals, this orthodoxy makes $(\exists x)(\ldots (x))$ a certain predicate of predicates of individuals. It is a predicate, here applied to the predicate F, which we may roughly equate with the higher-level notion of *instantiation*. Nothing instantiates the property *greatest prime* if and only if every sentence of the form "_ is greatest prime" is false. On this account *not*-$(\exists x)(\ldots (x))$, like $(\exists x)(\ldots (x))$, will also be a higher level predicate or predicate of predicates of individuals. It will be the compound predicate of predicates, non-instantiation. And whether a man knows it or not, what he is thinking about and struggling for an account of when he thinks about *nothing* is pre-cisely what this compound second-level predicate of first-level predicates stands for.[6]

---

[6] In first-order predicate calculus, where quantification is only over individuals $(\exists x)(F(x))$, and in second-order predicate calculus, where quantification is either over individuals, as in $(\exists x)(F(x))$, or over first-level properties or concepts, as in $(\exists F)(\exists x)(F(x))$, it is not possible actually to state the existence of this second-level property. But in a third-order predicate calculus it would be possible to do so if one wished. One could say Platonically that *there was* a second-level property of first-level properties of individuals (viz. non-instantiation)

Another even less controversial orthodoxy warns us that like any
other word in this position the word "nothing" may occur in
oratio obliqua when it occurs within the phrase "thinking [*or* speak-
ing] about . . .". If we say with Frege that in "thinking about
Theaetetus" the name "Theaetetus" designates the *sense* of the
name of the man Theaetetus who is thought about, then we shall
say that in "thinking about *nothing*" (similarly construed as
giving the content of a thought) the word "nothing" occurs
designating what is in fact the *sense* of a second-level concept-word.
(Other accounts are in fact possible, and Frege's has certain disadvantages, but none of these disadvantages are in point here.
Frege's theory stands here as a place-holder for whatever turns out
to be the best theory of indirect speech.)

By providing this second-level concept, and so this something,
to be the subject matter of thinking about nothing, and by providing the sense of the concept-word "nothing" to be the reference of
the word *nothing* in the oblique context "Socrates thinks about
nothing", I think that we simultaneously block the only source of
objection to the *saying → saying something* doctrine, and make quite
clear that the thinking about *nothing* which is vindicated by these
considerations is utterly different from thinking with no subject
matter to think about (which is an evident absurdity), and also

---

such that it qualified some first-level property (e.g. *largest prime number*).
It is not really worth making any more fuss about the use of this third-
order statement of the existence of a second-level concept than it is
worth making about the use of $\sim(\exists x)(\ldots (x))$ in the first-order
calculus to deny that any individual satisfies the concept *largest prime
number;* but if anyone is worried about whether there is such a concept
as *nothing* then this is his answer. So there is such a subject of thought as
nothing, even if nobody thinks about this concept. When we reflect that
even if there is no such thing as *x* that does not necessarily exclude the
possibility of someone's thinking *about x* (see text ensuing), we shall see
that thinking about *nothing* is in fact doubly underwritten.

Concept of a first-level concept with no extension is a property-like account
of *nothing*. Its extensional counterpart would be *the extension of the concept "concept with no extension"* or $\{\{\wedge\}\}$, the unit-set of the null set.
Both relate to *nothing* as applied within the domain of individuals; and
as it stands the quantifier analysis expounded here does not treat any
acceptable statements there may be of the form "nothing is both a
concept (or class) and a man". But in the present context there is unfortunately insufficient space to investigate the type-theoretical feasibility of more general definitions of *nothing*, e.g. by means of typical
ambiguity and/or a cumulative type-theory.

utterly different from thinking about what is *in fact* nothing, e.g. about ⟨Theaetetus is flying⟩. These are three different things. It is very obvious perhaps that the thought or judgement that Theaetetus is flying is a quite different thing from a non-thought and a quite different thought again from a thought about the difficult concept *nothing*. But I have believed it to be worth while to digress to this extent because *oratio obliqua* and second-level predication are both persistently important in the attempt to gain an authentic understanding of any of the puzzles Plato treats in the *Sophist*.

Step I being correct, I pass to the *Being = Truth* doctrine. We may overlook something distinctive in Plato's treatment of non-being unless we are alert to some special facts about the Greek language in this connexion.

For an English speaker it may not be an immediately natural idea to search for an object ⟨p⟩ annexed to any statement p, let alone to insist on raising the question whether this object ⟨p⟩ exists or not. It is still less natural to do so with the intention to call ⟨p⟩ *something being* or *something which is* if p is true. It is worth while to ask what makes this natural in Greek, as well as to inquire what specifically philosophical need there is to postulate something like ⟨p⟩ to stand as the object of such mental acts as truly judging, truly believing or truly saying that p.

In the *Theaetetus* formulation of the problem of non-being, Socrates asks whether it is possible to see without seeing anything. "Surely if a person sees any one thing he sees something which is", 188E8 *alla mēn ei hen ge ti horai, tōn ontōn ti horai.* It is the same, Socrates and Theaetetus agree, with hearing. It is also the same with touching. Both analogies are significant. It has often been pointed out that the mention of touching suggests that Plato's notion of judgement is affected by his conceiving of it as a peculiar sort of material transaction between the thinker and a chunk of reality. Plato seems to regard this chunk as just as capable of separate articulation and as detachable from everything else as the peel on a lemon or the crust on a loaf of bread. On this view what is annexed to a sentence in the act of judgement has to be something very substantial indeed. But, important though this touching analogy certainly is, it leaves us wanting to know why Plato chose it in the first place. What conditions a philosopher of Plato's constitution to be seized by a mental cramp so startlingly and distinctly materialistic? For this reason I think the seeing and hearing analogy is really a more helpful one. Seeing and hearing are closer to judging, they take dependent clauses, and the way in which they are physical transactions between a person and his environment is a subtler way. Although the kind of *that* clause which they admit, when they have one, certainly does not import anything you could as easily detach from the world as the peel from a lemon, there is an interesting peculiarity of Greek grammar which any Greek speaker might seize upon if he were already puzzled about what kind of a transaction judging was and had thought to use the analogy with seeing or hearing to illuminate it.

Greek treats clauses of reported speech or thought in three ways. (1) There is a construction with a *that* clause (*hoti* or *hōs*). This construction only differs from the English construction in the tense of the dependent clause (which has to be that of the original or directly quoted version). (2) There is a construction with an accusative and infinitive (or nominative and infinitive for identical subject in main and independent clauses) where the infinitive replaces the verb of the sentence reported to have been thought or said. Finally, (3) there is a construction with an accusative (or nominative) and concordant *participle* replacing the verb of the clause reported to have been thought or said.[7] (1) and (3) are often interchangeable, but most verbs which use (3) cannot (when used in the same sense) take (2). What matters at present is that *see* and *hear* belong to a group which uses (3). I see that Theaetetus sits = *horō ton Theaeteton kathēmenon* = (lit.) I see Theaetetus *sitting*. This is a construction of striking philosophical interest. Admittedly there is no particular incentive to misunderstand or pervert such perfectly ordinary Greek as *horō ton Theaeteton kathēmenon* unless one is already puzzled about the status of reports of what is said or thought. But if one is puzzled about this then what is more natural than to conceive of the comfortable and apparently unproblematic entity *sitting Theaetetus* being an ordinary *direct* object of sight? The next step is a natural one. One could guess that a philosopher who reached this point and was puzzled about the status of that-clauses in judgement might well use the analogy between seeing and judging to try to analyse all *that*-clauses by reference to construction (3). Once the

[7] For a hypothesis about the conditions in Attic Greek for membership of class (3) see below, note 9.

idea was suggested any philosopher speaking any language might find it a promising or interesting programme.

How near Plato came to thinking of this as a systematic approach to the objects of judgement can only be a guess, and not a guess to be pressed too hard. It is enough, whether or not he conceived of this as a deliberate or systematic method of analysis, that in discussing saying (*legein*) and judging or believing (*doxazein*), which in fact take construction (2), he immediately has recourse to an analogy with a set of verbs every one of which take participial construction (3). Nothing could cohere better than the desire to make this analogy cohere with his use of *on ti*, *something being* or *something which is*, to stand for the purport of a correct judgement, or *what an arbitrary true sentence says*. I am tempted to suggest that the neuter participle *on* stands proxy for an arbitrary participle applied to an arbitrary subject of an arbitrary true sentence which could be converted into the construction (3) form in *oratio obliqua*. This usage is helped along by the fact that it is frequently idiomatic to transpose Greek finite verbs such as *kathētai*, *sits* or *has sat down*, into a continuous form *esti kathēmenos* closely resembling the English *is sitting*. If the verb *einai*, *to be*, can be felt to be implicit in every verb, then its participle, *onta* or *on*, can be felt to be implicit in every true sentence awaiting the status of dependent clause in indirect speech. But every true judgement awaits this status potentially since every judgement can in principle be reported in case it is ever said or thought. That it is terribly easy to pass from saying this about true judgements to saying it about false judgements which *purport* to be true (and surely in themselves all do) accurately reflects the tension which holds between the *saying* → *saying something* and the *Being* — *Truth* doctrines (steps A and B).

It is a virtue of this hypothesis, which supports the general view I take of the sentential variant but is not essential to it, that it explains very well how Plato's use of *on* for what an arbitrary true sentence says can poise itself so delicately between the *existence* of a state of affairs affirmed by a true sentence F(*a*) and the *application* (and then *purported application*) of the predicate F of a sentence F(a) to the subject, *a*, of the sentence. Plato's eventual solution of the sentential variant of the problem of non-being will crucially depend on his being able to make use of the bridge which he has found here from the one view to the other view of what it is for there to be something which "Theaetetus flies/sits" says.

If construction (3) and the rest and Plato's search for analogies serve to explain how an *on ti*, $\langle p \rangle$, *something which is*, gets annexed to every true sentence p, then what does Plato think $\langle p \rangle$'s *prima facie* relation to p should be supposed to be? What relation do they have to have to one another to produce the puzzle from which the discussion takes off? Studiously vaguely, I have spoken of $\langle p \rangle$'s being *annexed* to p, but to judge from the problem Plato sees here it seems as if the relation which will make false judgement into a problem cannot be very different—call it what you will—from the name-thing relation. It seems that just as an *onoma* (name) in the *Cratylus* is an instrument of teaching and sorting out Reality (*didaskalikon ti estin organon kai diakritikon tēs ousias* 388A–C), whose correctness lies in the purpose of showing how things are (*tōn onomatōn he orthotēs toiautē tis ebouleto einai, hoia dēloun hoion hekaston esti tōn ontōn*, 422D1 ; cp. 428E2 *endeixetai hoion esti to pragma*), so on the view of sentences which gives the paradox a sentence may be seen as showing, or drawing the hearer's attention to, or *displaying* for him (hence the reporting use of the accusative and participle construction) some situation in Reality—a situation in the world of whose existence he will as a result of this act become *informed*. Of course this is not quite how Plato himself comes to think of a sentence—he propounds the paradox—but he has a duty to be interested in the *possibility* of such a view. It is the simplest view and the conception is not a conception one can simply throw away. Plato had already taken the first and most decisive step in superseding it in the *Cratylus*, where he came to see a sentence as a compound only one of whose constituents was a name, the other being a verb (*onomata kai rhemata* 425A); but to develop his complete theory Plato has to get completely clear about the defect of the simpler view, which treats the sentence itself as a name. The paradox of false opinion has to be rehearsed.

On what one might call the *display view* of sentence-meaning which seems to underlie the paradox the truth-conditions of the sentence p will be:[8]

$$True\ \mathrm{p} \equiv (\exists x)\ (x = \langle \mathrm{p} \rangle),$$

or less formally:

> p *is true if and only if*
> *something is the object*
> $\langle p \rangle$ *which* p *displays.*

---

[8] Or rather the truth-conditions of the *statement made* by the sentence p. But I shall never bother here to include this complication, on which nothing hangs in the present connexion.

The point of the paradox of false opinion is then to ask "What would it be like for it to be false that p? What would it be like for nothing to be the situation ⟨p⟩ which p displays?" This looks puzzling for a moment, but in fact crafty and fallacious manipulation (step E in particular) is required to make the question as embarrassing as Plato gives it the air of being. Certainly if p is false then there is no such object as ⟨p⟩. But does that necessarily contradict the *saying* → *saying something* thesis? The thesis only requires that there should be an answer to the question "what did he say?" And surely there *is* an answer. He said that Theaetetus was flying. It is readily granted that he could not *show* ⟨Theaetetus is flying⟩ if there were no such thing as flying Theaetetus to show. For one can only show what exists. But at best this only proves that *show* in the theory must be trivially modified to read *make as to show*. There is a citation which one could give of what he *made as to show*. And what he *made as to show*—that Theaetetus was flying—was something of whose existence he could persuade people without there being any actual flying Theaetetus to exhibit. If it is false that Theaetetus is flying then certainly what *Theaetetus is flying* purports to display *is not*, is not a real situation, is *nothing*. By what I called the *harmlessly transparent description of the object of saying* we may even go on to say that what Socrates (or whoever) judged was nothing, or even that he judged nothing. It is harmless if it is not misunderstood. But to claim that there is then nothing which "Theaetetus is flying" or its utterer purports to display or says is to make the new step which I called the *fallaciously opaque reading of the harmlessly transparent description*. For remember that in the sentence "*Theaetetus is flying* (or its utterer) says or purports to display ⟨Theaetetus is flying⟩" the designation "⟨Theaetetus is flying⟩" stands within *oratio obliqua*. (In Fregean terms, it stands there for the *sense* of the designation "⟨flying Theaetetus⟩".) So *even if* it were permissible to construe "nothing is ⟨Theaetetus is flying⟩" as of the form "*a = b*", or "the null-thing = ⟨flying Theaetetus⟩" in order to make the substitution —and it is not in fact permissible, but even if it were—we *either* must not convert "Socrates judged ⟨flying Theaetetus⟩" at all into "Socrates judged nothing"; *or* must not misunderstand the result, if we do use the possibility of transparent description to say "Socrates judged what was *in fact* nothing". We simply cannot extract from it the conclusion that he did not judge at all. (In Fregean terms *nothing* is not a proper name, and even if it were the senses of "⟨flying Theaetetus⟩" and "nothing" would not be the same; and to retain truth the inter-substitution would have to be an inter-substitution of identical *senses*, since it is these which are designated within the oblique context "Socrates judged . . .".)

II

There are such grave objections, then, to Plato's actual derivation of the paradox of false judgement in his passage from step A to step E that it may suddenly seem that there really is a tenable position to be defended in the supposition that a sentence p *refers* to a state of affairs ⟨p⟩ which exists if and only if p is true; just as "Ossian" is a perfectly good proper name which refers to Ossian, and has as its signification a poet at the court of St. Patrick who composed a certain epic. ("*Refers to* . . ." and "*has as its signification* . . ." are oblique contexts, remember. I am not subscribing to any belief in Ossian.) That Richard Bentley, Dr. Johnson and others were right in their view that the epic in question was a fake, and that there was never any such person, need have no tendency to show that those who upheld the authenticity of the work and spoke of Ossian were not using "Ossian" as a proper name. So far as I know this view of sentence-meaning has never really been given a proper run for its money. (See, however, Russell's first lecture on Logical Atomism, p. 187 in *Logic and Knowledge*, ed. Marsh [London, 1956].) To present this theory we might adapt an idea from the *Cratylus* (430E–431B, cp. 432E4) and think of purporting to display ⟨p⟩ in a case where there was no such situation as ⟨p⟩ as analogous to showing someone a picture of ⟨p⟩—which is something one might do even if p were true and ⟨p⟩ itself were kept back, in reserve as it were. The view is interesting enough for us to see what now happens to the analogies earlier mentioned.

The analogy with touching can hardly be preserved, for seeming to touch something is certainly not any sort of touching anything. And purporting to touch is no less problematic than purporting to show. But this analogy was never more than an embarrassment in any case. What about the other analogy? Could there be an analogy illustrative of the status of the object of saying which was an analogy between purporting to show and seeing or hearing? It is not quite clear, where nothing is a value for X, that one cannot see or hear X. There is seeing snakes, seeing visions, hearing voices, and so on, where the object of seeing or hearing may have no existence at all apart from the seeing or hearing. But this is not enough. For this particular kind of seeing or hearing makes no claim about anything external to the act of seeing or hearing. Only a seeing of a kind which requires to be scaled down to "I *thought* I saw X", for X which is a false statement or for an object X which is non-existent, can come anywhere matching *purporting to show* ⟨p⟩. For it is of the essence of purporting to show that p to *claim* and *commit oneself to* the objective and actual existence of ⟨p⟩. So the analogy would have to go:

See ⟨p⟩	:seem to see ⟨p⟩
:: Say that p, for true p	:say that p, for false p
:: purport to display ⟨p⟩, for existent ⟨p⟩	:purport to display ⟨p⟩, for ⟨p⟩ in fact non-existent.

The analogy in the form we are now forced to give it breaks down at exactly the point at which it is required to hold. Someone who seems to see ⟨p⟩, *qua* doing just this, is in no way *committed* to hold that there is any such situation as ⟨p⟩. He may distrust what seems to him because he knows he has been given a hallucinatory drug. He may even doubt whether he is seeing at all. Whereas one who purports to display ⟨p⟩ *is* committed to the existence of ⟨p⟩. I do not mean he is committed to *believe* in this—he may speak knowingly falsely or insincerely—but that *qua* saying that p he is obliged to maintain that there is such a state of affairs as ⟨p⟩. Otherwise he must give up his assertion that p. This failure of analogy with respect to ⟨p⟩ only reflects the deceptively fundamental truth that the first intention significance of *saying* that p is to be taken as *speaking the truth*—which in its turn reflects the even more fundamental fact that the primary dimension of assessment of success or failure in thought and speech is the true-false dimension, truth being the verdict designated the *winning* verdict. And of course what put the analogy wrong was the need to modify *see* to *seem to see*. But we had to modify it to get an analogue of *say falsely* and *purport to display*.[9]

---

[9] Interestingly the whole difficulty of analogy is marked by something in Greek which Plato's approach is calculated to make him ignore—the difference which grammar makes between mental verbs with infinitival construction (2) and mental verbs like *see* and *hear*

It might be worth looking harder for analogies with verbs taking the participial construction if the naming or *purporting to display* theory of sentence meaning had a better future than it has. But in spite of the flaw in Plato's criticism of the theory it is easy to construct another objection which will exactly fill the hole which is left when Plato's own argument is withdrawn or subtracted.

Suppose "Theaetetus is flying" displays ⟨flying Theaetetus⟩. Then what do we say about its negation, *it is not the case that Theaetetus is flying?* If we simply say that it displays ⟨non-flying Theaetetus⟩ then we leave unanalysed what makes the second sentence into a negation of the first. To analyse this we must somehow make ⟨flying Theaetetus⟩ into a *constituent* of ⟨Theaetetus does not fly⟩. Otherwise nothing answers to the fact that in order to be negated by it *Theaetetus flies* has to be a constituent of *it is not the case that Theaetetus flies*. Unless it were such a constituent there would be no basis for the fact that it is negated by the complex sentence. We then reach something like ⟨not ⟨Theaetetus flies⟩⟩—which is presumably the situation of there "being no such situation as ⟨Theaetetus flies⟩". But how exactly does the designation "⟨Theaetetus flies⟩" figure in the designation "⟨There is no such situation as the situation ⟨Theaetetus flies⟩⟩", which is surely the only reading we can give "⟨not ⟨Theaetetus flies⟩⟩"? By itself "⟨Theaetetus flies⟩" is

---

taking the participial construction (3). The grammar books do not make this point but the leading characteristic of a verb V belonging to group (3) is that, in spite of the opacity or obliquity generated by V, V(p) logically implies True p, and V(*a*) logically implies (∃*x*) V (*x*). Verbs which take the infinitive construction rarely or never have this characteristic, and of course *say*, *judge*, *believe*, etc., all take the infinitive construction—something which with hindsight and Plato's discussion before us we can see to be symptomatic of one completely general difficulty in any reductive programme built around construction (3).

Many of the points about saying which are alluded to here are made by Dummett in "Truth," *P.A.S.* 1958. They are slightly modified here to meet some frequent but rather simple-minded objections (about lying, irony etc.) which Dummett's rather compressed formulation occasioned. The very possibility of lying depends on the prior existence of linguistic institutions which lying can exploit and abuse, institutions which can confer on saying something the status of a performance standardly *aimed* at truth. And saying can *only* have this status if *truth* is the fundamental or first intention notion of success in saying. Once this institution is in existence there can be a second intention "institution" to get over a falsehood by being taken to be conforming one's utterance to the first institution.

by the nature of the theory an ostension or display of a situation. It is what "Theaetetus flies" purports to display. But this cannot be its role in "⟨not ⟨Theaetetus flies⟩⟩". For here the use of this complex designation would commit the user both to display flying Theaetetus, and simultaneously to display the non-displayability of flying Theaetetus. But this is an utterly self-undermining project. No non-absurd utterance can commit a speaker to commit himself to X and simultaneously commit him to undermine his own same commitment to X. And *Theaetetus is not flying* is non-absurd.

What we have to conclude from this is that in our ⟨. . .⟩ notation "⟨not ⟨Theaetetus is flying⟩⟩" does not display ⟨Theaetetus flies⟩ at all, just as "The King of France does not exist" does not pick out the King of France but predicates non-instantiation of the concept *King of France*. But whatever alternative role we assign to "⟨Theaetetus flies⟩" within the more complex designation, it cannot be the same role as it has when it figures by itself. But that was what we needed in order to explain negation. It follows that there is something wrong with what we intended in the first place by the ⟨. . .⟩ notation. But obviously exactly the same difficulty would affect any notation designed to express the display theory. We must give up the theory.

The same point can be made more simply if we use what is for us a rather more habitual terminology, and express the theory under discussion as the theory that an indicative sentence is simply a name of something which exists if and only if the sentence is true. The argument would then be simply this. If ⌜p⌝ is a name and ⌜not-p⌝ is a true negation of ⌜p⌝, then ⌜p⌝ must have the same naming role in both [p] and [not-p].[10] Otherwise the negatedness of ⌜p⌝ by ⌜not-p⌝ will not have been explained. Now if (absurdly) the theory

[10] The corner notation indicates that I am speaking not of the Roman letter "p" but of arbitrary expressions of the syntactic category indicative sentence. The argument relies on the fundamental asymmetry of reference and predication with respect to negation. The argument need not deny the possibility of a "stoic" negation *not*-(F*a*) verified by the non-existence of *a*, but only the possibility of any standard or truly nominal (i.e. subject + predicate) *analysis* either of the occurrence of the phrase denoting *a* in such *not*-(F*a*) or of its occurrence in the F*a* which this *not*-(F*a*) negates. But it is the standard or nominal occurrence of names (not the occurrence of Russellian or Quinean predicate-versions of them) on which the display or naming theory has to rely in the first place in order to get started in explaining saying and sentence-meaning.

makes ⌜p⌝ commit the speaker to identifying something whose
identifiability ⌜not-p⌝ commits the speaker to denying, then ⌜p⌝ cannot have the same kind of occurrence in both ⌜p⌝ and ⌜not-p⌝. But it
was this which was required to explain the polarity of negation.

III

Using this argument in lieu of Plato's puzzle of false opinion
against the designation or display view of sentence-meaning let us
now go on. The virtue of the display theory was that at least it explained how statements attach themselves to the world and suggested how in attaching themselves, they *put themselves in the power
of reality* to establish or overthrow their claim to stand as true. He
who judges has to direct his judgement *at* something (*ho doxazōn
epi ti pherei tēn doxan* as Plato insists at *Republic* 478B).[11] It seems to
me that to explain this is nothing less than an adequacy condition
for a theory of sentence-meaning; and however vague and indirectly satisfiable this requirement may be, that a theory must fail
unless its account of sentence-*truth* is organically and immediately
related to its account of what it is for *sense* to be conferred upon a
sentence. Now, I think, Plato's own general strategy in tackling the
problem is, in outline, absolutely clear. Even if one cannot fix the
sense of a sentence by attaching it as a whole to something in reality
—even if there is no one thing for one sentence-owned tentacle to
feel for—one can attach it more indirectly by means of its parts. A
constituent name (*onoma*) *names* or identifies something and a constituent verb (*rhēma*) *predicates* something of what the name
identifies.

> When someone says "a man learns" you will agree that this is
> a sentence, a basic or elementary one. . . . For in this way he
> indicates some state of affairs, past, present or yet to be, and he
> doesn't merely name or identify some individual man but
> actually brings matters to a conclusion by coupling a verb
> [of action] to his reference (*alla ti perainei sumplekōn ta rhemata
> tois onomasi*). He doesn't merely name but also says something
> (262D).

[11] Cp. Wittgenstein, *Tractatus Logico-Philosophicus* (trans. D. F. Pears
and B. F. McGuinness). 2.1511 *That* is how a picture is attached to
reality, it reaches right out to it. 2.1512 It is laid against reality like a
ruler. . . . 2.1514 The pictorial relationship consists of the correlations
of the picture's elements with things. 2.1515 These correlations are, as
it were, the feelers of the picture's elements, with which the picture
touches reality.

This line of attack was clear enough well before Plato came to write this passage of the *Sophist* (if the ordering *Republic, Parmenides, Cratylus, Theaetetus, Sophist* is anything like correct). See *Cratylus* 425A, and recall the first attempt at innocuous redescription of false judgement at *Theaetetus* 189C2:

> We say that false judgement is a kind of interchange of judgement, when someone confuses one existent *a* with another existent *b* and says that *a = b*. In this way it comes about that his judgement pertains always to existents (*on men aei doxazei*), but he misses the existent he was aiming for and gets hold of another instead and so may quite properly be said to be judging falsely (*heteron d' anth' heterou, kai hamartanōn hou eskopei dikaiōs an kaloito pseudē doxazōn*).

Plato's examples in *Theaetetus* are mostly identity statements (and there is nothing to prove that he did not realize at the time of writing that they all belonged to a special class), so they are not simple cases of the *name + verb* schema. But the rough strategy both here and in the *Sophist* is surely the same. It is to stop trying to attach the whole and to explain the sense of the whole by explaining and attaching its several parts. If each part is attached then his judgement is always of existents—*on men aei doxazei*. (What leads to the rejection of the 189C11 redescription, which might in outline have sufficed for the *Theaetetus* so far as the problem of non-being is concerned, is the other puzzle about *knowing and not knowing* the terms of a false proposition. The same goes, I think, for the rejection at 208 of Socrates' dream. The objectionable constituent feature need have had nothing to do with the fact that the dream's theory of judgement complexes incorporated a naming *cum* attaching of parts conception of sentence-meaning.)

So far as it goes this new "composite" conception is not obviously unsatisfactory. The role of the *Sophist* is not so much to announce the approach of 262D—it is after all familiar—as to develop what was previously a mere sketch of a theory, as yet unclear at every point, into something candid, explanatory and explicit. Perhaps its most important single contribution is Plato's development of the difference between the way in which words which are names and the way in which words which are predicates "attach" to their non-linguistic counterparts.[11a] There is even some point in the

---

[11a] The interpretation to be followed here depends partly on the supposition that Plato continued to think of non-linguistic counter-

comparison sometimes made with Frege's doctrine of saturated and unsaturated components of a proposition and Frege's analogy between predicates (concept-words) and arithmetical function signs. The comparison is a crazy anachronism; but it has a point. It shows a direction in which the asymmetries Plato insists upon *could* be developed. This is not the only respect in which the *Sophist* represents an advance, but to assess its contribution as a whole it is necessary to try to see how Plato himself articulated the problem of non-being in its various aspects. And it is essential not to let the sentential variant of the problem which is our chosen perspective, or our own philosophy of logic, distort our view of the organization of Plato's procedures. If we were not already on our guard against this we should instantly take warning from the fact that the passage from 237–38 we began by discussing leads immediately into a discussion of what might seem to us a quite different problem— the greatest perplexity of all, as Plato calls it (*aporiōn hē prōtē kai megistē* 238A2)—the fact that it is not even possible to use the expressions *to mē on*, *me einai*, or *ouk esti*, (*what is not, not to be, is not*), in order to deny that there is any such thing as *to mē on*. For if *what is not* is not the designation of anything how could we intelligibly get it into a sentence, even in order to deny its existence? For us this is the generalization of a wider and easily distinguishable problem.[12]

---

parts for both *onomata* and *rhemata* even after developing the distinction between these classes of expressions. For a particularly explicit statement see 257B–C "the particle *not* indicates something different from the words to which it is prefixed, or rather from the *things* (*pragmaton*) *denoted by the words which follow the negation.*"

[12] The answer (*vide* note 5) to the generalized problem is that we *can* use this second-order predicate *existence* or *non-existence*, and that by the introduction of third-level predicates we can even say that there is such a second-level predicate as this, that it is self-identical etc. In this sense it exists. Plato's wish at 238A ff. to say that *that which is not* "is not" can also be honoured, if we interpret the assertion as the boringly unproblematic assertion that $(\phi) \ [(\sim \exists x) \ (\phi x) \rightarrow (\sim \exists x) \ (\phi x)]$, i.e. that anything such as the concept *King of France* which is uninstantiated is uninstantiated. But it is not possible in any satisfactory notation to say what Plato is really *trying* momentarily to say. This is indeed an inadequacy condition of a satisfactory notation. For Plato's thought at this moment (in a formulation later repudiated, at 258D–E) is that *not anything* is identical with a certain ordinary object-like individual *, an object called *nothing*, which is (or would be if it existed) a subject of first-order predicates such as " =": that on the one hand one wants to say

But so far as Plato is concerned the problems are not so readily dissociable. To solve the 237–38 problem Plato thinks that one has somehow (241D) to "force through the view that that which is not in some sense is, and then again that that which is in some sense is not (*biazesthai to mē on hōs esti kata ti kai to on au palin hōs ouk esti pēi*)". And Plato thinks that the existence of false judgement demands nothing less than a complete re-examination of the *whole* problem of the logical grammar of the verb *to be*. Only this can discover to us the something which a false statement states. That this requires nothing less than a general inquiry into predication is explained by the fact that Plato will provide the something, whether the statement be true *or* false, not by the production of an object of embarrassment like ⟨Theaetetus is flying⟩ but by the demonstration that even if the predicate Flying *is not* with respect to Theaetetus there in some sense *is* (*esti kata ti*) this something, Flying, which *is not* with respect to Theaetetus. Plato has already determined to avail himself of the bridge already described from sentence-truth to predicate applicability. Here there arise many problems of detail. I shall not have space here to vindicate the view that Flying *is* because, although it does not qualify Theaetetus, it does qualify other things, birds, insects, etc., and determines a *genos* having extensional relations of overlap, exclusion etc., and intensional relations of identity and difference with other *genē* all of which also

that (x) $(x \neq *)$—there is no such thing as $*$; that on the other hand one can't even say that. For if nothing is nothing—if nothing at all is this object—then there is no such object. Everybody knows there is no such object and nobody who knows this ought to proceed as if to refer to it. But then he shouldn't use the schema $(\ldots \neq *)$. And surely (x) $(x = x)$ in any case, so that if $*$ fell within the ambit of the quantifier (x) it would have to satisfy the schema "$x = x$" and we should get "$* = *$", or (nothing = nothing), which contradicts (x) $(x \neq *)$. And again, if $*$ satisfies the schema, $* = *$ holds. Then $(\exists x)$ $(x = *)$. But then something is nothing! And (by an inference like *if something is John then John is something*) nothing is something! It is easy to see that no sign can both signify what *nothing* signifies and belong to the syntactic category of individual name, or belong within the range of (x). If "$*$" purports to do this there is only one thing we can do. We must *cross out* both this sign and the expression "the null thing". I would add that model theorists who believe they can cope with this situation by simply excluding $*$ from the range of (x) in a language L or theory T, and dispense with the Russell-Frege analysis here espoused, must apparently suppose that nonsense is all right provided it is talked only in the metalanguage!

qualify non-null extensions. But there is another point of exegesis even more central to my subject which does have to be pursued.

When the problem about saying shifts to predicates why does Plato approach false predication via *negative* predication? *Prima facie* falsity and negation would seem to be quite different problems. To explain this I must follow Plato into his discussion of negative predication. Inevitably this involves a considerable number of points which arise in the long discussion of Being which intervenes between 240 and 260. Since it is Plato's view that non-being is only clear to the extent that being is, it is all the less surprising that the discussion which leads into the 260s has to become a discussion of predication in general.

IV

First there occurs a discussion of *einai* (be) in what we ourselves might classify an existential use; then a proof that it is senseless to require of every true statement that it be of the form A is (predicatively) A. Next, ensuing on a demonstration that the kinds, F, G, H . . ., to which an individual *a* belongs (i.e. the predicates true of it) will have relations sometimes of *disjointness* (*amikta genē*), and sometimes of *inclusion* or *overlap* (at best sketchily distinguished), there follows an extended section in which Plato distinguishes five principal predicate-kinds from one another. Following the interpretation hinted by Owen (*op. cit.*, p. 71) I take these kinds to be

(1) *Motion*, which I shall represent K, writing *Theaetetus moves* as (Theaetetus) K;
(2) *Rest*, which I shall represent Σ, writing *Theaetetus is at rest* as (Theaetetus) Σ;
(3) *Being something*, which I shall represent O[some F] or O[. . .].[13]

[13] On this interpretation of being, "(Theaetetus) O[some F]" is the closest one can get to rendering *Theaetetus exists*. Owen, *loc. cit.* "In the *Sophist* Plato had gone some way to disentangling the first two of these uses [predicative "is" from " ="]. I do not myself think he was equally successful with the third [existential use]; he seems in the end content to assimilate it to (or scrap it in favour of) the others. That is, he treats "to be" and "not to be" alike as incomplete or elliptical expressions which always call for some completion; *to be* is just *to be something or other*." There is one qualification I should like to make of this. Certainly (3) does not give us a complete analysis of existential *is*, no

For determinate F, O[. . .] can be written O[F] and this invites contraction to F.[14] Thus *Theaetetus is a man* can be written either as

$$\text{(Theaetetus) O[Man]}$$

or as

$$\text{(Theaetetus) Man.}$$

The kind O[. . .] gives rise to two special *genē* or kinds which are not
as such co-extensive either with *being something* or with each other.
They are

(4) *Identity* or T (for Greek *tauton*);
Socrates is identical with Socrates being written here as

$$\text{(Socrates) O[[T] (Socrates)].}$$

---

more than 247D–E docs. For both are (more or less) first-level predicative analyses. But at least

$$a \text{ exists} \equiv a \text{ is something}$$

is biconditionally *valid*. The analysis goes ill with Plato's *otherness* account of negation and, Plato apart, it is a defect in it to suggest no
analysis of the expression which seems to stand for *a* in "*a* does not
exist" or in "*a* is not anything". But we are not completely happy ourselves about how exactly to turn this expression into a first-level
concept-expression ("*a*-izes") to which the second-level property of
instantiation can then be ascribed or denied. And in any case, who
would wish to claim the distinction of being the first to isolate the
existential use of *be* if he were obliged to go on to suggest for it a first-
level analysis which distinguished it from predicative *is* only by reimporting precisely the sort of absurdities against which the *Sophist*
(and step D) was directed in the first place? Until one can get the
highly sophisticated notion of a second-level concept of first-level
concepts, Plato's analysis (3) is the best analysis one *could* get as an
approximation for the complete or intransitive *is*. And hang the distinction which he misses—if one has not the equipment to avoid
talking pure nonsense in making it! But I follow Owen in supposing
that the problem of existence *per se* scarcely figures at all as a principal
theme of the *Sophist*.

[14] This kind (3) is probably the *einai pros heteron* (being with respect
to another) of 255C, and if so it is called this because in (*x*)O[F], the
F-place and *x*-place take different values, the first a kind name, the
second an individual name. (Owen, *loc. cit.*, and note 15 below, and
see also J. M. E. Moravcsik's notion of "relational being" in his article
"Being and Meaning in the *Sophist*," *Acta Philosophica Fennica* Fasc.
XIV [1962].)

As before, O[[T](. . .)] could be contracted to T(. . .), which makes clear that it is a kind like K, Σ, or any other kind F.[15] Thus *Socrates is identical with Socrates* becomes

(Socrates) T (Socrates).

Finally there is the analogous concept (enjoying uncertain symmetry with T in Plato's treatment).

(5) *Difference* or $\triangle$ (for Greek *diaphoron*); *Socrates is (a) different (man) from Theaetetus* being written as

(Socrates) O[[$\triangle$] (Theaetetus)]

and being contracted in the same way as before to

(Socrates) $\triangle$ (Theaetetus).

Just as O[some F] can be displaced, for a known and determinate choice G of value for the variable F, by O[G] and this in its turn by G *simpliciter*, so the process can work the other way round. The notation has been devised to suggest this. K or Σ, or any other determinate value of the variables F, G, can be supplanted by such expansions as O[K] and O[Σ]; and *Theaetetus moves* or

(Theaetetus) K

can be rewritten in the form

(Theaetetus) O[K],

which naturally entails

(Theaetetus) O[some F].

The notation thus indicates what Plato explicitly announces, that the discussion of five greatest kinds will be a discussion of *being* and *non-being* (cp. 254C). For on this account Σ and K (which are surely just examples or specimen predicates) are just as much specific determinations of the ubiquitous O as $\triangle$ and T were. There is no question of a sixth predicate or *genos* as copula or con-

---

[15] It is Owen's hypothesis that this kind, T, is the one which Plato refers to at 255C as *einai kath'hauto* (being with respect to itself?), so called because the gaps in (. . .) O[[T](. . .)] have to be filled with names of the same thing to get a truth. The interpretation seems to me to cohere with the only minimally relational status assigned by Plato to *sameness*. One of its advantages is that it avoids the comical notion that Plato assigns to " = " the status of relation which one thing has to *another*.

catenator of other *genē*. This role is assumed by *einai* itself qualified in various ways—by Σ, K, $\triangle$, T, or by other subsidiary kinds F or by a real variable F yielding O[some F].

v

We are now, Plato thinks, in a position to explain negation in a way not patently open to Parmenidean objection. The word *not* (*mē* or *ou*) adjoined to a predicate G signifies *being something other than G* (257B–D). In other words if and only if

$$\sim(\text{Theaetetus}) \text{ G}$$

then (provided we concentrate, as Plato seems to, on the kind of case when F and G belong to one range; see below, p. 301)

$$\text{there is an F such that } \{((F) \triangle (G)) \ \& \\ (\text{Theaetetus}) \text{ O[F]}\},$$

or what might be meant to be the same thing,

$$(\text{Theaetetus}) \text{ O[some F such that (F)} \triangle (G)].$$

There are difficulties and ambiguities here. About *not big* Plato says at 257D:

> *Stranger:* For instance, when we say that some object is not big then do we seem to express (*dēloun*) *small* any more than *middling-sized* by the predicate (*rhēma*) "not big"?

Theaetetus' reply is *kai pōs*—how could we mean *small* rather than *middling-sized?*—which I take to mean that *not big* no more means *middling-sized* than it means *small*. What it means is *other than big*—which is a *genos* introduced and affirmed of the subject by the negative *rhēma* "not big" and purportedly definable by means of the *genos* Other and the *genos* Big (cp. 257D–258A).[15a] The claims of

---

[15a] The incompatibility interpretation favoured by some commentators seems to be ruled out (a) by the fact that the Stranger goes on to say (257C–D) that if anybody alleges that "negation signifies the opposite" we shall deny that it signifies *opposite* and agree only that it signifies *something other than* X where X is what follows the negation sign; and (b) by the fact the whole project is surely to contrive the explanation with the apparatus provided by the five greatest kinds; and (c) by the fact that Plato would surely have sensed that incompatibility could only be explained through negation itself.

Not Big to be such a *genos* will be examined in section VIII below. What must concern us first, regardless of its eventual status, is the interpretation and amendment of the definition of the supposed *genos*. It does need amendment. But first interpretation.

In *something other than Big* (*tōn allōn ti to mē kai to ou protithemena tōn epiontōn onomatōn, māllon de tōn pragmatōn . . .*—something other than the word or thing preceded by the "not", 258B–C) the "something" apparently behaves as a variable whose values are predicates, and what is meant by *x is something other than Big* is *x is qualified by a predicate F* (or *falls under a genos F*) *which is a different predicate* (*genos*) *from Big*. In itself this statement about *x* does not say which predicate the diverse predicate F is—for the F is a real variable (as will be even more evident in the corrected version of Plato's analysis). If someone wishes he may insist that the statement is about *x* and so it must import some property. But that property is at best the second-order property of *having some property distinct from F*. (The cost if we try to make our notation run as long as possible without the full apparatus of quantification is of course that it becomes difficult to see that it is this which has to be the *genos* properly designated by "[some F, i.e. satisfies some F, such that (F) $\triangle$(G)]".) Nothing is better calculated to mask the complexity of what is involved (in what is in any case too simple an analysis) than to confuse the doctrine that "not big" means *something other than Big* with the doctrine that "not big" means something other than Big—e.g. it means such and such *genos* F, which $\neq$ Big. But the passage quoted from 257B certainly seems to rule out this interpretation (which would surely imply precisely that "not big" in the statement that *x* is not big means "middling-sized" or means "small" according, say, to context and according to the value of *x*). If it does rule it out then Plato is surely in the right. For to use this method to find a *genos* for the *rhēma* "not big" would be to abandon the search for an account of negation which combined non-circularity with even the smallest degree of generality (as would the equally improbable suggestion that "not big" means something disjunctively composite like *middling or small*). It would seem to import the need for an infinite or indefinite number of separate definitions of *not-φ*, *not-ψ* . . ., predicate by predicate, and even occasion by occasion.

It may be said at this point that to the extent that Plato is clear about the distinction I have drawn his doctrine is what I say it is;

but that it is not obvious how clear or how consistent he was on the point. I think there is virtue in this objection. The distinction is indispensable to the generality of Plato's theory, but it may be that it is an imperfect grasp of what precise proposal it is that he is making (linked perhaps with the true but irrelevant reflection that anything that is not F has something about it which makes it so) which explains Plato's extraordinary confidence that Not Big is a *genos*. Although the difficulties are in principle the same when the definition of the *rhēma* "not big" is corrected and [satisfies some F such that $((F) \triangle (G))$)] is supplanted by something both adequate and more complicated, the incorrect definition may also be a contributory factor in Plato's insensitivity to these difficulties (*vide* below, section VII). But, before we can get to the correction which is needed in Plato's analysis of *not*-G, another interpretive point must be cleared away.

In $(F) \triangle (K)$, which figures in the unrevised and the revised analysis, we see a contraction of $(F) O[[\triangle](K)]$ where the values of the variables in the two round-bracketed places are not individuals but kinds. Apart from the large general problem about this sort of shift into which I cannot enter here, there is also the special question whether the individuation of kinds is like the individuation of properties or like that of classes. If one had asked Plato whether the kinds Green and Sticky would be the same if all and only green things were sticky I think he would have replied *No* (cp. 250C6–7, for example). This suggests that their individuation is property-like. On the other hand there is his tendency to think of the extensions of contradictories like Σ and K as completely exhausting the field of existents (e.g. 250D), a view which is easier for a philosopher who maintains that "there are" *gonō* if the *genē* he believes in are classes than if they are properties. (A class dissolves so much more easily into its members than a property which is asserted to exist can dissolve into its extension.) Perhaps the proposal most faithful to Plato's other intentions, and to this tendency to think of the *genos* as nothing over and above its individuals, would be something like

$$(H) T (F) = \{ \square \ (\forall x)((x) \ H = (x)F) \}$$

as the condition of *genos* identity ($\forall x$ being a quantification only over objects of lowest level) and

$$(H) \triangle (F) \equiv \sim \{ \square (\forall x)((x) \ H \equiv (x)F) \}$$

as that of diversity. And now the correction. If these definitions are anything like correct (still more if the purely extensional conception which drops ▢ altogether were correct) then Plato's analysis of negation is palpably inadequate. Indeed it is wrong. Simple difference of F and G cannot suffice to make them exclude one another. Theaetetus' having some quality distinct from flying can hardly in itself rule out the possibility. that Theaetetus flies. He would have a distinct quality even if he were flying.

The most natural amendment—but not the only possible one, see below, VII *ad. fin.*, p. 301—is to suggest that

$$\sim(\text{Theaetetus})G = (\text{df}) \text{ for all } \textit{genē} \text{ F},$$

$$\text{if (Theaetetus) O[F] then (F)} \bigtriangleup \text{G},$$

and more generally

$$\sim(a)G = (\text{df})(\forall F)((a)O[F] \to (F) \bigtriangleup (G))$$

It may be held that this is really what Plato meant all along. However that may be, the supposed negative *rhēma* in

$$\sim(\text{Theaetetus}) \text{ F}$$

will not be anything even so deceptively simple seeing as [satisfies some *genos* F such that (F) $\bigtriangleup$ (G)]. But we can let this problem ride for the moment until we have returned to falsity and seen what hangs on Plato's contention that there are negative *rhēmata* with their own associated *genē*.

VI

Having said that every elementary sentence needs a noun and a verb, having distinguished the functions of these parts of speech as the introduction of an object (*pragma*) and an action (*prāxis*) respectively, and having given *Theaetetus is sitting* as a true and *Theaetetus is flying* as a false sentence, Plato declares that the true sentence *legei ta onta[1] hōs esti[1] peri sou* (263B4)—says what are[1] respecting Theaetetus as they are[1]—and that the false [*legei*] *hetera tōn ontōn* (263B7)—[says] things other than what are[1] [respecting Theaetetus]. The numerals written superscript to the verb *to be* index different occurrences of the verb which are about to be explained; they do *not* index senses.

The passage continues:

So [the false sentence] says things which are[1] not as things which are[1] (*ta mē onta*[1] *ara hōs onta*[1] *legei*)—[i.e. it says] things which are,[2] but different things which are[2] from the things which are[1] respecting Theaetetus (*ontōn*[1] *de ge onta*[2] *hetera peri sou*). For I think we declared that there are[3] many things which are[1] respecting each individual, and that there are[3] many things which are[1] not [respecting him or it] (*Polla men gar ephamen onta peri hekaston einai pou, polla de ouk onta*, 263B12, cp. 256E and 251A–B).

The translation I have offered is painfully literal but, because it is intended to suggest an interpretation, it is not neutral. The verb *to be* stands in its *be*[1] occurrences, I think, for a verb's (and therefore for a kind's) *application* to an individual. *Things which are, onta*, would have meant before 238–39 *what is the case*, i.e. the objects ⟨p⟩, ⟨q⟩ annexed to the true sentences p,q . . ., but Plato has now abandoned these in favour of verbs. The way in which e.g. the kind Sits comes to be called *something which is*[1] respecting Theaetetus if "(Theaetetus) Sits" is true would appear to be something like this:

((Theaetetus Sits) if and only if ((Theaetetus) O[Sits]).

So Sits is one determination of Being, as could be illustrated grammatically if we expanded the Greek perfect tense *kathētai = has sat down*, into the form *esti kathēmenos = is seated* or *is sitting down*. Now if we wish to refer variably to all the kinds in which some individual falls, his (*being*) *sitting*, (*being*) *sleeping*, (*being*) *thinking* . . . (to refer to his *being* [. . .]*ings*—the things which he is) then one way which could conceivably (in Plato's Greek) occur to us is to speak of the individual's *onta*, his *beings* or the *beings respecting him* (*onta peri autou*), where the participle stands variably for any determination of Being and the plural ending shows the multiplicity of the verbs variably indicated as true of the individual.

When Plato picks up *things which are*[1] *not* at 263B9 with *things which are*[2], *but different things which are*[2] *from the things which are*[1] [*about Theaetetus*] at 263B11, the *are*[2] surely has the same sense as the *are*[1]. In *Theaetetus is flying* the kind Flies is[1] because it applies to *something* even if it does not apply to Theaetetus. Finally *is*[3] is a very light use—*there is, es gibt*—but it could be underwritten in the same way.

Plato represents this account of falsity as being heavily dependent on his earlier account of negation at 256. Why does he do
this? What should we lose if the whole account of falsity
simply went:

> *Stranger:* The true sentence says what are with respect to
> Theaetetus as indeed they are.
> *Theaetetus:* Certainly.
> *Stranger:* And the false sentence says what are not with respect
> to Theaetetus, purporting that they are with respect to him.

Plato's starting point was not any supposed difficulty in saying truly
that Theaetetus was not flying. So what does *Other* (*thateron*) have
specifically to do with falsity? Do we have here anything more than
a simple confusion of *that which is not* of a false statement with the
that which is not of a true negative one?

I think we may see the answer in the passage 241, D6–7—"force
through the view that that which is not in some sense is . . ."
(already cited), and in 240E:

> *Stranger:* Does false judgement hold that things which are not
> are not (*mē einai ta mē onta*) or *does it hold that things which are
> not in a sense are* (*pōs einai ta medamōs onta*)?
> *Theaetetus:* Things which are not have in some sense to be if
> anyone is ever at all to say what is false.

There is a trouble about these claims which must first be attended
to. An ordinary non-absurd false sentence does not standardly
describe what it itself says as something which is not. Plato did not
think it did and had no interest I can see in representing that
Theaetetus or the Stranger thought this. So the words *things which
are not* in the italicised sentence have to be understood in a "transparent" way as *things which* (as a matter of fact) *are not*. That Plato
courts disaster so blithely in this way shows something familiar and
important about his innocence of indirect speech; but understanding the words so, I venture the hypothesis that at 263 Plato's
reasoning has moved along the following chain of equivalences.
Socrates says Theaetetus flies if and only if there is something
Socrates says (238). There is something Socrates says in saying
"Theaetetus flies" if and only if Socrates introduces things (*praxeis*)
purportedly being with respect to (or *holding of*) *Theaetetus* (even though
these things, it so happens, are not respecting Theaetetus). But

Socrates introduces such things, which in fact are not respecting Theaetetus, if and only if *there are* things which he introduces so, even though they may not be or hold respecting Theaetetus. It is these which were promised at 241D6–7 and 240E. But what is it for there to be such a *prāxis* for Socrates to introduce if there is no flying of Theaetetus' available for Socrates' *rhēma?* If the analysis of falsity has simply *stipulated* that the false sentence said what was not with respect to Theaetetus we should have been faced here with what Plato would regard as a bleak and difficult question. But matters may seem to be different if the analysis of negation is supplied by means of the biconditional "Theaetetus is flying" is false if and only if "Theaetetus is not flying" is true. For Plato supposes that a sufficient condition for the latter is simply (257C–D) the application of [satisfies some F Other than Flying], which does imply that Flying is at least a *praxis* and a *genos* which a *rhēma* can introduce, even though it is the wrong one for Theaetetus. So there is what is not with respect to Theaetetus.

This is one explanation, perhaps, of Plato's determination to explain falsity in terms of negation, but there is a stronger hypothesis which although it argues grave confusion on Plato's part is rather difficult to dismiss. If it is a correct hypothesis it suggests that Plato did not see many of the implications of what he said correctly at 258E about the meaning of "not big", nor the full purport of the belated recognition of indirect speech at 263B8, signalled in the phrase "says things which are not *as (hōs)* things which are." Remarking that he can say of "Theaetetus flies" that it predicates a *genos* which partakes of Different with respect to the one(s) which *actually* is (are) with respect to Theaetetus, it looks as if Plato thinks that he notices that, by here supplying Sits as what actually is with respect to Theaetetus, we get what corresponds to the right-hand side of

> (Theaetetus) Flies ≡ (Theaetetus) O[satisfies
> some F other than *Sits*].

But the right-hand side is equivalent for Plato to "Theaetetus does not sit" and it may be that he supposes that this proves that "Theaetetus flies" is in some strong sense equivalent to "Theaetetus does not sit". So, if this is right, he believes that false judgement is just the same thing as negating a true judgement. Directly or indirectly negative *rhēmata* must carry the whole burden of both denial and false assertion.

If this is really Plato's thought then he confuses the possibility of saying that what "Theaetetus flies" predicates is different from what is with respect to him, viz. Sitting, for a quite different possibility, that of saying that "Theaetetus flies" predicates [satisfies a *genos* Different from Sits] of him. The second is what we had in the analysis of negation but the first is all that he is entitled to, and does not specify at all what is meant by the predicate "flies". Only multiple confusion about indirect speech could make one suppose so.

Why does Plato go to these lengths to explain falsity? Whichever of these two hypotheses is the right one, and whatever his achievements in the *Sophist*, Plato has not utterly or completely broken the spell of the simple situation of a speaker's referring to an individual and drawing attention to something about the individual. He is in motion away from it but not yet far enough away. Plato's use of the words *hōs onta* of a speaker's *purporting* that *genē* hold or *are* respecting Theaetetus in the 263 passage is in itself a notable event. It is the nearest he comes to an explicit recognition of the intentionality of saying and judging verbs. But, although it would be absurd to make it a complaint, I am afraid that in spite of this he persists in seeing Socrates' being able to purport that "Flying is respecting Theaetetus" as *explained* by there being such a *genos* as Flying (rather than vice versa). If he had developed further what he momentarily grasped with the word *hōs* he could have seen some part of the fallacy in his derivation at step E of the original puzzle; and he might have come to see that it is just as likely that it is the possibility of representing that Theaetetus is flying which explains how there is any such *genos* as Flying. What makes a predicate is not in fact an extension for it. Nor need there really be any members of a *genos* Flying for there to be such a *rhēma*, or for a man to purport that Flying is one of the extensions of which Theaetetus is a member. (Modern logic, with a more sophisticated notion of class, would maintain that members are not necessary even for the existence of the class.) Nor for that matter does *x is not big* really have to contain *not big* as a *rhēma* (257B) with corresponding *genos* in order to say something about *x*. In the next section I shall criticize that supposition.

VII

Thinking of judgement and predication as subsumption of an individual under a *genos*-extension, Plato is obliged to hold that not only F which is falsely ascribed to something which is not in fact F but also *not*-F, truly ascribed, should be *rhēmata;* and each must introduce some *genos*. We have seen how this idea is sustained for false assertion and the part played there by the definition of negation in terms of Other. Unless the idea can be sustained for negation itself such a stand must certainly have been pointless for falsity. But impressive difficulties do face the conception (and all variations on the conception) that a *rhēma* or predicate *not*-F secures its stable meaning by importing a *genos* into discourse (the *genos* in Plato's theory being that subset or *morion* (257D) of Non-Being whose subsets are the extensions of all *genē* identical with themselves and non-identical with F). As remarked, Plato's notion of a *genos* is somewhat indeterminate between property and class interpretations, so I shall try to show that there are difficulties for both.

If a supposed difficulty in seeing the difference between meaning *something different from G* and meaning something different from G, or a difficulty in disambiguating O[some F distinct from G], makes it difficult to see that the original 257B–D definition concerns what is at best a second-order property (the property of having a property distinct from G), or if someone were willing to entertain the supposition that such a property would suffice; then the difficulties in Plato's project certainly become a hundred times more obvious with the appearance of the amendment,

$$\sim(x)\ G \equiv (\mathrm{V}F)((x)F \to (F)\ \triangle\ (G)).$$

What this amendment says is that all of x's properties are distinct from the property G. It predicates distinctness from G of each of them. If you insist you may again rule that it ascribes something to x—viz. the second-order property of having all of its first-order properties distinct properties from property G. But what sort of a property of an individual is this? To predicate it is not, certainly, to try to introduce a mere cavity or emptiness into discourse. But neither is this a *genos* which is anything like the unproblematic examples of *genē* introduced by such *rhēmata* as Plato actually cites, *walks, runs, sleeps, moves, rests*. Still less could anyone call it "an action" (*kai tálla hosa praxeis semainei* 262B).

The class interpretation of *genos* fares no better. If predicating F of y is placing y in the class of things $(\hat{x})(Fx)$—otherwise identifiable, one is compelled to hope, than by this designation—and if we insist that predicating *not*-F of y is placing y in the complement F of F, then for any fully general theory of negative assertion this has to be an *unrestricted* complement of F. But it is a fact of more than merely technical interest that no set theory at present believed free of contradiction can contain this set. The difficulty of allowing it arises from our inability to specify how such an entity could possibly be constructed on any systematic principle whatever, and it is symptomatic of a completely general difficulty in explaining the sense of a *rhēma*, *not*-F, by means of the idea that saying anything about *x* is always placing *x* in a class. For this makes no use whatever of the notion of *withholding x* from a class, and we may be forced to recognize that affirmation and denial of a predicate to an individual are equally primitive concepts. My own view would be that it is only an illusion that the second is reducible to the first—the very same illusion as the discredited idea that a class and its complement are always equally well defined. Affirmation or placing is unintelligible without a twin notion of denial or exclusion.

Returning to properties, I would add that it is one thing to use a pre-existing and well-founded theory of affirmative and negative judgement to extend the ordinary notion of property to include higher-order and negative properties of mounting degrees of abstractness, and quite another thing to make such an unnatural extension of the notion of property in order to *found* a theory of affirmative and negative judgement. I do not think the point I am urging is one which is unsympathetic or irrelevant to Plato. Only a few years later in the *Politicus* (262A–E) he himself explicitly insisted that a genuine *genos* could not be created by simple negation. It seems that either the *Politicus* is a retraction of the *Sophist* doctrine or else the incorrect definition conceals from Plato both the full force of the objection to such *genē* as Not Big and also the question-begging nature of a reply to Parmenides which simply *stipulates* that if $\sim$(a) F then there is automatically a property G such that (a) G $\equiv$ $\sim$(a) F. And in any ordinary sense of class or property this is simply not true. In the ordinary sense of property what property do the following things which are not red have in common? Helium, the number two, the Eiffel Tower, the Grand National, the concept *horse?*[16]

[16] An approach which may come to mind here is an explicitly postulational extension of the notion of property. It is not the only objection to this that, against Parmenides, it is simply question-begging. For example, if there is a property of not having the property, F, or if postulation can guarantee this, then is there also a property of not having the property of not having the property F? This should be the same as the property F, but what is there about the postulation which could *show* it? Do we have to postulate this too? (We can bring intuitionists into the argument by adding one more negation and

To the last argument it may be natural to retort that these heterogeneous items are not even the kinds of thing to have *red* either true or false of them and that we can limit our enquiry to the latter. This objection could hardly save Plato—what is the Platonic or *otherness* account of the occurrence of the word *not* in the sentence preceding this one?—but it does draw attention to an important interpretive possibility not so far canvassed. It may be that the most sympathetic amendment of Plato's theory is not so much

$$\sim(x)G \equiv (\forall F)((x)F \rightarrow (F) \triangle (G))$$

as

$$\sim(x)G \equiv (\exists F)((F \text{ belongs to the same range}$$

$$\text{as G belongs to) and } (F) \triangle (G) \text{ and } (x)O[F])$$

a range being a class of predicates falling under e.g. a determinable like size, or colour, or shape, or whatever. It is a leading mark of such ranges that any two predicates in one range have to compete with one another to qualify an individual. Not both can possess it. That Plato does sometimes write as if some such possibility were in his mind I shall not deny. Perhaps the amendment is a more natural one than the one first suggested. But when an author is as unclear as Plato is here about what he himself is proposing we may only be able to enumerate the possibilities open to him and evaluate them. And the new option is certainly no more trouble-free than the others. It does not explain such categorial denials as "points do not have size", and it seems to be impossible to provide a definition of the required notion of "range" without reimporting the idea of negation itself.

What I think that these difficulties show is that the Other is not enough. Predication must be explained from a clear paradigm which does not require the learning of a predicate to depend on the grasping of something, whether class or property, which is utterly indefinite or unrestricted. To fix the sense of a predicate is to attach to it some determinate and controllable contribution which it can make to the sense of a sentence. This is a condition of adequacy which can perfectly well accommodate negative predication if denial is allowed into the theory of judgement and assertion on the same terms as affirmation or ascription. But once it is accorded this primitive place it can exploit everything that is clear about the

---

appealing to the universally admitted truth that not-not-not-F(a) → not-F(a).)

theory of affirmative predication and completely displace Difference and the Other from the theory of negation.

VIII

For these reasons I do not myself believe that Plato came near to solving the problem of negation, or that he reached any satisfactory understanding of what problem this problem really is. The little clarity we now have about the nature of the problem of negation does not lead me to think that Plato's notion of the notion of *Other* is of fundamental importance in solving it. A theory of speech acts is a more likely focus for a satisfying answer. On the other hand we are not in a position to condescend to him on the subject. As J. L. Austin complained, we ourselves are all too apt to define negation in terms of falsehood and falsehood in terms of negation, and to fend off the charge of circularity by keeping the occasions of such interdefinition apart (rather than by getting really clear about what exactly is to be expected from an analysis of negation).

As for falsity, Plato's objective was as much to *find room* for falsity as to define it by means of his account of negation; and in the former project I believe he has more success. Admittedly he mistakes the gravity of some of the obstacles which he thinks he sees in the way of admitting the existence of falsity, and he does not always take the best or the shortest way round them. As a result his eventual theory is a more primitive theory than it otherwise might have been. But in the course of it he puts logic and philosophy onto the subject of parts of speech and the asymmetrical roles of names and other parts in the completed sentence.

It is stupid too to condescend to Plato's imperfect grasp of *oratio obliqua*, and especially stupid in the absence of the really satisfying derivation (which we ourselves still lack) of the failure of substitutivity in opaque contexts of a for b or ϕ for ψ, even though $a = b$ or $\phi = \psi$. What is it about *saying* which gives rise to this failure? Plato's "fallaciously opaque reading" (step E) cannot even rate as a misunderstanding until a theory of judgement is available which explains what this misunderstanding is a misunderstanding of, and says something about how words actually have their meaning in direct and indirect discourse.

In conclusion I should like to make one more point. Plato has sometimes been commended for giving up and demonstrating the untenability of a position called *semantic atomism*. He certainly demonstrated well enough that not all expressions were names and that compound expressions such as sentences were not names. But he retains the idea of analysing what is said into a structure of individually describable parts. It is precisely by concentrating on this that he dissolves the problem of sentence-reference. And if he had not retained it he would have deserved no credit on this score. For this approach is both correct and indispensable. When we describe the separate functionings of the parts of the sentence, particularly verbs or predicates, we have admittedly to describe the contribution they make as a contribution to the sense of *the whole*, the item which receives a truth-value. The whole is all-important. But Plato's method of describing the contribution of *onomata* and *rhēmata* respects all of its claims to this kind of priority. Indeed it marks them. But it is also true and important that there is an infinitude of sentences we can understand. At best we can have grasped some dozens of these as wholes. Most of the sentences we produce and understand are far too complex to grasp as wholes, and it is quite unrealistic to suppose that the utterance conditions of even so simple a sentence as "Tomorrow the baker will deliver three loaves" could be imparted without imparting an essentially structured thought represented by a sentence constituted of elements arranged in a correspondingly structured array. This is the force of semantic atomism.[17]

Plato's contribution to the problem of sentence meaning as such is mainly negative—p does not have a sense by being annexed to ⟨p⟩—or vague—ascribing an action to an actor, but how? But it is very important. It leaves room for the best sort of account we ourselves have to give—that the sense of *s* is fixed by explaining under what conditions the utterance of a token of the sentence-type *s* issues in truth. Indeed it prepares the way for such an account.

[This essay has not been previously published.]

[17] It is often felt that there is some conflict between the sense in which sentence-meaning is primary and semantic atomism. The most concise refutation of this which I know is Quine's ("Russell's Ontological Development," in *Bertrand Russell, Philosopher of the Century*, ed. R. Shoenman [London, 1967], p. 306) : "The unit of communication is the sentence and not the word. This point of semantical theory was long obscured by the undeniable primacy, in one respect, of words. Sentences being limitless in number and words limited, we necessarily understand most sentences by construction from antecedently familiar words. Actually there is no conflict here. We can allow the sentences a monopoly of full 'meaning' in some sense, without denying that the meaning must be worked out. Then we can say that knowing words is knowing how to work out the meanings of sentences containing them. Dictionary definitions of words are mere clauses in a recursive definition of the meanings of sentences."

NOTES ON CONTRIBUTORS

John L. Ackrill, Professor of the History of Philosophy at Oxford University and Fellow of Brasenose College, Oxford.

Reginald E. Allen, Professor of Philosophy at the University of Toronto.

Harold Cherniss, member of the permanent faculty of the Institute for Advanced Study, Princeton, New Jersey. Earlier he had been Professor of Classics at Johns Hopkins University and at the University of California at Berkeley.

Robert C. Cross, Regius Professor of Logic at the University of Aberdeen.

J. D. Denniston, late Fellow of Hertford College in Oxford University, and University Lecturer in Greek and Latin Literature.

Julius M. E. Moravcsik, Professor of Philosophy at Stanford University. Previously he taught at the University of Michigan.

G. E. L. Owen, Professor of Philosophy and the Classics at Harvard University. Previously he had been Reader, and then Professor, of Ancient Philosophy at Oxford University and a Fellow of Corpus Christi College.

Richard Robinson, formerly Professor of Philosophy at the Sage School of Philosophy, Cornell University, has been Fellow and Tutor of Oriel College in Oxford University, and University Lecturer in Philosophy, since 1948.

Colin Strang, Reader in Philosophy at the University of Newcastle-upon-Tyne.

Gregory Vlastos, Stuart Professor of Philosophy at Princeton University. He had previously taught philosophy at Queen's University, in Kingston, Ontario, and at Cornell University.

Anders Wedberg, Professor of Philosophy at the University of Stockholm.

David Wiggins, Professor of Philosophy at Bedford College, University of London. He had previously been a Fellow and Tutor of New College, Oxford.

A. D. Woozley, formerly Professor of Philosophy at St. Andrews University in Scotland, is now Professor of Philosophy at the Corcoran School of Philosophy, University of Virginia. He has served as editor of the *Philosophical Quarterly*.

SELECTED BIBLIOGRAPHY OF RECENT BOOKS AND ARTICLES IN ENGLISH ON PLATO'S METAPHYSICS AND THEORY OF KNOWLEDGE

I. BOOKS AND ARTICLES BY
CONTRIBUTORS TO THIS VOLUME.

Ackrill, John, "Plato and the Copula," *Journal of Hellenic Studies* 77 (1957, Part I), 31–55.

Cherniss, Harold, *Aristotle's Criticism of Plato and the Early Academy* (Baltimore, 1944).

The Riddle of the Early Academy (Berkeley, 1945).

"The Relation of the *Timaeus* to Plato's Earlier Dialogues," *American Journal of Philology* 78 (1957), 225–66.

"A Much Misread Passage of the *Timaeus*," *American Journal of Philology* 75 (1954), 113–30.

"Plato as a Mathematician," *Review of Metaphysics* 4 (1950/51), 395–425.

"*Timaeus* 38A8–B5," *Journal of Hellenic Studies* 77 (1957, Part I), 18–23.

Cross, R. C., "Logos and Forms in Plato," *Mind* 63 (1954), 433–50.

Cross, R. C., and A. D. Woozley, *Plato's Republic: A Philosophical Commentary* (London and New York, 1964).

Moravcsik, J. M. E., "*Symplokē eidōn* and the Genesis of *logos*," *Archiv für Geschichte der Philosophie* 42 (1960), 117–29.

"Being and Meaning in the *Sophist*," *Acta Philosophica Fennica* 14 (1962), 23–78.
"The 'Third Man' Argument and Plato's Theory of Forms," *Phronesis* 8 (1963), 50–62.

Owen, G. E. L., "A Proof in *peri ideōn*," *Journal of Hellenic Studies* 77 (1957, Part I), 103–11.

"The Place of the *Timaeus* in Plato's Dialogues," *Classical Quarterly* 2 N.S. (1953), 79–95.

"Plato and Parmenides on the Timeless Present," *Monist* 50 (1966), 317–40.

Robinson, R., *Plato's Earlier Dialectic*, Second Edition (Oxford, 1953).

"Forms and Error in Plato's *Theaetetus*," *Philosophical Review* 59 (1950), 3–30.

"The Theory of Names in Plato's *Cratylus*," *Revue Internationale de Philosophie* 9 (1955), 221–36.

"A Criticism of Plato's *Cratylus*," *Philosophical Review* 65 (1956), 324–41.

"Plato's Consciousness of Fallacy," *Mind* 51 (1942), 97–114.

Vlastos, G., "Anamnesis in the *Meno*," *Dialogue* 4 (1965), 143–67.

"Degrees of Reality in Plato," *New Essays on Plato and Aristotle*, edited by R. Bambrough (London and New York, 1965), 1–19.

"A Metaphysical Paradox," *Proceedings and Addresses of the American Philosophical Association* 39 (1966), 5–19.

"The Third Man Argument in the *Parmenides*," *Philosophical Review* 63 (1954), 319–49.

"Plato's 'Third Man' Argument: Text and Logic," *Philosophical Quarterly* 19 (1969), 289–301.

Wedberg, Anders, *Plato's Philosophy of Mathematics* (Stockholm, 1955).

II. BOOKS BY OTHER AUTHORS

(a) *Commentaries or Translations with Notes of Philosophical Interest.*

On the *Meno*: Bluck, R. S., *Plato's Meno* (Cambridge, England, 1961).

Klein, Jacob, *A Commentary on Plato's Meno* (Chapel Hill, 1965).

Thompson, E. S., *The Meno of Plato* (London, 1901; reprinted, Cambridge, England, 1961).

On the *Parmenides:* Cornford, F. M., *Plato and Parmenides* (London and New York, 1939).

On the *Phaedo:* Bluck, R. S., *Plato's Phaedo* (London, 1955).

  Hackforth, R., *Plato's Phaedo* (Cambridge, England, 1955).

On the *Phaedrus:* Hackforth, R., *Plato's Phaedrus* (Cambridge, England, 1952).

  Pieper, J., *Enthusiasm and Divine Madness: On the Platonic Dialogue, Phaedrus,* translated from the German by R. and C. Winston (New York, 1964).

On the *Philebus:* Hackforth, R., *Plato's Examination of Pleasure* (Cambridge, England, 1949).

On the *Republic:* Shorey, P., *Plato: The Republic,* Vols. I and II (London and Cambridge, Mass., 1930 and 1935).

On the *Sophist* and the *Theaetetus:* Cornford, F. M., *Plato's Theory of Knowledge* (London, 1935).

On the *Sophist* and the *Politicus:* Taylor, A. E. (edited by R. Klibansky and Elizabeth Anscombe), *Plato: the Sophist and the Statesman* (London, 1961).

On the *Timaeus:* Cornford, F. M., *Plato's Cosmology* (London, 1937).

  Taylor, A. E., *A Commentary on Plato's Timaeus* (Oxford, 1928).

(b) Books.

Brumbaugh, R. S., *Plato for the Modern Age* (New York, 1962).

Cornford, F. M., "Mathematics and Dialectic in the *Republic*," *Mind* 41 (1932), 37–52 and 173–90.

Crombie, I. M., *An Examination of Plato's Doctrines,* Vol. II: *Plato on Knowledge and Reality* (London, 1963).

Field, G. C., *The Philosophy of Plato* (London, 1949).

Friedländer, Paul, *Plato: An Introduction,* translated from the German by H. Meyerhoff (New York, 1958).

Grote, G., *Plato and the Other Companions of Socrates* (London, 1865).

Grube, G., *Plato's Thought* (London, 1935).

Gulley, N., *Plato's Theory of Knowledge* (London, 1962).

Hardie, W. F. R., *A Study in Plato* (Oxford, 1936).

Lyons, John, *Structural Semantics: An Analysis of the Vocabulary of Plato*, (Oxford, 1963).

Murphy, N. R., *An Interpretation of Plato's Republic* (Oxford, 1951).

Ross, W. D., *Plato's Theory of Ideas* (Oxford, 1951).

Runciman, W. G., *Plato's Later Epistemology* (Cambridge, England, 1962).

Schipper, Edith, *Forms in Plato's Later Dialogues* (The Hague, 1965).

Shorey, P., *The Unity of Plato's Thought* (Chicago, 1903; reprinted 1960).

What Plato Said (Chicago, 1933; 6th Impression, 1965).

Sprague, Rosamond, *Plato's Use of Fallacy* (London, 1962).

Stenzel, J., *Plato's Method of Dialectic*, translated from the German by D. J. Allan (Oxford, 1940).

Taylor, A. E., *Plato, The Man and His Work* (London, 1926; Third Edition, Revised and Enlarged, 1929).

(c) *Articles and Essays.*

Austin, J., "Are There *A Priori* Concepts?" *Philosophical Papers*, edited by J. O. Urmson and G. J. Warnock (Oxford, 1961), 1–22.

Anscombe, G. E. M., "The New Theory of Forms," *Monist* 50 (1966), 403–20.

Baldry, H. C., "Plato's 'Technical Terms,'" *Classical Quarterly* 31 (1937), 141–50.

Berger, Fred R., "Rest and Motion in the *Sophist*," *Phronesis* 10 (1966), 70–77.

Bluck, R. S., "*Logos* and Forms in Plato," *Mind* 65 (1956), 523–29.

"False Statement in the *Sophist*," *Journal of Hellenic Studies* 77 (1957, Part II), 181–86.

Brumbaugh, R. S., "Plato and the History of Science," *Studium Generale* 14 (1961), 520–27.

Butler, R. J., "The Measure and Weight of the Third Man," *Mind* 72 (1963), 62–78.

Cornford, F. M., "Mathematics and Dialectic in the *Republic*," *Mind* 41 (1932), 37–52 and 173–90.

De Laguna, Th., "Note on the Theory of Ideas," *Philosophical Review* 43 (1934), 443–70.

Demos, R., "Partly So and Partly Not So," *Mind* 68 (1959), 51–56.

Duff-Forbes, D. R., "The Regress Arguments in the *Republic*," *Mind* 77 (1968), 406–10.

Edelstein, L., "The Function of the Myth in Plato's Philosophy," *Journal of History of Ideas* 10 (1949), 463–81.

Ferguson, A. S., "Plato's Simile of Light, Part I and Part II," *Classical Quarterly* 15 (1921), 131–52, and 16 (1922), 15–28.

"Plato's Simile of Light Again," *Classical Quarterly* 28 (1934), 211–13.

Field, G. C., "Plato and Natural Science," *Philosophy* 8 (1933), 131–41.

Frank, E., "The Fundamental Opposition of Plato and Aristotle," *American Journal of Philology* 61 (1940), 34–53 and 166–85.

Gallop, D., "Plato and the Alphabet," *Philosophical Review* 72 (1963), 364–76.

Geach, P. T., "The Third Man Again," *Philosophical Review* 65 (1956), 72–82.

Hackforth, R., "The Aviary Theory in the *Theaetetus*," *Classical Quarterly* 32 (1938), 27–29.

"Platonic Forms in the *Theaetetus*," *Classical Quarterly* 7 (1937), 53–58.

"False Statement in the *Sophist*," *Classical Quarterly* 39 (1945), 56–58.

Hamlyn, D. W., "The Communion of Forms and the Development of Plato's Logic," *Philosophical Quarterly* 5 (1955), 289–302.

"Forms and Knowledge in Plato's *Theaetetus*," *Mind* 66 (1957), 547.

"*Eikasia* in Plato's *Republic*," *Philosophical Quarterly* 8 (1958), 14–23.

Hare, R. M., "Philosophical Discoveries," *Mind* 69 (1960), 145–62.

Hicken, Winifred F., "Knowledge and Forms in Plato's *Theaetetus*," *Journal of Hellenic Studies* 77 (1957, Part I), 48–53.

"The Character and Provenance of Socrates' Dream in the *Theaetetus*," *Phronesis* 3 (1958), 126–45.

Keyt, D., "Aristotle on Plato's Receptacle," *American Journal of Philology* 82 (1961), 291–300.

"The Fallacy in the *Phaedo*," *Phronesis* 8 (1963), 167–82.

Lacey, A. R., "Plato's *Sophist* and the Forms," *Classical Quarterly* 9 (1959), 43–52.

Lee, E. W., "On Plato's *Timaeus*, 49D4–E7," *American Journal of Philology* 88 (1967), 1–28.

"On the Metaphysics of the Image in Plato's *Timaeus*," *Monist* 50 (1966), 341–68.

Lloyd, G. E. R., "Plato as a Natural Scientist," *Journal of Hellenic Studies* 88 (1968), 78–92.

Lorenz, K., and J. Mittelstrass, "On Rational Philosophy of Language: The Programme in Plato's *Cratylus* Reconsidered," *Mind* 75 (1966), 1–29.

Luce, J. V., "The Theory of Ideas in the *Cratylus*," *Phronesis* 10 (1965), 21–36.

McDiarmid, J. B., "Plato in Theophrastus' *De Sensibus*," *Phronesis* 4 (1959), 59–70.

Malcolm, J., "The Line and the Cave," *Phronesis* 7 (1962), 36–45.

"Plato's Analysis of *to on* and *to mē on* in the *Sophist*," *Phronesis* 12 (1967), 130–146.

Miller, H. W., "The Aetiology of Disease in Plato's *Timaeus*," *Transactions and Proceedings of American Philological Association* 93 (1962), 175–87.

Mills, K. W., "Plato's *Phaedo*, 74B7–C6," *Phronesis* 2 (1957), 128–147 and 3 (1958), 40–58.

Morrow, G. R., "Necessity and Persuasion in Plato's *Timaeus*," *Philosophical Review* 59 (1950), 147–60.

Nakhnikian, G., "Plato's Theory of Sensation," *Review of Metaphysics* 9 (1955), 129–48 and 306–27.

Nehrlich, G. C., "Regress Arguments in Plato," *Mind* 88 (1960), 88–90.

Peck, A. L., "Plato and the *Megista Genē* of the *Sophist*," *Classical Quarterly* 2 (1952), 32–56.

"Plato's *Sophist*: The *Symplokē tōn Eidōn*," *Phronesis* 46–66.

"Plato versus Parmenides," *Philosophical Review* 71 (1962), 159–84.

Phillips, B., "The Significance of Meno's Paradox," *Classical Weekly* 42 (1948–49), 87–91.

Raven, J., "Sun, Divided Line, and Cave," *Classical Quarterly* 3 (1953), 22–32.

Rosenmeyer, T. G., "Plato and Mass Words," *Transactions of American Philological Association* 88 (1957), 88–102.

Ryle, G., "Plato's *Parmenides*," *Mind* 48 (1939), 129–51 and 302–25.
"Letters and Syllables in Plato," *Philosophical Review* 69 (1960), 431–51.

"Dialectic in the Academy," *New Essays on Plato and Aristotle*, edited by R. Bambrough (London, 1965), 39–68.

"Plato," Encyclopedia of Philosophy, edited by Paul Edwards (New York, 1967).

Sellars, W., "Vlastos and 'The Third Man' " and "A Rejoinder," *Philosophical Perspectives* (Springfield, Illinois, 1967), 23–72.

Sesonske, A., "Knowing and Saying," *Archiv für Philosophie* 12 (1963), 3–13.

Shorey, P., "Origin of the Syllogism," *Classical Philology* 19 (1924), 1–19.

"Platonism and the History of Science," *Proceedings of the American Philosophical Society* 66 (1927), 159–82.

Solmsen, Fr., "Plato and the Unity of Science," *Philosophical Review* 49 (1940), 567–71.

"Dialectic Without Forms," *Proceedings of the Third Symposium Aristotelicum* (Oxford, 1968), 49–68.

Stannard, J., "Socratic Eros and Platonic Dialectic," *Phronesis* 4 (1959), 120–34.

Steele, D. A., "A Mathematical Reappraisal of the Corpus Platonicum," *Scripta Mathematica* 17 (1951), 173–89.

Trevaskis, J. R., "The *megista genē* and the Vowell Analogy of Plato, *Sophist* 253," *Phronesis* 11 (1966), 99–116.

Turnbull, R. G., "Aristotle's Debt to the 'Natural Philosophy' of the *Phaedo*," *Philosophical Quarterly* 8 (1958), 131–46.

"The Argument of the *Sophist*," *Philosophical Quarterly* 14 (1964), 23–34.

Verdenius, W. J., "Notes on Plato's *Phaedo*," *Mnemosyne* IV, 11 (1958), 193–243.

ABBREVIATIONS USED IN THIS BOOK

Aristotle (Arist.)

APo. = Posterior Analytics
APr. = Prior Analytics
de An. = de Anima
EE = Eudemian Ethics
EN = Nicomachean Ethics
GA = de Generatione Animalium
GC = de Generatione et Corruptione
Int. = de Interpretatione
Metaph. = Metaphysics
MM = Magna Moralia
Ph. = Physics
Pol. = Politics
Rh. = Rhetoric
SE = de Sophisticis Elenchis

Isocrates (Isoc.)

Areop. = Areopagiticus

Plato (Pl.)

Alc. = Alcibiades
Ap. = Apology
Chrm. = Charmides
Cra. = Cratylus
Cri. = Crito
Criti. = Critias
Def. = Definitions
Ep. = Epistles
Epin. = Epinomis
Euthd. = Ethydemus
Euthphr. = Euthyphro
Grg. = Gorgias
Hp.Ma. = Hippias Major
Hp.Mi. = Hippias Minor
Ion
La. = Laches

Lg. = Laws
Ly. = Lysis
Men. = Meno

Phd. = Phaedo
Phdr. = Phaedrus
Phlb. = Philebus
Plt. = Politicus
Prm. = Parmenides
Prt. = Protagoras
R. = Republic
Symp. = Symposium
Sph. = Sophist
Tht. = Theaetetus
Ti. = Timaeus

Plotinus (Plot.)

Enn. = Enneads

Xenophon (X.)

Cyr. = Cyropaedia
Mem. = Memorabilia

Thucydides (Th.)

END OF VOLUME I

INDEX LOCORUM

Plato (cont'd)

Plato (cont'd)

Plato (cont'd)

Plato (cont'd)

Plato (cont'd)